CULTURAL HERITAGE AND CONTEMPORARY CHANGE
SERIES I, CULTURE AND VALUES, VOLUME 17
SERIES IIA, ISLAM, VOLUME 6

WAYS TO GOD

GEORGE F. McLEAN

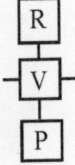

The Council for Research in Values and Philosophy

CULTURAL HERITAGE AND CONTEMPORARY CHANGE
SERIES I, CULTURE AND VALUES, VOLUME 17
SERIES IIA, ISLAM, VOLUME 6
General Editor
George F. McLean

WAYS TO GOD

Personal and Social
At the Turn of the Millennia

The Iqbal Lecture, Lahore

GEORGE F. McLEAN

The Council for Research in Values and Philosophy

Copyright © 1999 by
The Council for Research in Values and Philosophy

Box 261
Cardinal Station
Washington, D.C. 20064

All rights reserved

Printed in the United States of America

Library of Congress Cataloging-in-Publication

McLean, George F.
    Ways to God, personal and social, at the turn of the millennia / George F. McLean.
    p. cm. — (Cultural heritage and contemporary change. Series I, Culture and values; vol. 17) (Cultural heritage and contemporary change. Series IIA, Islam; vol. 6)
    Includes bibliographical references and index.
    1. Spiritual life--History of doctrines. 2. Philosophy and religion-History. I. Title. II. Series: Cultural heritage and contemporary change. Series IIA, Islam ; vol. 6.

BL624.M3975 1999
210—dc21

99-48111
CIP

ISBN 1-56518-123-9 (paper).

CONTENTS

INTRODUCTION   1
PROLOGUE: Religion as Coming Home: The Iqbal Lecture   11

PART I. PROTO-PHILOSOPHIES AS WAYS TO GOD
Chapter I. Method: From the Structure of   53
   Consciousness to an Archeology of Ways to God
Chapter II. The Totemic Way to God: 75
   The Religious Base of Thought and Culture
Chapter III. Greek Myth   107
   as a Proto-Philosophical Way to God
Chapter IV. The Ritual Hindu Way to God   133
   as a Proto-Metaphysics

PART II. CLASSICAL PHILOSOPHICAL AND MYSTICAL WAYS TO GOD
Chapter V. The Development of Greek and   165
   Judeo-Christian Philosophy: Bases for Ways to God
Chapter VI. Systematic Christian Philosophy   195
   as a Way to God
Chapter VII. Al-Ghazālī and Mulla Sadra: 235
   Islamic Mystical and Existential Ways to God

PART III. CONTEMPORARY PHILOSOPHICAL WAYS TO GOD
Chapter VIII. Human Subjectivity and   289
   Personal Ways to God
Chapter IX. Cultural Traditions and Civil Society   327
   as Social Ways to God
Chapter X. The Dialectic of Good and Evil: 381
   "Ultimate Concern" in History as a Way to God

APPENDICES
I: The Structure of Development   417
   by Jean Piaget
II. Moral Development at Different Age Levels   435
   by Margaret Gorman
INDEX   443

ACKNOWLEDGEMENTS

This work is the result of ongoing collaboration in which many have shared. Hence the author expresses his gratitude to:

(a) the Vice Chancellor, Faculty and Students of the University of the Punjab, Lahore, for evoking this work through their invitation and response to the Iqbal lecture on which it is based;

(b) the Universities, especially the Gregorian University in Rome and The Catholic University of America in Washington, and the philosophical Associations, especially The International Society for Metaphysics, The American Catholic Philosophical Association, and The World Union of Catholic Philosophical Societies, whose open vision inspired both this search into many sources and the effort to find their deep point of intersection as the pilgrimages of all peoples to the Holy Mountain;

(c) The Council for Research in Values and Philosophy (RVP) and its associated research teams in China and India, Central and Eastern Europe, Cairo and Rome, Africa and Latin America, Europe and North America, which have pioneered the contemporary philosophical ways which converge in this work;

(d) Richard and Nancy Graham whose gracious hospitality and world vision provided context and inspiration for the initial draft of this work; and

(e) Hu Yeping whose technical competence and constant care have brought this manuscript to completion.

Above all, on the occasion of the completion of his 70th year, the author thanks God as Source and Goal of all for life and vocation, and for the opportunities to discover and admire these many ways along which peoples of all cultures and civilizations, past and present, are drawn forward toward Him by whom we have first been loved.

George F. McLean
June 29, 1999

INTRODUCTION

If there be truth to the commonplace that the first millenium was focused upon God and the second upon man, then this beginning of the third millennium should be the opportunity to unite both. This would render religion more inspiring and transformative and thereby enable humankind to be more holy and social.

The radical character of the present challenge — and hence of today's opportunity — appears from a review of the 2000 year story of our era. The first millennium generally is characterized as God-centered. Its beginning is counted from the birth of Christ and its history can be told in two broad strokes: the first being the sweep of Christianity across the West; the second being the sweep of Islam across the Southern rim of the Mediterranean to the Atlantic on the West and across Asia to the Pacific on the East. Everywhere life was highly sacralized in form and symbol, as is typified by the Christian liturgical year and the Moslem practice of praying five times daily. All was God's will, which individuals and communities sought to know and to follow.

The second millenium came gradually to be centered upon human reason and its free exercise. This process began with the introduction of Aristotle's thought to Islam and thence to Christianity. The period was marked by such great and integrating thinkers as al-Farabi, Ibn Sina (Avicenna), Ibn Rushd (Averroes), Albert the Great and Thomas Aquinas with their massive *summas*, soaring cathedrals of the mind.

At midpoint in the second millenium, however, attention to reason was radicalized and became a reductionist rationalism. At that time clear and distinct ideas clearly ordered became the norm for the validity of all that would be considered to be worthy knowledge, which, in turn, became the norm for values. What was clear to the human mind was, of course, what was human rather than what was of divine or even physical nature. Hence, the Enlightenment heritage tended to consider the universe as total and humanity as self-sufficient; religion was looked upon as but a superstructure or projection of what was, in fact, human. As described by Milton in "Paradise Lost" this attempt of humanity to save itself or to become God is both primordial and catastrophic.

What is human becomes the center and measure of all, thoughtlessly abandoning God and viciously attacking nature. Nothing is sacred; all is subject to ever more restrictive and conflictive human self-interests.

The final implications of this orientation became clear in the closing century of the second millenium, marked by wars hot and cold, pogroms and holocausts, and exploitation of humankind and of the environment. People now are no longer willing to proceed further along this path. Having come to the brink, humankind senses its desperate need to find another path for collaboration among itself and with nature and God.

At this juncture we find ourselves on the threshold between challenge and opportunity. Progress can no longer be seen as merely a matter of the implementation of human life in terms of its material support and physical organization, or even of its network of personal communication and social interaction. All of these are ultimately ambiguous, with great potential for good, but also with a capacity to support evil bent upon human destruction. True progress must be founded in the creative power of God; it must be implemented by the development of human dignity, creativity and responsibility; and it must be centered upon what is ethically good and aesthetically moving because inspired by the Spirit. Precisely in these terms new and exciting ways open to a life with meaning and value for all.

Such human efforts point neither back to the second millennium with its ambiguous sense of "progress" forgetful of both God and nature, nor even to the first millenium focused upon God but less vividly conscious of humankind. Rather, they must begin with a recuperation of the sacred as appreciated in even the earliest of human settlements where it suffused and inspired the whole of life, giving it meaning and founding community. This sacredness of life must be followed through time as it unfolds in, and as, the multiple human cultures and civilizations. All of this must be harvested afresh.

The present work is an effort to take up this challenge in a way that looks forward, seizing the opportunity of this turn of the millennia to find ways, old and new, along which humanity can proceed. The task of our times is to provide direction and motivation for life; to inspire meaning for the many technical and communicative human creations; to provide norms and balance for interaction with the local, global and indeed galactic environment; to explore the true dignity and creativity of personal and social life in our time; and to do all this by renewing and unfolding the import of the divine origin, sacred meaning and transcendent goal of all.

The particular occasion of this work was an invitation from the University of the Punjab in Lahore, Pakistan, to deliver its Iqbal lecture. That underscored the spirit of Mohammed Iqbal who in the first half of the 20th century took up the challenge of human meaning in our times, drawing upon the great religious tradition of Islam and relating it to present thought. In his honor and under his inspiration the work of shaping these chapters into the present work was begun. Hence, the chapters often note their relation to the Islamic horizon and inspiration, as well as to issues faced commonly by Christian and Chinese, Indian and African cultures.

These issues now are unfolding ever more rapidly with the dramatic new developments in the relation of philosophy and reason to faith and religion, and to the dialogue of civilizations in a global community. These have been treated in other lectures, delivered especially in Islamic contexts at the University of the Punjab in Lahore, the al Azhar University in Cairo and Mofid University in Qom, as well as the universities and academies of Science of the newly independent states of Central Asia. Those lectures can be found in the companion volumes being published along with the present one and entitled respectively *Faith, Reason and Philosophy* and *Religion and the Relation between Cultures*. But first there is need to examine more comprehensively the many ways to God which have bee pioneered and elaborated through the centuries and which provide the bases for responding to present challenges.

The term "way" in the title should not be taken instrumentally in the sense of employing religion as a means for human fulfillment. That would invert the order of God and man after the manner of the secularizing influence of the Enlightenment. God is source and the goal, never a means. It is precisely in restoring this relation as creature to Creator that humankind rediscovers its real possibilities for fulfillment, peace and happiness.

The term "way" as employed here bears a number of

connotations. It connects from the past in order to bring forward the achievements of humanity, especially its discoveries concerning the deepest meaning and highest horizons of life; it bespeaks the ability of humankind to pioneer and create new realms; it points ahead and hence has about it an active, dynamic newness.

Moreover, the "way" which all seek leads not to alien places, but to our true home in which we find our deepest peace, contentment and fulfillment. Ultimately, it leads to God, who not only is immanently present in our inner hearts, but whose transcendence opens before us both limitless possibilities and the prospect of definitive fulfillment. With this last note "way" takes on its ample religious connotation and thereby echoes the most basic themes in the several cultures. Thus the ways to God in the different civilizations provide the basis of global cooperation in the common search both for God beyond this life and for godliness within it.

- For the Greek mind "the way" is the great arching road, referred to by Parmenides in the Proemium of his Poem; it passes through all and unites all, touching the heavens and even the underworld.

- For the Sufi it is the "Way" of spiritual growth lived in the Spirit, a holy life in time.

- For the Buddhist it is the sevenfold Path of spiritual growth.

- For the Catholic it bespeaks the five ways which Thomas articulated at the beginning of his *Summa Theologica* for relating all things back to God, St. Bonaventure's itinerary of the mind to God, St. Teresa of Avila's spiritual ascent of Mount Carmel, and even the "little way" of Theresa of the Child Jesus.

- For all nations it is the multiple paths by which all peoples, religions and civilizations in their separate pilgrimages converge toward the one Holy Mountain.

This work reflects research into these "ways" in many ancient and modern philosophical traditions, in Rome and Chennai (Madras), in Paris and Egypt, in China and Peru. Echoes of those studies appear in the various chapters. The effort, however, is not merely one of comparative philosophy, for as there can be but one infinite Being it would be inadequate and misleading simply to juxtapose multiple ways as if they were not intimately related and convergent. In the present global intersection of religiously founded civilizations there is special need and opportunity to search out how these are organically related.

This could be done after the manner of Hegel in his *Science of Logic* and *Phenomenology of the Mind*. That would enable one to see the inherent relatedness of the ways as the dialectical unfolding of the very nature of being as idea or spirit. But in these times, as noted above, the concern is to look not only for what is essential, necessary and universal, but especially for what is existential and unique in the free and creative exercise of life. Hence, it is important to examine how the consciousness and commitments of human life have developed as ways to God within the stories of persons and peoples. Part I "Proto-philosophies as Ways to God" undertakes that task. Chapter I "Method: From the Structure of Consciousness to an Archeology of Ways to God" reviews the developmental pattern of the cognitive abilities of children elaborated by Piaget and Kohlberg, which Fowler applied to religious development. It points out how the structure of human cognitive abilities is constituted sequentially first of the external senses such as sight and hearing, next of the internal senses such as the imagination for figurative or picture thinking, and finally of the intellect which grasps meaning. These three constitute the grid upon which philosophers from Aristotle to Descartes have structured their thought.

By following these cognitive capabilities developmentally the chapters of this work — analogously to Piaget's sequence of the stages of cognitive and affective development — unveil how the ways to God developed and were lived existentially. Moreover, as each stage remains as a substratum in the subsequent stages, the sequence is cumulative and progressive in character, so that each way not only includes the former, but unfolds their potentialities in ever new and richer ways.

Chapter II "The Totemic Way to God: the Religious Base of Thought and Culture" examines the beginning of this process in the totemic thought of the earliest peoples. Here the intellect, working in terms of what the external senses perceive, interprets all in terms of a totem, which might be a bird or an animal. All the members of that tribe are understood by identity with the one totem as their sacred center; their relations among themselves and with nature are understood on this basis and in these terms. Through the subsequent ages the intensity and natural spontaneity of this religious or proto-religious sense of life will be continually mined and rearticulated in the deepest formulas of human wisdom and relived ritually as the heart of the religions to follow.

Chapter III "Greek Myth as a Proto-Philosophical Way to God" unfolds this at the mythic stage of human consciousness where the intellect works in terms of what the imagination can picture. Here there developed a rich pattern of the gods as transcendent and personal beings, in terms of which all of human life and nature was interpreted. As seen in the great epics of Homer, all of nature was sacred and human destiny lay ultimately the will of the gods who ruled and were ruled in turn by yet further powers.

Chapter IV "The Ritual Hindu Way to God as a Proto-Metaphysics" studies how Hindu thought bridged between the mythic panoply of the gods and a yet higher metaphysical vision. Both of these are most ancient in the Hindu tradition and both have remained in complementary relationship in Indian thought up to the present time. This provides the affirmative spiritual roots of Buddhism and thus of Asian culture as a whole.

Part II "Classical Philosophical and Mystical Ways to God" extends the above pre-philosophical pattern of thought to the development of systematic philosophy proper. Chapter IV on Hindu philosophy remains relevant here as foundation and archetype of the East. Chapter V "The Development of Greek and Judeo-Christian Philosophy: Bases for Ways to God" follows the elaboration of systematic philosophy in the West in Greek and Christian thought. The key steps here are in the field of metaphysics and include: Parmenides' elaboration of the notion of Being as One, unchanging and eternal; Plato's elaboration of participation as the structure of the relation of the many to the One; and the development by the Christian Fathers of the appreciation of existence beyond essence. Together they progressively elaborated the elements needed by reason in its effort to understand and articulate the relation of all to God.

Chapter VI "Systematic Christian Philosophy as a Way to God" shows how these three elements were brought together in the high Middle Ages through the rediscovery by Islam, and in turn by Christianity, of the Aristotelian sciences. This made it possible to elaborate a rigorously integrated vision of the participation of humans in God as his images and vice-gerants on earth.

Chapter VII "Al-Ghazali and Mulla Sadra: Islamic Mystical and Existential Way to God," studies the Islamic reactions to this reintroduction of Greek philosophy. These range from al-Ghazali's departure from philosophy in order to follow the mystical Sufi way, to Mulla Sadra's intensive employment of Greek philosophy and the Christian sense of existence to shape a masterful structure in the Islamic tradition relating all to God and describing the ways thereto.

There is a fascinating interplay between Islam and Christianity in the Chapters of this second Part. Chapter V is a common background for both traditions, and the High Middle Ages saw massive and interlinked accomplishments in the two. Chapter VII describes the heroic decision of al-Ghazali to leave philosophy when he perceived that the work of Avicenna and other philosophers was unable adequately to provide for the great vision of responsible human freedom required by the eschatology of the Qu'ran. But it suggests as well that he may have moved too quickly to abandon philosophy, for a century later philosophical responses to his concerns would be worked out by Aquinas. These could be helpful as well in enabling the thought of Mulla Sadra to evolve more amply the role of the body in the life of the human person, both here and hereafter.

Part III "Contemporary Philosophical Ways to God" shows how the new appreciation of human subjectivity opens ways to God that are both personal and social. Chapter VIII "Human Subjectivity and Personal Ways to God" describes the way in which the sense of the person has been dramatically renewed in recent times by attention to personal subjectivity, which modernity had ignored in favor of the objective and universal categories of science. But subjectivity that is fully human entails also the intersubjective relations between persons of which social life is built. Hence, Chapter IX "Cultural Traditions and Civil Society as Social Ways to God" examines the development of culture and cultural traditions especially as these emerge from, and in turn shape, the exercise of social life.

In the modern humanist manner religion had been seen as superfluous or at most as a means for social life, leaving humankind trapped within itself. In contrast, the contemporary (as well as the ancient Hindu) mode of religious awareness sees the divine not only as transcending or above, but also as immanent or within, that is, as the depth dimension and foundation of being. In this light the creative exercise of social freedom as the very emergence of being into time is the expression of divine life. All then becomes theonomous and social life can be appreciated and lived as the unfolding in time of the eternal power of Being and love of God. This is a way to God, but, even more, it is the special way in which God is present in and through our lives together. In this humankind appears as only vice gerant ruling over the rest of creation, but as priesthood offering all back to God, including its own life in time.

It would be magnificent, but less real and less challenging, if human freedom were unambiguous and remained simply in the role of an expression of divine life. In fact, it is highly torn between good and evil. This is the burden of Chapter X "The Dialectic of Good and Evil: 'Ultimate Concern' in History as a Way to God." It follows Paul Tillich's dialectic of the existential exercise of human freedom not only as expression, but also as negation of its divine heritage. This is the concrete drama of everyday life, and hence of the life of each person and people. Thus, the ways to God become not simply paths over which one travels, but the continuing vital drama of Fall and Resurrection. In these terms human life achieves its meaning as a struggle in faith and hope to rise to a fuller life in God; this is its true vocation.

The overall order of this work is at once diachronic and synchronic. It is diachronic from the past, depicting a sequence of stages each opening its own new mode of relating to God. This begins from the earliest sense of unity which in terms available through the external senses coordinated and rendered meaningful in the totem all aspects of the earliest forms of social life. The subsequent chapters unfold this understanding progressively through the successive actuation of the intellect in terms of the gods in imaginative mythic thought and in terms of being in the properly intellectual terms of philosophical thought, both objective and subjective. Thus Part I constitutes an archeology of religious knowledge as pre-philosophical, and Part II shows the further developed of this into systematic philosophical ways to God.

This sequence of ways is also synchronic, for it is not simply an account of what is past, a sequence of insights which arise and then disappear. Rather, what once was seen remains and cumulatively provides a theoretical and practical base for what is yet to come. Moreover, as subsequent forms of thought can never adequately express all that was vividly conscious in the previous forms, the earlier ways must be retained, even in being superseded. Each remains as a building block or, better, a part of an organic system.

Finally, the ways in Part III move diachronically toward the future. They give life and hope for persons and society in facing the decisive choices of good or evil in private and public life. In the past the great civilizations have developed their distinctive identities precisely through such choices which constructed in the same stroke both its history and its culture. In the present global context each has its own integrating contribution to make to the cooperation between civilizations from which the future of humanity as a whole is emerging. Viewed thus prospectively the ways to God are redemptive as the restoration, reorientation and recommitment of one's freedom in the Good. Not only for individuals, but for peoples this constitutes the definitive process of homecoming in God.

Thus, the final phrase of the title, "at the turn of the millennia," suggests that the ways to God are not only historical and of the past or even perduring structures in the present, but future oriented paths for contemporary renewal and future progress. They are indeed responses to the present challenge to reintegrate heaven, humankind and nature for the third millenium.

Together the single chapters of this work, each concerned with a different way, coalesce to compose a single Way to God. This is the deep history of humanity which, from its origins to the present — and on into the new millenium — constitutes the real drama of the great human pilgrimage. Supporting humankind in its restless outer movements and peregrinations through time is this deeper and increasingly conscious inner return of heart and mind to God as Source and Goal. Beneath the surface phenomena which happen only once, this is the perduring and essential which endows all with ultimate meaning.

In this light the single ways are not alternate paths, but the continuing foundational story of humankind's ever more conscious return to the creator by whom it was first loved. It provides the inspiration which consistently encourages our creativity and supports our sacrifices, redemptively transforming both into ways to our true home. This is religion as homecoming.

PROLOGUE

RELIGION AS COMING HOME:
The Iqbal Lecture

Mohammad Iqbal's brilliant exploration of the beauty and majesty of the Islamic religious vision not only expresses the soul of the people of Pakistan, but stands as a beacon for all religious visions, wherever they may be. Even more, his determination to respond with vigor and creativity to the great challenges to human meaning in our times, and to do so not by compromising the religious vision, but precisely by plumbing in faith its richness, is a most appropriate example for all. Indeed, if there be truth in the commonplace that the first millennium was focused upon God and the second upon man, then Iqbal may be the harbinger our new millennium, pointing the way to a vision that reunites both.

But how can the past give birth to the future; in particular, how can earlier human vision, especially that of a person who has passed from this life, generate new insights deep enough to help elucidate what both transcends human life and makes it possible?

One thinks immediately that this might be done by adding from other traditions or subsequent times. But there is danger in this of constructing an odd creature, recalling the definition of the camel as a horse made by a committee. True growth may be catalyzed from without, but it must emerge from within, from the home, the hearth and the heart. Here a story, my story, might help to suggest how this could be true of the thought of Mohammad Iqbal.

A STORY

In recent years it has become the custom to tell one's story as a way of shedding light upon the vital sources of one's insight and inspiration, what one values, and what one is really about in one's life. My story in philosophy is one of coming home by leaving home; hopefully it might help in reconstructing Iqbal's *Reconstruction of Religious Thought in Islam*.

As a young man I left homeland in order to undertake my education in the premier Catholic university, the Gregorian in Rome.

There, the Jesuits labored mightily for the mystical number of seven years to introduce me to the philosophy and theology of the Graeco-Roman Christian tradition, reading Augustine in the light of Plato and Thomas Aquinas' *Summa Theologiae* in the light of Aristotle. This is one of the great traditions of religious thought; it is the one in which I was born as a philosopher and which I have always been grateful to know and to savor.

My doctorate in philosophy was a first step outward to the work of the Protestant Christian philosopher-theologian, Paul Tillich. I then remained to teach metaphysics and philosophy of religion at the Catholic University of America. These courses followed the Aristotelian model, beginning from the world and reasoning to God after the pattern of Aristotle's *Metaphysics* and Thomas' "five ways" to resolve the question: Does God exist?

After some twelve years (another mystical number) it was time to step out of the Western Christian tradition as a whole. At the University of Madras I was most graciously received by Prof. T.N.P. Mahadevan who, with personal conviction and passionate commitment, introduced me to the Hindu metaphysical tradition, especially the non-dualist (*advaita*) tradition of the great Shankara. This was a second decisive experience for me and one which, with the help of Prof. Balasubramaniam and other in Madras and elsewhere in India, I have renewed and extended whenever possible.

Surprisingly, however, in taking me away from home, these studies brought me home at a yet deeper and truer level. Opening the text of the *Sutras*, the great systematic *summa* of the Hindu tradition, I found that rather than arriving at the divine life only at the end in the Aristotelian manner, it began with God: the first *sutra* announced the inquiry into Brahma which the second *sutra* described as "that from which, in which and into which all is."[1]

Suddenly, as with Marx's process of standing Hegel on his head, I found that my reading of Thomas' five ways to the existence of God was being inverted and, to my surprise, that it was thereby deepened and corrected. Reading the *Sutras* enabled me to grasp that the deeper sense of Thomas' "ways" was not to deduce the infinite from the finite (a real contradiction in terms), but to reconnect all such things to the source of their being and meaning. The five ways were incisive arguments that from whatever point of view —

origin, level of perfection, or goal — God alone is self-explanatory. All else takes their origin from him, manifests his divine life, and searches for its fulfillment in transcending itself toward others and ultimately toward Him. Human life is thereby freed from egoistic self-enclosure and its corollary, mutual conflict. Instead, life is essentially open to, and reflects, that infinity of being and meaning in which all else is grounded.

The long road to the other side of the world had brought me finally home to the foundational truth of my own philosophical tradition. This experience provides the theme here, namely, leaving home in order to return enriched, and not so much by what is found elsewhere, but especially by the deeper meaning one is enabled thereby to draw out of one's own tradition. This recalls the history of Abraham, our common father in faith. Here, I would like to investigate the possibilities of such an approach for the thought of Mohammad Iqbal, following broadly his three stages: (a) faith or belief, (b) thought or rational understanding, and (c) personal discovery and assimilation.

ARCHEOLOGY OF HUMAN THOUGHT AS RECONSTRUCTION OF RELIGIOUS AWARENESS

In the modern secular context the foundational religious meaning of life has been extensively forgotten. Instead, the rare and quite recent phenomenon of a world view precinding from, or neutral to, the divine has come to be taken as the honest base line from which the religious issue should be considered. For Iqbal this is quite out of the question, analogous to defining the mind on the basis of but one of its limited (analytic) processes. Hence, he does not go far in the first chapter of his *Reconstruction of Religious Thought in Islam* before stating as its principle what the *Sutras* exemplified both in its text and in its structure, namely, that: "It is in fact the presence of the total infinite in the movement of knowledge that makes finite thinking possible."[2] The genius of his work is its powerful and intricate elaboration of this theme.

This paper will attempt to suggest three ways in which Iqbal's thesis might be supplemented: first, from the point of view of an archeology of religious thought in support of his conviction that thought is natively religious; second, by elements from systematic philosophy with a view to understanding which the meaning this religious insight gives to human life; third, by drawing upon a phenomenology of religious consciousness to see how assimilation of this insight might open new ways of creating human comity for the millennium now dawning.

To begin, in a typically brief but pregnant aside Iqbal notes that "to the primitive man all experience was supernatural."[3] Rather than being simply a reference to dead facts from the past, this points to the total cumulative human experience regarding the essential importance of religion as manifested by human life. Moreover, it suggests the common ground needed by the many cultures as they begin to interact more intensively. It is then the place to begin.

From earliest times human thought has always and everywhere had a sacred center. It is possible to track the evolution of this constant awareness by relating it to the three dimensions of the human mind. The first is the external senses of sight, touch and the like by which one receives information from the external world. The second is the internal senses of imagination and memory by which one assembles the received data. This is done in a manner which enables it to represent the original whole from which the various senses drew their specific data, to represent these and other data in various combinations, and/or to recall this at a later time. Finally, beyond the external and internal senses is the intellect by which one knows the nature of things and judges regarding their existence.[4]

Not surprisingly, upon examination it appears that the actual evolution of human awareness of the sacred follows this sequence of one's natural capacities for knowledge. In all cases it is intellectual knowledge that is in play, for religious awareness concerns not the characteristics or shapes of sensible objects, but existence and indeed the one who gave his name as "I am Who Am". This was articulated successively, first in terms of the external senses in the totemic stage of thought, then in terms of the internal sense in the mythic period, and finally in properly intellectual terms as the origin of philosophy or science.[5]

To follow this evolution it should be noted that for life in any human society as a grouping of persons there is a basic need to understand oneself and one's relation to others. It should not be thought that these are necessarily two questions, rather than one.

They will be diversely formalized in the history of philosophy, but prior to any such formalization, indeed prior even to the capacity to formalize this as a speculative problem, some mode of lived empathy rather than antipathy must be possible. Plato later worked out formally and in detail that the unity of the multiple is possible only on the basis of something that is one, but the history of human life manifests that present in the awareness of the early peoples and according to their mode of awareness there always has been some one reality in terms of which they understood all to be related.

Totemic Thought (see Chapter II below)

The primitive or foundational mode of self-understanding was the totem. The earliest understanding by peoples of themselves and their unity with others and with nature was expressed in terms of some objects of the external senses, such as an animal or bird. Peoples spoke of themselves by simple identity with the animal or bird which was the totem of their clan. Lévy-Bruhl expresses this in a law of participation: Persons saw themselves not merely as in some manner like, or descendent from, their totem, but instead asserted directly, e.g.: "I am lion." In these terms they founded their identity and dignity, considered themselves bound to all others who had the same totem, and understood by analogy of their totem with that of other tribes the relations between their two peoples for marriage and the like.[6]

Moreover, the totem, in turn, was not simply one animal among others, but was in a sense limitless: no matter how many persons were born to the tribe the potentiality or resources of the totem was never exhausted — without limit there was always room for one more. Further, the totem was shown special respect, such as not being sold, used for food or other utilitarian purposes which would make it subservient to the individual members of the tribe or clan. Whereas other things might be said to be possessed and used, the totem was the subject of direct predication: one might say that he had a horse or other animal, but only of the totem would one say that he is, e.g., lion.

The totem then was the unique limitless reality in terms of which all particular people and things had their identity and interrelation. It was the sacred center of individual and community life in terms of which all had meaning and cohesion. It made possible the sense of both personal dignity and interpersonal relations, which were the most important aspects of human life. This it did with a sense of direct immediacy that would be echoed, but never repeated, in subsequent stages of more formally religious thought.

Whether this be seen as religious or proto-religious, what it shows is that religion is not something added to a secular universe, but the basic and essential insight of even the simplest forms of human community. The issue then is not whether there be room for religion alongside public life or how to protect one from the other, but how religion functions as the root of human meaning and community.

Mythic Thought (see Chapter III below)

The totem was able to provide for unity and meaning while the life of all members of the tribe remained similar. But its manner of expressing unity became insufficient as society became more specialized and differentiated. The bonds between members of the tribe came to depend not merely upon similarity and sameness, but upon the differentiated capabilities of, e.g., hunters, fishers and eventually farmers. With this ability to be both united and differentiated came an appreciation as well of the special distinctiveness of the sacred with regard to the many individuals of which it was the principle and center. What in totemic thought previously had been stated simply by identity (I am lion) could now be appreciated as greater than, and transcending, the members of the tribe. This is reflected in the development of priesthood, rituals and symbols to reflect what was no longer seen simply as one's deepest identity.[7]

Such a reality could no longer be stated in terms corresponding to the external senses, but needed instead to be figured by the imagination. The terms drawn originally from the senses now were reconfigured in forms that expressed life above humankind and which stood as the principle of human life. Such higher principles, as the more knowing and having a greater power of will, would be personal; and as transcendent persons, they would be gods.

It would be incorrect then to consider this, as did Freud and Marx, to be simply a projection of human characteristics. On the contrary, the development of the ability to think in terms shaped by the imagination released human appreciation of the principle of life from the limitations of animals, birds and other natural entities available to the external senses and allowed the transcendence of the principle of unity to be expressed in a more effective manner. This was not to create the sense of transcendence; rather it allowed the unique and essential foundation of human meaning of which Iqbal spoke to find new expression in terms of the evolving capabilities of human consciousness.

Of this the *Theogony*,[8] written by Hesiod (ca. 776 B.C.), is especially indicative. Because the gods stated the reality of the various parts of nature, when Hesiod undertook to state how these were interrelated he in effect articulated the unity and interrelation of all in terms of the divine, which is the basic sense of religion.

His work has a number of important characteristics. First, it intends to state the highest possible type of knowledge. Thus, it begins with an invocation to the Muses to provide him with divine knowledge: "These things declare to me from the beginning, ye Muses who dwell in the house of Olympus."[9] Secondly and correspondingly, it is concerned with the deepest issues, namely, the origin and unity of all things: "Tell me which of them came first" he asked, and then proceeded to a poetic delineation of the most important religious issues, from the justification of the divine reign (later named "theodicy" by Leibniz) to the understanding of evil.[10] Thirdly, because it was written as the period of purely mythic thought was drawing to a close — within two centuries of the initiation of philosophy in Greece — Hesiod was able to draw upon the full resources of the body of Greek mythology, weaving the entire panoply of the gods into the structure of his poem. He collected and related the gods not externally in a topographical or chronological sequence, but in terms of their inner reality and real order of dependence. Thus, when in the *Theogony* he responds to the question: "how, at the first, gods and earth came to be," his ordering of the gods weds theogony and cosmogony to constitute a unique mythical religious understanding regarding the unity and diversity of all.

The order of the parts of the universe is the following. The first to appear was Chaos: "Verily at the first Chaos came to be." Then came earth: "but next wide-bosomed Earth the ever sure foundation of all," and starry Heaven: "Earth first bare starry Heaven, equal to herself." From Earth, generally in unison with Heaven, were born Oceanus and the various races of Cyclopes and gods, from whom, in turn, were born still other gods such as Zeus and the races of men.

The understanding of the unity of reality expressed by this poem is the very opposite of a random gathering of totally disparate, limited and equally original units. On the contrary, the relation between the gods, and hence between the parts of nature they bespeak is expressed in terms of procreation. Hence, every reality is appreciated as related positively to all others in its genetic sequence.

This relatedness of things does not depend upon a later and arbitrary decision, but is equally original with their very reality; indeed, it is their reality. Neither is it something which involves only certain aspects of the components of the universe: it extends to their total actuality. This includes actions: Rhea, for example, appeals to her parents for protection from the acts of her husband, Cronus, against his children. Hence, the understanding which the poem conveys is that of a unity or relation which is the original reality of things and on which their distinctive character and actions depend.

This unity is understood to be by nature prior to diversity for it appears through a genetic structure in which each god proceeds from the union of an earlier pair of gods, while all such pairs are descendents of the one original pair, Earth and Heaven. Further, the procreation of the gods proceeds from each of these pairs precisely as united in love, under the unitive power of Eros who is equally original with heaven and earth.

From what has been said we can conclude that unity pervades and precedes gods and men. All is traced back to Earth and Heaven as the original pair from whose union, under the impetus of Eros, all is generated. But what is the relation between Heaven and Earth? This question is at the root of the issue of unity as expressed in mythic terms. It promises to be able to take us to a still deeper and more properly religious understanding if we return to the text and use the proper etymological tools.

The text states the following sequence: Chaos, Earth, Heaven. Unfortunately, since the Stoics, Chaos has come to mean disorder and mindless conflict or collision. Aristotle, however, in his *Physics* referred to chaos as empty space (*topos*).[11] Etymologically, the term can be traced through the root of the Greek term '*casko*' to the common Indo-European stem, 'gap'. This stem was employed in a manner similar to a sonar signal in order to sound out mythic thought across the broad range of the Indo-European peoples. The term was found to express a gaping abyss at the beginning of time as for example the derivative '*ginungagap*' in Nordic mythology.[12] Kirk and Raven confirm this analysis and conclude that 'chaos' meant, not a state of confusion or conflict, but an open and perhaps windy space which essentially is between boundaries.[13]

Returning to the text of the *Theogony* in this light, it will be noted that it does not say "In the beginning" or speak directly of a state prior to Chaos, but begins with Chaos: "At first Chaos came to be". But there is no suggestion that Chaos was the original reality; on the contrary, the text is explicit that chaos came to be: "*He toi men prótista Cháos genet.*"[14] Further, Chaos is a space to which boundaries are essential. These, it would seem, are the gods which the text states just after Chaos, namely, Earth and its equal, Heaven. These are not said to have existed prior to chaos and to have been brought into position in order to constitute the boundaries of the 'gap'; rather, they are said somehow to follow upon or be arranged on the basis of chaos.

Thus, Kirk and Raven understand the opening verses of the body of the text, namely, "Verily at the first Chaos came to be, but next wide-bosomed Earth . . . and Earth first bare starry Heaven equal to herself" in an active sense to express the opening of a gap or space, which thereby gives rise to Heaven and Earth as its two boundaries.[15]

For its intelligibility, this implies: (a) that an undifferentiated unity precedes the gap, and (b) that by opening or division the first contrasting realities, namely, Heaven and Earth, were constituted. That is, on the basis of the gap one boundary, Heaven, is differentiated from the other boundary, Earth: by the gap the boundaries identically are both constituted and differentiated as contraries. As all else are derivatives of Chaos, Earth and Heaven in the manner noted above, it can be concluded that the entire differentiated universe is derivative of an original undifferentiated unity which preceded Chaos.

It would be premature, however, to ask of the mythic mind whether this derivation took place by material or efficient causality; that question must await the development of philosophy. But the original reality itself is not differentiated; it is an undivided unity. As such it is without name, for the names we give reflect our sense perceptions which concern not what is constant and homogenous, but the differentiated bases of the various sense stimuli. What is undifferentiated is not only unspoken in fact, but unspeakable in principle by the language of myth which depends essentially upon the imagination.

Nonetheless, though it is unspeakable by the mythic mind itself, reflection can uncover or reveal something of that undifferentiated reality which the *Theogony* implies. We have, for instance, noted its reality and unity. This lack of differentiation is not a deficiency, but a fullness of reality and meaning from which all particulars and contraries are derived. It is unspeakable because not bounded, limited and related after the fashion of one imaged contrary to another. This is the transcendent fullness that is at the heart of the Hindu *advaita* or nondual philosophy; it is also the total infinite to which Iqbal referred as that which makes finite thinking possible.

It is the source of that which is seen and spoken in our language which is based in the imagination and which Hindu thought refers to as the world of names and forms. Further, it is the source, not only whence the differentiated realities are derived, but of the coming forth itself of these realities. This is reflected in two significant manners. First positively, Eros, which itself is said to come from chaos, is the power which joins together in procreative union the pairs of gods, thereby reflecting the dynamic, manifestive and sharing character of the undifferentiated reality.

Negatively, this is indicated also by the acts which the *Theogony* describes as evil. For example, it says that "Heaven rejoiced in his evil doing", namely, hiding away his children in a secret place of Earth as soon as each was born, and not allowing them to come into the light. Cronus is termed "a wretch" for swallowing his children. In each case evil is described as impeding the process by which new realities are brought into existence. This implies that its opposite, the good, involves essentially bringing forth the real. The undifferentiated unity is the origin of the multiple and differentiated; in terms we shall encounter below, it is participative.

Finally, it can now be seen that all the progeny, that is, all parts of the universe and all humans, are born into the unity of a family. This traces its origin, not to a pair of ultimately alien realities and certainly not to human chaos as conflict, but to the undifferentiated Unity. Just as there is no autogenesis, there is no unrelated reality or aspect of reality. It would seem, then, that verses 118-128 of the hymn imply a reality which is one, undifferentiated and therefore unspeakable, but productive of the multiple and therefore generous and sharing. For the Greek mythic mind then, beings are more one than many, more related than divided, more complementary than contrasting.

As a transformation of the earlier totemic structure, mythic understanding continues the basic totemic insight regarding the related character of all things predicated upon a unity and fullness of meaning. By thinking in terms of the gods, however, myth is able to add a number of important factors. First, quantitatively the myth can integrate, not only a certain tribe or number of tribes, but the entire universe. Second, qualitatively it can take account of such intentional realities as purpose and fidelity. Third, while implying the unitive principle which had been expressed with shocking directness in totemic thought ("I am lion"), it adds the connotation of its unspeakable and undifferentiated, but generous, character.

The expression of all this in terms of the forms available to the mythic internal sense of imagination had its temptations. These were pointed out by Xenophanes who noted that by the time of Homer and Hesiod a perfervid imagination had gone from expressing the transcendence of the gods to attributing to them as well the many forms of evil found among men:[16] the very principles of meaning and value had begun to point as well to their opposites. Thinking in terms of the imagination was no longer sufficient. Instead, the intellect needed to proceed in its own terms, beyond sense and imagination, to enable the deeper sense of the divine and of nature to be expressed and defended against confusion and corruption. As the mind proceeded to operate in properly intellectual terms, rather than though the images of mythic thinking, science and philosophy replaced myth as the basic mode of human understanding.

Metaphysics (see Chapter V below)

Once begun, philosophy made spectacularly rapid progress. Within but a few generations, the human intellect had worked out a structure of the physical world using the basic categories of hot and cold, wet and dry available to the external senses, along with mechanisms of vortex motion.[17] Mathematical reason worked with the internal senses to lay down the basic theorems of geometry.[18] In brief, by developing properly intellectual terms the Greeks elaborated with new and hitherto unknown precision insights regarding physical reality.

But that had never been the root human issue. Totemic and mythic thought were not merely ways of understanding and working with nature, although they did that as well. Fundamentally they concerned the metaphysical and religious issues of what it meant to be, the divine and transcendent basis of life, and the religious terms in which it needed to be lived in time. After the work of others in conceptualizing the physical and mathematical orders, Parmenides was able to take up the most basic questions of life and being in properly intellectual metaphysical terms.

First, he bound the work of the intellect directly to being: "It is the same thing to think and to be" (fragment 3).[19] Hence, the requirements of thinking would manifest those of being. Second, he contrasted being with its opposite, nonbeing, as something in contrast to nothing at all (fragment 2). This principle of non-contradiction was a construct of the mind; like *pi* in geometry it was something good to think with, for it enabled the mind to reflect upon the requirements of both being and mind so as to avoid anything that would undermine their reality.

Speaking still in a mythic language, the Proemium of Parmenides' famous poem described a scene in which he was awakened by goddesses and sent in a chariot drawn by a faithful mare along the arching highway that spans all things. In this process he moved from obscurity to light, from opinion to truth. There, the gates were opened by the goddess, Justice, as guardian of true judgements and he was directed to examine all things in order to discern the truth.

Parmenides then images himself proceeding further along the highway[20] till he comes to a fork with one signpost pointing toward being as essentially beginning. Here, Parmenides must reason regarding the implications of such a route. As "to begin" means to move from nonbeing or nothingness to being, that is, were "to be" to include "to begin" that would mean that being included within its very essence *nonbeing* or nothingness. There would then be no difference between being and nothing; being would be without meaning; the real would be nothing at all. If conversely, from this notion of beginning such nonbeing is removed then it emerges as essentially not beginning, but eternal. This is the first requirement of being: the possibility of taking the fork which would have being as essentially beginning is excluded; being is by nature eternal and all that does begin can do so only in derivation therefrom.

The chariot then moves along the highway of being and the procedure is analogous at the two subsequent forks in the road where the signposts tempt one to consider being as changing and multiple, respectively. Each of these, Parmenides reasons, would again place nonbeing within being itself, thereby destroying its very character as being. Nonbeing is contained in the notion of change, inasmuch as a changing being is *no* longer what it had been and *not* yet what it will become. But for such nonbeing to pertain to the essence of being would destroy being. When, however, nonbeing is removed then being emerges as unchanging. Similarly, nonbeing is essential to the notion of multiplicity, inasmuch as this requires that one being *not* be the other. When, however, nonbeing is removed what emerges is one. These then are the characteristics of being: it is infinite and eternal, unchanging and one.

Being itself then transcends the multiple and changing world in which we live: it is in a manner more perfect than could possibly be appreciated in the graphic terms of the internal senses of imagination which defined the nature of human capabilities in the stage of myth.

In this way Parmenides discerned the necessity of Absolute, eternal and unchanging being — whatever be said of anything else. Neither being nor thought makes sense if being is the same as nonbeing, for then to do, say or be anything would be the same as not doing, not saying or not being. As the real is irreducible to nothing and being is irreducible to nonbeing — as it must be if there is any thing or any meaning whatsoever — then being must have about it the self-sufficiency expressed by Parmenides' notion of the absolute One.

A person can refuse to look at this issue and focus upon particular aspects of limited realities. But if one confronts the issue of being it leads to the Self-sufficient as the creative source of all else. Without this all limited beings would be radically compromised — not least, man himself. It is not surprising, therefore, that Aristotle would conclude his *Metaphysics* as a search for the nature of being with a description of divine life and call the whole a "theology".[21]

The issue then is not how the notion of the divine entered human thought; it has always been there, for without that which is One and Absolute in the sense of infinite and self-sufficient man and nature would be at odds; humankind would lack social cohesion; indeed, thinking would be the same as not thinking, just as being would be the same as nonbeing.

From the above archeology of human thought in its totemic, mythic and first philosophical stages it can be concluded with Iqbal that it has been religious insight regarding the Absolute which has made finite thinking possible. Leaving home and going deeply into the past thus brings us home to reconstruct the deep truth of faith regarding knowledge, namely, not only that it can also be about religion, but that in essence thought itself is the religious reconstitution of all in God: this is what knowledge most fundamentally is.

There are two implications of this archeology which I would like to note here. The first concerns the relation of a people to the message of a prophet. As the basis of the human self-understanding of the different cultures is essentially religious, a divine revelation through a great prophet comes not as alien and conflictual, but as a special divine help to appreciate, purify and strengthen a culture. The message of the prophet evokes the divine life which lies within; it enables each people to plunge more deeply into the infinite ground of their cultural traditions and to bring out more of its meaning for their life. Indeed, confidence (etymologically rooted in "faith" — con-fidence) and commitment to one's tradition as grounded in the infinite means precisely expecting it to have even more to say then a people has yet articulated. In this light, the Prophet's voice is a call to delve anew into one's tradition, to bring out more of its meaning for one's times and to live this more fully. This is a voice to which one can respond fully and freely.

In this sense I would take issue with Iqbal's seemingly overly Darwinian description of the first period of religious life as

> a form of discipline which the individual or a whole people must accept as an unconditional command

without any rational understanding of the ultimate meaning and purpose of the command. This attitude may be of great consequence in the social and political history of a people, but is not of much consequence in so far and the individual's inner growth and expansion are concerned.[22]

The archeology of human thought suggests that the response of a people to the message of the prophet is more precisely a renewal and reaffirmation of their deep self-understanding. This is truly a homecoming in whose very essence lies the deep freedom of the peace one experiences in returning home after a long and confusing day. But I suspect that Iqbal would not disagree with this for in reality it is an application to culture of what he concluded regarding thought, namely, that it is made possible by the presence therein of the total infinite.[23] This parallels his observation regarding the natural order, namely, that "there is no such thing as a profane world . . . all is holy ground," citing the Prophet: "The whole of this earth is a mosque."[24]

A second implication can be of special importance in these times of intensifying communication and interaction between peoples. If the future is to hold not Huntington's conflict of civilizations, but their cooperation in a shrinking world, then it is important to see how the civilizations deriving from prophets and religious traditions can relate one to another. Hermeneutics can be helpful here with its suggestion that in order to delve more deeply it is helpful to hear not only reformulations of what we ourselves say in our own horizon, but new formulations from other traditions regarding the basically shared truths of our divine origin and goal. As Iqbal is supported by an archeology of knowledge indicating that all knowledge is grounded in the divine, we can expect that religious texts from the traditions of other great prophets will evoke new echoes from the depths of our own tradition. In this light interchange with other traditions comes not as a threat. Rather, cultural interchange can enable us to make our pilgrimages, each more unerringly along our own path, to the one holy mountain[25] to which Iqbal refers as the total absolute. Other forms of cooperation can, and indeed must, be built upon this.

SYSTEMATIC PHILOSOPHY AND THE RELIGIOUS RECONSTRUCTION OF HUMAN PERSON
(see Part II below)

There is another implication of arriving at Iqbal's sense of the essentially religious character of thought through an archeology of human thinking. This relates to his concern to protect religion against the tendency of analytic rationality to reduce the mind to its empirical content and to bind it to the material, or at least to what could clearly and distinctly be conceived by the human mind. Iqbal's approach was to show the limited character of such a view, not only in terms of its objects, but especially as a description of thought itself. He did this by majestically describing the broad (religious) reaches of the mind. For this he reinterpreted time, light and freedom in ways that echoed the thought of his contemporaries, Bergson, Whitehead, Alexander, Royce and Einstein, whose thought he much enriched with the cultural resources of the Islamic tradition. This is a special power and grace of his thought.

There is here a significant contrast to al-Ghazālī (see Chapter VII below) whose *Munqidh* I most highly admire (and indeed with Professor M. Abulaylah of the al-Azhar have annotated and republished). In describing his itinerary to the mystical life al-Ghazālī considered thought to be limited and therefore in the end inadequate or even subversive for religious life. This implied a rupture of thought and faith which even Averroes (Ibn Rushd) was not able to repair. In our times this has become particularly worrisome, for the Enlightenment has radicalized this gulf by reducing all thought rigorously to contrary and hence limited concepts: the modern world in which we live has been built in these terms. It should not be surprising, indeed it is a point of honor, that Islam always has stood firmly against such "enlightenment". Some have reacted by rejecting modernity in bloc — even at times violently and self destructively. Iqbal's response is different. He is eloquent in his exposition of the essential importance of limited, categorial thought, precisely in its own sphere, and reaches out to welcome the positive contributions of modernity.

But he gives voice to infinitely richer domains of thought grounded in the divine. Thus the divine appears as it were dimly as the background of every limited human encounter; human life becomes theonomous and can be seen in its transcendent significance. For Iqbal, when related to their infinite ground, science and technology become concrete manifestations and articulations of the meaning of God in time.

But as he warms to this subject in his *Reconstruction* Iqbal edges ever closer to that mystical vision of Hallaj in which all is so suffused with divine light and meaning that man and nature seem almost divine. Iqbal reacts against any identification of the two and with the full force of the Islamic tradition of fidelity would answer: 'Never; there is but one God and no other!'

In this lies the contemporary drama of Islam as of all religious visions, for man today is intent upon an answer to the question of "how he is to be understood?" Note this is not the question of how God could create our world of finite beings. The answer to that question is hidden in divine love which we can seek to acknowledge (as we shall suggest below), but never to understand in itself: such understanding is the divine life itself. Rather, the question is how, in the light of this revelation of God's love, we can overcome the *hubris* by which the human ego claims to be absolute, and yet understand the reality of the human person as having the autonomy required for the responsibility and creativity required in order to survive and flourish — and to play his role in the echatology of the Qu'ran. How can men and women come truly alive so as to recognize themselves fully as images of God, yet not be God; and moreover how in the image of their creator, can they undertake a creative exercise of their proper freedom and responsibility?

This is a point of high metaphysics on which I would like to suggest a way to carry forward Iqbal's work after the image of leaving in order to return.

We all know and greatly admire the work of such Islamic scholars as al Farabi, Avicenna and Averroes, who drew upon and developed the Greek philosophical heritage (see Chapter V below). It is a part of our common heritage which, however, was interrupted in Islam when, after the interchange between al-Ghazālī and Averroes, this Graeco Islamic effort was broadly abandoned. In the metaphysical quest the relay was passed to another religious tradition, that of the Western Christian philosophers of the high Middle Ages: Thomas Aquinas, Scotus, and their schools.

Iqbal suggests two reasons why the path of Aristotle and

Averroes was found to be finally inimicable to the Islamic vision. First, the notion of an immortal agent intellect stood in the way of the value and destiny of the human ego[26] and hence of one's full personal spirituality and responsibility. Second the orientation to high metaphysical theory diverged from the concrete inductive orientation of Islam.[27] But the concrete point in time at which Greek thought was abandoned was that of the dispute over the agent intellect and hence it seems best to begin with this issue.

Here one could wonder whether the Islamo-Greek tradition was abandoned just a bit too soon, for in the Christian tradition of scholarship Aquinas's religious response was imminent, and would enable the Greek tradition to evolve into modern thought. In view of this a project of reconstruction in Islam could take particular interest in the work of Thomas Aquinas as part of its effort to discover how Islam can be truly at home in modern times and creative in modern terms. Any such insights would, in turn, be of great interest to other religious traditions, all of which are struggling with this issue each in its own way.

Hermeneutics tells us that in approaching an issue we need a question in order to focus our attention and be able to draw new insight. Iqbal provides the questions we should ask for the project of religious reconstruction; they concern existence and its implication for creation and the religious sense of man.

Existence and the Reconstruction of Being in God
    (see Chapter V below)

Iqbal sees as key to religious reconstruction the overcoming the relatively passive sense of reality found in the formal order characteristic of the Platonic strain of thought, and also reflected in modern rationalism. In that light limited realities passively replicate the archetypal forms or ideas, but add nothing new; finite reality is drained of its vitality and reduced to a shadow. Instead, Iqbal calls for a return to the active character of reality. This suggests that we look in the early Christian Fathers for the emergence of being as existence. It was indeed this which characterized the thought of Thomas and gave it such prestige in Christian circles

Although Greek philosophy grew out of an intensive mythic sense of life in which all was a reflection of the will of the gods, it nonetheless presupposed matter always to have existed. As a result, the focus of its attention and concern was upon the forms by which matter was determined to be of one type rather than another. For Aristotle, physical or material things in the process of change from one form to another were the most manifest realities and his philosophizing began therefrom. This approach to philosophy beginning from sense encounters with physical beings corresponded well to our human nature as mind and body, and could be extended to the recognition of divine life. But Iqbal wants more; for him "it is in fact the presence of the total infinite in the movement of knowledge that makes finite thinking possible." The Greek philosophical awareness of what it meant to be real would need considerable enrichment in order to appreciate the foundational significance for human though of its grounding in a fully transcendent and infinite Being.

It was just here that the development of the prophetic Judeo-Christian context had an especially liberating effect upon philosophy. By applying to the Greek notion of matter the Judeo-Christian heritage regarding the complete dominion of God over all things, the Church Fathers opened human consciousness to the fact that matter, too, depended for its reality upon God. Thus, before Plotinus, who was the first philosopher to do so, the Fathers already had noted that matter, even if considered eternal, stood also in need of an explanation of its origin.[28]

This enabled philosophical questioning to push beyond issues of form, nature or kind to existence and, hence, to deepen radically the sense of reality. If what must be explained is no longer merely the particular form or type of beings, but matter as well, then the question becomes not only how things are of this form or that kind, but how they exist rather than not exist. In this way the awareness of being evolved beyond change or form;[29] to be real would mean to exist and whatever is related thereto. Quite literally, "To be or not to be" had become the question.

By the same stroke, our self-awareness and will were deepened dramatically. They no longer were restricted to focusing upon choices between various external material objects and modalities of life — the common but superficial contemporary meaning of what Adler terms a circumstantial freedom of self-realization — nor even to Kant's choosing as one ought after the manner of an acquired freedom of self-perfection; all this remains within the context of being as nature or essence. The freedom opened by the conscious assumption and affirmation of one's own existence was rather a natural freedom of self-determination with responsibility for one's very being.[30]

One might follow the progression of this deepening awareness of being by reflecting upon the experience of being totally absorbed in the particularities of one's job, business, farm or studies — the prices, the colors, the chemicals — and then encountering an imminent danger of death, the loss of a loved one or the birth of a child. At the moment of death, as at the moment of birth, the entire atmosphere and range of preoccupations in a hospital room shifts dramatically, being suddenly transformed from tactical adjustments for limited objectives to confronting existence, in sorrow or in joy, in terms that plunge to the center of the whole range of meaning. (This can be stated in social terms as well — see Chapter IX below.) Such was the effect upon philosophy when the awareness of being developed from attention to merely this or that *kind* of reality, to focus upon the act of existence in contrast to non-existence, and hence to human life in all its dimensions and, indeed, to life divine.

Cornelio Fabro goes further. He suggests that this deepened metaphysical sense of being in the early Christian ages not only opened the possibility for an enriched sense of freedom, but itself was catalyzed by the new sense of freedom proclaimed in the religious message. That message focused not upon Plato's imagery of the sun at the mouth of the cave from which external enlightenment might be derived, but upon the eternal Word or Logos through and according to which all things received their existence and which enlightened their consciousness life.

> In the beginning was the word, and the word was
>   with God, and the word was God.
> The same was in the beginning with God.
> All things were made by him: and without him was
>   made nothing that was made.
> In him was life, and the life was the light of men.
> And the light shineth in darkness, and the darkness
>   did not comprehend it.
> That was the true light, which enlighteneth every

man that cometh into this world.[31]

Thus the power of being bursts into time through creator and prophet:

- it directs the mind beyond the ideological poles of species and individual interests, and beyond issues of place or time as limited series or categories;
- it centers, instead, upon the unique reality of the person as a participation in the creative power of God, a being bursting into existence, who is and cannot be denied;
- it rejects being considered in any sense as nonbeing, or being treated as anything less than its full reality;
- it is a self or in Iqbal's term an 'ego', affirming its own unique actuality and irreducible to any specific group identity; and
- it is image of God for whom life is sacred and sanctifying, a child of God for whom to be is freely to dispose of the power of new life in brotherhood with all humankind.[32]

It took a long time for the implications of this new appreciation of existence and its meaning to germinate and find its proper philosophic articulation. Over a period of many centuries the term 'form' was used to express both the kind or nature of things and the new sense of being as existence. As the distinction between the two was gradually clarified, however, proper terminology arose in which that by which a being is of this or that kind came to be expressed by the term 'essence,' while the act of existence by which a being simply is was expressed by 'existence' *(esse)*.[33] The relation between the two was under intensive, genial discussion by the Islamic philosophers when their Greek tradition in philosophy was abrogated.

This question was resolved soon thereafter in the work of Thomas Aquinas through a real distinction which rendered most intimate the relation of the two principles as act and potency and opened a new and uniquely active sense of being. This is not to say that al-Ghazālī was wrong in opposing Averroes or that Islam was wrong in choosing the side of al-Ghazālī in this dispute. Aquinas also had to overcome the Latin Averrorists in the course of his intellectual battles in Paris. But Iqbal's intuition of the cultural importance of reasoning in terms of being as actively existing suggests the importance of this juncture in the history of thought as the evolution of the religious vision both of God and of the reality of the human person and of society as participations therein. With this the Christian metaphysical tradition went on to develop technical tools important for understanding human life in this world.

Being and The Reconstruction of Man in God
 (see Chapter VI below)

The focus upon being as active had profound implications for the understanding of man in God. It had crucial importance first for the sense of the divine itself. In Plato's more passive vision the divine as active would be situated below the idea of the Good or the One which were objects of contemplation. We saw how taking being in a more active sense allowed Aristotle to appreciate divine life as an active thinking on thinking.

Iqbal and the Islamic tradition rightly feared that this notion, as a product of human reasoning, would be essentially limited and limiting. This is his incisive and trenchant critique of the cosmological and other modes of reasoning to God. Certainly reasoning in terms of forms and categories would be subject to this critique, but as just noted being had come to be perceived rather in terms of existence, which is affirmation without negation and hence without limitation.

Nevertheless, Iqbal makes a key contribution to any appropriate reading of a systematic Christian philosophy by insisting that the notion of God is not a product of human reasoning. Rather, as seen above through the archeology of human knowledge, the absolute is there as the center of human life in its earliest totemic mode; it flowers as humankind develops the mythic mode of thought; and it is there from the beginning in Parmenides' founding of Greek metaphysical thought. As notes Augustine in his dialectic of love: it is not we who first loved God, but He who first loved us: from him come life and light and love.

Viewed in this light, the classical "five ways" to God have been largely misunderstood. They are not proofs for the existence of God, much less ways constructing the reality of God. Instead they are ways in which all things are bound back to God (*re-ligio* as one of the etymologies of 'religion') all things, whether they be considered in terms of their origin, of their level of being, or their goal, purpose or meaning. Despite his critique of the cosmological arguments, Iqbal seems to intuit this when he writes that their true significance will appear only "if we are able to show that the human situation is not final."[34]

In this light, one need not fear that an affirmation of man whether by personal freedom or technological means will be detrimental to religion. Rather human life becomes the proclamation of God's wisdom, power, love and providence. On this basis Thomas proceeds systematically to shed the requirement not only of an external agent intellect, but also of a special divine illumination for each act of reason, and of seeds of possibility for all new realizations — all of which were ways by which the earlier Christian-Platonism had attempted to preserve a role for God in human progress. Instead the human person is seen as sacrament of God, His sign and symbol, as creative vice regent and artist in and of this world. Thus, Thomas does not hesitate to affirm of the human person whatever is required in order that, properly according to his own nature and in his own name, the person be able to fulfill these roles in this world. This is the proper autonomy of the human in the divine; we might say that in this the human person comes truly home in God.

Participation and the Reconstruction of Religious Vision
(see Chapter VI below)

The existential sense of being and its openness to the infinite has allowed more recently for a renewed appreciation of Thomas' structure of participation by which human autonomy is an affirmation, rather than a derogation of God. In any limited being, its essence or nature constitutes by definition a limited and limiting capacity for existence: by it, the being is capable of this much existence, but of no more. Such an essence must then be distinct from the existence which, of itself, bespeaks only affirmation, not negation and limitation.

But such a being, whose nature or essence is not existence but only a capacity for existence, could not of itself or by its own nature justify its possession and exercise of existence. The Parmenidean principle of noncontradiction will not countenance existence coming from non-existence, for then being would be reducible to non-being or nothing. Such beings, then, are dependent precisely for their existence, that is, precisely as beings or existents.

This dependence cannot be upon another limited being similarly composed of a distinct essence and existence, for such a being would be equally dependent; the multiplication of such dependencies even infinitely would multiply, rather than answer the question of how composite beings with a limiting essence have existence. Hence, limited composite beings must depend for their existence upon, or participate in, uncomposite being, that is, in a being whose essence or nature, rather than being distinct from and limiting its existence, is identically existence. This is Being Itself — the total infinite to which Iqbal refers as making finite being and thinking possible.

That uncomposite Being is simple, the One par excellence; it is participated in by all multiple and differentiated beings for their existence. The One, however, does not itself participate; it is the unlimited, self-sufficient, eternal and unchanging Being which Parmenides had shown alone was required for being. "Limited and composite brings are by nature relative to, participate in, and caused by the unique simple and incomposite being which is Absolute, unparticipated and uncaused."[35]

This sense of participation makes it possible to speak of the nonreciprocal relation of finite to infinite and to identify the essentially caused character of the former.[36] This is a crucial step beyond the Platonic tradition which rightly can be criticized for failing to develop adequate tools for distinguishing man from God. An existential metaphysics understands causality in terms of participation in the infinite. Hence, even while placing central emphasis upon union with the divine, by its conceptual and ontological structures it never loses sight of their distinction. Nevertheless, through making this distinction it sees every aspect of the caused or created being as totally derivative from, and expressive of, the infinite. Let man be man; indeed let all creatures be, for they glorify God the infinite and all mighty, the munificent and merciful!

For his sense of participation some early Christian Church Fathers numbered Plato among the prophets. As clarified and enriched by Aristotle's sense of being as active, by the Christian existential sense of being and by the work of his great medieval Islamic commentators, this metaphysics can provide the systematic clarification needed by Iqbal's insights regarding religion in order that they be articulated in the increasingly structured physical and social environment in which we live. In the face of the dilemma of human *hubris* vs religious passivity in our days, this provides indispensable help in responding to the need of those devoted in faith. For it can aid them to understand better the relation of their increasingly complex life to God and assist them in living their faith in our times: in a word, it is crucial to coming home and being at home religiously in our times.

PHENOMENOLOGY OF GIFT AS RELIGIOUS RECONSTRUCTION OF SOCIAL COHESION
(see Chapter VIII below)

For Iqbal making man at home in the world might be a proper task for "metaphysics . . . a logically consistent view of the world with God as part of that view." But he sees another stage in which

> metaphysics is displaced by psychology, and religious life develops the ambition to come into direct contact with the ultimate reality. It is here that religion becomes a matter of personal assimilation of life and power; and the individual achieves a free personality, not by releasing himself from the fetters of the law, but by discovering the ultimate source of the law within the depths of his own consciousness.[37]

Iqbal would probably be very interested in recent developments in phenomenology. For him

> the aspiration of religion soars higher than that of philosophy. Philosophy is an intellectual view of things; and as such, does not care to go beyond a concept which can reduce all the rich variety of experience to a system. It sees Reality from a distance as it were. Religion seeks a closer contact with Reality. The one is theory; the other is living experiences, association, intimacy. In order to achieve this intimacy thought must rise higher than itself, and find its fulfillment in an attitude of mind which religion describes as prayer — one of the

last words on the lips of the Prophet of Islam.[38]

Hence the search into human subjectivity is really at the heart of Iqbal's concern for the reconstruction of religion. He brilliantly rearticulated the Islamic vision in terms of the vitalism of his time as part of this century's renewed discovery and appreciation of human subjectivity. It is necessary to follow the emergence of this attention and to elaborate the possibilities of the phenomenology to which it led in order to extend Iqbal's work of religious reconstruction. This would liberate the human spirit from egoism, and bring it finally home — this time not only to self, but to others and to God.

Phenomenology

At the beginning of this century, it appeared that the rationalist project of stating all in clear and distinct objective terms was close to completion. This was to be achieved in either the empirical terms of the positivist tradition of sense knowledge or in the formal and essentialist terms of the Kantian intellectual tradition. Whitehead writes that at the turn of the century, when with Bertrand Russell he went to the first World Congress of Philosophy in Paris, it seemed that, except for some details of application, the work of physics was essentially completed. To the contrary, however, the very attempt to finalize scientific knowledge with its most evolved concepts made manifest the radical insufficiency of the objectivist approach.

Similarly, Wittgenstein began by writing his *Tractatus Logico-Philosophicus*[39] on the Lockean supposition that significant knowledge consisted in constructing a mental map corresponding point to point to the external world as perceived by sense experience. In such a project the spiritual element of understanding, i.e., the grasp of the relations between the points on this mental map was relegated to the margin as simply "unutterable." However, experience in teaching children led Wittgenstein to the conclusion that this empirical mental mapping was simply not what was going on in human knowledge. In his *Blue and Brown Books*[40] and his subsequent *Philosophical Investigations*[41] Wittgenstein shifted human consciousness or intentionality, which previously had been relegated to the periphery, to the very the center of concern. In this context the focus of his philosophy was no longer the positivist replication of the external world, but the human construction of language and of worlds of meaning.[42]

A similar process was underway in the Kantian camp. There Husserl's attempt to bracket all elements in order to isolate pure essences for scientific knowledge directed attention to the limitations of a pure essentialism and opened the way for his understudy, Martin Heidegger, to rediscover the existential and historical dimensions of reality in his *Being and Time*.[43] The religious implications of this new sensitivity was articulated by Karl Rahner in his work *The Spirit in the World* and by the Second Vatican Council in *The Church in the World*.[44]

For Heidegger the meaning of being and of life was unveiled in conscious human life (*dasein*) lived through time and therefore through history. Thus, human consciousness becomes the new focus of attention; the uncovering or "bringing into light" (the etymology of phenomenology) of the unfolding patterns and interrelations of being would open a new era of human awareness. Epistemology and metaphysics would develop in the very work of tracking the nature and direction of this process.

Thus, for Heidegger's successor, Hans-Georg Gadamer, the task becomes that of uncovering how human persons, emerging in the culture of a family, neighborhood and people, exercise their freedom and weave their cultural tradition. This is not history as a mere compilation of whatever humankind does or makes, but culture as the fabric of human symbols and interrelations by which a human group unveils being in its time.

Iqbal provides needed direction here by pointing out that a religious outlook is not an external search for power and control susceptible of empirical investigation and pragmatic interpretation. Rather religion entails an inner attitude which takes us to the very roots of our being and even to its source.

This points us deeply into human subjectivity, but what is its ultimate meaning for life? Is this new focus upon human subjectivity but another chapter in *Paradise Lost* in which humankind attempts to seize its own destiny in a way that excludes God? Or does to interact more consciously mean to attack others more devastatingly, killing not only bodies but spirits as well? Is the new awareness of cultures to open new periods of persecution and cultural genocide;

very concretely, "Can we get along" as peoples, cultures and civilizations?

Gift

"Appreciation"[45] is a key element in Iqbal's thought regarding religion. It unites the elements of our previous sections regarding systematic philosophy, namely, existence, the subsistence of man and the causal participation of human life in the divine. It does so, however, not as effective, objective realities to be known, but as subjective realities lived and savored in a manner that is itself as religious as prayer and contemplation. This is the intent of a phenomenology in terms of the consciously lived appreciation for our life as gift; it leads one to the total absolute, now however not only as a condition of knowledge, but as the source and hence the goal of love.

One can begin with the person as a polyvalent unity operative on both the physical and non-physical levels. Though the various sciences analyze distinct dimensions, the person is not a construct of independent components, but an identity: one's physical and the psychic realities are dimensions of oneself and of no other. Further, this identity is not the result of my personal development, but was had by me from my beginning; it is a given for each person. Hence, while I can grow indefinitely, act endlessly, and do and make innumerable things, the growth and the actions will be always my own; I am the same given or person who perdures through all the stages of my growth.

This givenness appears also through reflection upon my interpersonal relations. I do not properly create these, for they are possible only if I already have received my being. Further, to open to others is a dynamism which pertains to my very nature and which I can suppress only at the price of deep psychological disturbance. Relatedness is given with one's nature and received as a promise and a task; it is one's destiny. What depends upon the person is only the degree of his or her presence to others.[46]

Unfortunately, this givenness is often taken in the sense of closure associated with the terms 'datum' or 'data', whether hypothetical or evidential. In the hypothetical sense, a given is a stipulation agreed upon by the relevant parties as the basis for a process of argumentation: Granted X, then Y. Such are the premises of an argument or the postulates in a mathematical demonstration. In the evidential sense, data are the direct and warranted observations of what actually is the case. In both these meanings the terms 'given' or 'data' direct the mind exclusively toward the future or consequent as one's only concern. The use of the past participle of the verb stem (*data*) closes off any search toward the past so that when one given is broken down by an analysis new givens appear. One never gets behind some hypothetical or evidential given.

This closure is done for good reason, but it leaves open a second — and for our purposes potentially important — sense of 'given'. This is expressed by the nominative form, 'donum' or gift. In contrast to the other meanings, this points back, as it were, behind itself to its source in ways similar to the historians' use the term 'fact'. They note that a fact is not simply there; its meaning has been molded or made (*facta*) within the ongoing process of human life.[47] In this sense it points back to its origin and origination; it could be the road home.

However, this potentially rich return to the source was blocked at the beginning of the 19th century by a shift to an anthropocentric view. In this horizon facts came to be seen especially as made by man who is conceived either as an individual in the liberal tradition, or as a class in the socialist tradition — to which correspond the ideals of progress and praxis, respectively. Because what was made by man could always be remade by him,[48] this turned aside a radical search into the character of life as gift. Attention still remained only upon the future understood simply in terms of man and of what man could do by either individual or social praxis.

There are reasons to suspect that this humanism is not enough for the dynamic sense of a cultural heritage and the creative sense of harmony as cooperation with others. Without underestimating how much has been accomplished in terms of progress and praxis, the world-wide contemporary phenomenon of alienation, not only between cultures but from one's own culture and people, suggests that something important has been forgotten.

First, as notes Iqbal, by including only what is abstractively clear, these approaches begin by omitting that which can be had only in self-knowledge, namely, one's self-identity and all that is most distinctive and creative in a people's heritage. Focusing only upon what is analytically clear and distinct to the mind of any and every individual renders alien the notes of personal identity, freedom and creativity, as well as integrity, wholeness and harmony. These characterize the more synthetic philosophical and religious traditions and are realized in self-knowledge, deep interpersonal bonds,[49] and under the personal guidance of a teacher, spiritual director or guru.[50]

Second, there is the too broadly experienced danger that in concrete affairs the concern to build the future in terms only of what has been conceived clearly and by all will be transformed, wittingly or unwittingly, into oppression of self-identity and destruction of integrative cultures both as civilizations and as centers of personal cultivation. Indeed, the charges of cultural oppression from so many parts of the world lead one to doubt that the humanist notion of the self-given and its accompanying ideals can transcend the dynamics of power and leave room for persons, their freedom and creativity, especially for those of other cultures.

Finally, were the making implied in the derivation of the term 'fact' from 'facere' to be wholly reduced to 'self-making,' and were the given to become only the self-given, we would have stumbled finally upon what Parmenides termed "the all impossible way" of deriving what is from what is not.[51] Iqbal's essential insight — shared by the Hindu, Islamic and Judeo-Christian traditions — that all is grounded in the Absolute should guard against such self-defeating, stagnating and destructive self-centeredness.

Phenomenology of Person as Gift in God
   (See Chapter VIII below)

It is time then to look again to the second meaning of 'given' and to follow the opening this provides toward the source as implied in the notion of gift. Above, we noted that self-identity and interpersonal relatedness are gifts (*dona*). We shall now look further into this in order to see what it suggests regarding the dynamic openness required for cooperation between persons and cultures.

First, one notes that as gift the given has an essentially gratuitous character. It is true that at times the object or service given could be repaid in cash or in kind. As indicated by the root of the term 'commercial,' however, such a transaction would be based on some merit (*mereo*) on the part of the receiver. This would destroy its nature as gift precisely because the given would not be based primarily in the freedom of the giver.

The same appears from an analysis of an exchange of presents. Presents cease to be gifts to the degree that they are given only because of the requirements of the social situation or only because of a claim implicit in what the other might have given me. Indeed, the sole way in which such presents can be redeemed as gifts is to make clear that their presentation is not something to which I feel obliged, but which I personally and freely want to do. As such then, a gift is based precisely upon the freedom of the giver; it is gratuitous.

There is striking symmetry here with the 'given' in the above sense of hypothesis or evidence. There, in the line of hypothetical and evidential reasoning there was a first, namely, that which is not explained, but upon which explanation is founded. Here there is also a first upon which the reality of the gift is founded and which is not to be traced to another reality. This symmetry makes what is distinctive of the gift stand out, namely, that the giving is not traced back further precisely because it is free or gratuitous. Once again, our reflections lead us in the direction of that which is self-sufficient, absolute and transcendent as the sole adequate source of the gift of being. Phenomenological reflection leads us home to what Iqbal intuited, namely, that only a total absolute makes possible anything finite, including our very selves.

Further, as an absolute point of origin with its distinctive spontaneity and originality, the giving is non-reciprocal. To attempt to repay would be to destroy the gift as such. Indeed, there is no way in which this originating gratuity can be returned; we live in a graced condition. This appears in reflection upon one's culture. What we received from the authors of the *Vedas*, a Confucius or Mohammad can in no way be returned. Nor is this simply a problem of distance in time, for neither is it possible to repay the life we have received from our parents, the health received from a doctor, the wisdom from a teacher, or simply the good example which can come from any quarter at any time. The non-reciprocal character of our life is not merely that of part to whole; it is that of a gift to its source.[52]

The great traditions have insisted rightly both upon the oneness of the absolute reality and upon the lesser reality of the multiple: the multiple is not The Real, though neither is it totally non-reality. Anselm's elaboration of the notion of privation contains a complementary clarification of the gratuitous character of beings as given or gifted. He extended this notion of privation to the situation of creation in which the whole being is gifted. In this case, there is no prior subject to which something is due; hence, there is no ground or even any acceptance. Anselm expressed this radically non-reciprocal nature of the gift — its lack of prior conditions — through the notion of absolute *privation*.

It is *privation* and not merely negation, for negation simply is not and leads nowhere, whereas the gift is to be, and once given can be seen to be uniquely appropriate. It is absolute privation, however, for the foundation is not at all on the part of the recipient; rather it is entirely on the part of the source.[53]

To what does this gift correspond on the part of the source? In a certain parallel to the antinomies of Kant which show when reason has strayed beyond its bounds, many from Plotinus to Leibniz and beyond have sought knowledge, not only of the gift and its origin, but of why it had to be given. The more they succeeded the less room was left for freedom on the part of the person whose very life is given or gift. Others attempted to understand freedom as a fall, only to find that what was thus understood was bereft of value and meaning and hence was of no significance to human life and its cultures. Rather, the radical non-reciprocity of human freedom must be rooted in an equally radical generosity on the part of its origin. No reason, either on the part of the given or on the part of its origin makes this gift necessary. The freedom of man is the reflection of the pure generosity by which he is given: if in general man is the image of God, then in particular human freedom is the image of God's love.

At this point philosophy begins to gain that intimacy which Iqbal sees as characterizing religion. The intellect takes on that union which is more characteristic of a mystical state. One appreciates one's freedom as given and responds freely and spontaneously. This enables one to respond in love to the love by which one's heart has been given. This, in turn, evolves into generosity in the image of the outgoing love of one's creator.

Yet in all this the metaphysics of existence keeps cause and effect distinct from one another so that one is not absorbed into the divine love by which one is given, but instead is affirmed as being in one's own right and hence as a distinct, unique, generous and creative source in this world.

Thus religion as appreciation entails not withdrawal from the world, but its engagement and transformation. This appears from a continuation of the phenomenology of self or ego as gift, which implies in turn a correspondingly radical openness or generosity. Man as gift is not something which is and then receives. It was an essential facet of Plato's response to the problems he had elaborated in the *Parmenides* that the multiple can exist only *as* participants of the good or one. Receiving is not something they *do*; it is what they *are*.[54] As such at the core of their being they reflect the reality of the generosity in which they originate.

Cultural Harmony and Creative Interchange
  as Gratitude to God (see Chapter VIII below)

Understanding oneself as gift entails understanding oneself also as giving of oneself in openness to others. As noted below in Chapter IX, the sense of gift makes it possible to extend the notions of duty and harmony beyond concern for the well-being of those with whom I share and whose well-being is in a sense my own. The good is not only what contributes to my perfection, for I am not the center of meaning. Rather, being as received is essentially out-going.

This has two important implications for our topic. Where the Greeks' focus upon their heritage had led to depreciating others as barbarians, the sense of oneself and of one's culture as radically given or gifted provides a basic corrective. Knowing and valuing oneself and one's culture as gifts implies more than merely reciprocating what the other does for me. It means, first, that others and their culture are to be respected simply because they too have been given or gifted by the one Transcendent source. This is an essential step which Gandhi, in calling outcasts by the name "harijans" or "children of God," urged us to take beyond the sense of pride or isolation in which we would see others in pejorative terms.

But mere respect may not be enough. The fact is that I and another, my people or culture and another, originate from, share in and proclaim the same "total absolute". That this creates not out of need, but out of love implies that the relation between cultures as integrating modes of human life is in principle one of complementarity and outreach. Hence, interchange as the effort to live this complementarity is far from being hopeless. In the pressing needs of our times only an intensification of cooperation between peoples can make available the needed immense stores of human experience and creativity. The positive virtue of love is our real basis for hope.

A second principle of interchange is to be found in the participated — the radically given or gifted — character of one's being. As one does not first exist and then receive, but one's very existence is a received existence or gift, to attempt to give back this gift, as in an exchange of presents, would be at once hopelessly too much and too little. On the one hand, to attempt to return in strict equivalence would be too much for it is our very self that we have received as gift. On the other hand, to think merely in terms of reciprocity would be to fall essentially short of my nature as one that is given, for to make a merely equivalent return would be to remain centered upon myself where I would cleverly trap, and then entomb, the creative power of being.

Rather, looking back I can see the futility of giving back, and in this find the fundamental importance of passing on the gift in the spirit in which it has been given. One's nature as given calls for a creative generosity which reflects that of one's source. Truly appropriate generosity lies in continuing the giving of which one has received through shaping one's cultural tradition creatively in response to real present day needs. As these involve not only ourselves, but others, this means cooperating in kind with the creative gifts at the heart of other cultures so that all may be truly at home. This requires a vast expansion or breaking out of oneself as the only center of one's concern. It means becoming appreciative and effectively concerned with the good of others and of other groups, with the promotion and vital growth of the next generation and of those to follow. Indeed, it means advancing Iqbal's insight regarding religious thought one step further to a total harmony of humankind with nature which reflects the total absolute as the condition of possibility of all.

*Implications of Religious Reconstruction for Life
 in Our Times* (see Chapter X below)

The implications of such generosity are broad and at times surprisingly personal. First, true openness to others cannot be based upon a depreciation of oneself or of one's own culture. Without appreciating one's worth there would be nothing to share and no way to help, nor even the possibility of taking joy in the good of the other. Further, cultural interchange enables one to see that the elements of one's life, which in isolation may have seemed to be merely local customs and purely repetitive in character, are more fundamentally modes in which one lives basic and essential human values. In meeting others and other cultures, one discovers the deeper meaning in one's own everyday life.

This is more than mere discovery, however. One recognizes that in these transcendental values of life — truth and freedom, love and beauty — one participates in the dynamism of one's origin and hence must share these values in turn. More exactly, one can come to realize that real reception of these transcendental gifts lies in sharing them in loving concern in order that others may realize them as well. This means passing on one's own heritage not by replicating it in others, but by promoting what others and subsequent generations would freely become.

Finally, that other cultures are quintessentially products of self-cultivation by other spirits as free and creative images of their divine source implies the need to open one's horizons beyond one's own self-concerns to the ambit of the freedom of others. This involves promoting the development of other free and creative centers and cultures which, precisely as such, are not in one's own possession or under one's own control. One lives then no longer in terms merely of oneself or of things that one can make or manage, but in terms of an interchange between free persons and people's of different cultures. Personal responsibility is no longer merely individual decision making or for individual good. Effectively realized, the resulting interaction and mutual fecundation reaches out beyond oneself and one's own culture to reflect ever more perfectly the glory of the one source and goal of all.[55]

This calls for a truly shared effort in which all respond fully, not only to majority or even common needs, but to the particular needs of each. This broad sense of tolerance and loving outreach, even in the midst of tensions, is the fruit of Iqbal's religious attitude of appreciation as mediated through a phenomenology of gift. It has been described by Pope John Paul II as a state in which violence cedes to peaceful transformation, and conflict to pardon and reconciliation; where power is made reasonable by persuasion, and justice finally is implemented through love.[56]

NOTES

1. *The Vedanta Sutras of Badarayana* with commentary by Sankara, tran. by G. Thibaut (New York: Dover), I, 1, 2.

2. See the edition edited by M. Saeed Sheikh (Lahore, Pakistan: Iqbal Academy and Institute of Islamic Culture, 1989), pp. 4-5.

3. *Ibid.*, p. 13.

4. This threefold structure followed both in Aquinas' *Commentary on Boethius' work* On the Trinity, qq. 3 and 5, and Descartes' systematic procedure for placing under doubt all that arises from the three sources of knowledge until what is derived from each source could be certified as true. Aristotle's dictum regarding humans as physical and spiritual held that there is nothing in the intellect which is not first in the senses.

5. Indeed, one might define philosophy and science precisely as knowledge of the various aspects of reality in terms proper to human reason and hence expressive of the nature or existence of the things themselves.

6. L. Lévy-Bruhl, *How Natives Think* (New York: Washington Square Press, 1966), ch. II.

7. *Ibid.*, ch. XII. See also Werner Jaeger, *The Theology of the Early Greek Philosophers* (London: Oxford Univ. Press, 1967), ch. I; and G.S. Kirk and J.E. Raven, *The PreSocratic Philosophers* (Cambridge: At the University Press, 1960), pp. 26-32.

8. Hesiod, *Theogony* (New York: Liberal Arts Press, 1953); also *The Theogony*, trans. Hugh G. Eyelyn-White (Loeb Classical Library; Cambridge, Mass: Harvard University Press, 1964), pp. 89-99, 107-115.

9. *Ibid.*, 11, 104ff.

10. *Ibid.* See also George F. McLean and Patrick J. Aspell, *Ancient Western Philosophy: The Hellenic Emergence* (New

York: Appleton, Century, Crofts, 1971).

11. Werner Jaeger, *The Theology of the Early Greek Philosophers* (London: Oxford University Press, 1967), pp. 12-13.

12. Jaeger, p. 13 and Kirk and Raven, 26-32.

13. G.S. Kirk and J.E. Raven, *ibid.*

14. *Hesiod, the Homeric Hymns and Homerica*, trans. by H.G. Evelyn-White (London: Heinemann, 1920), p. 86.

15. Kirk and Raven, *loc.cit.*

16. Xenophanes, fragments 11, 14-16 in George F. McLean and Patrick J. Aspell, *Readings in Ancient Western Philosophy* (Englewood Cliffs, N.J.: Prentice-Hall, 1970), p. 31.

17. Anaximander, fragments, see McLean and Aspell, pp. 22-28.

18. See McLean and Aspell, *Ancient Western Philosophy* (Englewood Cliffs, NJ: Prentice Hall, 1971), ch. III.

19. Parmenides, fragments, see McLean and Aspell, *Readings in Ancient Western Philosophy*, pp. 39-44.

20. Fragment 8; see Alexander P.D. Mourelatos, *The Route of Parmenides: A Study of Word, Images, and Argument in the Fragments* (New Haven: Yale, 1970).

21. *Metaphysics*, XII, 7, 1072 b 26-29.

22. Iqbal, p. 143.

23. Iqbal, pp. 4-5.

24. Iqbal, p. 123.

25. *Isaias* 27:13.

26. Iqbal, p. 3.

27. Iqbal, pp. 102-103, 113.

28. G. McLean, *Plenitude and Participation: The Unity of Man in God* (Madras: The University of Madras, 1978), pp. 53-57.

29. Aristotle had taken the compossibility of forms as a sufficient response to the scientific question of 'whether it exists'. See Joseph Owens, *The Doctrine of Being in the Aristotelian Metaphysics; A Study in the Greek Background of Medieval Thought* (Toronto: P.I.M.S., 1978).

30. Mortiner J. Adler, *The Idea of Freedom: A Dialectical Examination of the Conceptions of Freedom* (Garden City, New York: Doubleday, 1958), I, 609.

31. John I:1-5, 8.

32. C. Fabro called the graded and related manner in which

this is realized concretely an intensive notion of being. Cornelio Fabro, *Participation et causalité selon S. Thomas d'Aquin* (Louvain: Pub. Univ. de Louvain, 1961).

33. Cornelio Fabro, *La nozione metafisica de partecipazione secondo S. Tommaso d'Aquino* (Torino: Societá Ed. Internazionale, 1950), pp. 75-122.

34. Iqbal, pp. 25.

35. Fabro, *La Nozione* and *Participation et causalité*.

36. This, it would seem, may be better than saying as does Iqbal that "the true infinite does not exclude the finite; it embraces the finite without effacing its finitude." This would enable him also to escape the entanglements he finds in the so-called "cosmological argument." Indeed, the argumentation requires a metaphysical stage in order to have a positive conclusion. Iqbal, pp. 29-30.

37. Iqbal, p. 143.

38. Iqbal, pp. 48-49.

39. Tr. C.K. Ogden (London: Methuen, 1981).

40. (New York: Harper and Row).

41. Tr. G.E.M. Anscombe (Oxford: Blackwell, 1958).

42. Brian Wicker, *Culture and Theology* (London: Sheed and Ward, 1966), pp. 68-88.

43. (New York: Harper and Row, 1962).

44. *Documents of Vatican II*, ed. W. Abbott (New York: New Century, 1974).

45. Iqbal, p. 61.

46. Maurice Nedoncelle, "Person and/or World as the Source of Religious Insight" in G. McLean, ed., *Traces of God in a Secular Culture* (New York: Alba House, 1973), pp. 187-210.

47. Kenneth L. Schmitz, *The Gift: Creation* (Milwaukee: Marquette Univ. Press, 1982), pp. 34-42. I am particularly indebted to this very thoughtful work for its suggestions. I draw here also upon my "Chinese-Western Cultural Interchange in the Future" delivered at the International Symposium on Chinese-Western Cultural Interchange in Commemoration of the 400th Anniversary of the Arrival of Matteo Ricci, S.J., in China (Taiwan: Fu Jen Univ., 1983), pp. 457-72.

48. Karl Marx, *Theses on Feuerbach*, nos. 6-8 in *F. Engels, Ludwig Feuerbach and the Outcome of Classical German Philosophy* (New York: International Publishers, 1934), pp. 82-84.

Schmitz, *ibid.*

49. A. S. Cua, *Dimensions of Moral Creativity: Paradigms, Principles and Ideals* (University Park, PA: Pennsylvania State Univ. Press, 1978), chaps. III-V.

50. W. Cenkner, *The Hindu Personality in Education: Tagore, Gandhi and Aurobindo* (Delhi: South Asia Books, 1976).

51. Parmenides, *Fragment* 2.

52. Schmitz, pp. 44-56.

53. Anselm, *Monologium*, cc. 8-9 in *Anselm of Canterbury*, eds. J. Hopkins and H. W. Richardson (Toronto: E. Mellen, 1975), I, pp. 15-18. See Schmitz, 30-34.

54. R. E. Allen, "Participation and Predication in Plato's Middle Dialogues" in his *Studies in Plato's Metaphysics* (London: Routledge, Keegan Paul, 1965), pp. 43-60.

55. Schmitz, pp. 84-86.

56. John Paul II, "Address at Puebla," *Origins*, VIII (n. 34, 1979), I, 4 and II, 41-46.

PART I

PROTO-PHILOSOPHIES AS WAYS TO GOD

CHAPTER I

METHOD:
From the Structure of Consciousness to an Archeology of Ways to God

In order to explore the multiple ways to God it is important first to identify the distinctive modes of awareness of the divine in order to decipher the religious phenomena, and respond thereto in one's own pilgrimage. Further, some sense of the chronological sequence of the emergence of these ways is needed in order to be able to appreciate the character and goals of the distinctive religious movements, not only in one's own life, but in the history of people. Finally, there is need to appreciate the mutually complementary character of these ways and of the religious cultures they characterize in order to have principles of mutual understanding and global cooperation. Such principles are to be found not in God who is eternal, simple and unchanging, but in humans who are dispersed through space, complex in their physical and psychological make-up, and who progress or develop through time.

Professor Semou Pathe Gueye points out that this is the heart of the work Hegel, not only in his *Encyclopedia of Philosophy*, but in his *Science of Logic* on the form of knowing and in his *Phenomenology of the Spirit* on the form of consciousness, all of which show that all forms of consciousness and affectivity are ways of moving toward the truth which foundationally and ultimately is God. Religion and philosophy then are the highest forms of consciousness and the truth of history. In this Hegel integrates subject and object, man and nature, the world and God.

This is not to say that religion obeys reason, but rather that with philosophy it is the highest form in which reason expresses itself. Conversely the attempt of reason to proceed outside of a religious vision grounded in the Absolute has always been disastrous because it results in placing the limited as the unlimited, the relative as the absolute, man as God. This is characteristic of Enlightenment reason and perhaps most baldly and tragically expressed in Nietzsche and Sartre.

All of this can be seen in the writings of Hegel which should be read and pondered. The present work has, however, a somewhat different orientation, not one that contradicts the deep truth of what Hegel details in principle and in essence, but one which looks for the way in which this is lived in fact and in existence. Its intent is to search for the significance of the fact that human life in God is lived through time and in multiple modes. Hence, it will be important to see not only how the earlier and simpler modes of awareness are included in the more sophisticated ones which follow, but how their content is proper to them and cannot otherwise be captured; not only how the multiple converge toward a higher synthesis, but the significance of their diversity; not only their unity in principle, but the living of their diversity.

For this reason it has seemed that the model of lived development as analyzed psychologically by Piaget and others might be especially suggestive in directing our attention. Its assistance in following the diachronic as well as synchronic pattern of the multiple ways to God promises to bring us to the existential richness of what Hegel so richly unfolded in terms of essence and idea.

The pattern of sequenced development identified by Jean Piaget and others in the growth of the individual person shows, for instance, that only at a certain age is the capacity for abstract reasoning developed, at which point the child's kinetic, cognitive and effective modes of action are transformed. This is reflected also in the development of higher levels of moral reasoning, which the cross cultural studies of Lawrence Kohlberg show to take place as life becomes socially more complex and persons take on more sophisticated administrative responsibilities. The very possibility for such differentiation, however, is grounded in the structure of the human person and one's complex capacities for knowledge. This was the fundamental principle for the ordering of the sciences in the Aristotelian tradition and for the controlled development of scientific knowledge by Descartes.

The Developmental Model of Jean Piaget

Hence, this chapter will look primarily at the sequence of the progressive awakening of cognitive capabilities charted through the work of Jean Piaget and summarized by him in "The Mental Development of the Child."[1] It will concern, first, Piaget's general explanatory theory for the progression from one cognitive level to the next; second, the cognitive, affective, behavioral and physiological components or dimensions of a personality; and third, a sketch of the differentiated and sequenced levels which obtain in the development of these components. This should enable understanding of how the synchronic distinction of modes of thought based on the psychological structure of the human person becomes as well a diachronic pattern. This is found not only in personal psychological growth, but in the development through time of a progression in people's consciousness of God and in their living of this awareness in their social life.

A Theory of Development. To help understand the progression from one stage to the next Piaget elaborated a theory based upon the notion of equilibrium, its loss and reconstitution.

Any stage in the growth of persons constitutes an equilibrium or integrated state of its component factors in which the persons are able to make their contribution to others and to the whole society. An equilibrium is upset by a need, such as hunger which leads to the activity required in order to satisfy the need and to restore the equilibrium. Where the need can be satisfied by competencies already possessed, such as eating to satisfy hunger, doing so simply restores the previous equilibrium with the same competencies had before at that level. However, where the need can no longer be satisfied by capabilities already possessed, new ones must be developed. The subsequent state integrating these new capabilities, constitutes a new and higher equilibrium. This overall structure of development holds true of the range of transformations from a child's learning to walk, through the green revolution in agriculture, to the stages in the history of astronomy.

Development implies elements of both continuity and differentiation. There is continuity because in the higher stage the capabilities of the previous stage are not lost, but perfected. The infant's ability to move its limbs in crawling is not lost, but remains as a substructure and are perfected when the child learns to walk. These abilities are perfected still further when he or she learns to run and then adds the syncopation needed in order to be able to dance. Throughout, the earlier capabilities are retained and increasingly perfected. Where this is not the case what is had is not development but mere change, not improvement but mere substitution.

Conversely, development also implies differentiation because the adoption of one from among the many different possible modes of activity for responding to a need means that this type of activity will be the more developed. As further needs arise it will be easier to respond by further developments in this same line than by activating other capabilities which, though in principle equally effective, concretely are less available to this person or people. A family, for example, may solve its food problems by either more intensive farming or more intensive fishing, but seldom by both. The same is true with the virtues of patience and courage. Progressively, one capability or mode of action atrophies as the other is repeatedly employed and developed. Thus, over time and in interaction with their physical and social environment, each people evolves distinctive cultural patterns along with its history.

Components of Personality. In order to render the general theory more concrete Piaget distinguishes four dimensions of a personality:

- (1) The cognitive, by which we are aware of things as they exist over against ("ob-ject") ourselves as knower, even if these be about ourselves. This is the life of our senses and intellect, namely, of sensation and intelligence. When intellectual knowledge achieves reflexion upon itself, it is no longer only objective, but subject centered as well.

- (2) The affective, by which we respond to things with feelings and emotions, such an empathy and love, or rejection and hate.

- (3) The behavioral, by which we act personally and eventually socially.

- (4) The physiological, by which we are constituted bodily or organically.

Levels of Development. All four components or dimensions of personality are linked together and develop in unison. In his general theory, Piaget works out a sequence of levels built especially upon the cognitive component, reflecting the modern rationalist emphasis. Each step in the development of the capacities for knowledge enables corresponding developments in the articulation of feeling and the implementation of action. However, development in modes of feeling also facilitate action, including cognition; and development of demands for action evokes a more sophisticated pattern of feelings and new cognitive capabilities. Hence, one might question the unidirectional development from cognition to affectivity and behavior and see alternate sequences in terms of deeper senses of the constitution of human identity.

In any case, Piaget sees each step in the development of one's cognitive abilities as being accompanied by a corresponding step in the other dimensions of one's personality. This proceeds in a series of four progressive steps from infancy — years 1-2 (*Mental Development*, pp. 8-17), to early childhood — years 2-7 (pp. 17-38), to middle childhood — years 7-12 (pp. 38-59), and to adolescence — year 12- (pp. 60-76).

Two examples show briefly how this works: 1. cognitive development during the stage of infancy, and 2. the stages of affective development throughout all of childhood. A brief, yet more detailed sketch of the overall process is reconstructed through passages from Piaget in Appendix I at the end of this volume.

1. *Development in Infancy.* The first example is found in Piaget's brief summary of the development which takes place during the first two years of life. Cognitively, during the first three months of infancy everything is perceived in terms of self. Correspondingly, affectivity is a matter of reflexes, such as fear of losing one's equilibrium or of falling off a table or ledge, in terms of which behavior is instinctive. As a result physiologically nutritional needs are central with the infant proceeding from perceptions of hunger, to discomfort, to cry for nourishment.

By the second three months the infant develops cognitively the first organized percepts of the other as is seen in the actions of turning toward sounds, repeating what gives good results, or recognizing and adapting to others. This is accompanied affectively by differentiation in the emotions of pleasure and pain, and behaviorally by the first motor habits.

After the first six months the infant evolves practical intelligence of self in relation to others. This is accompanied by elementary affective and sensori motor organization, such as, e.g., experimenting with sight by developing action schemata in order to work out what can be seen by one or both eyes.

Figure I. Development during Infancy
(J. Piaget, *Six Psychological Studies*, pp. 8-17)

Infancy	Cognitive	Affective	Behavioral	Physiological
1-3 mos.	perceives all in terms of self	first emotions; instincts, reflexes	instinctive according to reflexes	nutritional needs
3-6 mos.	first organized percepts	differentiated emotions	first motor habits	
6-18/24 mos.	sensori-motor and practical intelligence of self in relation to others	elementary affective organization		

2. *Development of Affectivity.* A second example is Piaget's summary description of the affective development experienced throughout childhood. Affectivity first undergoes elementary organization so that joy and sadness are linked to interest and disinterest, and to effort and fatigue. This manifests both initial self-awareness and awareness of other things and persons. The evolution of affectivity during the first two years corresponds to the parallel evolution of motor and cognitive functions, which extends through childhood and adolescence. Piaget describes it thus:

 During the initial stage of reflex techniques there

are corresponding elementary instinctive strivings linked with nutrition as well as the kind of affective reflexes that constitute the primary emotions. . . .

At the second stage (precepts and habits), as well as at the beginnings of sensorimotor intelligence, there is a corresponding series of elementary emotions or affective percepts linked to the modalities of activity itself: the agreeable or the disagreeable, pleasure and pain, etc., as well as the first realizations of success and failure. To the extent that these affective states depend on action per se and not as yet on awareness of relationships with other people, this level of affectivity attests to a kind of general egocentricity.

With the development of intelligence, however, and with the ensuing elaboration of an external universe and especially with the construction of the schema of the "object," a third level of affectivity appears. It is epitomized, in the language of psychoanalysis, by the "object choice," i.e., by the objectivation of the emotions and by their projection onto activities other than those of the self alone. When "objects" become detached more and more distinctly from the global and undifferentiated configuration of primitive actions and percepts and become objects conceived as external to the self and independent of it, the situation becomes completely transformed.

On the one hand, in close correlation with the construction of the object, awareness of "self" begins to be affirmed by means of the internal pole of reality, as opposed to the external or objective pole. On the other hand, objects are conceived by analogy with this self as active, alive and conscious. This is particularly so with those exceptionally unpredictable and interesting objects — people.

> The elementary feelings of joy and sadness, of success and failure, etc., are now experienced as a function of this objectification of things and of people, from which interpersonal feelings will develop. The affective "object choice" which psychoanalysis contrasts with narcissism is thus correlated with the intellectual construction of the object, just as narcissism correlated with the lack of differentiation between the external world and the self. This "object choice" is first of all vested in the person of the mother, then (both negatively and positively) of the father and other relatives. This is the beginning of the sympathies and antipathies that will develop to such an extent in the course of the ensuing period (pp. 15-16).

A more complete description of these stages of child development in Piaget's own terms can be found in Appendix I at the end of this volume.

Piaget summarizes the overall pattern of cognitive and affective development, and their interrelation, as follows:

> In conclusion, let us point out the basic unity of the processes which, from the construction of the practical universe by infantile sensorimotor intelligence, lead to the reconstruction of the world by the hypothetico-deductive thinking of the adolescent, via the knowledge of the concrete world derived from the system of operations of middle childhood.
>
> We have seen how these successive constructions always involve a decentering of the initial egocentric point of view in order to place it in an ever-broader coordination of relations and concepts, so that each new terminal grouping further integrates the subject's activity by adapting it to an ever widening reality.

Ways to God 61

Figure II. Development throughout Childhood

	Cognitive (thinking)	*Affective* (feeling, willing)	*Behavioral*	*Psychological*
Infancy years 1-2 (pp. 8-17)	sense percepts from self to others	instincts, emotions with elementary organization	1st motor habits for relation to others, workd	nutritional basis
Early Childhood years 2-7 pp. 17-38	intuitive concrete non-reversible picture pp. 22-23	stably organized interpersonal feelings of e.g., obedience pp. 33-38	socialization of behavior on intuitive moral values	
Middle Childhood years 7-12 pp. 38-59	abstract intellectual, concepts, reversible on concrete things pp. 41-54	will for moral and social choices pp. 54-60	distributive justice and cooperation pp. 38-41	
Adolescence year 12- pp. 60-76	formal thought with abstract hypothetico-deductive constructions pp. 61-64	autoincarnation of ideals and entry into the society of adults pp. 64-70	according to ideal	e.g., integration of sexuality

Parallel to this intellectual elaboration, we have seen affectivity gradually disengaging itself from the self in order to submit, thanks to the reciprocity and coordination of values, to the laws of cooperation. Of course, affectivity is always the incentive for the actions that ensue at each new stage of this progressive ascent, since affectivity assigns value to activities and distributes energy to them.

But affectivity is nothing without intelligence. Intelligence furnishes affectivity with its means and clarifies its ends. It is erroneous and mythical to attribute the causes of development to great ancestral tendencies as though activities and biological growth were by nature foreign to reason. In reality, the most profound tendency of all human activity is progression toward equilibrium. It is reason, which expresses the highest forms of equilibrium, reunites intelligence and affectivity.

LAWRENCE KOHLBERG'S MODEL OF COGNITIVE DEVELOPMENT

The pattern of Piaget's research has been employed and confirmed by Lawrence Kohlberg's work on moral development and derivatively by J. Fowler[2] on religious development. Kohlberg tested out especially the pattern of the ability of children at different ages to make judgements regarding issues of justice. He organized his stages from instinctive, to obediential behavior, to distributive justice and finally to the ability to act according to ideals. These stages are summarized in the following schema:

Level I: *Preconventional*

Stage 1: Heteronomous or punishment-and-obedience orientation. The physical consequences of action, particularly as to punishment and reward by others, determine the moral status of an act.

Stage 2: Instrumental relativism. Right action is what is personally beneficial, although this may include reciprocal exchanges of benefit to others in a "marketplace" or trading arrangement.

Level II: *Conventional*

Stage 3: Interpersonal conformity. Moral goodness consists in carrying out what others expect of someone in a role or position, and in the approval of these others.

Stage 4: "Law-and-order" orientation. Obeying the fixed laws of the society or group and maintaining social order constitutes right action.

Level III: *Post-Conventional or Principled*

Stage 5: "Social contract" orientation. Right action is action in accordance with the law as constituted by tacit or explicit agreement among agents with different values and opinions.

Stage 6: Universalistic ethics. Moral standards are those which are self-chosen and universalizable.[3]

Margaret Gorman has worked this out in an impressive set of schemata which extends from young children through young adults to middle and even old age (see appendix II at the end of this volume and her article explaining the schemata, "Life-long Moral Development").[4]

APPLICATION TO THE PROGRESSION OF PEOPLES

Obviously, it is a big step from Piaget's stages of cognitive development in children, Kohlberg's scheme for cognitive moral development, and Gorman's life long pattern of overall moral growth, to the concern of this work, namely, to learn more about ways to God. It is important not to overextend the analogy between these.

Nevertheless, the theory of cognitive and moral development can be helpful as we stand before the broad array of such ways, each with its own special character and contribution. Like an anthropologist who enters a native camp, one must know what one is looking for, what can be significant and how the relevant pieces of evidence can be fitted together. Without that everything can be written down, but none of it will have meaning.

Piaget's work on relations between knowledge, affectivity and behavior, their various stages, and the transition from one to another can have a suggestive heuristic value in our investigation. For, it suggests the range and mode of cognitive, affective and behavioral activity at various stages, as well as correspondences between these. As a result a mode of behavior can be appreciated not just as a bizarre fact, but as corresponding to a distinctive mode of understanding and the corresponding affective response — and vice versa.

This suggests that at each step in the development of peoples — as of this work — we look for the need, which entails a disequilibrium, and for the development of related capabilities of awareness, affectivity and behavior aimed at restoring the equilibrium. Understanding this should enable greater appreciation of the mode of religious response developed at that point in human progress. By no means does this suggest that God is a human creation. The divine infinitely transcends human capabilities; what evolves are human abilities to appreciate and respond to the divine. Like a mirror or a microscope we do not create what we observe. Rather, we develop multiple modes of observation in order to respond to, and thereby to live with, in and by the divine.

There is much more on this in the chapters which follow. Here, however, it is essential to observe a number of cautions. First, one must not consider the infant to be inhuman because he or she has not developed higher levels of cognition, affectivity or action. In terms of the level of development of the infant's capabilities of awareness and strength he or she responds to his or her mother as fully and unconditionally as does the mother in response, given her more developed capabilities. Both hold to each other with all the strength and affectivity of which they are capable. Indeed, the gospel will call on the adult to be as a little child in recognition of the difficulty of retaining the uncompromising and single minded devotion had as a child when one reaches higher and more complex levels of psycho-social development.

Similarly, it must not be thought that a person or people is less human before developing some of the higher levels of reasoning and affectivity. The child at whatever stage organizes his or her whole life according to his or her level. A five year old is fully human, deserving of all the protections to life possessed by one of 17 or 35 years; indeed, their needs and rights to protection and education are greater, and accordingly the by-word: "Children first".

Correspondingly, on the part of whole peoples, to identify their distinctive mode of thinking at a particular stage of their development is by no means to dehumanize them. Thus, it is unfortunate that the term "primitive" has taken on the connotation of being less human. Its basic etymology should be retained which bespeaks what is basic, primary and essential. In this sense a people that is "primitive" in social structure can tell us much about what is essential to being human, about what is most to be protected and promoted.[5] It is unfortunate then that for use of this term the works of Lucien Lévy-Bruhl[6] and Placide Tempels[7] were for some time taken negatively. We shall see more on this in the next chapter.

Finally, it must be understood that peoples can organize and live their whole life only in terms of the capabilities they have developed. Hence, it must be expected that the organization of the life of a group whose cognitive capabilities are focused in terms, e.g., of imagination or "picture thinking" will be lived accordingly. Whereas a young child needs to care for only a limited area of activity in terms of his or her imagination, an entire people in an analogous stage of development must care in those terms for all the needs of childcare, social organization and culture. The Golden Age of Greece with its great creations of art and public administration was lived entirely in imaginative, mythic terms, for science was not yet possible, yet we struggle, and in many ways in vain, to match that level of civilization. Hence, the steps we shall take in the sequence of the following chapters regarding ways to God is not a univocous transfer from a level of child development to the culture of a people, but an analogous relation according to which the stages of cognitive, affective or motor development specify the modes which the range of a people's reasoning, affectivity and social relations can achieve.

Indeed, Paul Tillich goes further in pointing out that as persons or people's move from one level to the next, the mode into which they move, while providing special and needed capabilities, is not able to carry forward all that was developed in terms of the prior level. For this reason, Piaget's note that earlier stages are not dispensed with, but remain as substrata for the proper realization of those which follow is especially indicative of the importance of a cultural heritage and its indispensable character for authentic human development. From this follows the crucial need of protecting cultural traditions and attending to their proper transposition and adaptation.

All of this suggests that the different ways to God are not indifferently related between themselves, that each cannot be undertaken at any point in life or at any social or historical stage. Rather, it appears:

(a) that there are a series of basic cognitive capacities or powers, technically called faculties;

(b) that each of these has a characteristic mode of activity;

(c) that they are actuated in sequence in the life of each individual;

(d) that this constitutes stages of development, each with its own characteristic, cognitive, affective and behavioral dimension;

(e) that the earlier stages remain as foundations in what might be called "higher" stages, which are characterized by the deployment and implementation of qualitatively more perfect abilities in each dimensions;

(f) that the "lower" stages may never be able to be fully transferred with all their content to the "higher" levels, and therefore must continue to be lived in earlier terms lest they be lost (that there is an element of totem in myth and of myth in science, which is only now being rediscovered); and

(g) that this is a matter not only of individual development, but characterizes the life of peoples as a whole, which suggests an embeddedness in the culture which cannot be adequality articulated in conceptual terms, but is appreciated aesthetically.

Hence earlier people may articulate their personal and social lives entirely, and indeed very richly, in terms of the first levels of thought or understanding, and order their physical, social and religious relations thereby. In a parallel manner, each of the ways to God is essentially a profound and integral responses to the religious call of its time and remains an integral dimension of the religious response in our times. To be fully conscious of one's religious life today and creative in its development for the future requires then some sense of these components.

APPLICATION TO THE STRUCTURE OF KNOWLEDGE

We can begin to sort out the distinct ways to God by identifying first the basically different cognitive capabilities on which they are based. According to these basic human capabilities for knowledge — technically called faculties — the structure of the levels of knowledge of the sciences and of the ways to God can be charted. Basically they are threefold, being divided between sense and intellect, while the senses are further subdivided between those that are external and internal.

The external senses are classically the five senses of sight, hearing, smell, taste and touch, though recent psychology would add to the list. They present to us the world outside and do so directly or by intuition. The object must be physically present to be seen or touched, or if mediated by a mirror or television these must be close to us with an unobstructed line of sight. Further, we can see only what is on the screen at that time. Thus, sensation is a physical or material capability, and, as with all things in the physical world, is characterized by space and time. These are the external senses.

We must not only gather impressions from our various senses, however, but combine them in an integrated image of the single object. This is the work of common sense. Further, we are able to continue to work with what we have sensed in the past, but which remains in our memory available to recall. Finally, we are able not only to repeat the images of the past, but to recombine these in limitless ways. From the memories of the red color of a barn, a horse and a bird in flight we can form with our imagination the composit image of a flying red horse, though no such a thing has ever existed.

This work of the internal sense capability is essential if we are not merely to remain in the given situation, but to begin to find new ways of arranging our physical and social relations. Without these capabilities we would be simply condemned to whatever be our circumstances. The internal senses, however, remain senses, and their presentation of objects retain physical or spatial characteristics. Hence, the imagination always works with some shape, figure or picture, even if it be a word. Indeed it was by combining this figurative character had in geometry with the arithmetic precision of algebra that Descartes was able to develop algebraic geometry and to know within a month its capabilities and limits.

A major difference is found, however, between sense knowledge, whether external or internal, and intellection. The former are material modes of knowledge and hence characterized by space and time; intellection, in contrast, is precisely freed from such characteristics: it is not material but spiritual. Thus it is able to grasp the nature of things unspecified as to space and time; and to establish symbolic relations so as to develop language and entire cultures and ways of life. It is able to think in terms of being, unity and truth, goodness and beauty. This enables the mind to grasp the meaning of the physical world, to establish laws and rights, to create beautiful buildings and symphonies, and to evaluate things in terms not only of passing time but of eternity. By this a human, while fully animal, can transcend not only the animal kingdom, but especially oneself and one's ego. Thus, one's life and the lives of others can be appreciated in their global dimensions and sacred meaning.

This threefold division of the powers of knowledge was central to the establishment of the pattern of the sciences in ancient as well as modern philosophy. Aristotle's division of the sciences proceeded on the basis of this division.

First, it recognizes that the intellect is distinct from the senses and that its knowledge is not held to the concrete singularity of its object as are the senses. I can touch only this or that tree, but in both cases I can know it as a tree rather than a rock. That is to say, the intellect abstracts from the individuality of its objects and hence is able to develop knowledge that is not simply of a collection of single things, but concerns the nature of a whole class of things. This makes it possible to develop sciences as coordinated bodies of knowledge of general types or species.

The sciences, however, are themselves grouped together. Things as presented by the external senses are characterized by their external qualities whereby one is able to distinguish e.g., trees from animals. Knowledge of the former will come within the field of botany and of the latter within zoology; both life sciences in turn will be distinct from geology as a science of inorganic realities.

Secondly, if the intellect works with objects presented not with the qualitative information provided by the external senses, but only with the quantitative factors received by the internal senses, then one is no longer in the physical sciences but in mathematics. Here one abstracts not only from the singular individuality of the object as do the physical sciences, but also from whether the object be plant or mineral. It is concerned only with such quantitative factors as sizes and shapes; its work is mathematics.

Thirdly, when the intellect prescinds or abstracts from the characteristics of all sense knowledge, both external and internal, and its physical objects to consider things simply as existing, rather than as characterized either qualitatively or quantitatively, it has gone beyond the physical to the meta-physical.

Aristotle's classical threefold division of the sciences was further developed by Thomas Aquinas in the Middle Ages (see Chapter V below). It is central also to the *Meditations* of Descartes, the father of modern philosophy. In initiating his famous method of doubt in *Meditation* I he noted that it was necessary to assure the truth of knowledge and hence to bracket or put all under doubt until its truth value could be assured. But though it was not possible to do so singly for each instance of knowledge, he could employ a class action approach by establishing a doubt about the principles or sources of whole areas of knowledge. These — not incidentally — were of three levels. The objectivity of the external senses was subject to doubt because of the experience of dreams. The internal senses could be subjected to doubt because of the fantastical imagination of artists and other image makers who could make up images unrelated to any reality. The intellect, however, which saw clearly could be doubted only on the supposition of an evil genius able to deceive us in our thinking Correspondingly, the re-establishment of modern philosophy through his subsequent series of Meditations consisted precisely the recertification in reverse order of these three levels of knowledge.

To distinguish these three basic modes of human knowledge is identically to open three corresponding ways to God as each constitutes a distinct mode of awareness in terms of which the divine can be articulated. Thus in relation to the external sense, the totemic intellect used visible objects to express the divine; in relation to the internal sense of imagination the mythic intellect developed the stories of the gods, while in terms proper to the intellect the philosophical mind proceeded to express the divine as Being itself.

CONCLUSION: A MODEL FOR THE DEVELOPMENT OF WAYS TO GOD

It is time now to bring together this synchronic series of ways of knowing and compare it to the diachronic developmental series in human life and its history. From the above, on the one hand, we have the threefold synchronic series of: (a) the division of the powers of knowledge and (b) the corresponding division of the sciences. On the other hand, we have the two diachronic sequences of: (a) the emergence of different modes of thinking throughout human history and (b) the recent developmental insights of Piaget, Kohlberg and Fowler. Comparing these two sequences we find a threefold pattern each with its own way to God. (1) To the work of the intellect as proceeding with, and according to, the data of the external senses there corresponds the totemic mode of thinking, social organization and overall sense of life which was characteristic of earlier and simpler forms of social life, but which remains later as a substructure. (2) To the work of the intellect as proceeding with, and according to, the internal sense of imagination and its picture thinking there corresponds the later mythic mode of thought. Finally, (3) to the work of the intellect proceeding in, and according to, its own intellectually developed capabilities there corresponds the scientific mode of thought. This, in turn, as noted above, can be of three levels of abstraction or separation, namely, the physical, the mathematical and the metaphysical. To all of this, which is according to cognitive development, should be added affective development on the part of feelings and will, which would generate a second parallel schema, as well as a third schema based on the physical and kinetic order.

From the above the following cognitive schema emerges:

Cognitive Faculty	Corresponding Activity	Pattern of Human Consciousness
1. external sense	sensing	totem
2. internal senses myth	picturing	
3. intellect	abstract reasoning	complex scientific systems
	a. simple apprehension..	physics mathematics
	b. judgement	metaphysico-religious

This schema, as with the classical structure of the sciences, is built on the pattern of powers or faculties for objective knowledge, that is, for knowledge of reality as distinct from the subject. However, it has been characteristic of more recent thought (echoing in part the orientation of St. Augustine long ago) to turn from the objective to the subjective, that is to the self-reflective and free awareness of the properly human consciousness as central reality in all creation. This is reflected in Heidegger's *dasein* or self-conscious human being where Being properly enters into time. Classically, this was seen as the human precisely as image of God. Further analysis of the structural and hermeneutic characteristics of the method of this study of ways to God is found in the succeeding chapter, drawing upon Lévi-Strauss and Paul Ricoeur on the concrete issue of the interpretation of totemism.

We should not underestimate how great is this inversion of horizons from the objective to the subjective. In terms of our physical nature Aristotle and Thomas had considered change, i.e., the physical, to be what is most obvious; all was judged from there.

The present inversion from objectivity to subjectivity points rather to reality as self-conscious (Part III). Hence, it directs our attention to the divine, and particularly to the Trinitarian interchange of knowledge and love, as the archetype of reality. It follows that it is through a degree of participation or imitation of the divine that all is to be understood and responded to, whether in mind, in heart or in body.

The significance of ways to God is that they enable our human outlook to be truly God-centered; that is, to appreciate ourselves and others, including nature, in terms of our divine origin and goal, and hence as holy and indeed sacred. In this light we find the real meaning and value of all our capabilities or powers.

Further, the ways to God not only provide a foundation for knowledge, but evoke love or charity as the form of all the virtues. Thus they invite us to mystical union of love with God. Hence, these many ways to God bring us truly home.

Each of these ways will need to be identified in detail along with their corresponding activities and patterns of social consciousness. This will be the burden of the subsequent chapters. Indeed, doing so will constitute an archeology of consciousness, not only in the sense of identifying the sequence in which each emerges, but also of digging deeply into ourselves for our capabilities for responding to God and bringing these to light.

Further, following the suggestive developmental theory of Piaget it may be possible to gain some insight into how and why these modes have succeeded, without entirely replacing, one upon the other. If so, we could better appreciate the fundamental religious meaning of these ways, what must be retained of each way in those which succeed, and the new vistas on the divine that are opened by each succeeding way. This will make it possible to respect and promote each of these ways to God, while relating them ecumenically one to another.

Finally, if these are not only ways to God, but entire modes of human awareness and their corresponding cultures and civilizations then they will constitute a high wisdom. They will enable us to see how knowledge itself and hence all of human life — knowledge along with its corresponding affectivity and action — is a process from and to God. This endows human life with that sacredness in meaning and dignity which makes it at once the personal subject of rights and the bearer of social responsibilities, both inspired by ultimate concern for God who is made manifest and is glorified through all.

NOTES

1. Jean Piaget, "The Mental Development of the Child," *Six Psychological Studies*, trans. A. Tenzer (New York: Vintage Books, 1967), chap. I. (Page numbers in the text refer to this work.)

2. J. Fowler, "Stages in Faith: the Structural-developmental Approach," in T.C. Hennesey, ed., *Towards Moral and Religious Maturity* (New York: Paulist Press, 1977b).

3. L. Kohlberg, "High School Democracy and Educating for a Just Society," in Ralph L. Mosher, ed., *Moral Education: A First Generation of Research and Development* (New York: Praeger Publishers, 1980), p. 21. Kohlberg claims to have validated these stages cross-culturally.

4. Margaret Gorman, "Life-long Moral Development", *Psychological Foundations of Moral Education and Character Development: An Integrated Theory of Moral Development*, Richard T. Knowles and George F. McLean, eds. (VI. 2; Washington, D.C.: The Council for Research in Values and Philosophy, 1992), pp. 267-319.

5. M. Heidegger, *An Introduction to Metaphysics* (Garden City, NY: Doubleday, 1961), p. 130.

6. Lucien Lévy-Bruhl, *How Natives Think* (New York: Washington Square Press, 1966), p. 62.

7. Placide Tempels, *La Philosophie Bantoue* (Elisabethville: Lovania, 1945).

CHAPTER II

THE TOTEMIC WAY TO GOD:
The Religious Base of
Thought and Culture

In the modern, often secular, context which is now passing the foundational religious meaning of life was extensively forgotten. Instead, the rare and relatively recent phenomenon of a world view prescinding from, or neutral to, the divine was taken as the honest base line from which religious issues should be considered. For Mohammad Iqbal this was quite out of the question, for it is to define the mind on the basis of but one of its limited processes, namely, the analytic. Hence, he does not go far in the first chapter of his *Reconstruction of Religious Thought in Islam* before stating as its principle what the *Vedanta Sutras* exemplified both in their text and their structure, namely, that: "It is in fact the presence of the total absolute in the movement of knowledge that makes finite thinking possible."[1] The genius of Iqbal's work is its powerful and intricate elaboration of this theme.

The present work will attempt to suggest three ways in which Iqbal's thesis might be supplemented: first, from the point of view of an archeology of pre-philosophical thought in support of his conviction that thought is natively religious; second, by elements from systematic philosophy with a view to understanding the meaning this religious insight gives to human life; and third, by drawing upon a phenomenology of religious consciousness to see how assimilation of this insight opens new ways of creating human comity for the millenium which is now dawning. These constitute parts I-III of this work.

In a typically brief but pregnant aside, Iqbal notes that "to the primitive man all experience was supernatural."[2] Rather than being simply a reference to dead facts from the past, this points to the cumulative human experience regarding the essential importance of religion as manifested by human life. Moreover, it suggests the common ground which the many cultures need as they begin to interact more intensely. This then seems the place to begin.

From earliest times human thought almost universally has had a sacred center. It is possible to track the evolution of this constant awareness by relating it to the three dimensions of the human mind described in Chapter I above. The first is the external senses of sight and touch by which one receives information from the surrounding world. The second is the internal senses of imagination and memory by which one assembles the received data in a manner which enables it to present the original whole from which the various senses drew their specific data, to imaginatively re-present these and other data in various combinations, or to recall this at a later time. Finally, beyond the external and internal senses there is the work of the intellect by which one knows the natures of things and judges regarding their existence.[3]

Not surprisingly, upon examination it appears that the actual evolution of human awareness of the sacred follows this sequence of one's natural capacities for knowledge. In all cases it is intellectual knowledge that is in play, for religious awareness concerns not the colors or shapes of sensible objects, but existence and indeed the one who gave his name as "I am Who Am". But intellectual knowledge was articulated successively, first in terms of the external senses in the totemic stage of thought, then in terms of the internal senses in the mythic period, and finally in properly intellectual terms at the origin of philosophy (and of science as philosophy).[4]

To follow this evolution it should be noted that for life in any human society as a grouping of persons there is a basic need to understand oneself and one's relation to others. It should not be thought that these are necessarily two questions, rather than one. They will be diversely formalized in the history of philosophy, but prior to any such formalization, indeed prior even to the capacity to formalize this as a speculative issue, some mode of lived empathy rather than antipathy was essential, even for bare survival. Plato later worked out, formally and in detail, that the unity of the multiple is possible only on the basis of something that is one. But the history of social life manifests that, present in the awareness of the early peoples and according to that mode of awareness, there was always some one reality in terms of which all was understood to be related.

RETURN TO THE SOURCES

On December 19, 1925, in Calcutta, the first All-India

Philosophy Congress was held in order to rediscover and further develop the rich philosophic patrimony of the subcontinent. The direction given by its President, the great Bengali poet Rabindranath Tagore, was to look to the philosophy of the people.[5] His words would be echoed by those of Ghandi pointing to the village and its values. In this, as in many matters, Tagore and Ghandi showed keen good sense which time is proving to be prophetic.

It was good sense, for were a person raised in a village to visit New Delhi or New York he or she would need a city dweller in order to get around and make arrangements for lodging. On a trip to the source of the Amazon, however, only a native accustomed to travelling by foot and canoe and to finding food and shelter in the forest would be of help. The more sophisticated the guide the less he or she could be of assistance; guides from Delhi or New York would be totally helpless.

There is more here than mere common sense. Horticulturalists have found that the more highly refined a strain of rice the more reduced are its capabilities for adaptation. Conversely, wild grains have great capacity for adaptation and survival. Hence, they are looked upon genetically not as deficient, but as treasuries of the capacities needed to develop grains adapted to new or more difficult environments. In archeology new findings are continually manifesting human capacities for iron work and for art long before these had been expected on the basis of earlier evolutionary theories. These and similar findings have suggested the need to reconsider the oversimplified model of an univocal and self-sufficient evolutionary process from the less to the more perfect. They call, especially, for a reassessment of views predicated thereupon regarding the origin and the nature of humankind's foundational understanding of its nature and meaning

This reassessment as regards the basis of human self-understanding is further urged by the combination of, on the one hand, the great antiquity of such sacred texts as the *Vedas* and the *Upanishads* and, on the other hand, their unique continuing capacity to judge what is worst and to inspire what is most noble in human behaviour. "Like a rich man who knows how to bring both new and old things out of his treasure house" they bear witness to a transcendent dimension of human reason. Through the ages this has made possible the drama of life in the simplest household while relativising the accomplishments of even the greatest human empires. It transcends time, but grounds every temporal vision.

Gradually, even grudgingly, we adjust our chronology of human life lived with care and concern upon learning for example that at the time of the arrival of the Aryans, roughly between 2000 and 1800 BC, the peoples of the Indus valley already had cities such as Harappa and Mohanjodaro with urban design, drainage and public facilities often surpassing those of the present.[6] C. Kunan Raja points out that, as prior to the *Vedas* there existed a great people and an advanced civilization, the hymns of the Rig Veda are not anticipations, but "a scanty remnant from an earlier date of an immense store of philosophy, grand, sublime, profound, clear and definite." Thus, "The latter-day systems of philosophy must be traced to earlier stages through the *Upanishads* to the *Rgveda* and also to a much earlier stage of Pre-Vedic philosophy."[7] If we are to choose the appropriate tools for such a task it will be important for us to know how much earlier this might be.

Everything said thus far simply pales before the realization that Harappa and Mohanjodaro existed during only the last one-half of one percent of the 200,000 years since the time men left their polished stone instruments in the Mysore areas to the south, which, in turn, is but one-tenth of the way to those in East Africa whose fossils can be traced back some 2,000,000 years.[8]

As the love of wisdom, philosophy and especially its metaphysics must search out the content of the comprehension which bore man up in this successful voyage across so vast a sea of time. What was the bark; what was its tiller, and by what was it guided and corrected? How did its crew hold together through the countless stormy trials, and how did they manage to emerge with such complex and elegant cultures?

For discovering this prehistoric understanding writ in the lives of countless generations it will not be sufficient to search for its echoes in the texts of hymns and myths which we can trace only to relatively recent times. Anthropology will be necessary, but it will not constitute a sufficient tool, for, as Arthur Keith has noted correctly,[9] the issue is too philosophical to be decided by empirical means alone. To anthropology there must be added philosophy, especially as hermeneutics. Fortunately, recent progress in this field, following some key insights of Heidegger, make it possible to articulate more precisely the goal of our search, to elaborate a method for its discovery, and to begin to apply the method to the phenomenon of totemism in primitive societies. In this it will be our intention not simply to discover thought that is past, but to identify there that indispensable principle for human life which grounds cultures and transcends time.

METHOD

Heidegger's assessment of the relation between Plato and the pre- Socratics provides both a key to his articulation of the task to be undertaken and an illustration of the method he elaborated for its accomplishment. Pre-Socratic philosophy reflected in a general and unsophisticated manner the variety and powerful vitality of reality. To improve upon this vision Plato had focused on forms, natures or ideas. He elaborated all this with such great dialectical brilliance that Whitehead has termed all Western philosophy since then a set of footnotes to his writings. Unfortunately, the progress made in the conceptual clarification of the variety of nature was accompanied by a corresponding loss of sensitivity to the power and activity of nature, that is, to its existential reality. To remedy this loss Heidegger held that we must now return to the vision of the pre-Socratics in order to retrieve its dynamic existential element. Substantive forward progress in Western philosophy today, that is, the development of insight that is radically new, will depend not upon incremental conceptual development of forms, but upon reaching back prior to Plato in order to develop what he had omitted.[10]

This example from Heidegger's thought is replete with indications for a methodology for our project. First one needs to look at thought historically. This does not mean merely the forward direction of Hegel's search for ever more formal articulation. Like genetic strains in horticulture, these become increasingly enslaved to ever more specific conditions as they become more remote from their origins. On the contrary, what is most essential must be sought where in principle the forward process of scientific conceptualization cannot operate. It must be sought in that which is essentially unscientific according to the terminology of the "scientific interpretation that brands as unscientific everything that transcends its limits."[11] Radical newness is to be found, if anywhere, not in further elaboration of what already has been conceptualized, but in a step backward *(der Schritt zurück)* into that which was in some way present at the beginning of philosophizing and has remained unspoken throughout. "Far from having been thought or even having been thinkable, this reality has been obscured by the objectifying effect of much of the thought which has been developed thusfar."[12]

The task then will be not merely to restate in a more perfect manner what already has been stated less perfectly, but to open ourselves to the reality toward which our historical efforts at conceptualization and indeed the very project of conceptualization as such is not directed. Thus, one finds in the term 'metaphysics' reference to that which lies "beyond" *(meta)* the project of definition and conceptualization of the material order which Aristotle had carried to its principles in this *Physics*. The *Brhadaranyaka Upanishad* states that "when to the knower of Brahman everything has become the Self then . . . what should one think and through what, . . . through what . . . should one know the Knower?"[13] Similarly the *Brahma Sutras* state as a first principle that "(Brahman is not known from any other source) since the scriptures are the valid means of Its Knowledge."[14]

One method for developing a greater awareness of this foundation of thought consists in looking back as far as possible to its origins in order to rediscover what subsequently has been left unsaid because, it seems, too rich for the limited capacities of categorization. This is a return to our beginnings precisely in order to begin again in a new and more radical manner. To do this one must avoid projecting the limitations of one's own conceptualizations upon the origins. Hence, the manner of approach must not be only that of defining, which, literally, is to delimit, though systems of philosophy need this in their structured processes of reasoning. Instead, philosophy must broaden its approaches to that of enquiry, that is, of opening to what has been left unsaid.

It would appear important, therefore, to look back into human experience for the mode and content of thought which preceded not only the beginnings of philosophy in the proper sense of the term, but the forms of mythic symbolization which specify the distinctive cultures which derive from them. To do this we must employ data from anthropology regarding life in primitive societies throughout the world. This, in turn, will require the development of a philosophic hermeneutic adapted to discovering in the simplest forms of the lived experience of humankind what is foundational, and therefore common.

The term 'primitive' itself is in need of rehabilitation along etymological lines as first and hence basic for all else. It is a fundamental fallacy, notes Heidegger, to believe that history begins with the

> backward, the weak and helpless. The opposite is true. The beginning is strongest and mightiest. What comes afterward is not development but flattening the results from mere spreading out; it is inability to retain the beginning ... (which) is emasculated and exaggerated into a caricature.[15]

How can these beginnings be known? Because they precede not only the philosophical tradition, but even the pre-philosophical oral tradition expressed in the myths, it is necessary to invert the general hermeneutic directive to attend to the words themselves. Instead, the following special hermeneutic principles must be followed in analyzing and interpreting the philosophic significance of our origins, namely: (a) the manner of acting will be more significant than what is said; (b) the manner of thinking and feeling will not be separable from the manner of acting; and (c) the preconditions or conditions of possibility of this manner of thought, feeling and acting will be the most significant of all.

To implement this the remainder of this chapter will take the following four steps. First, an anthropological analysis of the totem, as the means used by the primitives for social self-identification and coordination, will determine the structural characteristics of their life and thought. Second, an internal analysis of these structures and their transformations will show that they depend for their meaning upon a unity or whole. Third, further hermeneutic reflection will identify where this unity is to be sought in the life of the primitive. Finally, awareness of this unity will be located in the notion of the totem as a plenitude and in the participational vision of reality which that entails.

THE FORMAL STRUCTURE OF PRIMITIVE THOUGHT

Anthropologists during the 19th century remarked the constant tendency of primitive peoples in the most disparate places to identify themselves and their relations with other humans and with nature in terms of a totem. This might be a bird, animal or, at times, even an inanimate object or direction. As all areas of life in these simplest societies were predicated upon the totem, their culture has come to be called totemic. Lévi-Strauss's *Totemism* is a history of the anthropological work done on this notion in the XXth century,[16] and thereby a history of anthropology itself since 1910.

It begins with a severely reductionist critique of the notion of totem by positivist anthropological theory.[17] The notion, however, proved to be so essential that it could not be dispensed with. Hence there followed four steps by which successive schools of anthropology progressively reconstructed the formal structure of the totem. Not surprisingly the steps are those by which one constructs a formal analogy of proper proportionality of the form A : B :: C : D.

First, A. P. Elkin identified the simple logical relation A : C between e.g., a bird and a tribe. This had both an analytic function for classifying groups so as to set rules for inter-marriage, and a synthetic function expressing continuity between man and nature. Lévi-Strauss points out that this empirical approach contributed some appreciation of the synthetic significance of the totem in expressing relatedness between man and nature and continuity between past and present. Nevertheless, this interpretation was inadequate for indicating why this entailed that ancestors have totems with animal forms and why the solidarity of the social group needed to be affirmed in a plurality of forms. In time this made it necessary to add new functional dimensions to the first empirical explanations.[18]

Second, Malinowski added subjective utility or pragmatic value to this relation, pointing to the biological significance of the totem as good to eat or to its psychological importance in controlling fears. (To this Radcliffe-Browne added the insight that totemism constituted an instance of the ritualization of relations between man and animals.) Malinowski interpreted this in functional terms to mean not that totems are objects of ritual and sacred because they had already been made social emblems, but that totemic societies chose animals to serve as social emblems because they already were objects of ritual and that this in turn was due to the fact that they were important material and spiritual influences in their lives: they were good to eat. In this light the social factor is primary, while the ritual and religious dimension is secondary and a function of natural interest. (When some schoolboys explained in utilitarian terms the sacred status of cows because of their milk and other useful by-products, Rabindranath Tagore has one of his characters, an older classical Hindu remark that one can tell thereby that the boys had been educated by the British.)

However, the difficulty with utilitarian explanations is that they cannot explain sorts of totems which were not useful, edible, etc.[19] Consequently, a psychological dimension was added, namely, that the totem helped to allay fears. But this explanation also confronted a daunting series of difficulties.[20] (a) Anxiety cannot be the cause, but only a concomitant, for it itself is due to the way one subjectively perceives a disorder. (b) An explanation cannot be found in a connection of articulate modes of behavior with unknown phenomena, for what is incomprehensible cannot be the explanation, but only an indication of the need to seek the explanation elsewhere. (c) Members of a group people do not act according to their individual feelings; rather, they feel according to the way they are allowed, obliged or accustomed to feel. Customs and norms come first and give rise to internal sentiments and the circumstances in which these can be displayed. (d) It is not feelings which give rise to rites, as if religious ideas were born of effervescent social surroundings, but rites which generate feelings, i.e. religious ideas are presupposed for such emotions. Therefore emotions are not explanations, but the results of either body or mind. Lévi-Strauss concludes that the real cause must be sought either in the organism by biology or in the mind by psychology or anthropology.

However, he has already demonstrated that a biological, behaviorist or utilitarian psychological analysis of human emotions does not suffice, for these are generated in terms of circumstances beyond the self, not vice versa. Hence, he points his structuralist analysis to objective analogy. This leads to its prerequisites and thereby to the metaphysical level. Thus to explain the special use of certain types of animals anthropologists went beyond subjective utility to objective analogy.

Third, the relation of a tribe and its totem was stated by M. Fortes and R. Firth merely in terms of direct resemblance or external analogy of the members of a tribe or clan to their totem. For example, just as tribe C is similar to the eagle (A : C), so tribe D is similar to the sparrow (B : D) or A : C :: B : D.

Fourth, A.R. Radcliffe-Browne corrected this by noting that the analogy was not between sets of similarities, but between sets of differences. Just as the high-flying eagle (A) is different from, but related to, the low-flying sparrow (B), so the members of two tribes (C and D) are both distinct and related, i. e., A : B :: C : D. The totem then was not necessarily good to eat, but it was good to think.

These four steps reconstructed the essential analogy of forms in the totemic relation. But this was not yet structuralism, i. e. structure alone, for content had not yet been reduced to form. Lévi-Strauss took that step and directed attention to the logical connection between the pairs of opposites i. e. between A : B on the one hand and C : D on the other. He located the principle of the unity between the species chosen as totems and their tribes in a formal condition, namely in their having in common at least one formal characteristic which permitted them to be compared.[21]

If, in fact, this condition and hence the unity of such structures requires other factors beyond the order of form and structure, the investigation of such factors would require methods of analysis different from structuralism. We have begun, however, with the formal in order to be able to draw upon the extensive developments in the abstract theoretical side of the science of anthropology. With the tools of philosophical hermeneutics we can now reflect upon the formal structures in order to establish whether further meaning is to be sought in totemism fact and if so where it is to be found.

TOTEMIC STRUCTURE AND EXISTENTIAL PLENITUDE

The Principle of Form. There are, indeed, reasons to believe that more is required than can be articulated in Lévi-Strauss's purely formal structural analysis. First of all, his thought in classifying the pairs of species is categorical in nature and therefore has all the limitations of definition which concerned Heidegger. Bernard

Lonergan described it as a method of determination which therefore has limited denotation and varies with cultural differences. Lévi-Strauss's condition for the totemic relation between the pairs A : B and C : D, namely that the pairs have in common at least one characteristic in terms of which they can be compared, cannot be fulfilled by categorial thought alone. Because categorial thought consists of forms which are contraries and hence limited, none of its objects could constitute the common element required for the total unity of structures. In principle the search for the basis of the unity, even of formal structures, cannot be carried out in terms of the limited denotations of abstractive knowledge. Instead it requires transcendental thought or intending which is "comprehensive in connotation, unrestricted in denotation, invariant over cultural change."[22]

The need for this comprehensive cognitive unity is confirmed by Jean Piaget from the nature of structuralism itself. He criticizes Lévi-Strauss for attending too exclusively to structure, form and essence, which abstract factors, he claims, can be explained psychologically by the mere permanence of the human intellect. What is more fundamental for structuralism is the fact that structures are generated by a system of operational structural transformations. These transformations require a principle which cannot be impersonal for it is the cognitive nucleus common to all subjects. Neither can it be individual for, through the series of transformations in which the structure is constituted on ever new and broader levels, this subject is progressively decentered.[23] Hence, in principle it must be beyond any contrary or any concept; it must be unique and comprehensive. Much as Nicholas of Cusa's "folding together" or *complicatio*, the system of structural transformations points to a unity which is not reducible to any individual.

This first level of reflection upon the structural analysis of totemism in terms of form alone points to what Heidegger referred to above as "the unthought". He identifies a number of its characteristics. It must be one, unlimited, and spirit; it is the principle of all transformations and the basis of the unity, form and content of all structures.

A further and hermeneutic level of reflection by Paul Ricoeur in his essay, "Structure and Hermeneutics," identifies where this principle of the totemic relation is manifested. Above we questioned the self-sufficiency of the notion of a common characteristic by which the totemic species and the tribe are compared. Ricoeur continues this question noting that, while structural relations are based proximately upon semantic analogies, more fundamentally they depend upon real similarity of content.[24] For this reason, the totemic relations or homologies between species in categorial terms presuppose as the conditions of their possibility a more fundamental unity of meaning; this, in turn, presupposes a corresponding unity or whole of meaning and of being. There is

> no structural analysis . . . without a hermeneutic comprehension of the transfer of sense. . . . In turn, neither is there any hermeneutic comprehension without the support of an economy, of an order in which the symbol signifies . . . (for) symbols symbolize only within wholes which limit and link their significations.[25]

Further, this fundamental whole or plenitude of meaning is both cognitive and affective, for humans first perceive meanings through feelings. Hence, the concrete logic of the primitive will have not only cognitive, but affective aspects, and both will be essential to our search. Earlier in this century, the philosopher anthropologist, Lucien Lévy-Bruhl, pointed out that the two were not yet distinguished in what he termed the "collective representations" (more about this below) by which the members of a particular tribe interpret and respond to other persons and to nature. The totemic logic of proportionality between humans and animals unfolds against the background of a general cognitive-affective sense of kinship between humans and totemic animals. It is to this collective representation of kinship that we must look in order to discover the awareness of the unity or plenitude of reality and meaning upon which the totemic relation was grounded.

The Principle of Existence. The scientific constructs and models which help to interpret life abstract from time or are synchronous. It must be urged that they express the form only and not the content or the reality; they are not life, but only "a secondary level of expression, subordinate to the surplus of meaning found in the symbolic stratum."[26] The actual appearance of this meaning takes place only in diachronous relations, that is, those in which the "disinterested, attentive, fond and affectionate love (of kinship) is acquired and transmitted through the attachments of marriage and upbringing."[27] For that fundamental and foundational meaning we must look to this existential process, to the life of the family in its simplest human contexts of tribe and clan. Remaining unthought, it is the principle of all beings and meanings.

Further, the search for this principle must inquire without imposing delimiting categories. Hence, our questions must not concern individual realizations, for the "unthought" is never adequately expressed in any individual life or any combinations thereof. Instead our questions must concern the conditions of possibility for concrete life as lived within the unity of a tribe, indeed of any and all tribes. This exceeds even the diachronous succession of generations, while being pointed to by those concrete tribal lives as the condition of their possibility.

This search is the very essence of all ways to God and will be the continued concern of all that follows in this and subsequent chapters. We begin with a concrete analysis of the phenomenon of totemism.

TOTEMISM

The Question

We direct our attention to the simplest societies, sometimes called "primitive". As noted above the word "primitive" is to be taken not in the sense of deficient or crude, but of that which is first and manifests what is fundamental or basic, and hence indispensable. Our method then will be to search for what is basic in the sense of being required or essential for human life in society.

In investigating any matter it is necessary to have a question so that the investigation can be directed to significant evidence, which then is assembled in order to provide meaningful insight. Like a searchlight, a question does not create the object, but enables it to stand out for observation and interpretation.

The basic issue might be stated in the following manner. On the one hand, the life of people who live together, whether in a tribe or clan, a village or city, or even on a global level, requires an attitude between persons and peoples which is not one of antipathy, for then cooperation would be impossible and murder would reign. Nor can it be one merely of indifference, for then we would starve as infants or languish in isolation as adults. Rather there is need of a way to consider others in a positive manner in order to be able to establish cooperative relations and, where possible, care and concern.

On the other hand, persons are individual, distinct and irreducible one to another or to a community, party or commune. This constitutes the perennial human dilemma which was writ large in the Cold War between the extremes of the individualism of the liberal "free world" and of the collectivism of the communist world, with the "third" world basically proxy to one of the two or to the tension between them.

The overriding and perennial question is how distinct people with their proper autonomy can look upon each other not negatively or indifferently, but positively and with concern both to promote the good of the other and to see the other as good for oneself? That is, what links us together; in what terms and on what level can people think of the good both of oneself and of all?

The Response

What is striking is that throughout the world in the earliest and simplest of societies peoples answered this question in a similar way, or by a common means. Each tribe identified a totem and in terms of this understood their relations among themselves, to other peoples and to nature. We must look more closely at this phenomenon.

It is unfortunate that the work of Lévy-Bruhl which first pointed this out has been received with such anxiety in the African context for it would appear to contain basic keys precisely for appreciating the present foundational importance of African thought for all other modes of human awareness. Lévy-Bruhl was himself a specialist in positivist thought and its logic. However, in analyzing the thought patterns reported at the turn of century by persons returning to Europe from other parts of the world he identified a mode of thought which was not merely an assembling and sorting out of multiple atomic components, but was marked by a central sense of unity. To his credit, rather than dismiss this as superstitious or insignificant he opened the way to recognizing this crucial and foundational sense of reality. Compared to his positivist logic, this was something other, which he unfortunately termed pre-logical. Some took the explicit horizontal implication of the term and wilfully turned it into a vertical, evaluative category. Try as he did, in his *Cahiers* and elsewhere, to correct this meaning imposed upon his thought and even to do away with the term "pre-logical" which was being misinterpreted, he was never able to do so.

Instead, the term was caught up in the important and positive assertion of the significance of African thought, but with a complex political shift. For many years in order to assert the equality of African culture with that of other regions it was denied that there was anything proper to its logic. Even after independence from colonial rule, Europe was still taken as the standard and the concern of many was to assert that African thought was no different. The situation was complicated further by the desire of many to affirm that Marxist analysis was appropriate for interpreting the African reality, which of course would be undercut were it to be recognized that Africa had a distinctive logic. A decade was lost discussing whether there was anything which could be called African philosophy. What was not appreciated was that if African culture had distinctive characteristics it might make a special contribution to world philosophy, and even, as a suggested here, to enabling other philosophies to appreciate their own foundations and consequently to appreciate more fully their own content. In this light "primitive" mind is more properly appreciated not negatively or pejoratively, but positively as meaning primary and foundational.

Lévy-Bruhl pointed out first that the mode of thinking was one of "collective representation".[28] This is important to note, for since the Enlightenment Western thought has been basically analytic in nature. With Descartes we look for clear and distinct ideas regarding the minimal units of an object of reason or a problem and then seek to assemble these with equal clarity. Our mind becomes specialized in grasping limited things as divided and contrasted one against the other. We tend to lose capacities for the synthetic processes of thought and hence for attention to the unities within which the pieces have their origin, meaning and purpose, and *a fortiori* for the One "from which, in which and into which all exist", according to the opening words of the Hindu *Vedanta Sutras*.[29]

In contrast, in the term collective representation, "representation" is used intentionally as more general and inclusive than concepts or even cognition; it includes sense as well as intellectual knowledge, affective reactions as well as knowledge, and indeed motor responses as well as knowledge and affectivity.

Further these representations are "collective" in a number of senses. First, they are socially conditioned: the same event may be a cause of fear in one tribe and of laughter in another. Second, they concern the total meaning of an event and for the whole of life. Third, they are not conceptual exclusions identifying each thing in contrast to all others after the manner of analytic compartmentalization mentioned above, but synthetic in that they see each as participating in a whole. The importance of this synthetic or unitive character is reflected in the fact that to be ostracized is to be excluded not only from a particular community, but from human dignity itself. Literally, the evil of slavery lies not in bondage but in the loss of the bond to one's community, whereas the unity of persons or of a people is the fundamental key to one's humanity.

Further, such attitudes must be more than merely subjective. If they have promoted, rather than destroyed, human life through the aeons of so-called primitive life, they are ways in which humans cannot only feel, but be, well. They must then reflect something essential and objective regarding human reality, and this must be the more true of that which makes them possible. What then is the condition of possibility of these positive attitudes between persons or towards one another in a tribe or clan?

This question was studied by Lévy-Bruhl in his work, *How Natives Think*, on the cognitive-affective collective representations of the first and simplest societies. His investigations led him to the totem as that in terms of which these peoples saw themselves to be united according to what he termed the "law of participation". In the most disparate places and climes tribes identified an animal or thing as their totem, its specific nature being differentiated according to the locale. Their perception of their relation to this totem was not simply that of one to one's ancestors from whom one derives, to one's name by which one is externally designated, or to a later state which one will enter following death. Lévy-Bruhl notes that under questioning totemic peoples reject all such relations as inadequate. Rather, the members of the tribes insisted that quite directly they are their totem. "They give one rigidly to understand that they are araras (a bird that is the totem of this people) at the present time, just as if a caterpillar declared itself to be a butterfly." They understand their relation to the totem to be one of simple identity, which he describes as "a mystical community of substance."[30]

This participational mode of identity is both a way of thinking and a way of being. It is the former in that it does not work in terms merely of spatial relations. For example, no matter how far a hunter is from his camp, what his wife does or does not eat is thought to effect his success or failure. This does not mean that a spatial sensitivity is absent; indeed it is amazingly acute and some South Sea islanders are said to be able to navigate over great distances without landfalls or navigational equipment. Rather what this indicates is that their thought processes regarding unity and relatedness are not controlled by, or reducible to, spatial considerations. Things could be caused and moved at a distance: telekinesis, which some now would call witchcraft, was considered an actual happening. Nor is this thinking held to temporal relations, for one's ancestors live now and effect our lives. Finally, it is not merely a functional relation, for they think not externally only, in terms of themselves and what others can do for them, but in terms of a real internal unity with others.[31]

Again this does not mean that there is no sense of time or of the sequence of events. Rather the sense of time is not simply external or of exclusion, of parts or moments outside of parts, but of inclusion. In sacred time moments perdure through time and are ritually present. This is particularly manifest in creation myths which express the basic reality of life and are formative of every facet of life. This was detailed by the Dogon sage, Ogotemmêli, and recorded by Marcel Griaule in *Dieu d'eau: entretiens avec Ogotemmêli.*[32]

Finally, such thinking is not in terms of functional relations in which one thing is done in order to cause another. Hence, the fact that a hoped for result does not follow in space or time, does not appear to discourage the repetition of the practice. A totemic people does not appear to base its understanding of the meaning and purpose of things on practical success or failure. Thus, as noted above, whereas some anthropologists would say that something was chosen as a totem because it was good to eat or for some other practical purpose, Lévi-Strauss noted rather that the totem was not good to eat, but good to think.

Thus, totemic people think not just in terms of themselves and others as separate, but in terms of the whole and of unity in the whole. This surpasses spatial, temporal or functional, i.e., external, relations. It is rather a unity of being. Primitive peoples are, and understand themselves to be, a unity with, in and by the totem.

Hence participation in the totem is not only a way of thinking, but also a way of being; indeed it is the former because it is the latter. This expression of one's identity in term of one's totem, such as "I am lion" or "I am araras", is not only to assume a common name as might a sports team; nor is it to indicate something past or future as if I used to be a lion, or am descended from lion, or after death will become a lion; nor is it to indicate that I am presently some part of lion such as its eye or tail; nor finally is it to state kinship with lions.[33]

Instead, such statements, totemic peoples insist, express an actual and essential identity which is veritably symbiotic in character. The life of the person is that of the totem. Thereby, all the members of a tribe are most profoundly one with the others from their beginning and by the very fact that they have come to exist, just a I am a brother or sister to all the other children in my family not on the basis of something I do, but by my very emergence into being.

This unity then is in no wise merely an abstract identity of essence or nature, such as would be reflected by a structuralist analysis of forms. Rather, it is a concrete, living, existential identity or participation in the totem. It is in these terms that the primitive interprets his or her entire life, determining both the real significance of the actions he or she performs and hence what he or she should and should not do.

> In analyzing the most characteristic of the primitive's institutions — such as totemic relationship . . . — we have found that his mind does more than present his object to him: it possesses it and is possessed by it. It communes with it and participates in it, not only in the ideological but also in the physical and mystical sense of the word. The mind does not

imagine it merely; it lives it. . . . Their participation in it is so *effectually lived* that it is not yet properly imagined.[34]

This insistence upon unity with the totem manifests a state of both thought and feeling prior to the dominance of objectification whereby things and persons are seen as objects over against me. Unity has not yet been dominated by multiplicity; it is a concrete identity, indistinguishably both objective and subjective.

This mode of understanding was first termed by Lévy-Bruhl, not anti-logical or a-logical, but "pre-logical."[35] In this he reflected his own initial positivist bias that there could exist only a series of single and externally related units, and consequently that any logic must consist simply of such terms. In his posthumously published *carnets*, however, he retracted the term 'pre-logical', for his investigations had shown that the primitives did indeed have a consistent pattern of meaning. Apostle has analyzed this in detail in his work on African philosophy, *African Philosophy, Myth or Reality?* and concluded to the need to recognize in it a proper, if not a perfect, logic.[36]

Primitive societies were not held together by understanding everything as a series of units of which the totem is but one. Rather, the totem was understood to be the one in which all the others had their identity, their meaning, and their unity among themselves. Such a reality cannot be just one being among many others. As that in terms of which all members in the tribe — no matter how many — have their meaning, the totem is for that tribe the fullness or plenitude of reality and meaning in which all live or participate as a community. It is the key to the meaning of all, the intensive center of all meaning. It does not participate in the individuals; rather, the individuals participate in it. In Augustine's classic terms: I have not first loved You; it is You who first loved me. Due to this symbiosis of people with their totem, the primitive's knowledge of reality expressed in the totem is immediate, rather than inferential.

In turn, a person's relation to other members of the tribe and to nature is understood in terms of their relation to their totem. Through participation in the common totem the many members of the tribe are intimately related one to another; like brothers, they see themselves to be more deeply united than distinguished.

This is reflected in very varied forms of contact, transference, sympathy and telekinesis as, in the above example, when the success of a hunter is understood to depend more radically upon what is, or is not, eaten by his wife at home than upon any other factor. These and other examples manifest an intense understanding of the unity and relatedness of the members of the tribe in a manner not dependent upon surface spatio-temporal or empirical factors. It is not that such relationships are not also known and acted upon by the primitive. But they see the basic reality of their life as a participation in the totem and on this they base their interpretation of the nature and the reality of their relationships to all else.

CHARACTERISTICS OF THE TOTEMIC WAY

Unity. This concept brings important insight to the question of unity and distinctiveness which have so divided the modern mind, characterized by a rationalist and analytic mode of thinking. The totem is not one in a series, but the unique reality in which each and all have their being — and, by the same token, their unity with all else.

This is the key to social unity. Each is not indifferent to all else or only externally or accidentally related to others in terms of temporal or spatial coincidence or functional service. Rather all are in principle and by their very being united to all, to whom they are naturally and mutually meaningful. Hence, one cannot totally subject anybody or indeed any thing to one's own purpose; one cannot take things merely as means in a purely functional or utilitarian manner. Instead, all persons are brothers or sisters and hence essentially social. This extends as well to nature in an ecological sensitivity which only now is being recuperated.

What is impressive in this is that all are united but without the loss of individuality that has been the case in modern collectivisms. Instead, each individual, rather than being suppressed, has meaning in the unity of the totem. Hence, nothing one does is trivial, for every act is related to the whole. No one is subservient as a tool or instrument; all are members of the whole. As each act stands in relation to the whole whose meaning it reflects, everything is of great moment. There is justice and there are taboos, for there are standards which are not to be compromised.

Religion. What then should be said of the totem as the key to a meaning in which all participate: is it religious, is it divine? Some would answer in the affirmative and for a number of reasons:

- it is the key to the unity of persons, recalling the religious statement of the brotherhood of man in the fatherhood of God;
- it has the absolute meaning of the religious center: the one God of Judaism, Christianity, Islam and Hinduism;
- it is the key to the sacred meaning and dignity of all.

In all these ways the totem is the religious center.

Perhaps, however, it might be called proto-religious, in that while this principle of unity is privileged and not reducible to humans, neither is it explicitly appreciated as being distinct from, and transcending the contents of this world.

On the other hand, the effort of the mystic at the high end of the religious spectrum is precisely to overcome separation from God. The direction is immanent, namely, to unite one's life with the divine, and to do so perhaps less by achieving transcendence than by entering more deeply into the center of one's own interiority. In this light totemic thought emerges in its true importance as something not to be escaped from, but to be recaptured and lived in new ways in the midst of our much more complex society and more technically organized world.

An a posteriori *Way.* The road we have taken has many of the characteristics of the classical *a posteriori* ways to the existence of God. (a) It began from a reality that did actually exist, namely, the successful and progressive life of peoples through the thousands of centuries which constitute almost the entirety of human experience. (b) It sought the principles of this existence, namely, the content of the understanding which made possible their successful human life. (c) It concluded in that totemic unity and fullness in which people had both their being and their unity. Thus, it established the plenitude of, and participation in, the foundational totem as principle both of the human mind and of social life.

This road differs, however, from the classical five ways of Thomas Aquinas.[37] (a) Being essentially anthropological in character, it began with people in the primitive stage of their development. (b) Being essentially hermeneutic in method, it attended to the conditions of possibility for the understanding manifested in their life. (c) This combination of anthropological and hermeneutic factors concluded to the plenitude, not as it is in itself, as a cause distinct from its effect — the much later science of metaphysics will be required for that — but only as appreciated by the primitive mind in its totemic mode.

This difference should not be considered to be merely negative. The thought of the primitive is not merely a poorer form of what people in subsequent ages would do better with improved tools. Heidegger pointed to an important sense in which it is only by returning to the origins that important progress can be made. I would like to suggest three ways in which this is true of a return to the totemic vision if made through the combined tools of anthropology and philosophical hermeneutics.

Implications of the Totemic Way

Metaphysical Content. Human progress is made in part through the ability to understand in increasingly more formalized terms and systems the relationships which obtain in society, in nature, and between the two. If these scientific elaborations are not to be merely empty signs, hypothetical systems or external relations, they must draw upon the meaning of life itself, first expressed humanly in terms of the totem. This will be required not only for their certainty as noted by Descartes, but for their content and unity as pointed out by the classical realist philosophies. This will be particularly necessary if the process of development is to implement, rather than to supplant, human values and transcendent aspirations.

What has been said of the sciences should, with appropriate adaptation, be said of metaphysics as well. It is the task of metaphysics as a science to establish with rigor its processes of definition, reasoning and conclusion. The intelligibility of the entire science is dependent upon the intelligibility of its subject, being. In turn, it is the search for that intelligibility which has ever led the mind to reasoning regarding the plenitude of being of Plato's "One" or "Good",[38] Aristotle's "life divine",[39] Heidegger's "Being",[40] or Iqbal's "total absolute".[41]

All are clear that this plenitude cannot be constituted by any limited instance or any combination thereof. Plato's notion of *reminiscentia* may be more helpful than is generally thought, however, if employed in terms not of the hypothesis of a prior existence of the individual in a world of ideas, but of the real experience of our totemic ancestors. The totemic peoples subjected to the acid test of time the proposition that if human life is to be lived it must be lived in terms of a unity, a whole, a Plenitude of reality in which all have their being and meaning. This was the cultural heritage they bequeathed to subsequent ages. South Asian thought reflects this in being characterized by a quest for the highest value of life, for *moksa* or spiritual freedom. The Greeks reflected this in their myths, in the context of which Plato was able to proceed from multiple instances of goodness to the one Goodness Itself which, as the sun, gives light to all in this cave of time. The so-called later Heidegger came finally to focus on this as the ground from which all beings emerged into time. Iqbal saw it as the basis for all human knowledge.

A Return to the Source. This is not only a question of the past. Gandhi has pointed out that a new nation cannot be built unless it finds its soul. Menendes y Pelago said this well:

> Where one does not carefully conserve the inheritance of the past, be it poor or rich, great or small, there can be no hope of giving birth to original thought or a self-possessed life. A new people can improvise all except intellectual culture, nor can an old people renounce this without extinguishing the most noble part of its life and falling into a second infancy similar to senile imbecility.

What Gandhi added was that this spirit or culture is to be found not only in books, but in family and village life. Though some have taken this as an issue of economics, in fact it is one of metaphysics.

How is such a metaphysics to be elaborated? Here the original suggestion of Heidegger assumes particular importance. He noted that philosophic traditions, in proceeding to ever more intensive analysis and clarity trade existential content in order to gain formal clarity. From within the scholastic contexts of both East and West it is protested — I believe rightly, but heretofore in vain — that the vital significance of the classical analyses is not appreciated. Meanwhile, more and more all such analyses were previously classified as at best ideological superstructures which obscure attention to the reality of life.

In response, following Heidegger's suggestion, we have stepped back to a point, prior to Plato's and Aristotle's development of selective analyses, at which life was lived in communion, rather than seen in abstractions. We have stepped back beyond myth to totem. There, a crude but robust sense of the plenitude of reality and of participation therein is to be found. It gave men who had naught else an awareness of their unity one with another and an appreciation of the importance of the actions of each. With that, and that alone, they were able, not only to traverse the vast seas of time, but to arrive with such treasures in the form of epics, myths and hymns — rightly considered sacred texts — that our several cultures have lived richly merely on the interest of such a patrimony.

Even to live wisely on the interest, however, it behooves one to be as clear as possible concerning the capital; this is especially true in philosophy. Both as a sequential process of evolving human understanding and as Heidegger's process of retrieve, it is essential to know what came before in order to plan one's next step and have the materials with which it can be fashioned. A significant body of scholarship works on the basis of a supposed evolution from polytheism to monism. Others would hold that monism is the more original and that the evolution consisted in the progressive introduction of a plurality of gods. The two suppositions are used by their proponents, not only to order chronologically the Vedic hymns and passages in the *Upanishads,* but to interpret the meaning of their key phrases and ideas. The same can be said regarding such key notions as matter and spirit, monism and pluralism.

In fact, the totem is none of these, but expresses the unity and plenitude from which subsequently some will evolve an explicit monotheism, while others will develop theories regarding the development of the physical universe. Both will have their roots in the unity which is the totem, but neither will exhaust its potential meaning. More importantly, neither will be completely deprived of the unspoken totemic context of their meaning. Hence, as we shall see, it is erroneous to interpret Vedic thought or pre-Socratic philosophy as a proto-materialism.

The Divine as Present. Precisely because this vision of unity in plenitude is foundational for human life, the steps taken in the initial phases of its clarification and articulation will be statements of what is essential in order that life be lived and lived well in a particular culture. As the *Vedas* express these conditions of possibility, Professor T.N.P. Mahadevan marked well that they can no more rightly be said to be produced than Newton can be said to have produced, rather than to have discovered, the law of gravitation. They are indeed discovered or "heard" (*Sruti*) as one bores deeply into the accumulated sediment of our long experience of living, till finally "like joyous streams bursting from the mountains" the sense of Unity comes forth as revelation of the Real.[42]

Theologians are in difficulty, however, if they restrict their views simply to the words of their scriptures, for faith then becomes fideism. As century succeeds century the words lose their existential content, become empty signs, and are filled with ideas which are at best ephemeral and possibly even dangerous. In times they come to be progressively less understood and then ignored. For the active philosopher dedicated to wisdom and to comprehension these dangers are greater still. It is the philosopher's special task to work out the order of being and meaning, to clarify the significance of the steps in reasoning processes, and to test and ground their principles. We do this so that the One in all and all in One, the plenitude and the participation by which we live and breathe and have our being may pervade our minds, inspire our hearts, and guide our steps.

It is supremely wise of philosophers such as Suresvara to recognize that their reasoning processes are only preparatory, ground-clearing operations, whereas the knowledge of the One arising from Sruti or sacred text is immediate and non-relational. It is not the product of their reasoning, but is made known by Scripture through implication. Here the philosopher meets the real challenge of metaphysics and joins with the seer in concern for that which surpasses name and form.

As negative statements must be based upon positive content, the philosopher's negative statements that Brahman is "other than the unreal, the insentient, and the finite" would appear to need to be based upon positive awareness of "non-relational, non-verbal content".[43] The philosopher must ask in what way such meaning is present to the awareness of the one who hears *Sruti*. The strong emphasis in Indian thought upon unity would seem to suggest or facilitate the appreciation of presence which is unveiled, that is, revealed by the words of the sacred text.

It has been the burden of this chapter to suggest that this presence can be further appreciated if we look, not to the individual alone, but to the mother-lode of human experience lived intensively in family and clan. There it is commonly found that parents, though even when relatively inarticulate, nonetheless convey to their children a vibrant and concrete, if equally inarticulate, sense of such characteristics of existence as its unity, truth, and goodness. The above analysis showed how the totem expressed in a non-verbal manner an awareness of the plenitude of being in which all are united. It indicated also the manner in which some of this meaning might now be retrieved.

If, indeed, some non-verbal awareness of unity and participation is present as the basis of all truly humane life, then:

- metaphysics may not be an esoteric concern; the realities with which it deals may be much more present than the data for which one needs telescopes, expeditions, laboratories and computers;

- *karma yoga* or the way of action may be integral to *jnana yoga* or the way of knowledge; and

- emancipation, as reflecting the true nature of man,[44] may be being lived in the simplest and most familiar surroundings.

In the words of Chakravarti Rajagopalachari of Madras:

> Whether the epics and songs of a nation spring from the faith and ideas of the common folk, or whether a nation's faith and ideas are produced by its literature is a question which one is free to answer as one likes. . . . Did clouds rise from the sea or was the sea filled by waters from the sky? All such inquiries take us to the feet of God transcending speech and thought.[45]

In sum, the totem was not simply one animal among others, but in a sense limitless: no matter how many persons were born to the tribe, the totem was never exhausted. Further, the totem was shown special respect, such as not being sold or used for food or other utilitarian purposes, which would make it subservient to the individual members of the tribe or clan. Whereas other things might be said to be possessed and used, the totem was the subject of direct predication: one might say that one had a horse or other animal, but only of the totem would one say that one is, e.g., lion.

The totem, then, was the unique, limitless reality in terms of which all persons and things had their being and were interrelated. It was the sacred center of individual and community life in terms of which all had meaning and cohesion. It made possible both the personal dignity and interpersonal relations which are the most important aspects of human life. It did this with a sense of direct immediacy that would be echoed, but never repeated, in subsequent stages of more formally religious thought.

Whether this be seen as religious or proto-religious, it is more foundational even than a way to God, for it states the basically religious character of all human life. What is shown is that religion is not something distant which is added to a universe which humankind first experiences as basically secular, but that religion is the basic and essential insight of even the simplest forms of human community. It makes clear that the issue is not whether there be room for religion alongside public life or how to protect one from the other, but how religion functions as the root of human meaning and community.

NOTES

1. (Lahore: Ashrof, 1944^2), p. 6
2. *Ibid.*, p. 17.
3. This threefold structure of the sciences in the Aristotelian tradition is elaborated in Aquinas's *Commentary on Boethius's Work on the Trinity*, qq. 3 and 5. Descartes's procedure for placing all under doubt follows the same sequence of the three sources of knowledge. This depends as well on Aristotle's dictum that there is nothing in the intellect which is not first in the senses. For more detail see chapter I above.

4. Indeed, one might define philosophy and science precisely as knowledge of the various aspects of reality in terms proper to human reason, and hence as expressive not merely of my subjective sensations, but of the nature and existence of things themselves.

5. P.K. Mukherji, *Life of Tagore* (New Delhi: India Book Co., 1975), p. 153.

6. *The Vedic Age*, ed. R.C. Majumdar and A.D. Pusalker (vol. I of *The History and Culture of the Indian People*; Bombay: Bharatiya Vidya Bhavan, 1957), pp. 169-198.

7. C. Kunhan Raja, *Asya Vamasya Humn* (*The Riddle of the Universe*): *Rgveda I, 164* (Madras: Genesh, 1956), pp. xxvii-xxxix; and *Poet-Philosophers of the Rgveda: Vedic and Pre-Vedic* (Madras: Ganesh, 1963), pp. x-xi

8. Stephen Fuchs, *The Origin of Man and His Culture* (Bombay: Asia Publishing House, 1963), pp. 47-49; G.E. Daniel, "Archaeology" in *Macropaedia, The New Encyclopedia Britannica* (Chicago: Encyclopedia Britannica, 1977), vol. I, p. 1082.

9. Arthur B. Keith, *The Religion and Philosophy of the Vedas and Upanishads* (Harvard Oriental Series, vol. XXXII; Cambridge, Mass.: Harvard University Press, 1925), p. 195.

10. "Our asking of the fundamental question of metaphysics is historical, because it opens up the process of human being-there [in its essential relation — i.e., its relations to the essential as such and as a whole —] to unasked possibilities, futures, and at the same time binds it back to its past beginning, so sharpening it and giving it weight in its present. In this questioning, our being-there is summoned to [its history in the full sense of the word, called to history and to] decision in history." Martin Heidegger, *An Introduction to Metaphysics* (Garden City, NY: Doubleday, 1961), pp. 36-37 and 32.

11. *Ibid.*, p. 136.

12. "The criterion of the unthought demands that the heritage of thought be liberated in respect of what still lies in reserve in its 'has been' (*Gewesenee*). It is this which holds tradition initially in its sway and is prior to it, though without being thought about expressly as the originative source." Heidegger, "Letter on Humanism", trans. by E. Lohner, in W. Barrett and H. Aiken, *Philosophy in the Twentieth Century* (New York: Harper & Row, 1971), pp. 270-302.

13. *Br. Up.*, IV, v. 15.

14. *Brahma-Sutra*, I, i, 3.

15. Heidegger, *Introduction to Metaphysics*, p. 130.

16. Claude Lévi-Strauss, *Totemism* (Boston: Beacon Press, 1963).

17. In that context earlier research into the origins of Indian thought such as that of A. Keith (*op. cit.*, vol. I, pp. 195-97) tended to discount the significance of the totem, pointing, e.g., to the absence of one or another specific factor, such as ritual eating, which was in no sense essential to the notion. The subsequent anthropological work described here, by which the notion has been scientifically reconstructed, provides the basis for restating the question. This is the more true as Keith himself argues, even regarding the meaning of Brahman, from the fact that a notion such as that of a supernatural power pervading the universe is generally found in all other tribes in other parts of the world to its having been a basic factor in early Indian thought. *Ibid.*, vol. II, p. 446.

18. *Totemism*, pp. 56-58.

19. *Ibid.*, pp. 59-65.

20. *Ibid.*, pp. 66-71.

21. *Ibid*, pp. 87-88. Cf also *The Savage Mind* (Chicago: University of Chicago Press, 1970), p. 93. In *Totemism* (p. 82) he notes that E. E. Evans-Pritchard had held that the primitives looked upon the totemic animals and the tribes as collateral lines descending from God as their common origin, which implied that their reality or content was essentially related. This would correspond to some degree to Heidegger's "unthought" which founds the meaning of all things and unites them among themselves. For the structuralist, however, content is not distinct from form.

22. Bernard Lonergan, *Method in Theology* (New York: Herder & Herder, 1972), p. 11. Sergio Moravia cites passages from Lévi-Strauss which indicate some recognition of this need. They speak of spirit as subject of the universal categories, and of the transformation of structures as the unconscious activity of the spirit. *La ragione nascosta, scienza e filosofia nel pensiero di Claude Lévi-Strauss* [Firenze: Sansoni, 1969], pp. 325ff.

23. Jean Piaget, *Structuralism* (New York: Harper and Row, 1970), pp. 139-142.

24. "A careful examination of *The Savage Mind* suggests

that at the base of structural homologies one can always look for semantic analogies which render comparable the different levels of reality whose convertibility is assured by the "code". The "code" presupposes a correspondence, an affinity of the contents, that is, a cipher." Paul Ricoeur, "Structure and Hermeneutics" in *The Conflict of Interpretations, Essays in Hermeneutics* (Evanston, Ill.: Northwestern University Press, 1974), p. 56. See also Hans-Georg Gadamer, *Truth and Method* (London: Sheed and Ward, 1975).

25. *Ibid.*, p. 60.
26. *Ibid.*, pp. 48 and 56, n. 18.
27. Lévi-Strauss, *The Savage Mind*, p. 37
28. Lucien Lévy-Bruhl, *How Natives Think* (Les functions mentals dans les societes inferieures; New York: Washington Square Press, 1966), p. 62.
29. *Sutras*, I, 1, 2.
30. *How Natives Think*, p. 62.
31. *Ibid.*, pp. 61-63.
32. Marcel Griaule, *Dieu d'Eau: Entretiens avec Ogotemmêli* (Paris: Fayad, 1966).
33. *How Natives Think*, pp. 4-7.
34. *Ibid.*, pp. 324, 362.
35. *Ibid.*, ch. III.
36. L. Apostle, *African Philosophy: Myth or Reality?* (Brugges, Belgium: Story, 1980).
37. See ch. VI below.
38. Plato, *Republic*, 508.
39. *Metaphysics* XII, 7.
40. *Being and Time*, trans. J. Macquarrie and E. Robinson (New York: Harper and Rowe, 1962).
41. *Reconstruction of Philosophy*, p. 6.
42. T.N.P. Mahadevan, *Invitation to Indian Philosophy* (New Delhi: Heinemann, 1974), p. 14. The simile is taken from the *Vedas*.
43. R. Balasubramanian, *The Taittirīyopanisad Bhāsya-Vārtika of Sureśvara* (Madras: Center for Advanced Study in Philosophy, University of Madras, 1974), p. 180.
44. S. Dasgupta, *A History of Indian Philosophy* (Delhi: Motilal Banaridass, 1975), I, 58.

45. C. Rajagopalachari, *Ramayana* (Bombay: Bharatiya Vidya Bhavan, 1976), p. 312.

CHAPTER III

GREEK MYTH
AS A
PROTO-PHILOSOPHICAL WAY TO GOD

THE IMAGINATION

Following the directions of Tagore and Gandhi to look to the philosophy of the people, Chapter II concerned a major paradox in human understanding. It suggested, with Heidegger, that the way for philosophy to go forward was to take a step backward. For radical newness is to be found, not in doing more of the same, but in reaching more deeply into our heritage. To do so it was essential to mine the long totemic experience of life and to draw out what has not been, and perhaps cannot be, thematized and treated with the analytic tools of science. In doing this, Chapter II led to the totem as the principle of plenitude, or in Iqbal's terms, the total absolute, in terms of which humanity has understood its lives during the more than 99.8 percent of human experience which preceded the composition even of the *Rg Veda*.

The present chapter will concern a later period, that of myth, hymn and epic, as an evolution or transmographation of the totemic way, somewhat as a moth develops into the quite different form of the butterfly. Where the earlier nonverbal tradition of the totem illustrated how living in unity rather than in discord needed to be based on an absolute unity and plenitude, the verbal tradition of myth begins the progressive articulation of this proposition. The process will be followed in subsequent chapters to the initiation of philosophy and its development down to the present.

In this process we shall encounter a new set of issues. In Chapter I we asked first and in principle how development takes place enabling new questions to be asked and new insights to be acquired, and what is the relation between the content of earlier and subsequent stages of thought? Here we must look concretely at the nature of the transition from the primitive to the mythic stage of consciousness, and at how this unfolding of totemic thought opens a new way to God or new level of religious awareness. This Chapter will focus upon Hesiod's *Theogony*; the following chapter will look at some analogies, yet with important differences, in the *Nāsadīya-sūkta* or creation hymn, *Rg Veda* X, 129.[1]

Epistemologically a new way of thinking came to be required. In the totemic phase of human existence each person or family did all that was required for their life. The intellect worked in terms of what was directly presented by the external senses and the totem was articulated according to a physical object such as a bird or fish, according to what could be seen in the locale. Now new needs confronted the human mind. With the specialization and the division of labor, more complex patterns of human relations with their broader possibilities and responsibilities become necessary.

In these circumstances it was not sufficient to think in terms only of what could be articulated in terms available from the senses. The capabilities Piaget described as abstract intellectual concepts reversible on concrete things would be needed. Even more, the principle of unity, previously thought of in terms of a totem named from a sensibly present object, must now be appreciated in its distinction from all immediately sensible nature. Both of these made it necessary for the intellect to free itself from the concrete terms of physical objects and to engage the distinctive capabilities of the imagination as an internal sense. Thereby, the mind can variously combine what it has received through the senses to construct images and models with which the intellect can work on complex patterns of human relations and meaning.

A very general but suggestive analogy is the move from dancing to figure skating. In skating one is freed from the short strides and relatively slow speeds of the person on foot: one's body is endowed with the long graceful strokes along with the velocity which make possible moves quite out of the question even for the gymnast or ballerina. In literature the *Iliad* and *Odyssey*, written in terms of the gods, illustrate what this can mean for the human spirit.

The progression of Kant's *Critiques* gives a more properly philosophical insight into the possibilities opened by thinking in terms available not to the external senses, but to the imagination. Often imagination is considered ephemeral, unreal and distractive. In his first *Critique* Kant points out the actual role played by the imagination in the development of science. In his third *Critique* he points out its role in working out the alternatives essential for creative choice and especially for the deeper roots of freedom. It seems helpful then to step out of our chronological sequence at this point and to turn to Kant for help in reflecting upon the work of the imagination in order to draw out its essential role in freedom from other tasks at performs in human knowledge. This progression is analyzed in some detail in chapter IX below.

The Scientific Imagination

It is unfortunate that this range of Kant's work had been so little appreciated. Until recently, the rationalist impact of Descartes directed almost exclusive attention to the first of Kant's *Critiques*, namely, the *Critique of Pure Reason*, concerned with the conditions of possibility of the physical sciences. Its rejection of metaphysics as a science was warmly greeted in positivist and other materialist circles as a dispensation from any search beyond what was reductively sensible and, hence, phenomenal in the sense of being inherently spatial and/or temporal.

Kant himself, however, quite insisted upon going further. If the terms of the sciences were inherently phenomenal, then his justification of the sciences was precisely to identify and to justify, through metaphysical and transcendental deductions respectively, the sets of categories which enable the phenomenal world characterized by space and time to have intelligibility and scientific meaning. But since sense experience is always limited and partial, the universality and necessity of the laws of science must come from the human mind. Such *a priori* categories then belong properly to the subject precisely inasmuch as it is not material or spatiotemporal.

We are here at the essential turning point for the modern mind. Kant takes the definitive step in identifying the subject as more than a wayfarer in a world which it encounters as a given and to which one can but react. Rather, he shows the subject to be an active force engaged in the creation even of the empirical world in which it lives. The meaning or intelligible order of things is due not only to their creation according to a divine intellect, but also to the work of the human intellect and its categories. If, however, the human is to have such a central role in the constitution of this world, then certain human elements will be required, and their require ment itself will certify their reality.

First there must be an imagination which can bring together the flow of disparate sensations. This plays a reproductive role which consists in the empirical and psychological activity by which it reproduces within the mind the amorphous data received from without, but now according to the forms of space and time. This merely reproductive role is by no means sufficient, however, for, since the received data is amorphous, any mere reproduction would lack coherence and generate a chaotic world: "a blind play of representations less even than a dream".[2] Hence, the imagination must have also a productive dimension which enables the multiple empirical intuitions to achieve some unity. This is ruled by "the principle of the unity of apperception," that is, of understanding or intellection: "all appearances without exception, must so enter the mind or be apprehended that they conform to the unity of apperception."[3] This is done according to the abstract categories and concepts of the intellect, such as cause, substance and the like, which rule the work of the imagination at this level in order that it constitute a unity.

Second, this process of association must have some foundation in order that the multiple sensations be related or even relatable one to another, and, hence, enter into the same unity of apperception. There must be some objective affinity of the multiple — an "affinity of appearances" — in order for the reproductive or associative work of the imagination to be possible. However, this unity does not exist, as such, in past experiences. Rather, the unitive rule or principle of the reproductive activity of the imagination is its reproductive or transcendental work as "a spontaneous faculty not dependent upon empirical laws, but rather constitutive of them and, hence, constitutive of empirical objects."[4] That is, though the unity is not in the disparate phenomena, they can be brought together by the imagination to form a unity only in certain manners if they are to be able to be informed by the categories of the intellect.

Kant illustrates this by comparing the examples of perceiving a house and a boat that is receding downstream.[5] The parts of the house can be intuited successively in any order (door-roof-stairs or stairs-door-roof), but my judgment must be of the house as having all of its parts simultaneously. Similarly, the boat is intuited successively as moving downstream. However, though I must judge its actual motion in that order, I could imagine the contrary. Hence, the imagination, in bringing together the many intuitions goes beyond the simple order of appearances and unifies phenomenal objects in an order to which concepts can be applied. "Objectivity is a product of cognition, not of apprehension,"[6] for, though we can observe appearances in any sequence, they are unified and, hence, thought in orders which are ruled by the categories of the mind.

In sum, in the first *Critique* it is the task of the reproductive imagination to bring together the multiple elements of sense intuition in some unity or order capable of being informed by a concept or category of the intellect with a view to making a judgment. On the part of the subject, the imagination here is active, authentically one's own and creative. Ultimately, however, its work is not free, but necessitated by the categories or concepts as integral to the work of sciences which are characterized by necessity and universality.

The Aesthetic Imagination

In the third *Critique*, that of *Aesthetic Judgment*, the imagination has a similar task of constructing the object, but not in a manner necessitated by universal categories or concepts. In contrast, here the imagination, in working toward an integrating unity, is not confined by the necessitating structures of categories and concepts. It ranges freely over the full sweep of reality in all its dimensions to see whether and wherein relatedness and purposiveness or teleology can emerge so that the world and our personal and social life can achieve thereby its meaning and value. Hence, in standing before a work of nature or of art, the imagination might focus upon light or form, sound or word, economic or interpersonal relations. It can combine any of these as a natural environment or a society, whether encountered concretely or expressed in symbols.

Throughout all of this, the ordering and reordering by the imagination can bring about numberless unities. Unrestricted by any *a priori* categories, it can nevertheless integrate necessary dialectical patterns within its own free and, therefore, creative production; it can engage scientific universals within its unique concrete harmonies. This is properly creative work. More than merely evaluating all according to a set pattern in one's culture, it can choose the values and order reality accordingly. This is the very constitution of a culture itself.

It is a productive, rather than merely reproductive, work of the human person living in his or her physical world. Here, I use the possessive form advisedly. Without this capacity one would exist in the physical universe as another object, not only subjected to its laws but restricted and possessed by them. One would be not a free citizen of the material world, but its mere functionary or servant. In contrast, in his third *Critique* Kant unfolds how one can truly be master of one's life in this world, not by being arbitrary or destructive, but precisely as a creative artist bringing being to new realization in ways which constitute new growth in freedom.

In the third *Critique*, the productive imagination constructs a true unity by bringing the elements into an authentic harmony. This cannot be identified through reference to an intellectual category because freedom then would be restricted within the universal and necessary laws of the first *Critique*.[7] In order for the realm of human freedom to be extended to the whole of reality, this harmony must be able to be appreciated aesthetically by the pleasure or displeasure of the free response it generates. It is our contemplation or reflection upon the pleasure or displeasure, our elation at the beautiful and sublime or our disgust at the ugly and revolting, which shows whether a proper and authentic ordering has or has not been achieved.

One could miss the integrating character of this pleasure or displeasure and its related judgment of taste[8] by looking at it ideologically as simply a repetition of past tastes in order to promote stability. Or one might see it reductively as a merely interior and purely private matter at a level of consciousness available only to an elite class and related only to an esoteric band of reality. That would ignore the structure which Kant laid out at length in his first "Introduction" to his third *Critique*.[9] There he described this *Critique* as not merely juxtaposed to the first two *Critiques* of pure and practical reason, but as integrating both in a richer whole.

Developing the level of aesthetic sensitivity enables one to take into account ever greater dimensions of reality and creativity and to imagine responses which are more rich in purpose, more adapted to present circumstances and more creative in promise for the future. This is manifest in a good leader such as a Churchill or Roosevelt — and, supereminently, in a Confucius or Christ. Their power to mobilize a people lies especially in their rare ability to assess the overall situation, to express it in a manner which rings true to the great variety of persons, and, thereby, to evoke appropriate and varied responses from each according to his or her capabilities. The danger is that the example of such genius will be reduced to formulae, become an ideology and exclude innovation. In reality, as personable, free and creative, and as understood precisely in terms of the aesthetic judgment in contrast to pure and practical reason, their example is inclusive in content and application as well as in the new responses it continually evokes from others.

When aesthetic experiences are extended to broader visions of life and passed on as a human heritage, gradually they constitute a cultural tradition. Some thinkers, such as William James and Jürgen Habermas,[10] fearing that attending to these traditions might distract from the concrete needs of the people, have urged a turn rather to the social sciences for social analysis and critique in order to identify pragmatic responses. But this points back to the necessary laws of the first two *Critiques*. In many countries now engaging in reforms and even nation-building, such "scientific" laws of history have come to be seen as having stifled creativity and paralyzed the populace.

Kant's third *Critique* points in another direction. Though it integrates scientific universal and necessary social relations it does not focus upon them, nor does it focus directly upon the beauty or ugliness of concrete relations, or even directly upon beauty or ugliness as things in themselves. Its focus is rather upon our contemplation of the integrating images of these which we imaginatively create, that is, our culture as manifesting the many facets of beauty and ugliness, actual and potential. As noted above, the aesthetic evaluation of these is in terms of the free and integrating response of pleasure or displeasure, the enjoyment or revulsion they generate most deeply within our whole person. Confucius probably would feel very comfortable with this if stated in terms of an appreciation or feeling of harmony.

In this way, freedom itself at the height of its sensibility is not merely an instrument of a moral life, but serves through the imagination as a lens or means for presenting the richness of reality in varied and intensified ways. Freedom, thus understood, is both spectroscope and kaleidoscope of being. As spectroscope it unfolds the full range of the possiblities of human freedom, so that all can be examined, evaluated and admired. As kaleidoscope, it continually works out the endless combinations and patterns of reality so that the beauty of each can be examined, reflected upon and chosen when desired. Freely, purposively and creatively, imagination weaves through reality focusing now upon certain dimensions, now reversing its flow, now making new connections and interrelations. In the process reality manifests not only scientific forms and their potential interrelations, but its power to evoke our free response of love and admiration or of hate and disgust.

In this manner freedom becomes at once the goal, the creative source, the manifestation, the criterion and the arbiter of all that imaginatively we can propose. It is *goal*, namely to realize life as rational and free in this world; and it is *creative source*, for with the imagination it unfolds the endless possibilities for such human expression. It is also *manifestation*, because it presents these to our consciousness in ways appropriate to our capabilities for knowledge of limited realities and in the circumstances of our life. Moreover, it is *criterion*, because its response manifests a possible mode of action to be variously desirable or not in terms of a total personal response of pleasure or displeasure, enjoyment or revulsion; and finally it is *arbiter*, because it chooses to affirm or reject, to realize or avoid this mode of self-realization. In this way, freedom emerges as the dynamic center of our human existence. It can really be expected then that this power of creative freedom, when sparked by a new level of activity on the part of the imagination, will open a new way for the person to God.

TRANSITION FROM TOTEM TO MYTH AS OPENING A NEW WAY TO GOD

Chapter I examined the classical distinction of the three levels of knowledge and the identification by Piaget and Kohlberg of the levels of psychological development of the child. These provide a schema for identifying and relating the ways to God which have been elaborated by humankind. Piaget's general theory of development sheds light on the cultural transitions which enable and reflect new ways to God and their successive unfolding of a basic human awareness of God as source, foundation and goal of human life. The transition from totem to myth is a first such step beyond the universal primitive (foundational) experience of God. Many of the elements of this transition were sketched out by the philosopher-anthropologist, Lucien Lévy-Bruhl, in the last chapter of his *How Natives Think*.[11]

As noted in Chapter I Piaget describes the dynamism of development as a process of moving from an equilibrium in which the multiple internal and external factors of one's life are integrated, through a disequilibrium caused by the introduction of new factors, to a higher equilibrium by the development of new capabilities where necessary.

Chapter II then described the character of human awareness in its primitive, basic or totemic stage. Each group focused on a single principle, namely, the totem, through identification with which all members of the group had their identity and were related to all others in the group. This included the unity of the divine principle so central to Islam, but found also in the first commandment of the Judeo-Christian decalogue[12] and in the Hindu insight that Brahman is that from which, in which and into which all are.[13] Its social implications for the brotherhood of man in the fatherhood of God are so central and obvious that one who says he loves God, but hates his brother, is not just confused, but a liar:[14] for one cannot but see the contradiction in such a statement.

This primitive insight is the most fundamental, and the heart of all that subsequently will be developed in religious life and practice. It is so essential to each way to God which subsequently will unfold that it cannot be forgotten without that ceasing to be a way to God. From this follows the importance of Piaget's observation that any transition must not discard, but retain the essence of the prior state, and add thereto new capabilities and insights to form a new mode of thinking, feeling and acting. One begins from the equilibrium of the prior state of harmony in God, and moves through a disequilibrium to reestablish the equilibrium at a higher level of conscious awareness.

This chapter and those that follow then are not about the addition of a new way to God alongside that which was described in totemic terms. Rather they are an evolution of that way. In the present case the move is from the equilibrium of the totemic state in which unity was stressed, through the disequilibrium introduced with the differentiation and specialization of roles, to a new equilibrium. Unity is continued, but by employing the work of imagination engages the developing diversity in order to form a more integrated and stable union. The totem had been able to provide for unity and meaning while the lives of all members of the tribe remained similar. But its manner of expressing unity became insufficient as society became more specialized and differentiated. The tribe came to depend not merely upon similarity and sameness, but upon the differentiated capabilities of, e.g., hunters, fishers and eventually farmers.

Transcendence. With this ability to be both united and differentiated came an appreciation as well of the special distinctiveness of the sacred center with regard to the many individuals of which it was the principle. What in totemic thought previously had been stated simply by identity (I am lion) could now be appreciated as greater than and transcending the members of the tribe. This is reflected in the development of priesthood, rituals and symbols to reflect what was seen no longer simply as one's deepest identity, but as the principle thereof.[15]

Such a transcendent reality could no longer be stated in terms of such physical realities as parrot or lion corresponding to the external senses, but rather was figured by the imagination. The terms drawn originally from the senses now were reconfigured in forms that expressed life which was above the human and served as the principle of human life. Such higher principles, as knowing and having the power of will, were personal; as transcending persons in these capabilities they were called gods.

It would be incorrect to consider this, as did Freud and Marx, to be simply a projection of human characteristics. On the contrary, the development of the ability to think in terms shaped by the imagination released human appreciation of the principle of life from the limitations of animals, birds and other natural entities available to the external senses. These had always been special: to eat or sell them was taboo. Now the imagination was engaged to allow the transcendence of the principle of unity to be expressed in a more effective manner. This did not create the sense of transcendence, but allowed the unique and essential foundation of human meaning of which Iqbal spoke to find new and improved expression through an evolution of human capabilities.

Hence, what previously had been grasped simply in direct symbiotic unity, now with more distinctive self-awareness came to be appreciated not only to be immanent to each and all, but to transcend them as well. Whereas the totem was considered to be so simply one with the primitive, now symbol and ritual appear.[16]

As the imagination was essentially involved in this, the personal divine was pictured in the anthropomorphic forms of gods, and their interaction was the material of which myths were woven. If the totem had been proto-religious, the myth was religious for it opened the mind to transcendent, if anthropomorphic, principles of life and meaning.

In contrast to the taboos and the social unity based upon an unthinking totem, the unity founded in the gods could have elements of comprehension and command, of love and mercy; it could extend to all humans while being specific with regard to each person.

To ask of those in this stage of equilibrium how this could be so would be to suppose a later and philosophical type of thinking. What is important for the present is that, having attained the mythic level of development, the peoples were able to articulate with vastly greater complexity the unity which had been expressed as simple and direct identity in the totem. That unity could now be textured or woven, as it were, with the many rich threads of meaning available by the work of the imagination expressed in myths.

It should be noted that the evidence from this stage of development does not point to the use of mythical forms merely as literary devices. That would presuppose a prior understanding of things simply in their own, that is, in proper terms — a mode of understanding which had not yet evolved. Rather, myth at this point was the only mode of understanding — what Tillich would call "unbroken myth."[17] The many realities of the world were understood directly in terms of the identities of the gods and the interrelations between them. Thus, the interpretation of the gods was the highest wisdom and the questions were asked, as noted the *Rg Veda*, "not jestingly. . . . Sages, I ask you this for information."[18]

Immanence. Myth added a new appreciation of transcendence to remembrance of the unity stated so forcefully in the totem as that in terms of which all has its meaning. To this dimension of transcendence there corresponds an appreciation of the immanence of the divine, for these two characteristics of transcendence and immanence are not opposed one to the other, but correlative. This is true throughout our experience: the more transcendent a reality the more present it is. Thus, organic material such as a stone simply rests upon the earth, whereas the plant sinks its roots into the immediate soil to draw nutrition and eventually enriches the soil, while the animal finds its water and nutrition over a broad territory. With persons and their cognitive and affective life this relation is vastly intensified, as can be seen in the pervasive mutual influence between teacher and student, or lover and beloved. Continuing in this same direction, it is possible to see as correlative both the infinite transcendence of the supreme principle of unity and meaning and its immanence.

This religious insight entails in turn the rich and sacred dignity of each person and of the social interaction of persons. Conversely, our self respect and the respect and love we extend to others constitute an immanent context for the discovery of the divine and for our response thereto.

In no way is this an alternative to what was made possible by the totemic way. All of that however now emerges with much greater articulation both as regards the divine and as regards the human wayfarer. Henceforth, in mythic cultures all will be understood in terms of the gods. The classical literature of Greece would be written exclusively in these terms — indeed, they had no other — and Homer would produce the *Iliad* and *Odyssey* as an irreplaceable, because unsurpassable, cornerstone of Western Culture, similar to the great *Mahabarata* epic of the East. We shall look into the *Theogony* in order to see more concretely this way to God, but first we must look more in detail into the nature of myth.

THE NATURE OF MYTH

Myth might be described as "the operation of an imaginative consciousness which spontaneously conceives the world and man in the form of persons and events having a symbolic meaning."[19] Let us look at this in detail:

- *An imaginative Consciousness*: As noted above this is not intellectual knowledge as such, nor is it simply sense knowledge, but the intellect working according to, or in the terms presented by, the internal senses of memory and imagination. The imagination draws from the external senses information which it variously combines to constitute new integrated pictures. These, in turn, represent the external world not only as it already exists in itself, but also as it can be reordered and recombined by the human consciousness.

- *Spontaneous Conceptions*: Sensible realities are not first grasped directly in their own terms and then expressed through a god as their sign; instead, all is grasped in, and as, personal forms. E.g. the sea is not first known in its own right and then re-presented by Poseidon, rather the sea is Poseidon and Poseidon is sea: there is no other appreciation of sea separate from Poseidon.

- *Persons*: This enables the expression not only of some abstract empirical or physical data as would a thermometer or weather vane, but a joint cognitive, affective and behavioral involvement in reality. Myths express the meaning, value, purpose and creative contribution of the object. This can be appreciated by contrasting a weather report of a storm at sea with Homer's much richer if less technically exact description of the struggle between Poseidon and Zephyr or Vaughn Williams' "Sea Symphony".

- *Events*: What is important is not merely an individual, but the story line of the person's interaction with other persons and with all parts of nature. Thus, in the Bible what is important is less the individual figure or verse than the story line recounting the work of divine Providence.

- *Symbol*: This is not a sign which it joined arbitrarily to that which is signifies, as green and red indicate respectively "go" and "stop" in traffic lights but could have been the converse. In contrast, a symbol participates in, or shares, the reality it symbolizes, bespeaking a mode of immanence as, e.g., with the flag of a nation.

Myths constitute a rational, though not a critical inquiry. It is not critical because they do not state things by their proper names, but rather by the names of the gods: e.g. the sea by Poseidon. Consequently, there can be no strict critical control over the conclusions to be drawn from the evidence.

Nevertheless, their thought content is rational and coordinated.

The *Theogony* as we shall see is not just a random gathering of the names of the gods, but a systematic ordering in order to constitute an overall pattern conveying a deep sense of reality. Like the "days" of creation in the *Genesis* account, the sequence of the names and events may not be entirely consistent according to the laws of physics. But the *Theogony* and *Genesis* were not works of scientific cosmology; science had not yet developed and at the time was not a human capability. Nevertheless, myths were meant to convey deep and perduring truths, and were intentionally and effectively ordered to do so. Thus, in his *Works and Days*, the first treatise on labor, Hesiod found it necessary to identify vicious competition, for which there was no symbol, in order to contrast it to productive emulation symbolized by Eris. To do so he developed a sister goddess to Eris, a bad Eris. The rational content of the myths can be seen also in the Greeks articulation in terms of myth of a world view integrating the cosmos and humans. This was rich in expressing meaning and values and enabled people to live a human life in their physical and social unities. Indeed, it remains so indispensable a part of the world cultural heritage that broadly throughout the world today the *Iliad* is often the first book assigned in secondary school literature courses. It is a good place to begin an effort to be more richly human.

In sum, one might describe myth as a picturing understanding of reality in personal terms.

THE THEOGONY

In view of what has been said above, the *Theogony*, written by Hesiod (ca. 776 B. C.), is especially illustrative. Because the gods stated the reality of the various parts of nature, when Hesiod undertook to state the relationship which obtained between them he undertook in effect to articulate the theme of this study, namely, the way in which all things constitute a royal road to the divine. Indeed, whereas much of later thought so isolated the human from the rest of nature that it would leave the wayfarer as a beleaguered pilgrim in an alien and threatening land, the myth spoke of all in terms of divinity. In this it is closer to the totem as regards ways to God and reflects a recognition of the sacredness of earth and of nature which is one the most exciting of the recent sensitivities emerging in this post ideological period (see, e.g., Vaclav Havel's remarks on *Gaia*).

Hesiod's work has a number of important characteristics. First, it intends to state the highest possible type of knowledge. Thus, it begins with an invocation to the Muses to provide him with divine knowledge. "These things declare to me from the beginning, ye Muses who dwell in the house of Olympus."[20]

Secondly and correspondingly, it is concerned with the deepest issues, namely the origin and unity of all things. "Tell me which of them came first", he asks. Then he proceeds to a poetic treatment of issues ranging from the fact of evil to the justification of the reign of the gods (later named "theodicy" by Leibniz),[21] which include all the problems, such as that of evil, with which the religious awareness of the period was concerned.[22]

Thirdly, because it was written as the period of purely mythic thought was drawing to a close — within two centuries of the initiation of philosophy in Greece — it manifests the extent to which mythic thought could understand basic issues. Hesiod was able to draw upon the full resources of the body of Greek mythology, weaving the entire panoply of the gods into the structure of his poem. He did not, however, simply collect and relate the gods externally in a topographical or chronological pattern. Rather, his organization of the material was ruled by an understanding of their inner meaning and real order of dependence. Thus, when in the *Theogony* he responds to the question of "How at the first gods and earth came to be,"[23] his ordering of the gods weds theogony and cosmogony. It constitutes a unique manifestation of the way to God laid out by the mythic mind as understanding all as emerging from and of the divine. In order to examine this in detail we shall cite here the sections of the text that are central to our purposes.

The Text of Theogony, 11, 104-230, 455-505[24]

a. *Exhortation to the Muses.*

> Hail, children of Zeus! Grant lovely song and celebrate the holy race of the deathless gods who are for ever, those that were born of Earth and starry Heaven and gloomy Night and them that briny Sea did rear. Tell how at the first gods and earth came to be, and rivers, and the boundless sea with its

raging swell, and the gleaming stars, and the wide heaven above, and the gods who were born of them, givers of good things, and how they divided their wealth, and how they shared their honors amongst them, and also how at the first they took many-folded Olympus. These things declare to me from the beginning, ye Muses who dwell in the house of Olympus, and tell me which of them first came to be.

b. *First came Chaos, then Earth and Heaven, the first parents of the Titans or elder gods.*

Verily at the first Chaos came to be, but next wide-bosomed Earth, the ever-sure foundation of all the deathless ones who hold the peaks of snowy Olympus, and dim Tartarus in the depth of the wide-pathed Earth, and Eros (Love), fairest among the deathless gods, who unnerves the limbs and overcomes the minds and wise counsels of all gods and all men within them. From Chaos came forth Erebus and black Night; but of Night were born Aether and Day, whom she conceived and bare from union in love with Erebus. And Earth first bare starry Heaven, equal to herself, to cover her on every side, and to be an ever-sure abiding-place for the blessed gods. And she brought forth long Hills, graceful haunts of the goddess-Nymphs who dwell amongst the glens of the hills. She bare also the fruitless deep with his raging swell, Pontus, without sweet union of love. But afterwards she lay with Heaven and bare deep-swirling Oceanus, Coeus and Crius and Hyperion and Iapetus, Theia and Rhea, Themis and Mnemosyne and gold-crowned Pheobe and lovely Tethys. After them was born Cronus the wily, youngest and most terrible of her children, and he hated his lusty sire.

Myth as Founding All in God

Diversity in Unity. The order which Hesiod states in the *Theogony* is the following. The first to appear was Chaos: "Verily at the first Chaos came to be." Then came earth: "but next wide-bosomed Earth the ever sure foundation of all," and starry Heaven: "Earth first bare starry Heaven, equal to herself." From Earth, generally in unison with Heaven, were born Oceanus and the various races of Cyclopes and gods, from whom, in turn, were born still other gods such as Zeus and the races of men. In this manner, Hesiod articulates the sequence of the origin of all parts of the universe. Eros and the various modalities, such as Night and Day, Fate and Doom, also are pictured as arising from Chaos.

If, then, we ask what is the understanding of reality expressed by this poem, it will be noted that Hesiod expresses the very opposite of a random gathering of totally disparate and equally original units. On the contrary, the relation between the gods and between the parts of nature they bespeak is expressed in terms of procreation. As a result, every reality is related positively to all the others in its genetic sequence.

This relatedness does not depend upon a later and arbitrary decision; it is equally original with their very reality: they originate genetically from, and in, this unity. Neither does it involve only certain aspects of the components of the universe; it extends to their total actuality, including their actions. Rhea, for example, appeals to her parents for protection from the acts of her husband, Cronus, against their children. The understanding which the poem conveys, therefore, is that of a unity or relation which originates with their very being and on which the distinctive beings and their actions depend.

Indeed, unity is understood to be by nature prior to diversity. This is indicated by the genetic character of the structure in which each god proceeds from the union of an earlier pair of gods, while all such pairs are descendants of the one original pair, Earth and Heaven. Further, the procreation of the gods proceeds from each of these pairs precisely as united in love. Finally, this is done under the unitive power of Eros, who is equally original with heaven and earth.

Note that there is a sequence: the text says that the gods "came to be" or "first came to be". Further, this is not a merely temporal, external or atomic sequence, but a genetic one. They "came forth from", bare or were born from. This extends through all the gods, who stand for all the parts of nature. Thus, the parts of nature have a meaning and cohesiveness among themselves and with humans who also were born in these genetic lines.

From what has been said we can conclude that unity pervades gods and men: all is traced back to Earth and Heaven as the original pair from whose union, under the impetus of Eros, all is generated.

Unity as Absolute. But what is the relation between Heaven and Earth? As the genetic lines derive from these two original gods, if these gods are related between themselves then each thing in the universe is related to everything else. But if heaven and earth are not related then each thing is related only to its own line, but is alien to the other half of reality, which then would be indifferent or even antipathetic.

A similar crucial question is being dealt with here: is the world a battlefield between two alien forces in which one's basic attitude in life must be defence and manipulation, or is it in principle a unity in relation to which the proper attitude is love and generous cooperation. This, in sum, is the working out of the proper attitude in a situation in which diversity must be recognized and promoted. (In moral education it corresponds to Erikson's notion of trust and hope.[25] The infant who is well cared for can develop an attitude of trust and on this basis evolve a moral character that is open to all, trustful, cooperative and creative. If not, lacking trust, the focus is on self-protection and the manipulation of everyone else toward this goal.)

The Greek answer, which is foundational for the sense of unity in Western civilization lies in the mythical relation of Heaven and Earth. This can take us to a still deeper understanding in which the unity of all reality constitutes a path to God provided we return to the text and use the proper etymological tools.

The text states the following order: Chaos, Earth, Heaven. Unfortunately, since the Stoics, Chaos has since come to be taken to mean disorder and mindless conflict or collision, thus obscuring its original meaning in the earlier text of the *Theogony*. Etymologically, the term can be traced through the root of the Greek term '*casko*' to the common Indo-European stem, '*gap*'. Using this stem, as it were, as a sonar signal to sound out mythic thought throughout the broad range of the Indo-European languages, we find that the term is used to express a gaping abyss at the beginning of time as, e.g., with the derivative *'ginungagap'* in Nordic mythology.[26] Kirk and Raven confirm this analysis and conclude that for Hesiod 'chaos' meant, not a state of confusion or conflict, but an open and perhaps windy space which essentially is between boundaries.[27] Aristotle in his *Physics* referred to chaos as empty space (*topos*).[28]

Returning to the text in this light, it will be noted that it does not say speak directly of a state prior to Chaos, but begins with the emergence of Chaos: "At first Chaos came to be". However, there is no suggestion that Chaos was the original reality; on the contrary, the text is explicit that chaos came to be: *"He toi men prótista Cháos genet."*[29]

Further, Chaos is a space to which boundaries are essential. These boundaries, it would seem, are the gods which the text states just after Chaos, namely, Earth and its equal, Heaven. These are not said to have existed prior to chaos and to have been brought into position in order to constitute the boundaries of the '*gap*'; rather, they are said somehow to be arranged as contraries on the basis of chaos.

Thus, Kirk and Raven understand actively the opening verses of the body of the text: "Verily at the first Chaos came to be, but next wide-bosomed Earth . . . and Earth first bare starry Heaven equal to herself." They take this to express the opening of a gap or space, which *thereby* gives rise to Heaven and Earth as its two boundaries.[30]

For its intelligibility, this implies: (a) that an undifferentiated unity precedes the gap, and (b) that by opening or division of this unity the first contrasting realities, namely, Heaven and Earth, were constituted. That is, on the basis of the gap one boundary, Heaven, is differentiated from the other boundary, Earth. Hence, by the gap the boundaries are identically both constituted and differentiated as contraries. As all else are derivatives of Chaos, Earth and Heaven in the manner noted above, it can be concluded that the entire differentiated universe is derivative of an original undifferentiated unity which preceded Chaos.

It would be premature, however, to ask of the mythic mind

whether this derivation took place by material, formal or efficient causality; that question must await the development of philosophy. But clearly the original reality itself is not differentiated; it is an undivided unity. As such it is without name, for the names we give reflect our sense perceptions which concern not what is constant and homogenous, but the differentiated bases of the various sense stimuli. What is undifferentiated is not only unspoken in fact, but unspeakable in principle by the language of myth, for this depends essentially upon the imagination.

Nonetheless, though it is unspeakable by the mythic mind itself, reflection can uncover or reveal something of that undifferentiated reality which the *Theogony* implies. We have, for instance, noted its reality and unity. Its lack of differentiation is not a deficiency, but a fullness of reality and meaning from which all particulars and contraries are derived. It is unspeakable because not bounded, limited and related after the fashion of one imaged contrary to another. This is the transcendent fullness that is at the heart of the Hindu *advaita* or nondual philosophy; it is also the total infinite to which Iqbal referred as that which makes finite thinking possible.

It is the source of that which is seen and spoken in our language, and which Hindu thought refers to as the world of names and forms. Further, it is the source, not only from which the differentiated realities are derived, but of the coming forth itself of these realities. This is reflected in two significant manners. Positively, Eros, which itself is said to come from chaos, is the power which joins together in procreative union the pairs of gods, thereby reflecting the dynamic manifestive and sharing character of the undifferentiated reality.

Negatively, this is indicated also by the acts which the *Theogony* describes as evil. For example, it says that "Heaven rejoiced in his evil doing", namely, hiding away his children in a secret place of Earth as soon as each was born, and not allowing them to come into the light. Cronus is termed "a wretch" for swallowing his children. In each case evil is described as impeding the process by which new realities are brought into existence. This implies that its opposite, the good, involves essentially bringing forth the real. The undifferentiated unity is the origin of the multiple and differentiated; in terms we shall encounter below, it is participative.

Unity as Sharing. It can now be seen that all the progeny, that is, all parts of the universe and all humans, are born into the unity of a family. They trace their origin, not to a pair of ultimately alien realities and certainly not to chaos as conflict, but to undifferentiated Unity. Just as there is no autogenesis, there is no unrelated reality or aspect of reality. It would seem, then, that verses 118-128 of the hymn imply a reality which is one, undifferentiated and therefore unspeakable, but nonetheless essentially generous, sharing and productive of the multiple. For the Greek mythic mind then, beings are more one than many, more related than divided, more complementary than contrasting.

Thus far we have focused on unity, as our concern is especially with ways to God. We begin, perhaps too egocentrically, in our separate realities and look for our relation to the One. But the path that leads us there is in reality two way. We have found that it is more basically a genetic pathway coming from the One; this is its deeper truth. Hence, concern with the multiple realities and hence with individuality is integral to the concern of the *Theogony* which indicates much that is important thereto. But the key is its picturing of the multiple, both persons and parts of nature, as generated from the One. This has a number of implications.

First, it shows the One which is the source of all reality and hence reality itself to be expansive and generative, i.e., good. Second, it bespeaks participation, i.e., that it is of the nature of reality to share itself with others, to bear other identities as offspring which, in turn, share and bear still others.

From this it follows that the key to a good life is not holding off or refusing to share. Indeed, this is precisely the way evil is depicted: not as strife, but rather as hiding the children had by heaven and earth, and as Cronus swallowing his children as they came forth from Rhea so that they would not assume his office of king. Strife is not the source of evil, but follows from evil deeds as, e.g., the children of Cronus castrate him for having acted evilly. Thus, even negatively, the character of being is manifest to be good and sharing.

From this appears the proper basis of individuality. It is not opposition or selfish hording; rather individuals are significant to the degree that they participate, share and show forth the goodness of their divine origin.

In addition this affirmation of the distinctiveness of individuals is not absolute, but derivative. Their generation is via separation in, and of, the originally undifferentiated unity, it is carried out under the impulse of Eros as a unifying factor bringing together the gods in procreative union. Hence, contrary to Hobbes and his sense of man as wolf to man in a war of all against all, or to pragmatic cooperation only for some external, e.g. economic, benefit, individuals are not isolated, much less opposed to one another. Rather, they are in principle positively related and unitive. Hence, in sacramental practice matrimony always has been considered a sign of the church, which is Christ.

In sum, the overall picture is that of an original unity with many gods which, as with the parts of nature thy bespeak, come from the One via generative unions of the gods. This constitutes an open unity, parallel to that of all in the totem, but capable of taking explicit account of the differences in reality and integrating them. Finally, the identity of each is had not by holding to what it is, but in proclaiming, through sharing, what it has from the Divine. There is a strong sense of this in African cultures and in the image of the Cross as dying in order to live.

As a transformation of the earlier totemic structure, mythic understanding continues the basic totemic insight regarding the related character of all things predicated upon one center for the meaning of all. By thinking in terms of the gods, however, myth is able to add a number of important factors. First, quantitatively, the myth can integrate, not only a certain tribe or number of tribes, but the entire universe. Second, qualitatively, it can take account of such intentional realities as purpose, fidelity love and care. Third, while still affirming the unitive principle which had been expressed in totemic thought with shocking directness ("I am lion"), it expresses or connotes rather its transcendent, unspeakable, undifferentiated and generous character.

CRITIQUE OF THE ADEQUACY OF MYTH AS A WAY TO GOD

The expression of all this in terms of the mythic forms available to the internal sense of imagination had its temptations. These were pointed out by Xenophanes.[31] One set of fragments from his writing gives classical and somewhat biting expression to its imaginative character.

> But mortals believe the gods to be created by birth, and to have their own (mortals') raiment, voice and body (Fr. 14, Clement, *Stromateis*, V, 109, 2).

> Aethiopians have gods with snub noses and black hair, Thracians have gods with grey eyes and red hair (Fr. 16, *ibid.*, VII, 22, 1).

> But if oxen (and horses) and lions had hands or could draw with hands and create works of art like those made by men, horses would draw pictures of gods like horses, and oxen of gods like oxen, and they would make the bodies (of their gods) in accordance with the form that each species itself possesses (Fr. 15, *ibid.*, V, 109, 3).

But this is not the real problem. Xenophanes noted that by the time of Homer and Hesiod a perfervid imagination had gone from expressing the transcendence of the gods to attributing to them as well the many forms of evil found among men.[32]

> Both Homer and Hesiod have attributed to the gods all things that are shameful and a reproach among mankind: theft, adultery, and mutual deception (Fr. 11, Sextus, *Adv. Math.*, IX, 193).

In effect, the very principles of meaning and value had come to point as well to their opposites.

As a result it was no longer sufficient to think in terms of the imagination. The intellect needed to proceed in its own terms, beyond sense and imagination, in order to state formally the absolute unity which was the deeper sense of what totemic thought had stated so directly in saying, "I am lion" and especially to defend what had been stated in terms of the gods of nature in the anthropomorphic ventures of the imagination. As the mind began to operate in properly intellectual terms, rather than through the images of mythic thinking, it was able to overcome the anthropomorphisms of the myth. This enabled Xenophanes to make explicit that the supreme principle of unity and meaning was transcendent, one, all wise and provident.[33]

> There is one god, among gods and men the greatest, not at all like mortals in body or in mind (Fr. 23, Clement, *Strom.*, V, 109, 1).

> He sees as a whole, thinks as a whole, and hears as a whole (Fr. 24, Sextus, *Adv. Math.*, IX, 144).

> And he always remains in the same place, not moving at all, nor is it fitting for him to change his position at different times (Fr. 26, Simplicius, *Phys.*, 23, 11, 20).

> But without toil he sets everything in motion, by the thought of his mind (Fr. 25, *ibid.*, 23, 23, 20).

Philosophy as a distinct and proper discipline had begun. Proceeding in terms proper to the intellect, in time philosophy would supplant, but never eliminate, myth as the main mode of human understanding. Multiple new ways to God could then be elaborated.

NOTES

1. Authur A. MacDonell, *A Vedic Reader* (Oxford: At the Clarendon Press, 1917), pp. 207-211. Citations from *Rg Veda* X, 129 will be taken from this text.
2. Immanuel Kant, *Critique of Pure Reason*, trans. N.K. Smith (London: Macmillan, 1929), A 112; cf. A 121.
3. *Ibid.*, A 121.
4. Donald W. Crawford, *Kant's Aesthetic Theory* (Madison: University of Wisconsin, 1974), pp. 87-90.
5. Kant, *Critique of Pure Reason*, A 192-93.
6. *Ibid.*, A112, 121, 192-193. Crawford, pp. 83-84, 87-90.
7. See Kant's development and solution to the autonomy of taste, *Critique of Judgment*, nn. 57-58, pp. 182-192, where he treats the need for a concept; Crawford, pp. 63-66.

8. See the paper of Wilhelm S. Wurzer "On the Art of Moral Imagination" in G. McLean, ed., *Moral Imagination and Character Development* (Washington: The Council for Research in Values and Philosophy, 1992) for an elaboration of the essential notions of the beautiful, the sublime and taste in Kant's aesthetic theory.

9. Immanuel Kant, *First Introduction to the Critique of Judgment*, trans. J. Haden (New York: Bobbs-Merrill, 1965).

10. William James, *Pragmatism* (New York: Washington Square, 1963), Ch. I, pp. 3-40. For notes on the critical hermeneutics of J. Habermas see G. McLean, "Cultural Heritage, Social Critique and Future Construction" in *Culture, Human Rights and Peace in Central America*, R. Molina, T. Readdy and G. McLean, eds. (Washington: Council for Research in Values, 1988), Ch. I. Critical distance is an essential element and requires analysis by the social sciences of the historical social structures as a basis for liberation from determination and dependence upon unjust interests. The concrete psycho- and socio-pathologies deriving from such dependencies and the corresponding steps toward liberation are the subject of the chapters by J. Loiacono and H. Ferrand de Piazza in *The Social Context and Values: Perspectives of the Americas*, G. McLean and O. Pegoraro, eds. (Washington: Council for Research in Values and Philosophy, 1988), Chs. III and IV.

11. (New York: Washington Square Press, 1966).

12. *Exodus* 20.

13. *Vedanta Sutras*, I, 1, 2.

14. I John: IV, 20.

15. *How Natives Think*, ch. XII.

16. *Ibid*.

17. Paul Tillich, "Theology and Symbolism," in *Religious Symbolism*, ed. F. Ernest Johnson (New York: Harper and Row, 1955), p. 109.

18. C. Kunhan Raja, *Asya Vamasya Hymn* (*The Riddle of the Universe*), *Rgveda* I-164 (Madras: Ganesh, 1956), pp. 5-6; see also G. McLean, *Plenitude and Participation*; *The Unity of Man and God* (Madras: University of Madras, 1978), pp. 34-38.

19. George F. McLean and Patrick Aspell, *Ancient Western Philosophy* (New York: Appleton, Century, Croft, 1972), p. 8. See also by the same authors *Readings in Ancient Western Philosophy*

(New York: Appleton, Century, Croft, 1971) and Ernst Cassirer, *Mythical Thought*, vol. II of *Philosophy of Symbolic Forms* (New Haven, Conn.: Yale, 1965), pp. 3-59.

20. *Theogony*, n. 114, in *Readings in Ancient Western Philosophy*, p. 4.

21. *Ibid.*, n. 115.

22. Werner Jaeger, *The Theology of the Early Greek Philosophers* (London: Oxford University Press, 1967), pp. 12-13.

23. *Readings in Ancient Western Philosophy*, p. 4.

24. Hesiod, *The Theogony*, trans. Hugh G. Evelyn-White (Loeb Classical Library; Cambridge, Mass.: Harvard University Press, 1964), pp. 85-99, 107-151.

25. E.H. Erikson, *Childhood and Society* (New York: Norton, 1963), p. 247; and *Identity, Youth and Crisis* (New York: Noton, 1968).

26. Jaeger, p. 13.

27. G.S. Kirk and J.E. Raven, *The PreSocratic Philosophers* (Cambridge: At the University Press, 1960), pp. 26-32.

28. *Physics* IV, 1, 208b31.

29. *Hesiod, the Homeric Hymns and Homerica*, trans. by H.G. Evelyn-White (London: Heinemann, 1920), p. 86.

30. *Readings in Ancient Western Philosophy*, p. 5.

31. *Ibid.*, p. 31.

32. *Ibid.*

33. *Ibid.*

CHAPTER IV

THE RITUAL HINDU WAY TO GOD AS A PROTO-METAPHYSICS

I. RG VEDA X, 129: NUSADIYA SŪKTA (HYMN OF CREATION)

The analysis in Chapter II of totemism as a proto religious phenomenon showed it to be as a way to God, not an isolated experience of the solitary individual as religion has come to be thought by many in our times. Rather it was the commonly shared experience of all peoples and the first condition of human thought.

In the last chapter we looked into the transition to the mythic way to God beyond that of totemic thought. We saw the totemic understanding of the unity of reality evolve into mythic thought as a higher and later level of development. As we looked, in particular, into Greek myth as the root of Western philosophy, it would be helpful at this point to look with a similar purpose to the *Vedas*, the corresponding root of Eastern thought.

Here my words must above all be questions concerning issues for scholars within the Eastern tradition, but both Socrates and Zen have shown questions to be at the heart of philosophizing.

THOUGHT AND ACTION AS WAYS TO GOD

Chapter I followed Piaget's and Kohlberg's description of psychological development and saw that it had a number of parallel tracks. The one which is generally attended to and to which Piaget himself would seem to have given priority was the cognitive: the development of improved capabilities of knowledge was seen as the basis for greater sophistication in the affective and kinetic orders. While true, that is but part of the story, for the general theory of development works on the basis of equilibrium, how it is lost creating a need, and how at times it can be regained only by developing a higher cognitive capability such as a capacity for abstract reasoning. From this point of view the higher cognitive capability becomes the effect rather than the cause in the process of development. This centers on affectivity understood as the tendency toward a good (the equilibrium in general and specific objects in particular) or toward a goal that is absent. Affectivity, in turn, is set within the pattern of existential life activities in which we are engaged. Thus the pattern of development can be traced, and perhaps more effectively, through affective concerns than though cognitive capabilities. But affectivity directs attention further to types of action that are not merely of mind or will, but of the full human person, mind and body. Such integrally human actions are the root of the more partial mental processes.

Here, one touches upon the long dialectic in the Hindu tradition between thought and action. This concerns not the commonplace that must be taught to every child, namely, to think before one acts, but rather the higher reaches of the spiritual life. It is here that the real dilemma of the human condition emerges, namely, how can the self-aware human being live his or her destiny. As a participant in God, one is less than God in one's being and hence in one's capabilities. Yet inasmuch as one is both from God and directed towards God, one can live truly and fully only by relating to that which transcends one, and which does so infinitely.

As the human person is both body and spirit two ways or paths can be taken in response. One is that of the body and rituals, the other is that of the spirit through mind and heart. Fortunately, these ways need not be mutually exclusive if the person is truly one in nature and being. Indeed, given the limitations of the human person each way can have only partial success and will need to be complemented by the other.

In the Hindu tradition this has entailed, on the one hand, a florid set of rituals and signs all expressing the divine. These employ to the full the capabilities of the human imagination, which we saw as basic to the mythic way discussed in Chapter III. However, as one attempts to enumerate the rituals — someone has counted over forty in the morning bath — it begins to be evident that Hindu culture envisages not a secular life which is made sacred by a number of particular rituals, but that all of life is not only sacralized, but sacred. Yet as human life is essentially relative and not absolute, some argue that it is essential for the mind to enter in order to point beyond actions, even the sacred ritual actions of our life. Beyond the actions of the body, it is up to the human spirit — not merely as marked by the picturing capabilities of the imagination, but as fully spiritual and open to being — to continue on towards God, and so it must.

Nevertheless, the dialectic continues, for the spirit too is finite or limited in power; not only its concepts, but all its acts are limited. In the subsequent chapters we shall see philosophy attempting to come to terms with this in the form of negative intellectual judgements and the work of the heart rushing along mystic pathways. But one side of the Hindu experience argues inexorably that the human mind must always lag behind on any way to God and therefore that two strategies are essential. The first is to shorten, indeed eliminate, the distance by turning from transcendence, according to which God is infinitely distant, to immanence, in terms of which God is infinitely present. The second is to proceed not by mind in which we define and hence delimit the content of our thoughts, but by actions which point but do not define. Though I can point to a person, I cannot and must not attempt to define or delimit that person by my concepts. By actions we are ushered into the realm of sacred ritual, which must always be added over and above whatever can be achieved by human consciousness.

Further, among the numberless signs and rituals, sacrifices have special importance because they proceed not positively, but negatively. We can never be adequate in our attempts positively to affirm the full reality of God. But most philosophers agree that a negative statement can be more true, because less ambiguous than positive ones. In ritual the negative act by which the object of sacrifice is destroyed is decisive and definitive. It does not linger on to define and delimit that in favor of which it is made; in that sense it leaves open if more indeterminate the positive reality to which it points.

Of course, this may not be the end of the dialectic, for the meaning of the sacrifice can always be misinterpreted and this, in turn, will require prayerful reflection in order to achieve a more correct understanding of the actions and their significance. Thus, the two sides of the Hindu debate between mind and action, reflection and ritual, concept and sacrifice, or more deeply, the two ways to God go on, each needing the other.

Here we shall follow the path of sacrifice in terms not of the physical action itself, but of its significance. For this we shall look to the hymns which accompanied the acts of sacrifice and express their significance. Hence, the perspective will not be that of *a posteriori* reasoning to God as in some of the succeeding chapters, where the outlook is that of the creature looking for its self-sufficient cause. Here, by virtue of the act of sacrifice the bond of physical reality is broken and one reenters the universe, as it were, from the horizon of its source and beginnings. Such is the creation hymn, *Rg Veda* X, 129.

The *Vedas* were poetry with a purpose. They sought not to entertain, or even to guide after the manner of an ethics. Rather, pertaining to sacrificial rituals, their intent was to express in words meaning and reality as radical as that expressed symbolically in the sacrificial act itself. There, as in a negative theology, phenomenal existences were destroyed in order to make manifest the absolute reality. The purpose of sacrifice was to transcend the realm of ordinary meaning, which in comparison is an ignorance, and to proclaim the deep origin, order and sense of this life.

> Unripe in mind, in spirit undiscerning, I ask of these the Gods' established places.... I ask, unknowing, those who know, the sages, as one all ignorant for the sake of knowledge, what was that One who in the unborn's image hath stablished and fixed firm these worlds' six regions.[1]

Further, there would appear to be here a potentially significant contrast to the Greek mind. While using the language of myth and expressing realities in the personal terms of the gods, the *Vedas* also employed concrete and proper terms, e.g., for the parts of the universe; indeed, the whole of *Rg Veda X, 129*, is written in non-mythic terms. This enabled the Rishis to state content which nowhere appears in the records we possess of the early Greek mind, characterized totally by the mythic and symbolic modes of thought.

In view of what has been said in the previous chapter concerning the importance of retrieving the content of earlier thought, attention to the *Vedas* can be of special importance for a further reason. Probably they go back as oral transmissions,[2] to the thirteenth century B.C. and the immigration of the Aryans from Persia during the following few centuries. Yet Keith claims that no significant progress was made during the subsequent period of the

Brahmanas which closed about 500 B.C. Thus, "the *Rg Veda* carries us nearly as far as anything excogitated in this period"[3] prior to the *Upanishads* with which philosophy proper is generally thought to have begun.

For this reason we shall now turn to the *Vedas* and in particular to the *"Nāsadiya Sūkta"* or "Creation Hymn," *Rg Veda* X, 129. This hymn has been considered to be "by far the most important composition in this class in the whole *Veda*"[4] — "the finest effort of the imagination of the Vedic poet, and nothing else equals it."[5]

METHOD

Here we shall look for the hymn's understanding of:

(a) that from which all derive,
(b) the origination of the universe,
(c) the resultant relation between things, and
(d) the nature of reality itself.

We shall be interested in seeing what light might be shed on this by taking into account also the earlier context of primitive thought and, comparatively, what relation there might be to the mythic process from unity to diversity developed in the alternate Greek branch of the Aryan family and reflected by Hesiod's *Theogony*.

Our project is not a simple one from first to last, and some specific hermeneutic considerations should be noted. The problems begin with the establishment of the text itself. One *mantra* may have been lost[6] and the commonly used text has been accused of depending excessively upon the quantity of syllables in each verse. By failing to take account of the quality of the syllables — especially those that were accented, e.g., a short syllable or vowel which at that time was still reflected in the pronunciation — Esteller claims that unwarranted changes were made in the Sanskrit text when it was finally fixed by Panini in ancient times.[7] This question must be left to Sanskrit scholars for further study, but Esteller has published a reconstructed text taking this into account.

In reading the text a sensitivity to metaphysical issues will be indispensable. A. K. Coomaraswamy remarks:

For an understanding of the *Vedas* a knowledge of Sanskrit, however profound, is insufficient. . . . Europe also possesses a tradition founded in first principles. That mentality which in the twelfth and thirteenth centuries (AD) brought into being an intellectual Christianity, would not have found the *Vedas* difficult.[8]

In keeping with the developmental model elaborated in the first chapter above, we shall be interested in determining the distinctive manner in which the mode of thinking in this hymn surpasses that of the primitive or totemic mind, and differs from subsequent developments.

This, of course, does not discount the value of later systematic commentaries. They drew upon the full strength of the resources available to them in order to elucidate, in a manner consistent with their own doctrines, both the issue being treated in the text and related new problems which had arisen. It is precisely in these successive commentaries that Indian philosophy has progressed through the ages. They are our richest and clearest statements of the cumulative wisdom available on the issues treated in the text. This applies to the exegesis of our text in the *Śatapatha Brāhmana*, and even more to Sāyana's commentaries on this text and in the *Taittiriya Brāhmana*.[9]

Nevertheless, here we are engaged in the somewhat different task, described in the second chapter, of stepping back to the content of human thought which preceded the development of philosophic systems. It is crucial that this be done in terms of the early texts themselves, both in order that they might, without circularity, provide a basis for the subsequent systems and in order to retrieve as a basis for really new progress what the philosophic systems themselves did not undertake to articulate and develop.

Another important approach, suggested by V. Agrawala draws upon M. Ojha's *Daśavāda-Rahasya*. He identifies ten "doctrines which served as nuclei for the thoughts of the Rishis when poetic statements of *Srshti-Vidyā* were being attempted in a rich variety of bold linguistic forms." They constitute ten "language games" — to use more recent terminology — which were employed in the *Sāmhitās* and *Brāhmanas*, and referred to in the first two *mantras* of the "Nasadiya Sūkta." These are: *Sdasad-Vāda*: speech in terms of existence and non-existence; *Rajo-Vāda*: the primeval material cause; *Yyoma-Vāda*: space as the ultimate substratum; *Parāpara-Vāda*: such pairs as absolute-relative, transcendent-immanent, or higher-lower; *Āvarana-Vāda*: measure or container; *Ambho-Vāda*: water; *Amrita-Mrityu-Vāda*: death and immortality, matter and energy; *Ahorāta-Vāda*: time; *Deva-Vāda*: the gods; and *Brahma-Vāda*: the transcendent reality.[10]

These ten nuclei provide notably more proximate contexts for interpreting the text of *Rg Veda X*, 129 than do the much later six orthodox and three heterodox systems. They can be especially useful in identifying both the implicit content of the terms and their allusions. In particular, they were the tools with which that mentality carried out its reflection upon the issues of unity and of participation contained therein. Hence, they will be particularly central to our project of determining the metaphysical content of the vision in its own terms, though from our later and hence more self-conscious standpoint.

TEXT OF THE *HYMN OF CREATION* *(Rg Veda, X, 129)*[11]

> [1]There was not the non-existent nor the existent then; there was not the air nor the heaven which is beyond. What did it contain? Where? In whose protection? Was there water, unfathomable, profound?
>
> [2]There was not death nor immortality then. There was not the beacon of night, nor of day. That one breathed, windless, by its own power. Other than that there was not anything beyond.
>
> [3]Darkness was in the beginning hidden by darkness; indistinguishable, this all was water. That which, coming into being, was covered with the void, that One arose through the power of heat.
>
> [4]Desire in the beginning came upon that, (desire) that was the first seed of mind. Sages seeking in

their hearts with wisdom found out the bond of the existent in the non-existent.

⁵Their cord was extended across: was there below or was there above? There were impregnators, there were powers; there was energy below, there was impulse above.

⁶Who knows truly? Who shall here declare, whence it has been produced, whence is this creation? By the creation of this (universe) the gods (come) afterwards: who then knows whence it has arisen?

⁷Where this creation has arisen; whether he founded it or did not: he who in the highest heaven is its surveyor, he only knows, or also he knows not.

CONTENT ANALYSIS

The hymn would appear to be constructed of three parts. The first (*mantras* 1-3, verse 2) treats the state prior to creation; the second (*mantra* 3, verse 3 — *mantra* 5) describes the creative process; the third (*mantras* 6-7) constitutes an epistemic reflection.

Part I: Prior to Creation. A number of things are to be noted here. First, reality in this state prior to creation repeatedly is affirmed to be undifferentiated. This is proclaimed by negating successively all that is related as contrary to anything else: there was neither air nor heaven beyond, neither death nor immortality, neither night nor day. There was no place. Some see this undifferentiated character as being stated more directly by rejecting even the principle for such distinctions: there was no beacon of night or day. Esteller would read this as stating directly that there is "no distinguishing sign of the night nor of the day"; Sāyana would say only: "There was no consciousness of night and day." Finally, that its nature is undistinguishable *(apraketam)* is pictured by stating that it was darkness hidden in darkness and that it was water: "Indistinguishable, this all was water." By pointing out that water is the stage of creation prior to earth, Sāyana substantiates that this reference to water implies undifferentiation. Together this use of proper terminology constitutes a real advance in stating the unity over the improper and symbolic language used in the totemic and mythic visions analyzed above.

There are even certain more positive indications of the nature of the undifferentiated. First, it is termed "that one" *(tad ekam)*. This should be taken as a positive affirmation of being, for the text adds that "other than that there was not anything beyond" *(Mantra 2)*. Secondly, it is also referred to as being of the nature of life by the statement, "that one breathed."

Thirdly and of special importance, it indicates the self-sufficiency of "that one" which "breathed by its own power" *(Mantra 2)*. Radhakrishnan accepts the description "windless," and understands it as bespeaking Aristotle's unmoved mover — a point which A: Keith rejects as anachronistic.[12] Esteller reads this as "unconquerable by his inborn power." Sāyana may arrive at a similar point by holding that "breathless" implies the negation of all limiting factors, that is, all except the self; it is that which exists depending on, or supported by, its own being. This is important lest the originating experience of the *Ṛg Veda* be erroneously interpreted as being no more than a proto-materialism of the Sāṃkhya type — as is often said — and the Absolute merely a later superimposition for selfish purposes.

Finally, it might be asked whether in the first *mantra* the expression of undifferentiation by the words "there was not the air nor the heaven which is beyond" is not of further significance. In a threefold division of earth, air and heaven[13] it is by means of the introduction of the notion of air or space *(rajo)* that heaven is differentiated from earth. If this be the case, then, as with the notion of the beacon of day and night in the second *mantra,* the statement "there was no air" negates the principle of division and differentiation of heaven from earth, and hence a differentiated condition for heaven and earth.

If there be substance to this suggestion it would have two implications. First and most important, it should mean the philosophically important introduction from the very beginning of this hymn of the principle, not only of the unity, but of the differentiation of being. This would indicate that the two were not seen to be incompatible one with the other. Secondly, it could imply some correspondence to the above-mentioned, and not unrelated, notion of chaos as space *(gap)* found in this role in Hesiod's *Theogony*.[14] If this is found in widely diverse parts of the Indo-European diaspora it would be proportionately ancient and foundational for human thought.

Part II: The Creative Process (mantra 3, verse 3 - mantra 5). This is concerned with "the origin of the evolved world from the unevolved" and introduces two issues: first, in what does this origination consist; second, how is it realized?

The first issue is answered in terms of the differentiation of that which repeatedly had been described in the first part of the hymn as undifferentiated. In *mantra* 4 this is spoken of as the bond of the existent with what previously had been called non-existent. *Mantra* 5 describes the differentiations of above and below, of impregnators *(redodhà)* and powers *(mahimaná)*, of energy *(svadha)* and impulse *(práyatih)*. Sayana is keenly sensitive to the value implications of this differentiation; others would see these pairs as also being contrasted as male and female cosmogonic principles.[15] In that case the text would not merely state an initial differentiation of what previously had been undifferentiated. In the *Theogony* heaven and earth were related as male and female and from them all else is generated. Similarly, the original pair in the *Rg Veda X*, 129, if related in principle as male and female, would imply that all further plurality and differentiation can be understood fruitfully on the basis of a genetic unity. Only the main lines are traced, however, and that only in *Rg Veda X, 72*.

As with the *Theogony*, the nature of the unity which the male and female cosmogonic principles imply depends upon the degree of the unity of this original pair. Here it is most significant that the image conveyed by the hymn from beginning to end is not that these two principles are simply different and then brought together. On the contrary, what precedes or that from which their differentiation arises is a state of undifferentiation. Most fundamentally they are one rather than many. Continuity with the totemic vision and the experience it embodied could provide a basis for this vision.

On the second issue, namely, how this initial division was realized, the text is not silent, though it speaks after the manner of poetry, rather than of technical scientific prose.

First, in '*tuchyēnābhu*' the word '*tuchya*' introduces the notion of "void", or that which is not. To this is added the instrumental suffix "by it," to state "by means of the void." Finally there is the verb '*bhū*' or "become, arise," that is, what comes into being everywhere. A. Coomaraswamy would interpret the following words, "All that existed covered *(apihitam yad āsīt)*" as veil or *āvarivah* in *mantra 1*, namely, the world as that which covers the ultimate reality. Does this mean that the void plays a role in the transition — which is creation — from the differentiated to the differentiated state? If so, it would correspond well to *mantra 5* regarding the division of the above and the below as cosmogonic principles.

This raises the further question of whether the notion of the void here is related in any way to the notion of chaos as 'gap' or 'open space' found in the *Theogony*'s description of the origin of the universe, especially as that notion reflected a very ancient, and hence common foundational element in Aryan thought. Here in *mantra* 3 it is not merely an open space as in *mantra* 1, but the more philosophically suggestive notion of void. This suggests the notion of non-being which later will be of great systematic philosophic importance regarding these very issues. Sāyana interprets it as *Maya* which will play the major systematic role in these issues a millenium later in Shankara's *Advaita*. Here, however, it remains a poetic and imaginative statement.

Second, whatever be said of verse 3, verse 4 of *mantra* 3 and all of *mantra* 4 may contain more substantive indications of the manner of differentiation of the universe through the notions of will and mind. Heat is often used as the simile for that ardor of will with which one grasps (*kāmās*), holds to, or is attached to existence. When the reality is present this attachment is enjoyment, that is, it is one and holds itself in bliss. Verse 1 of *mantra* 4 proceeds to state that the origin was not deficient but *sam*, which Sāyana understands as meaning complete or having fullness. Further, *avartatādhi* should be understood, not as coming upon a reality from without, but as arising from within. This would mean that from the point of view of its origin creation is seen in this hymn as taking place, not out of need, but out of the plenitude of perfection, which would imply that it is pure gift as discussed in Chapter VIII below.

But what does *Kāmas* indicate regarding the nature of reality itself and hence of created reality? It should be noted that, when the object of the ardor of the will is absent or not yet possessed, grasping or attachment has the nature of desire. We have seen that the void has a separative role in the origination of differentiation, and that the original state is one of undifferentiation in contrast to the present differentiated state. In continuity with the totemic unity, then, the differentiated parts remain most fundamentally attracted one to another. In this case the text would be suggesting that it pertains to the internal nature of reality itself to be unitive and for the differentiated realities to be positively related or attracted to one another. This is what the Greeks expressed in a relatively external manner in their mythic notion of the god, Eros. It would also be the metaphysical basis for the social life of the family or village.

Further, verse 2 proceeds to say that desire is the first seed of mind. As regards the nature of reality itself does this imply that bliss *(ānanda)* as enjoyment of being in some sense follows upon or expresses consciousness *(cit)* of existence *(sat)*? For the originating Self this would imply that the creative causality of its active will is fully conscious. This, in turn, would provide the basis for the order and intelligibility which characterize the realm of creation.

In the order of created or differentiated beings the fact that desire is the first seed of mind integrates knowledge within the overall project of unity and orients it finally toward not analysis but synthesis, as it would appear to imply a striving of one person to know the other. This, in turn, is predicated ontologically upon the fact that the mind and its object originally were an undifferentiated unity as noted in the first part of the hymn and as was inherited from totemic thought. Thus, knowledge itself is most fundamentally the effort to grasp the other in its differentiated and hence partial expression of the original and undifferentiated unity. In this light the desire or will of one differentiated being as regards others should be not that of self-seeking, but of aiding, of serving the other, so that it might share or participate more fully in perfection.

Finally, both mind and desire may be combined in wisdom in verses 3 and 4 of *mantra 4:* "Sages seeking in their hearts with wisdom found out the bond of the existent in the nonexistent." Does this mean only that by reflecting on the problem they found the origin of the differentiated universe? This is possible, but the explicit distinction and ordering of desire and mind would suggest more, namely, the interior road to wisdom which is so characteristic of the Indian philosophers and of great interest in the West from Saint Augustine to present day phenomenologists (see Part III below).

What was said above regarding developmental modes of thought and the dependence of the poetic imagination upon the senses suggests that the answers to further questions, such as monism or pluralisms, monotheism or henotheism, and material or efficient causality will require the development of subsequent modes of thought for work in philosophy proper. This will be the concern of the chapters to follow. The human mind, however, will never be able to supplant poetry or exhaustively to articulate its meaning in scientific terms. Thus, such poetic hymns as the *Theogony* and *Rg Veda, X, 129* will ever remain inexhaustible and essential storehouses or treasuries for philosophers and for all people in their effort to find the way in which their lives can lead to God and to one another.

Part III. Epistemological Reflection. Manras 6-7. In the end the hymn steps back from the task of establishing the literal truth of the description of myth in mantras 1-5, saying: who truly knows?

On one level as it has been concerned with creation this seems to argue that no created intellect can know what preceded it as such — no created mind can know the act of creation itself upon which it depends. A fortiori it cannot know the working of the mind and heart which generated the act of creation. Only the Creator could know such truth.

But mantra 7 goes further to open the possibility that the creator too does not know. This could be read in two senses. One is that the creator is less than knowing: some impersonal force, brute and crude. This would fit the recent evolutionary paradigm in which all is read in terms of matter from which humankind but barely emerges. The other sense is that the creator of knowledge may rather be above knowledge, not a union of subject and object but subsistent truth itself. This would correspond to the body of the *Vedas* and the basic Hindu conviction that the divine is existence, consciousness and bliss. This is the truly decisive point in the constitution of a culture for it sets the parameters in terms of meaning and value: not of darkness and conflict, but of light and love. This is the basic issue of who and what we are and of what our life is about.

IMPLICATIONS

From the above archeology of human thought in its totemic and mythic stages it can be concluded, with Iqbal, that it has been religious insight regarding the Absolute which has made finite thinking possible. Leaving home and going deeply into the past now brings us back home to reconstruct the deep truth of our faith regarding knowledge: not only that knowledge can be also about religion, but that in essence thought itself is the religious reconstitution of all in God: this is what knowledge most fundamentally is.

There are two implications of this archeology which I would like to cite here. The first concerns the relation of a people to the message of a prophet. As the basis of the human self-understanding of the different cultures is essentially religious, a divine revelation through a great prophet comes not as alien and conflictual, but as a special divine help to appreciate, purify and strengthen a culture. The message of the prophet evokes the divine life which lies within; it enables each people to plunge more deeply into the infinite ground of their cultural traditions and to bring out more of its meaning for their life. Indeed, confidence (etymologically rooted in "faith") and commitment to one's tradition as grounded in the infinite means precisely expecting it to have even more to say then a people has yet articulated. In this light, the Prophet's voice is a call to delve anew into one's tradition, to bring out more of its meaning for one's times and to live this more fully. This is a voice to which one can respond fully and freely.

In this sense might I be permitted to take issue with Iqbal's seemingly overly Darwinian description of the first period of religious life as:

> a form of discipline which the individual or a whole people must accept as an unconditional command without any rational understanding of the ultimate meaning and purpose of the command. This attitude may be of great consequence in the social and

political history of a people, but is not of much consequence in so far as the individual's inner growth and expansion are concerned.[16]

The archeology of human thought suggests that the response of a people to the message of a prophet, far from being without rational understanding, is more precisely a renewal and reaffirmation of their deep self-understanding. This is truly a homecoming in whose very essence lies the deep freedom of the peace one experiences in returning home after a long and confusing day. But I suspect that Iqbal would not disagree with this for in reality it is an application of what he concluded regarding thought as being made possible by the presence therein of the total infinite.[17] This applies first to culture and then even to the natural order. "There is no such thing as a profane world . . . all is holy ground," wrote Iqbal, citing the Prophet: "The whole of this earth is a mosque."[18]

A second implication can be of special importance in these times of intensifying communication and interaction between peoples. If the future is to hold not Huntington's conflict of civilizations, but their cooperation in a shrinking world, then it is important to see how the civilizations deriving from prophets and religious traditions can relate one to another. Hermeneutics can be helpful here with its suggestion that in order to delve more deeply it is important to hear not only reformulations of what we ourselves say in our own horizon, but new formulations from other traditions regarding the basically shared truths of our divine origin and goal. As Iqbal is supported by an archeology of knowledge indicating that all knowledge is grounded in the divine, we can expect that religious texts from the traditions of other great prophets will evoke new echoes from the depths of our own tradition. In this light, interchange with other traditions comes not as a threat. Rather, cultural interchange can enable one to make one's pilgrimages more unerringly along one's own path, to the one holy mountain[19] — to which Iqbal refers as the total absolute. Other forms of cooperation can, and indeed must, be built upon this.

II. *BHAGAVAD GITA*

The first half of this chapter, in reflecting on the creation hymn, was set in the content of the ritual action of sacrifice which the hymn accompanied and expressed. There is another, indeed the most known, text which begins from the actions of daily life, but which also leads the reader to the divine source, and hence to its meaning of life. This is the *Bhagavad Gita*, to which we shall now look.

Anyone who has travelled in India undoubtedly has received myriad times the good advice: "Do one thing: read the *Gita*." It holds a unique place in Hindu literature. The main body of this literature emerges, as noted above, from the ritual practices, especially those of sacrifice, and thus is made up of four sections. First is the *Vedas* or Vedic hymns which were used in the sacrifices and state its basic truths: *Rg Veda* X, 129, examined above, is an example of this literature. Second are the *Brahmanas* detailing how the rituals were to be carried out. Third are the *Aranyakas* or allegorical statements of the meaning of the *Vedas*. Lastly, come the *Upanishad* which were really appendices to the *Aranyakas* and provided in a more direct, non-allegorical manner the philosophy of the *Vedas*. These four correspond as well to the four ideal stages of life: student, householder, forest ascetic, and mystic contemplation.

Beyond this are two other key text. One is the *Sutras*, or "strings", which are very short, cryptic statements of the central elements of the Vedic vision. Like the *Sententiae* of Peter the Lombard in medieval Europe they served as the basis for the systematic exposition of the philosophy.

The other is the *Bhagavad Gita*. This is part of the great epic poem the *Mahabarata*, which recounts the history of the Bharata clan. Progressively this moves ineluctably toward a great battle between the Pandavas, the aggrieved party, led by Arjuna, and the Kauravas.

In the moments just prior to the battle all pretense, self deception and minor concern must fall away. As in a great Shakespearean soliloquy it is then that the deepest truths of life are revealed. Here it is Arjuna, coming from a long preparatory forest retreat and tested to the extremes, who questions; it is the Lord Krishna himself who answers. Just as in the *Theogony* and the creation Hymn ultimate wisdom was sought of the gods, so it is here. It is the beauty and deep insight into the Truth contained in Krishna's response that alone gives this its standing as the central text of the Hindu tradition. Let us listen to the text itself.

THE DILEMMA

Arjuna asks the Lord Krishna to be his chariot driver and they go to survey the line of the battle. He sees not only his own family and friends, but arrayed against them a set of relatives, teachers and people he loves and admires:

I.
$_{21}$Drive my chariot, Krishna immortal, and place it between the two armies.
$_{22}$That I may see those warriors who stand there eager for battle, with whom I must now fight at the beginning of this war.
$_{23}$That I may see those who have come here eager and ready to fight, in their desire to do the will of the evil son of Dhrita-rashtra.
$_{24}$When Krishna heard the words of Arjuna he drove their glorious chariot and placed it between the two armies.
$_{25}$And facing Bhishma and Drona and other royal rulers he said: 'See, Arjuna, the armies of the Kurus, gathered here on this field of battle.'.
$_{26}$Then Arjuna saw in both armies fathers, grandfathers,
$_{27}$sons, grandsons; fathers of wives, uncles, masters,
$_{28}$brothers, companions and friends. When Arjuna thus saw his kinsmen face-to-face in both lines of battle, he was overcome by grief and despair and thus he spoke with a sinking heart.
$_{29}$Life goes from my limbs and they sink, and my mouth is sear and dry; a trembling overcomes my body, and my hair shudders in horror;
$_{30}$My great bow Gandiva falls from my hands, and the skin of my flesh is burning; I am no longer able to stand, because my mind is whirling and wandering.
$_{31}$And I see forebodings of evil, Krishna. I cannot foresee any glory if I kill my own kinsmen in the sacrifice of battle.
$_{32}$Because I have no wish for victory, Krishna, nor for a kingdom, nor for its pleasures. How can we want a kingdom, Govinda, or its pleasures or even life.
$_{33}$When those for whom we want a kingdom, and its pleasures, and the joys of life, are here in this field of battle about to give up

their wealth and their life?

₃₄Facing us in the field of battle are teachers, fathers and sons; grandsons, grandfathers, wives' brothers; mothers' brothers and fathers of wives.

₃₅These I do not wish to slay, even if I myself am slain. Not even for the kingdom of the three worlds: how much less for a kingdom of the earth!

₃₆If we kill these evil men, evil shall fall upon us: what joy in their death could we have, O Janardana, mover of souls?

₃₇I cannot therefore kill my own kinsmen, the sons of king Dhrita-rashtra, the brother of my own father. What happiness could we ever enjoy, if we killed our own kinsmen in battle?

₃₈Even if they, with minds overcome by greed, see no evil in the destruction of a family, see no sin in the treachery to friends;

₃₉Shall we not, who see the evil of destruction, shall we not refrain from this terrible deed?

₄₀The destruction of a family destroys its rituals of righteousness, and when the righteous rituals are no more, unrighteousness overcomes the whole family.

₄₁When unrighteous disorder prevails, the women sin and are impure; and when women are not pure, Krishna, there is disorder of castes, social confusion.

₄₂This disorder carries down to hell the family and the destroyers of the family. The spirits of their dead suffer in pain when deprived of the ritual offerings.

₄₃Those evil deeds of the destroyers of a family, which cause this social disorder, destroy the righteousness of birth and the ancestral rituals of righteousness.

₄₄And have we not heard that hell is waiting for those whose familiar rituals of righteousness are no more?

₄₅O day of darkness! What evil spirit moved our minds when for the sake of an earthly kingdom we came to this field of battle ready to kill our own people?

₄₆Better for me indeed if the sons of Dhrita-rashtra, with arms in hand, found me unarmed, unresisting, and killed me in the struggle of war.

₄₇Thus spoke Arjuna in the field of battle, and letting fall his bow and arrows he sank down in his chariot, his soul overcome by despair and grief.

Arjuna's ethical dilemma is grave indeed. First, he does not want to kill his kinsmen (I, verse 31). Second, he does not want to have killed those who support him in the fight and for whom he is fighting (33). Third, he does not want to kill those who attack him, even though they do evil, for then there would be no one to perform the sacrifices. Above we saw how the sacrifices express the source of meaning. Here Arjuna points out that an end to the sacrifices would eliminate the appreciation of the source of meaning and hence the personal and social dignity, meaning and worth by which we approach immortality. This, in turn, would destroy the social order, just as the loss of the totem of a tribe, leads to social disorder. (38)

Hence both personal and social life would be destroyed. Therefore he concludes that it is better not to act, to stand unarmed and to be killed, than to cause such a total destruction of his people. (46)

At this point the lord Krishna begins to speak and in the 72 verses of chapter II of the *Gita* presents, succinctly but classically, the main themes of Hinduism and hence the ritual way to God with which the chapter is concerned. The passage stands out so preeminently in Hindu literature that, through part of an immense epic, it has come to be considered part of the *Sruti* or revealed texts:

II.

$_1$Then arose the Spirit of Krishna and spoke to Arjuna, his friend, who with eyes filled with tears, thus had sunk into despair and grief.

$_2$Whence this lifeless dejection, Arjuna, in this hour, the hour of trial? Strong men know not despair, Arjuna, for this wins neither heaven nor earth.

Fall not into degrading weakness, for this becomes not a man who is a man. Throw off this ignoble discouragement, and arise like a fire that burns all before it.

$_3$I owe veneration to Bhishma and Drona. Shall I kill with my arrows my grandfather's brother, great Bhishma?

$_4$Shall my arrows in battle slay Drona, my teacher?

$_5$Shall I kill my own masters who, though greedy of my kingdom, are yet my sacred teachers? I would rather eat in this life the food of a beggar than eat royal food tasting of their blood.

₆And we know not whether their victory or ours be better for us. The sons of my uncle and king, Dhrita-rashtra, are here before us: after their death, should we wish to live?

₇In the dark night of my soul I feel desolation. In my self-pity I see not the way of righteousness. I am thy disciple, come to thee in supplication: be a light unto me on the path of my duty.

₈For neither the kingdom of the earth, nor the kingdom of the gods in heaven, could give me peace from the fire of sorrow which thus burns my life.

₉When Arjuna the great warrior had thus unburdened his heart, 'I will not fight, Krishna,' he said, and then fell silent.

Krishna then begins to respond by preparing Arjuna for deeper understanding. He does this by noting: first that Arjuna is not in an enlightened state, but is dominated by concern for his people (I 31, II 6); second, that he would drop out of action due to the problems of the moment, rather than taking a longer view of life in its totality; further, that he may be under the influence of such ignoble emotions as fear and discouragement; and finally, that he gives in to grief, desolation and even to despair (II 1, 7). The reason for this would seem to be too external a sense of meaning. Thus, for example, he is preoccupied by the need to assure the continuation of sacrifices even where this might contradict their meaning. Hence, Arjuna asks the Lord, Krishna, to shed light on the path that is his duty. Krishna proceeds to do so in what certainly is one of the greatest pieces of world literature.

THE RESPONSE

The Text

II.

₁₀Krishna smiled and spoke to Arjuna — there between the two armies the voice of God spoke these words:

₁₁Thy tears are for those beyond tears; and are thy words of wisdom? The wise grieve not for those who live; and they grieve not for those who die — for life and death shall pass away.

₁₂Because we all have been for all time: I, and thou, and those kings of men. And we all shall be for all time, we all for ever and ever.

₁₃As the Spirit of our mortal body wanders on in childhood, and youth and old age, the Spirit wanders on to a new body: of this the sage has no doubts.

₁₄From the world of the senses, Arjuna, comes heat and comes cold, and pleasure and pain. They come and they go; they are transient. Arise above them, strong soul.

₁₅The man whom these cannot move, whose soul is one, beyond pleasure and pain, is worthy of life in Eternity.

₁₆The unreal never is: the Real never is not. This truth indeed has been seen by those who can see the true.

₁₇Interwoven in his creation, the Spirit is beyond destruction, No one can bring to an end the Spirit which is everlasting.

₁₈For beyond time he dwells in these bodies, though these bodies have an end in their time; but he remains immeasurable, immortal. Therefore, great warrior, carry on thy fight.

₁₉If any man thinks he slays, and if another thinks he is slain, neither knows the ways of truth. The Eternal in man cannot kill: the Eternal in man cannot die.

₂₀He is never born, and he never dies. He is in Eternity: he is for evermore. Never-born and eternal, beyond times gone or to come, he does not die when the body dies.

₂₁When a man knows him as never-born, everlasting, never-changing, beyond all destruction, how can that man kill a man, or cause another to kill?

₂₂As a man leaves an old garment and puts on one that is new, the Spirit leaves his mortal body and wanders on to one that is new.

₂₃Weapons cannot hurt the Spirit and fire can never burn him. Untouched is he by drenching waters, untouched is he by parching winds.

₂₄Beyond the power of sword and fire, beyond the power of waters and winds, the Spirit is everlasting, omnipresent, never-changing, never-moving, ever One.

₂₅Invisible is he to mortal eyes, beyond thought and beyond change. Know that he is, and cease from sorrow.

₂₆But if he were born again and again, and again and again he were to die, even then, victorious man, cease thou from sorrow.

₂₇For all things born in truth must die, and out of death in truth comes life. Face to face with what must be, cease thou from sorrow.

$_{28}$Invisible before birth are all beings and after death invisible again. They are seen between two unseens. Why in this truth find sorrow?

$_{29}$One sees him in a vision of wonder, and another gives us words of his wonder. There is one who hears of his wonder; but he hears and knows him not.

$_{30}$The Spirit that is in all begins is immortal in them all: for the death of what cannot die, cease thou to sorrow.

$_{31}$Think thou also of thy duty and do not waver. There is no greater good for a warrior than to fight in a righteous war.

$_{32}$There is a war that opens the doors of heaven, Arjuna! Happy the warriors whose fate is to fight such war.

$_{33}$But to forgo this fight for righteousness is to forgo thy duty and honor: is to fall into transgression.

$_{34}$Men will tell of thy dishonor both now and in times to come. And to a man who is in honor, dishonor is more than death.

$_{35}$The great warriors will say that thou hast run from the battle through fear; and those who thought great things of thee will speak of thee in scorn.

$_{36}$And thine enemies will speak of thee in contemptuous words of ill-will and derision, pouring scorn upon thy courage. Can there be for a warrior a more shameful fate?

$_{37}$In death they glory in heaven, in victory they glory on earth. Arise therefore, Arjuna, with thy soul ready to fight.

$_{38}$Prepare for war with peace in thy soul. Be in peace in pleasure and pain, in gain and in loss, in victory or in the loss of a battle. In this peace there is no sin.

$_{39}$This is the wisdom of Sankhya — the vision of the Eternal. Hear now the wisdom of Yoga, path of the Eternal and freedom from bondage.

$_{40}$No step is lost on this path, and no dangers are found. And even a little progress is freedom from fear.

$_{41}$The follower of this path has one thought, and this is the End of his determination. But many-branched and endless are the thoughts of the man who lacks determination.

$_{42}$There are men who have no vision, and yet they speak many words. They follow the letter of the *Vedas*, and they say: "There is nothing but this."

₄₃Their soul is warped with selfish desires, and their heaven is a selfish desire. They have prayers for pleasures and power, the reward of which is earthly rebirth.

₄₄Those who love pleasure and power hear and follow their words; they have not the determination ever to be one with the One.

₄₅The three *Gunas* of Nature are the world of the *Vedas*. Arise beyond the three Gunas, Arjuna! Be in Truth, eternal, beyond earthly opposites. Beyond gains and possessions, possess thine own soul.

₄₆As is the use of a well of water where water everywhere overflows, such is the use of all the *Vedas* to the seer of the Supreme.

₄₇Set thy heart upon thy work, but never on its reward. Work not for a reward; but never cease to do thy work.

₄₈Do thy work in the peace of *Yoga* and, free from selfish desires, be not moved in success or in failure. *Yoga* is evenness of mind — a peace that is ever the same.

₄₉Work done for a reward is much lower than work done in the *Yoga* of wisdom. Seek salvation in the wisdom of reason. How poor those who work for a reward!

₅₀In this wisdom a man goes beyond what is well done and what is not well done. Go thou therefore to wisdom; *Yoga* is wisdom in work.

₅₁Sees in union with wisdom forsake the rewards of their work and free from the bonds of birth they go to the abode of salvation.

₅₂When thy mind leaves behind its dark forest of delusion, thou shalt go beyond the scriptures of times past and still to come.

₅₃When thy mind, that may be wavering in the contradictions of many scriptures, shall rest unshaken in divine contemplation, then the goal of Yoga is thine.

₅₄How is the man of tranquil wisdom, who abides in divine contemplation? What are his words? What is his silence? What is his work?

₅₅When a man surrenders all desires that come to the heart and by the grace of God finds the joy of God, then his soul has indeed found peace.

₅₆He whose mind is untroubled by sorrows, and for pleasures he has no longings, beyond passion, and fear and anger, he is the sage of unwavering mind.

₅₇Who everywhere is free from all ties, who neither rejoices nor sorrows if fortune is good or is ill, his is a serene wisdom.

₅₈When in recollection he withdraws all his senses from the attractions of the pleasures of sense, even as a tortoise withdraws all its limbs, then his is a serene wisdom.

₅₉Pleasure of sense, but not desire, disappears from the austere soul. Even desires disappear when the soul has seen the Supreme.

₆₀The restless violence of the senses impetuously carries away the mind of even a wise man striving towards perfection.

₆₁Bringing them all into the harmony of recollection, let him sit in devotion and union, his soul finding rest in me. For when his senses are in harmony, then his is a serene wisdom.

₆₂When a man dwells on the pleasures of sense, attraction for them arises in him. From attraction arises desire, the lust of possession, and this leads to passion, to anger.

₆₃From passion comes confusion of mind, then loss of remembrance, the forgetting of duty. From this loss comes the ruin of reason, and the ruin of reason leads man to destruction.

₆₄But the soul that moves in the world of the senses and yet keeps the senses in harmony, free from attraction and aversion, finds rest in quietness.

₆₅In this quietness falls down the burden of all her sorrows, for when the heart has found quietness, wisdom has also found peace.

₆₆There is no wisdom for a man without harmony, and without harmony there is no contemplation. Without contemplation there cannot be peace, and without peace can there be joy?

₆₇For when the mind becomes bound to a passion of the wandering senses, this passion carries away man's wisdom, even as the wind drives a vessel on the waves.

₆₈The man who therefore in recollection withdraws his senses from the pleasures of sense, his is a serene wisdom.

₆₉In the dark night of all beings awakes to Light the tranquil man. But what is day to other beings is night for the sage who sees.

₇₀Even as all waters flow into the ocean, but the ocean never overflows, even so the sage feels desires, but he is ever one in his infinite peace.

₇₁For the man who forsakes all desires and abandons all pride of possession and of self reaches the goal of peace supreme.

[72] This is the Eternal in man, O Arjuna. Reaching him all delusion is gone. Even in the last hour of his life upon earth, man can reach the Nirvana of Brahman — man can find peace in the peace of his God.

The Wisdom of Sankhya — the Vision of the Eternal

The direct response of Krishna to Arjuna in his dilemma is the message of *Karma Yoga*. *Yoga* means Yoke or placing under control; *Karma* means action in the broad sense of deeds, sacrifices, duties and prayer. The nature of *Karma Yoga* is to act or to carry out one's duties without looking for the fruit of one's action, either immediately here in this life or even afterwards in a higher life with God (II 47). To focus upon the results of one's action is to be subject to self-interest, to things or to results that we can accomplish. If instead one can proceed to doing one's duty then one can act with complete equanimity, equilibrium or balance of mind. This is a path between, on the one hand, activitism in this life or even in making sacrifices to obtain goods in the next world and, on the other hand, non-action, passivism or even rejecting all life activities in favor of contemplation. Hence, Krishna advises not renunciation of action, but renunciation in action.

But on what basis should one follow this path (II 1-38)? This must be not merely the way I feel, or the way I look upon things, but the way things really are. This is the path of the eternal, on which is based the path of wisdom, the vision of the eternal and freedom from bondage.

Its method is to move from my multiple states of experience and feeling (hot and cold, pleasure and pain) which are transient (II 1) to my self as that which continues through all these states and is their basis, to move from the many subjective states to the one self who experiences them (14-15). But then Krishna directs Arjuna to go higher still, to rise to the absolute Self (16-18) above even one's own self, which he relativises as a seen between the two unseens (28) which precede and follow after this life. Like Descartes, this is the search for what really is. The absolute or Brahman is described as *sat* or existence that is one, *cit* or consciousness, and *ananda* or bliss. This is the character of the absolute, of divine life; hence it is also the essence of our true life as deriving therefrom and directed thereto.

Existence (*sat*) is stated in terms of predurance and unity. It continues the first step noted above as being from the transient to the permanent; it identifies as goal that which is not of limited duration. Where the individual self was a limited "seen between two unseens",(28) this is definitive in existence. The real never is not; it is immortal and eternal beyond time and destruction. As with Xenophanese the one is never changing or moving, but is ever one (16-19, 24, 30).

Consciousness (*cit*) is seen as the one source of all meaning. The whole process has been one of consciousness, from feeling the varied states of hot and cold, pleasure and pain, to the self. This appears here especially as justice or the ability to make the right judgement in terms of one's duty or of doing what is right (31). It is honor as greater than death (33-26). Such right judgement is based on wisdom (39) which is the vision of the eternal. Ultimately it is founded in the all knowing Spirit or Self — like Xenophanese' God who knows all and moves all by His mind.

Bliss (*ananda*) is the ultimate Source and Goal of all. All comes from God who shows joy in sharing, indeed whose essence, as in Greek myth, is to share rather than to hide or inhibit. The ultimate aim of all then is joy in God or divine life (55); a good life gives peace on earth and glory in heaven (37).

In this broad light the particulars of life are ignored only if taken all by themselves and made into absolutes. This is particularly true of the ego or self, if taken as opposed to all others. This would be to make the ego an end in itself and reduce life to simply a matter of achieving particular pleasures. When, however, particular actions and persons are seen in and through the One then they take on great importance as manifestations of the Brahman, i.e., of existence, consciousness and bliss. Only in these terms are they truly real, just and good. Hence, the point is not to achieve some goal, but to exist or live in a way that is true and just; only this is really meaningful. Only acting in a way that is good, i.e. as a dynamic expression of joy, is really to exist: the rest is illusion.

What then of action which, concretely for Arjuna, is to enter into battle. The response is direct, do your duty (31-33), that is, do what is true, just and righteous. Not to do so is dishonor; and seen in terms of God and eternal life dishonor is worse than death (33-

36). In sum, when to battle is one's duty, then that is what one must do. It is the moral quality of the action that is important, not its outcome, for victory is glory on earth, in death is glory in heaven (37-38).

The metaphysics presented thus far has great ethical implications. The first half of this second chapter of the *Gita* distinguishes three levels of life: first, that of the various sensations such as hot and cold, pleasure and pain; second that of the individual human self; and third that of the absolute Self or Brahma.

Considering things on the first level there is only an interplay of physiological states, of the senses and of behavior. There is no question of honor: indeed, honor is pretense when taken in terms of Creon in the *Antigone*. But this is to isolate these realities from their real foundations.

On the second level, that of the individual self or *atman*, people are seen only in terms of time and place and hence as egos opposed one to the other. To be united they must be seen in terms of reality which transcends this level.

This third level is what was spoken of in the totem and myth; here it is Brahman or the absolute at the third level of reality and of awareness. This is existence; it is consciousness, truth and justice; and it is bliss or joy and love as dynamic gift. The first two levels must be seen to originate from this third, which they express; only in as much as they do so do they really exist and be matters of truth and goodness.

Evil in contrast, as was seen in the Greek myths, is suppression of this emergence from the real, from truth and goodness and hence a negation of justice and goodness. It is dishonor on earth and hell thereafter (34).

After a life lived in truth, however, death is simply the termination of the time sequence. It is negation not of reality, but only of the unreal, that is, of the self as opposed to others. Death then is affirmation of reality (37).

On this basis the text proceeds in its second part to provide particular ethical directions on how to live *karma yoga* (39-72):

- avoid thinking only of this life or state (II 42-44); these are delusions in comparison to the eternal or if thought of without the eternal (52);

- what is important is to achieve wisdom, i.e., to see all according to the eternal, which entails bringing all things together into an unity or harmony (61-66);
- this is done by 're-collection', that is, by recalling the senses from the particulars (59-61); and hence
- they are truly one who practice *karma yoga* (47-49).

This is the eternal in man, O Arguna. Reaching him all delusion is gone. Even in the last hour of this life upon earth, man can reach the Nirvana of Brahman — man can find peace in the peace of his God (72).

NOTES

1. C. Kunhan Raja, *Asya Vamasya Hymn* (*The Riddle of the Universe*), *Rgveda* I-164 (Madras: Ganesh, 1956), pp. 5-6; see also G. McLean, *Plenitude and Participation*; *The Unity of Man and God* (Madras: University of Madras, 1978), pp. 34-38.

2. Surendranath Dasgupta, *A History of Indian Philosophy* (Delhi: Motilal Banarsidass, 1975), I, 10.

3. Arthur B. Keith, *The Religion and Philosophy of the Veda and Upanishads* (Harvard Oriental Series, Vol. XXXII; Cambridge: Harvard University, Press, 1925), II, 442.

4. Kaegi, p. 89.

5. Keith, p, 437.

6. Griffith, II, 576, n. 5.

7. A. Esteller, "The Text-critical Reconstruction of the *Rgveda*," *Indica*, XIV (1977), 1-12. See also the Bandorkar Institute of Oriental Studies Jubilee Volume, 1978.

8. *A New Approach to the Vedas: An Essay in Translation and Exegesis* (London: Luzac, 1933), p. vii.

9. Vasudeva S. Agrawala, *Hymn of Creation* (*Nāsadīya Sūkta, Rigveda X, 129*) (Varanasi: P. Prakashan, 1963), pp. 40-57. This remains true even while recognizing the value of observations by Roth and Müller: see Griffith, Vol. I, pp. x-xi. I am particularly indebted to Dr. R. Balasubramanian of the University of Madras for his extremely generous and detailed exposition of Sāyana's commentary on *Rig Veda* X, 129.

10. *Ibid.*, pp. 5-18. Other more detailed analyses of *Rig Veda*

X, 129 are found in Sampurnand, *Cosmogony in Indian Thought* (Kashi Vidyapith), pp. 61-80; C. Kunhan Raja, *Poet Philosophers*, pp. 221-31; and Coomaraswamy, pp. 52-59.

    11. A.A. MacDonell, *A Vedic Reader* (Oxford: At the Clarendon Press, 1917), pp. 207-211.

    12. Rhadakrishnan, *Indian Philosophy* (London: Allen and Unwin, 1977), I, 101; Keith, p. 436 and n. 3.

    13. Kaegi, p. 34.

    14. See Chapter III above. Note the etymological similarity of the Sanskrit root of Brahman, 'brah', to the Old Norse, 'brag' and the close parallels between German spells and those of the *Artha Veda*.

    15. MacDonell, pp. 209-210.

    16. Iqbal, p. 180.

    17. *Ibid.*, p. 6.

    18. *Ibid.*, p. 155.

    19. *Isaias*: 27, 13.

PART II

CLASSICAL PHILOSOPHICAL AND MYSTICAL WAYS TO GOD

CHAPTER V

THE DEVELOPMENT OF GREEK AND JUDEO-CHRISTIAN PHILOSOPHY:
Bases for Ways to God

INTRODUCTION

The archeology of human thinking described in the preceding three chapters support Iqbal's sense of the essentially religious character of thought. He is concerned to protect religion against the tendency of analytic rationality to reduce the mind to its empirical content and to bind it exclusively to physical reality, or at least to what could be conceived clearly and distinctly by the human mind. Iqbal's approach was to show the limited character of such a view, not only in terms of its objects, but especially as a description of thought itself. He did this by majestically describing the broad (religious) reaches of the mind. For this he reinterpreted time, light and freedom in ways that echoed the thought of such of his contemporaries as Bergson, Whitehead, Alexander, Royce and Einstein. He much enriched their thought with the cultural resources of the Islamic tradition. This is a special power and grace of Iqbal's thought.

There is here a significant contrast to al-Ghazālī whose *Munqidh* I much admire. In describing his itinerary to the mystical life, al-Ghazālī considered thought to be limited and therefore in the end to be inadequate or even subversive of religious life. This opinion implied a rupture of thought and faith which even Averroes (Ibn Rashd) was not able to repair. In our times this has become particularly worrisome, for the Enlightenment has radicalized that gulf by reducing all thought rigorously to contrary, and hence limited, concepts: the modern world in which we live has been built in terms of these clear and distinct concepts. It should not be surprising, indeed it is a point of honor, that Islam always has stood firmly against such "enlightenment". Some have reacted by rejecting modernity *en bloc* — even at times violently and self-destructively.

Iqbal's response is different. He is eloquent in his exposition of the essential importance of limited, categorial thought, precisely in its own sphere, and reaches out to welcome the positive contributions of modernity. But he also gives even greater voice to the infinitely richer domains of thought grounded in the divine. Thus the divine appears, as it were dimly, as the background of every limited human encounter; human life becomes theonomous and can be seen in its transcendent significance. For Iqbal, when related to their infinite ground, science and technology become concrete manifestations and articulations of the meaning of God in time.

But, as he warms to this subject in his *Reconstruction*, Iqbal edges ever closer to that mystical vision of Hallaj (the misunderstood Islamic mystic executed for blasphemy) in which all is so suffused with divine light and meaning that man and nature seem almost divine. Iqbal reacts against any identification of the two; with the full force of the Islamic tradition of fidelity, he would answer: 'Never; there is but one God and no other!'

In this lies the contemporary drama of Islam, as of all religious visions, for man today is intent upon an answer to the question: "how is he to be understood?" Note, this is not the question of how God could create our world of finite beings. The answer to that question is hidden in divine love which we must seek to acknowledge (as we shall suggest below). But we can never comprehend that love, for such understanding could only be the divine life itself. Rather, the question is how, in view of God's love, can we overcome the *hubris* by which the human ego claims to be absolute, and yet at the same time understand the reality of the human person as having the autonomy required for the responsibility and creativity required in order to survive and flourish. How can men and women come truly alive so as to recognize themselves not as God, but in His image, and thereby be enabled to undertake the creative exercise of their proper freedom and responsibility? This is a point of high metaphysics on which I would like to suggest a way to carry forward Iqbal's work as a way to God.

We all know and greatly admire the work of such Islamic scholars as Al Farabi, Avicenna and Averroes in drawing upon and developing the Greek philosophical heritage. This is part of our common heritage which, however, was interrupted in Islam. After the interchange between al-Ghazālī and Averroes this Graeco-Islamic effort was broadly abandoned. In the metaphysical quest the relay was passed to another religious tradition, that of such

Western Christian philosophers of the high Middle Ages as Thomas Aquinas, John Duns Scotus and their schools.

Iqbal suggests two reasons why the path of Aristotle and Averroes was found to be finally inimicable to the Islamic vision. First, the notion of an immortal agent intellect stood in the way of the value and destiny of the human ego,[1] and hence of the recognition and development of one's full personal spirituality and responsibility; second, the orientation to high metaphysical theory diverged from the concrete inductive orientation of Islam.[2] As the concrete point in time at which Islam abandoned Greek thought was that of the dispute over the agent intellect, it seems best to begin with that issue.

Here one could wonder whether the Islamo-Greek tradition was abandoned just a bit too soon, for Aquinas's fully religious response to the problems which worried al-Ghazālī would follow within the century in the Christian tradition of scholarship. It would enable the Greek tradition to evolve into modern thought. In view of this a project of reconstruction in Islam could find the work of Thomas Aquinas particularly interesting as part of its effort to discover how Islamic thought, such as that of Iqbal, can be at home in contemporary times and creative in the new millennium. Any such insights would, in turn, be of great interest to other religious traditions, each of which is struggling with this issue in its own way.

Hermeneutics tells us that in approaching an issue we need a question in order to focus our attention and to be able to draw out new insight. This concerns existence and its implication for creation, and hence for the path or way of a systematic metaphysics to the Source and Goal, the *Alpha* and *Omega*, of all.

GREEK PHILOSOPHY OF PARTICIPATION IN THE ABSOLUTE

The PreSocratics: The Initiation of Western Philosophy

This way to God has long roots in the human cultural tradition to which we must return in order to be able to understand how the philosophical ways grow out of the totemic, mythic and ritual traditions sketched in Chapters II, III and IV. In Chapter I we saw how a process of development takes place when a need arises, and that the development will be relatively minor if the need can be resolved by competencies already possessed. When, however, a new competency must be evoked and developed a dramatic shift in human cultures can occur. This would appear to be the case as the intellect steps beyond the mythic pictures drawn by the imagination to proper terms that state directly the realities involved. Not incidentally, this was identically the point of initiation of philosophy proper.

Following the suggestion of Heidegger that, in confronting major issues, real progress can be made only by a "step back." The second chapter found that, in terms of the totem, "primitive" thought was aware that all things formed a unity on the basis of a unique plenitude of being and meaning which was the basis of their reality. The third and fourth chapters concerned intermediate stages to philosophy, namely myth and hymn. These were seen as enabling the content of totemic consciousness to be understood to transcend and be the origin of a differentiated universe. Hence, the authors of the myths came to be termed *"protoi theologisantes"*.[3] Chapter IV looked into the Hindu Vedic hymns spirit, written for the ritual sacrifices such as the *Creation Hymn, Rg Veda*, X, 129 and reflected in the beauty and drama of the *Bhagavad Gita*.

In the East most do not consider philosophy in the proper sense of the word to have been initiated until the *Upanishads* around the 6th century BC when the issues were separated from the proximate context of ritual and treated by, if not for, themselves. Aristotle described the wise man, the lover of wisdom or the philosopher, as one capable of universal and difficult knowledge, of greater than ordinary certitude, of identifying causes, and of seeking knowledge for its own sake.[4] This set of characteristics need not be definitive for every culture, and Aristotle suggested it only as an inductive model.

It is time now to turn directly to the development of such philosophic thought in order to determine the distinctive way to God constituted by properly philosophical thought and its corresponding cultures. It is not that no attention had been given to these issues in earlier times. Indeed, as they concern the most essential requirements for human life, their understanding had been the central human concern in all ages; this was the burden of the previous chapters.

But the essential and, at the time, yet unclarified role played by the imagination in the mytho-poetic mind had stood in the way of the development of a set of proper and precise intellectual terms. Once this problem was overcome it became possible to proceed by well coordinated processes of knowledge such as analysis and logical inquiry, synthesis and theory building,[5] to immediate and self-certifying awareness.[6] Once established, these processes would construct systems for, in the order of thought as in that of reality, unity is the touchstone of reality. In time each system would generate its own school, and in this manner the main body of philosophic work has been carried out. This chapter will concern the development of the capacity for systemtatic work in philosophy and the contribution it can make to an improved objective understanding of plenitude and participation.

The thought of those, such as Pascal or Kierkegaard, whose ingenious intuitions purposely lacked a corresponding structure of reason for their articulation and defense in order to protect their unique and deep content of subjectivity proved to be of limited impact at the time.

If development follows upon need, the words of Xenophanes provide insight into the evolution of the Greek mind from myth to philosophy. As recounted at the end of Chapter III above, he showed how the imaginative element in myth had enticed men to envisage the gods in an inauthentic manner. Rather than principles of unity, truth and goodness, some gods had come to be exemplars of strife, deceit and all manner of evil. "Both Homer and Hesiod have attributed to the gods all things that are shameful and a reproach among mankind: theft, adultery, and mutual deception."[7]

Something quite analogous is to be found in the history of Indian philosophy. After a long period of Hinduism the imagination had so corrupted the original purity and sacred character if its rites that a reform was needed, which was provided by Buddha. The Lord Buddha himself predicted that his Sangha would last for only 1000 years, and indeed some 1000 years later it was ripe for the reform realized by Shankara.

Xenophanes removed the imaginative factors and stated the meaning of the gods in more proper and specifically intellectual terms. Thus, he proceeded to affirm that

> There is one god, among gods and men the greatest, not at all like mortals in body and mind. . . . He sees as a whole, thinks as a whole, hears as a whole. . . . He always remains in the same place. But without toil he sets every thing in motion by the thought of his mind.[8]

In these terms he demonstrated that a way had been found, namely, philosophy, to state these crucial realities in terms which were susceptible to clear and controlled reasoning. Philosophy had been born.

Once begun, philosophy made spectacularly rapid progress. Within but a few generations, the human intellect had worked out a structure of the physical world using the basic categories of hot and cold, wet and dry, made available by the external senses, along with mechanisms of vortex motion.[9] Mathematical reason worked with the internal senses to lay down the basic theorems of geometry.[10] In brief, by developing properly intellectual terms the Greeks elaborated with new and hitherto unknown precision insights regarding physical reality.

But that had never been the root human issue. Totemic and mythic thought were not ways of understanding and working merely with nature, although they did that as well. Fundamentally, they concerned the metaphysical and religious issues of what it means to be, the divine basis of life, and the religious terms in which it needs to be lived.

Characteristically, the Greek philosophical mind carried out this search in abstract, rather than concrete, terms. By focusing upon a certain aspect of reality and omitting all else it developed clear and cohesive understanding. Even in employing such basic terms as air, fire, and water it considered them as principles which, when combined in various ratios of hot and cold, humid and dry, constitute whatever concretely exists. Where a single element, such as fire or water, was singled out this was due to its ability to explain the many states of things. Thus, for example, water, because it can exist in solid, liquid and gaseous states, was able to provide some unified and universal understanding for the entire realm of physical reality. Dasgupta would claim, against Shankara, that the *Upanishads* viewed the development of real beings in the world as a similar process of combining elements.[11]

This abstract approach to understanding the unity of all was carried to an initial summit in the reasoning of Anaximander (611-547 BC). He proceeded beyond the four basic elements and their combinations, noting that what is most basic in reality must perdure through all physical states, unite them all, and enable one to be significant for another. The principle must, therefore, be neither hot nor cold, neither wet nor dry; it must be without any of the boundaries or limits expressed by names and forms which delimit or define things as contraries. This unlimited was stated negatively as the *apeiron* or "unbounded," that is, the non-specified or undifferentiated.[12]

The search, for a positive statement of this unity continued. Pythagoras (c580-500) thought it consisted in numbers. Even Heraclitus, the classical proponent of diversity, was engaged in the same search for unity, for through all diversity he sought the unity of the *logos*. Thus, he considered fire to be the basic principle because, though darting up and dying down, it manifests throughout a certain unified form or shape. Both Pythagoras and Heraclitus recognized a certain unity and difference in what was numbered or changing, but on their level of abstraction the issue of the reality of that unity and diversity could not be directly confronted. That would be the work of Parmenides.

Parmenides: Being as One, Infinite and Eternal

Parmenides is the father of metaphysics in the West precisely because he remedied this situation by deepening the level of thought in order to be able to speak, not merely of this or that kind of thing, but of being or reality as such. It is important to note that for Parmenides this knowledge (*noeton*) is not simply a product of human reasoning. Like the *Theogony* and the *Vedas*, it is the divine knowledge found in the response of the goddess, Justice. Euripides held that the *nous* in each person is divine, and for Aristotle it is by the *nous* that we immediately recognize the first principles and premises upon which deductions are based.

In the *proemium* of his famous poem Parmenides moves seamlessly, but dramatically from myth to philosophy. Speaking still in the language of myth, Parmenides described a scene in which he was awakened by goddesses and sent in a chariot drawn by faithful mares along the arching highway that spans all things. In this process he moved from obscurity to light, from opinion to truth. There, the gates were opened by the goddess, Justice, as guardian of true judgements, and he was directed by her to examine all things in order to discern the truth.

Such an examination must be a search for *noeton* or the intelligible in contrast to the *aistheton* as the perceptible, the physical or bodily. The latter knowledge is deceptive and dependent upon the physical organs of the body; in contrast *noein* is true knowledge of reality itself. It is of *noein* that he says, "It is the same thing to think and to be."[13] Neither *aistheton* nor, *a fortiori*, Locke's exclusively sensible perception or verification, but intellection is the norm of being and hence of meaning: *noein is* meaning, notes Guthrie.[14] This has been the crucial and decisive foundation for Western thought up to the present — and hence the measure of the crisis at this entrance into the 3rd millenium A.D. For Western thought since its beginnings the path of intelligibility has been that of being; conversely what is not intelligible, what is without meaning, is not real. Because the requirements of intelligibility are those of being and vice versa, a science of being is possible which will concern all reality without remainder. No valid question of being is in principle without an answer for "It is the same thing to think and to be."[15] Inasmuch as that science depends upon *noeton* (intelligence) rather than *aistheton* (sensibility), it must be a meta-physics.

With intelligibility as the criterion of being, Parmenides proceeded on the basis of that which is immediately intellected, namely, "that Being is; . . . nothingness is not possible."[16] He concluded that being itself, and as such, does not include negation or hence differentiation. That is "to be" cannot be the same as "not to be". This principle of non-contradiction was a construct of the mind. Like *pi* in geometry it was good to think with. It enabled the mind to reflect upon the requirements of both being and mind, and to avoid anything that would undermine their reality. He thereby was able to reason as follows: any coming into or going out of being, any divisions or motion, indeed any differentiation would need to be predicated upon either what is or what is not. But, on the one hand, this could not be based upon being for, as being already is, no differentiation is possible thereby. But neither could difference be based upon what is not, because, precisely because that is not, it cannot generate, differentiate, do or be anything.[17] Hence, being itself and as such cannot begin, change or be multiple.

Parmenides then imagines himself proceeding further along the highway of being[18] until he comes to a fork with a signpost pointing toward "beginning" or to a supposed way of being which would include in its essence that it begins. Parmenides reasons regarding the implications of such a route that because "to begin" means to move from nonbeing or nothingness to being, then were "to be" to include "to begin" that would mean that being included within its very essence nonbeing or nothingness. There would then be no difference between being and nothing: being would be without meaning; the real would be nothing at all. If conversely, from this notion of beginning such nonbeing is removed, then it would not begin, but would be eternal. The possibility of taking the fork which would have being as essentially beginning is excluded; being cannot be essentially beginning but must have eternity about it. This is the first requirement of being. Hence, all that begins must be derived from Being.

The chariot then moves along the highway of being and the procedure is analogous at the two subsequent forks in the road where the signposts tempt one to consider being as changing and as multiple, respectively. Each of these, Parmenides reasons, would place nonbeing within being itself, which would destroy its very character as being. Nonbeing is contained in the notion of change, inasmuch as a changing being is *no* longer what it had been and *not* yet what it will become. But for nonbeing to pertain to the essence of being would destroy being. When, however, nonbeing is removed then being emerges as unchanging. Similarly, nonbeing is essential to the notion of multiplicity, inasmuch as this requires that one being *not* be the other. When, however, nonbeing is removed what emerges is one. These then are the characteristics of being: it is infinite and eternal, unchanging and one.

Being as such transcends the multiple and changing world in which we live: it exists in a manner more perfect than could possibly be appreciated in the graphic, figurative and hence extended terms of the internal sense of imagination which characterized the mind in its mythic mode or stage of development.

In this way Parmenides discerned the necessity of Absolute,

Eternal and Unchanging Being — whatever be said of anything else. Neither being nor thought make sense if being is in any way the same as nonbeing, for then to do, say or be anything would be the same as not doing, not saying or not being. If what is real is irreducible to nothing and being is irreducible to nonbeing — as it must be if there is any thing or any meaning whatsoever — then being must have about it the self-sufficiency expressed by Parmenides's notion of the absolute One.

One can refuse to look at this issue and focus upon particular aspects of limited realities. But if one confronts the issue of being it leads to the Self-sufficient as the creative source of all else. Without this all limited beings would be radically compromised — not least, human beings themselves. It is not surprising, therefore, that the painstaking journey of Aristotle in his *Metaphysics* in search of the nature of being would conclude to divine life.[19]

The issue then is not how the notion of the divine first entered human thought; it has always been there. This is true not only as fact, as seen in totemic and mythic thought, but in principle as shown by Greek philosophy. For without that which is One, humanity would be at odds with nature, and humankind would lack social cohesion. Without that which is Absolute, in the sense of infinite and self-sufficient, thinking would be the same as not thinking, and being would be the same as nonbeing.

It is unfortunate that attention has been directed almost solely to Parmenides's negation of differentiation, and that this has been taken as a negation of differentiation between beings and hence of multiple beings, rather than the separation of being from nonbeing. What is central is his direct and lucid clarification

- that being is, is one, and is intelligible;
- that it is Absolute in perfection, and self-sufficient, standing in definitive contrast to nothingness;[20]
- that as such it is self-explanatory or able to justify itself before *nous;* and
- that it is the ground of all metaphysics or understanding of being.

In stating this Parmenides was able to confront directly and for the first time, not merely the fact of differentiation among beings, but the issue of the reality of such differentiation. It is neither surprising nor of great importance that he was not able to resolve this issue. What is important is that due to his contribution the Western mind was able to go to work on the issue. No longer limited to asking about particular differences between specific beings or groups of beings, it could now begin to enquire directly concerning the reality and bases of differentiation. In time this would lead to the discovery of one's own uniqueness and the nature of one's relation to others. Progress in philosophy — as philosophers East and West observe — lies in understanding how this unity is lived, not destroyed, and that whatever meaning there be to the many is had in terms of the one.

Simplicius and others concluded from the first half of his Poem that for Parmenides not only that there must be one being which was absolute, but that there could be nothing else. This, however, does not at all fit with the second, longer half of the Parmenides' Poem, which treats at great length the many changing beings of the universe. Hence, it would appear to be a more correct reading of the first section of his text that being requires the one infinite unchanging and eternal Being, i.e., an Absolute which transcends the world of multiple and changing beings, and on which the universe of changing reality depends. But how the universe of multiple beings described in the second part of his Poem is related to the One is not worked out by Parmenides. It could be expected, however, that whoever would work out this relation of the many to the One would thereby be the father of the Greek — and hence of the Western — philosophical tradition.

Plato and Aristotle

It is no accident then that the great figures, Plato (429-348) and Aristotle (384-322), who marked out the major paths in Western philosophy should follow Parmenides in rapid succession. Once directly confronted with the unity of reality and hence with the issue of the reality of differentiation, the Greek mind had either to accept the skeptical position of the sophists which excluded any basis for organized civil life, or to begin some steps toward the resolution of the issue. These steps proceeded along the route of Plato's notion of participation of the many in the One. Based on this some Church

Fathers listed Plato among the precursors of Christ, while Whitehead considered all subsequent Western philosophy to be essentially a series of footnotes Plato's work.

Plato and the Notion of Participation. On the one hand, the search was directed toward those factors by which an individual being is most properly him- or herself — ultimately toward the discovery of 'non-being' as the principle by which beings are distinct one from another in the sense of 'not-that-being'[21] by which one thing is not the other: by which Tom is *not* John. Along with being, this type of non-being is a component principle of each one in the order of multiple things. In response to Parmenides, Plato saw this as the key to the difference and distinctiveness between beings.

On the other hand, that the community of things is similar or alike requires a source which itself is one. Because John, Agnes and Thomas are alike as humans, their forms share, partake, or participate in the one form of humanity. This form is not limited to the perfection of any one person, but is itself the fullness of the perfection of humankind. Like the totem, it is able to be participated in by an indefinite number of humans. To participate means to have one's being in derivation from, and hence as image of, absolute Being itself. Hence, I am by imaging or participating; imaging is not what I do, but what I am.

For Plato moreover, the object of the mind is the idea or form as the exemplar which "completely is" the reality of all that can be realized in that manner. Similarly, this form is "perfectly knowable."[22] The many instances are related as images to that one, either as sensible objects or as more to less differentiated forms. What is essential, as is manifest in Plato's later solution of the problems raised in his *Parmenides*, is that the relation of participation (*mimesis* or *methexis*) not be added to the multiple being as already constituted, but be constitutive of them: their reality is precisely to image.

This implies that the original forms are ontological dimensions of reality which transcend the series of concrete individuals. They are spoken of as ideas or forms in contrast to concrete particulars. The highest of these ideas is the Good or the One in which all else share or participate precisely as images thereof.[23] This permits a more balanced and less imaginative interpretation of Plato's references in his *Republic* to the "remembering" of ideas. Rather than being taken literally to imply prior states of the soul, they express the personal development of one's awareness of the reality of a higher ontological realm and its significance for one's life. They have memory's directness and certitude, but their source is the Greek *nous*, for they characterize the relation of the intellect to the source of all being and meaning.

By philosophizing in this mode of participation one escapes becoming become trapped in the alternative of either constructing personal but arbitrary intellectual schemata, or elaborating an impersonal science. Philosophizing is rather a gradual process of discovery, of entering ever more deeply into the values which we have in order to comprehend them more clearly in themselves and in their source. Because progressive sharing or participating in this source is the very essence of human growth and development, the work of philosophizing and the religious sensibility implicit in this notion of participation is neither an addenda to life nor merely about life. Rather, as was seen regarding totem and myth, philosophy and religion are central to the life process of human growth itself and at the highest level; from this process it draws its primal discoveries.

Aristotle and the Systematizing of Participation. Though Plato began the philosophical elaboration of the notion of participation, as his method was dialectical he did not construct a system. His terms remained fluid and his dialogues ended with further questions. It was left to his pupil, Aristotle, to develop the means for more rigorous or systematic work in philosophy. For this Aristotle elaborated a formal logic for the strict codification of forms or terms, their cognition in judgments, and the coordination of judgments into patterns of syllogistic reasoning. With this tool he was able to outline the pattern of the sciences which have played so dominant a role in the Western world to this day.

Further, whereas Plato's philosophy of participation as imaging had been conducive to using "reflections" or shadows, e.g. of trees on the surface of a stream, as a simile of the physical world.[24] This appeared to Aristotle to threaten the reality of the material and differentiated universe. Hence, he soon abandoned the use of the term "participation" and gave great attention to the changing of physical things, which he saw to be the route to the discovery of the active character of forms and being. By a careful coordination of the sciences of the physical world through a study of their general principles and causes in the *Physics*, and by relating the *Physics* to the *Metaphysics*, he clarified the relation of all changing things to a first principle. This principle is described in *Metaphysics XII* as subsistent knowledge and divine life.[25] To this all things are related as to their ultimate final cause which they imitate, each according to its own nature. Thus, the source, if not the system, of participation received important philosophical elaboration.

This notion of participation according to which the many derive their being from the One which they manifest and toward which they are oriented and directed would subsequently provide the basic model for what the Chinese refer to as "outer" transcendence or the relation of creatures to God. In Plato's thought, however, the order of forms was relatively passive, rather than active. Hence, the supreme One or Good was the passive object of contemplation by the highest Soul, which was conscious and active. Most scholars, therefore, consider the highest Soul or contemplator in Plato's thought, rather than the highest One or Good upon which it contemplates, to correspond to his notion of God.

Aristotle's philosophy, in contrast, began with changing beings available to the senses and discovered that such being must be composed of the principles of form as act and of matter as potency. As a result, his sense of being was axised upon form as a principle of act in the process of active physical change — which literally was "trans-formation". Consequently, when in his *Metaphysics* he undertook the search for the nature of being or what was meant by being, he tracked this from accidents such as colors which can exist only in something else to substances which exist in themselves. Inevitably, this same process led him to the highest of such substances which is or exists in the most perfect manner, that is, as knowing and indeed as knowing on knowing itself (*noesis noeseos*). This he referred to as life divine.[26] It is the culmination of his philosophy because it brings him to the very heart of the order of being — the goal of becoming and acting — and, hence, of reality itself. Joseph Owens[27] would conclude from his investigation of being as the subject of Aristotle's metaphysics that for Aristotle being was primarily the one Absolute Being and was extended to all things by a *pros hen* analogy; that is, all things are beings precisely to the extent that they stand in relation to the Absolute and divine One, which transcends all else.

In Aristotle's philosophy being was primarily substance; what changed was the composit or *synolon* of form and matter, but substance was not the composite but the form only.[28] As a result, his detailed scientific or systematic process of coordinating various types of being and identifying their principles was predicated upon forms according to their capacity for abstract universalization. The physical universe could be understood only as an endless cycle of formation and dissolution, of which the individual was but a function. Therefore, the freedom and significance of the individual were not adequately accounted for.

Further, while the individual's actions were stimulated and patterned — each in its own way — upon the one objectless Knower (*noesis noeseos*) as final cause, the many individuals were not caused thereby, derived therefrom or known by that principle of all meaning. Thus, though intense human concern is expressed in hellenic dramas which reflect the heritage of human meaning as lived in the family and in society, Greek philosophic understanding was much more specialized and restricted, particularly as regards the significance of the person.

More could not be expected while being was understood in terms of form alone. If, however, the meaning of the human person in this world of names and forms is of key importance today in both East and West; if the protection and promotion of the person become increasingly problematic as our cultures become more industrialized, technological and global; and if the search for freedom and human rights is central to our contemporary search to realize a decent society — then it will be necessary to look to further developments of the notion of being and of divine life. These will create higher levels of equilibria by retrieving and making explicit more of what was meant by Parmenides's One than had been articulated in the Greek philosophies of Plato and Aristotle. Indeed, the fact that the thought of Plato and Aristotle was not brought into synthesis by Aristotle himself suggests that it simply was not possible to do so in terms of being as understood merely as form as was the case in those times. Thus, in order to draw upon the full contribution of both Plato's notion of participation and Aristotle's systematic structures it is necessary to look to a later equilibrium predicated upon a significantly deepened understanding of being, namely, being not as form, but as existing.

THE CHRISTIAN PHILOSOPHY OF EXISTENCE AS LIFE IN GOD

M. Iqbal considers the key to religious reconstruction to be the overcoming of the relatively passive sense of reality found in the formal order characteristic of the Platonic strain of modern rationalism. As noted above, in this light limited realities passively replicate the archetypal forms or ideas, but add nothing new; finite reality is drained of its vitality and reduced to a shadow. M. Iqbal wrote his dissertation on Mulla Sadra who most vigorously and insistently attacked formalist categorical thinking in terms of essence. Instead, Mula Sadra was concerned to shift attention to existence.[29] It is in this sense that Iqbal calls for a turn to the active character of reality. This suggests that we look in Christian philosophy for the emergence of being as act, indeed as existence or the act of all acts. This was the special contribution of Christian philosophy and the key to its many innovations; it characterized the thought of Thomas and gave it its prestige in Christian circles

Although Greek philosophy grew out of an intensive mythic sense of life in which all was a reflection of the will of the gods, nonetheless, it presupposed matter always to have existed. As a result, its attention and concern was focused upon the forms by which matter was determined to be of one type rather than of another. For Aristotle, physical or material things in the process of change from one form to another were the most manifest realities and his philosophizing began therefrom. This approach to philosophy, beginning from sense encounters with physical beings, corresponded well to our human nature as spirit and body, and could be extended to the recognition of divine life. But Iqbal wants more; for him "It is in fact the presence of the total infinite in the movement of knowledge that makes finite thinking possible."[30] The Greek philosophical awareness of what it meant to be real would need considerable enrichment in order to be able to appreciate the foundational significance for human thought of its grounding in a fully transcendent and infinite Being.

The new equilibrium would have three components: (a) the

development in the awareness of the meaning of being as existence; (b) its fruition through Plato's insight regarding the participation of the many in Parmenides's One; and (c) the systematization of both (a) and (b) by the tools of Aristotle's scientific philosophy. As Plato's contribution (b) had been continually employed, what was required was the discovery of being as existence (a) which took place with the early Christian Fathers, and the rediscovery of Aristotle's works (c) which took place a thousand years later.

Being as Existing: To Live

Dependence on the Divine. Development in the understanding of being required transcending the Greek notion which had meant simply to be of a certain differentiated type or kind. This meaning was transformed through the achievement of an explicit awareness of the act of existence (*esse*) in terms of which being could be appreciated directly in its active and self-assertive character. The precise basis for this expansion of the appreciation of being from form to existence is difficult to identify in a conclusive manner, but some things are known.

Because the Greeks had considered matter (*hyle* — the stuff of which things were made) — to be eternal, no direct questions arose concerning the existence or non-existence of things. As there always had been matter, the only real questions for the Greeks concerned the shapes or forms under which it existed. Only at the conclusion of the Greek and the beginning of the medieval period did Plotinus (205-270 A.D.), rather than simply presupposing matter, attempt the first philosophical explanation of its origin. It was, he explained, the light from the One which, having been progressively attenuated as it emanated ever further from its source, finally had turned to darkness.[31] This obviously is not very satisfactory, but whence came this new sensitivity to reality which enabled him even to raise such a question?

It is known that shortly prior to Plotinus the Christian Fathers had this awareness. They explicitly opposed the Greeks' simple supposition of matter; they affirmed that, like form, matter too needed to be explained and traced the origin of both form and matter to the Pantocrator.[32] In doing this they extended to matter the general principle of *Genesis*, that all was dependent upon the One who created heaven and earth, the Spirit who breathed upon the waters. In doing this two insights appear to have been significant.

Beyond Form and Matter. First, it was a period of intensive attention to the Trinitarian character of the divine. To understand Christ to be God Incarnate it was necessary to understand Him to be Son sharing fully in the divine nature.

This required that in the life of the Trinity his procession from the Father be understood to be in a unity of nature: the Son, like the Father, must be fully of one and same divine nature. This made it possible to clarify, by contrast, the formal effect of God's act in creating limited and differentiated beings. This could not be in a unity of nature for it resulted, not in a coequal divine Person, but in a creature radically dependent for its being. But to push the question beyond being one simply of nature or kind of being is to open directly the issue of the reality of beings, and hence not only of their form, but of their matter as well. This is to ask not only how things are of this or that kind, but how they exist at all rather than not exist. It constituted an evolution in the human awareness of being, of what it means to be real. This was no longer simply the compossibility of two forms, which Aristotle had taken as a sufficient response to the scientific question "whether it existed"; instead to be real means to exist or to stand in some relation thereto.

By the same stroke, our self-awareness and will were deepened dramatically. They no longer were restricted to focusing upon choices between various external objects and life styles — the common but superficial contemporary meaning of what Adler terms a circumstantial freedom of self-realization — nor even to Kant's choosing as one ought after the manner of an acquired freedom of self-perfection. Both of these remain within the context of being as nature or essence. The freedom opened by the conscious assumption and affirmation of one's own existence was rather a natural freedom of self-determination with responsibility for one's very being.[33]

One might follow the progression of this deepening awareness of being by reflecting upon the experience of being totally absorbed in the particularities of one's job, business, farm or studies — the prices, the colors, the chemicals — and then encountering an imminent danger of death, the loss of a loved one or the birth of a child. At the moment of death, as at the moment of birth, the entire atmosphere and range of preoccupations in a hospital room shifts dramatically. Suddenly they are transformed from tactical adjustments for limited objectives to confronting existence, in sorrow or in joy, in terms that plunge one to the center of the entire range of meaning. Such was the effect upon philosophy when human awareness expanded and deepened, from concern merely with this or that *kind* of reality, to the act of existence in contrast to nonexistence; and hence to human life in all its dimensions; and, indeed, to God Himself.

The Philosophical Impact of Redemption: Radical Freedom. Cornelio Fabro goes further. He suggests that this deepened metaphysical sense of being in the early Christian ages not only opened the possibility for a deeper sense of freedom, but itself was catalyzed by the new sense of freedom proclaimed in the religious message.

I say "catalyzed", not "deduced from," which would be the way of science rather than of culture. Where the former looks for principles from which conclusions are deduced of necessity, a culture is a creative work of freedom. A religious message inspires and invites; it provides a new vantage point from which all can be reinspected and rethought; its effects are pervasive and enduring. This was the case with the Christian *kerygma*.

That message focused not upon Plato's imagery of the sun at the mouth of the cave from which external enlightenment might be derived, but upon, the eternal Word or *Logos*, the Son who entered the cave unto death so that all might rise to new existence.

> In the beginning was the word, and the word was
>   with God, and the word was God.
> The same was in the beginning with God.
> All things were made by him: and without him was
>   made nothing that was made.
> In him was life, and the life was the light of men.
> And the light shineth in darkness, and the darkness
>   did not comprehend it.
>   . . .
> That was the true light, which enlighteneth every

man that cometh into this world.[34]

But this was more than light to the mind. Christ's resurrection was also a freeing of the soul from sin and death. Fabro suggests that reflection upon one's free response to the divine redemptive invitation was key to the development of the awareness of being as existence. The radically total and unconditioned character of this invitation and response goes beyond any limited facet of one's reality, and/or particular consideration according to time, occupation or the like. It is rather the direct self-affirmation of one's total actuality. Its sacramental symbol is not one of transformation or improvement; it is not a matter merely of reformation. Instead, it is resurrection from the waters of death to radically new life. This directs the mind beyond any generic, specific or even individual form to the unique reality that I am as a self for whom living is freely to exercise or dispose of my very act of existence. This opened a new awareness of being as that existence by which beings stand outside of nothing ("ex-sto") — and not merely to some minimum extent, but to the full extent of their actuality, which Fabro calls an intensive notion of being.

This power of being bursting into time through Creator, Redeemer and Prophet:

- directs the mind beyond the ideological poles of species and individual interests, and beyond issues of place or time as limited series or categories;
- centers, instead, upon the unique reality of the person as a participation in the creative power of God — a being bursting into existence, which is and cannot be denied;
- rejects being considered in any sense as nonbeing, or being treated as anything less than its full reality;
- is a self, or in Iqbal's term an 'ego', affirming its own unique actuality and irreducible to any specific group identity; and
- is image of God for whom life is sacred and sanctifying, a child of God for whom to be is freely to dispose of the power of new life in brotherhood with all humankind.

It took a long time for the implications of this new appreciation of existence and its meaning to germinate and find its proper philo sophic articulation. Over a period of many centuries the term 'form' was used to express both kind or nature and the new sense of being as existence. As the distinction between the two was gradually clarified, however, proper terminology arose in which that by which a being is of this or that kind came to be expressed by the term 'essence,' while the act of existence by which a being simply is was expressed by 'existence' *(esse)*.[35] The relation between the two was under intensive, genial discussion by the Islamic philosophers when their Greek tradition in philosophy was abrogated at the time of al-Ghazāli (see Chapter VII below).

This question was resolved soon thereafter in the work of Thomas Aquinas through a "real distinction" between existence and essence as principles of being. This rendered most intimate the relation of the two principles related as act and potency respectively, which opened a new and uniquely active sense of being. This is not to say that al-Ghazālī was wrong in opposing Averroes or that Islam was wrong in choosing the side of al-Ghazālī in that dispute; Aquinas also had to overcome the Latin Averroists in the course of his intellectual battles in Paris. But Iqbal's intuition of the need to proceed in terms of being as active suggests the importance of this juncture in the history of thought. With this renewed sense of being as existence, rather than as merely form, the Christian metaphysical tradition went on to develop a systematic philosophy with the technical tools needed for understanding human life in this world.

The Philosophy of Participation: To Live in God

The Historical Challenge. But what was the relation of existence and essence — and of the beings thus structured — to Parmenides's One? This is the essential question if the new insight regarding existence is to constitute a way to God. In order to achieve this the previous philosophical accomplishments regarding participation in plenitude must not be lost, but integrated within a cohesive structure. For this, both the participational insight of Plato and the systematic tools of Aristotle will be required. Since Plato and Aristotle had worked together as teacher and student for twenty years it might be expected that their two contributions would have been inseparably linked. In fact, such was not the case. While the body of Aristotelian texts lay sequestered in Pergamon for 150 years, the Platonic influence was gradually extended as the heart of Greek culture through Asia Minor to Alexandria.

Thus the philosophical atmosphere in which the thinking of the Church Fathers took place was Platonic, and in some contrast to the Aristotelian. Especially through the works of St. Augustine Plato's thought pattern became the general context of the Christian thought through the first millennium in medieval Europe. The knowledge of Aristotle in the West during that period had in large part been restricted to Boethius's translations of the *Organon*, and the body of medieval thought itself could be called a Christian Platonism.

In this situation it can be understood how new was the situation when the expansion of Islamic culture into Spain and the contact with the East resulting from the First and Second Crusades led to the introduction, within the short span of one century, of practically the whole body of Aristotle's works. This was not the mere discovery of some new principles or concepts which, by the proper genius of the medieval mind, developed according to the demands of the previously existing Platonic thought pattern. Rather, it was the sudden opening of a new world, which had been scientifically articulated according to its own genius and its own pattern prior to Christian culture. Though genetically related, it was not just a new arrival to be reared according to family patterns, but a full grown relative with whom one discussed as with an equal.

If recent studies have done much to point out the need of considering Aristotle against the background of the intellectualism of Plato, they have not eliminated the profound diversity in the basic pattern and orientation of the two bodies of thought.[36] When they met in thirteenth century Paris it was in a sharp and escalating dispute between those, led by Siger of Brabant, who professed a relatively pure Aristotelianism as interpreted in the work of Averroes and those who reflected the Christian Platonism of the first millennium. Like most disputes in which important issues are at stake either side would lose too heavily if it were really to defeat the opposition. For what would it profit the Latin Averroists to gain philosophical leadership if they did so at the price of their Christian tradition? Or how could the Christian Platonists carry out their hope of uniting all to God if they were to close the door on the new scientifically articulated world which was being stretched out before them?

In these circumstances what was needed was a creative mediator, which task fell to Thomas Aquinas. Working in the realm of ideas he could not simply divide the disputed area between the two sides, but would have to relate both in a fruitfully integrated whole. This meant, first, that he would have to oppose each party on some points. Thus, the task of conciliation required a campaign with fighting on both flanks. It has been suggested that this battle, fought by St. Thomas in his second stay in Paris, was "one of the most decisive battles of the world."[37] Upon it hinged the access of future Western thought to its combined heritage of both wisdom (Plato) and science (Aristotle), the ability of the renewed Aristolelianism to draw its values from the earlier Christianized Platonism, and the fruition of both in an increasingly rich articulation of the meaning of existence.

But the visions of Plato and Aristotle could be brought into mutually fructifying union only on the basis of a radically new insight drawn from the root meaning of human experience. This was available in the understanding of being as existence, as described above, which was sufficiently profound and open to draw out further implications of both earlier orientations. The result was Thomas's systematic philosophy of participation.

A Structure for Thinking about Ways to God. With the three major components in hand, namely, being understood in terms of existence, the Platonic notion of participation, and Aristotle's structure for scientific knowledge, Thomas proceeded to develop a systematic metaphysics whose integrating structural principle was that of participation. In view of what has been said above, the test of such a system would be its ability to retrieve and elaborate some of the content of Parmenides's awareness of the One in a manner that allows for multiple or differentiated being. We shall consider, then: first, the systematic character of his metaphysics as a science of being (this will provide the basis for his five ways to God, which are to be discussed in the following chapter); second, the internal structure of participating beings.

As a systematic tool for developing such a science Thomas had at his disposal Aristotle's model of the syllogism (B is C; and A is B; therefore A is C) as the basic logical form for scientific reasoning. A science is constructed as a study of its subject (A); in the case of metaphysics this is being as that to which it pertains to be. The work of the science is to establish knowledge concerning the attributes, principles, and causes of this subject. It must state what is true of the subject necessarily and always; indeed, what cannot be otherwise.[38] This is done by the mediation of the middle term (B) as the essential or quidditative understanding of the subject (A). Whatever can be seen to pertain as an attribute (C) to the middle term (B), which in turn is the nature of the subject (A), pertains to the subject (A) necessarily and always. The resulting judgments constitute the body of the conclusions of the science.

There is a classic danger in systematic metaphysics, and it lies just at this point of establishing its subject. The danger is that what is taken as the subject will be only some limited form of reality which the philosopher has comprehended. As a result his scientific metaphysics will systematically reduce reality to his limited vision. Such reductionism is the characteristic difficulty both of materialism and idealism, indeed of rationalisms of every sort. Thomas protected his thought against this in two ways.

First, he recognized that if the subject of the science must be susceptible of qudditative human understanding then in principle it could include only limited beings. Hence, if an absolute is to enter the purview of this science it will be as the cause, rather than as a component of the subject. This is a humbling beginning for metaphysics, but it enables it to retain its scientific rigor. At the same time it protects the transcendent and unlimited character of the Absolute from being cut down to the limitations of the capacity of the human mind for quidditative knowledge. This is where alternate metaphysical systems tend to skepticism or to idolatry.

Secondly, even of the limited being which is the subject of the science there is no attempt to establish an initial and inclusive definition. The sequence of drafts of Thomas's *Commentary on Boethius's De Trinitate*[39] show him first attempting and then abandoning the attempt to constitute the subject of metaphysics in the same manner as the subjects of the other sciences, namely, by Aristotle's abstractive apprehension of a determined and delimited form or nature. To obtain the subject of a metaphysics open to all beings and to being as such he gradually was forced to employ, not abstraction, but judgment for that is concerned directly, not with form, but with existence as affirmation. As a result the notion of being is not univocal and delimited as is a form, but analogous or open to affirming in positive terms the full range of existence: being as whatever is and in whatever way it is.

Further — and this will subsequently be of importance regarding the Absolute or Plenitude of perfection — the form of the judgement by which the subject of metaphysics is separated out is negative; it negates or sets aside whatever might in principle restrict or limit the affirmation that is being. It is the judgement that the being with which the science will be concerned will not be limited only to those things which are of a changing or material nature, that is, to the working of the intellect in conjunction with the senses. Because there are both material and non-material things, there follows the negative judgement that in order to be real a being need not be material. Hence, being as being, or that according to which it is being, is not material or changing. This judgement is negative in that it negates limitation to only one type of being, namely, to material being (but it does not exclude material beings).

Being as the subject of the science of metaphysics is thereby liberated in principle from restriction to a particular kind of existence in contrast to others. It is opened for any and all being, for every aspect of being, and for whatever might prove either to characterize or to be required by being precisely as being.

As a science it will constitute a systematic process of inquiry. With being as its subject it will proceed without shackles, able to respond with faithful accountability before Parmenides's principle of contradiction, and to consider all inasmuch as it is being rather than non being. It will consider in positive terms every evidence of being whether dependent or Absolute, effect or cause. Indeed, the path from the one to the other will itself be a way to God.

The Internal Structure of Being

Participation as Life in God. The systematic construction of participation begins with an analysis of the structure of multiple, differentiated or finite beings. By conjoining Parmenides's analysis of the impossibility of being differing, either by being or by nothing, with the evidence of the fact of differentiation, Plato concluded that there must be some principle by which one being (X) is not another being (Y). The principle will be non-being in the sense, not of nothing, but of not-that-being, as I am not you. The relation of this principle to being, however, had not been explained. By the beginning of the thirteenth century the question had evolved into that of the relation between the essence or nature by which the existence is differentiated and the act of existence itself. Drawing upon both Parmenides and Aristotle, Thomas contributed a solution whose structural principle was that of participation.

Being as such, as Parmenides had noted, was not limited and not differentiated: affirmation was not negation. Thus, if an existence is found to be limited — that is, negated with regard to any more of existence than the certain existence it exercises — this must be due to some other principle than existence. Further, if this principle, even though it is other than existence, does exist then it must be made to exist by existence, to which it is then related as a passive capacity or potency. Finally, if the result is a limited being it must consist conjointly of both this principle as a delimiting capacity or potency and its corresponding act or existence.

Aristotle had discovered this relation of potency to act as the way in which matter and form, as two principles, constitute one changing or physical being. Thomas extended the meaning of act and potency from that specific relation to the more general one between the various constituent principles. He did so by employing the relation of act and potency to explicate the relation he had discovered between essence and existence as constituents of limited or finite being. In this way he was able to identify the internal constitution of being, the subject of metaphysics.

This step was as crucial for metaphysics as was the discovery of atoms for physics. Neither existence nor essence is itself a being, nor even intelligible by itself alone. Rather, beings are composed of existence and essence, not as beings, but as intrinsic principles or constituents of beings. Existence is the act by which essence is made to be, and essence is the limiting and defining capacity or potency by which the existence is distinct from all other existents and is of a particular kind.

Attempts to think in terms of existence without essence have produced anarchic personal affirmation without order, just as thought in terms of essence without existence has produced order that is totalitarian, lifeless and oppressive. Neither existence nor essence can be or be thought without the other. Attempts to do so produce monstrous caricatures of being which have come to characterize our century and turn what is a garden of paradise into a jungle ravaged by ferocious aberrations.

Philosophizing in a Religious Culture. Before moving in the next chapter to the impact of this for the realization of beings in time and, hence, of life and meaning in God, let us reflect for a moment on the dynamics at play in the impact of this Christian vision upon philosophy. We must ask first whether, when situated within a cultural context grounded in a revealed vision, philosophy, as knowledge gained by the natural light of reason, ceases to exist and is transformed into a theology based upon revelation? Certainly, that which involves formally the mysteries of the Trinity and the plan or economy of Redemption in Christ can be known only by revelation and is, therefore, a matter of theology. Today, however, we are more conscious of the significance of the cultural and social context within which thought takes place. One who is raised in a loving and generous family will be more able and more liable to make place for love and generosity in one's interpretation and response to life, just as one who lives in a more calculating, manipulative and exploitive environment is less likely to factor love into one's thinking. Today, we recognize that, like economics and even mathematics, philosophy is created by real persons who live in specific places and times, and that it is stimulated by their physical, social and hence cultural circumstances. Philosophy reflects the deepest experiences and free commitments of its creators.

The sense of meaning experienced through earlier ages and articulated in the myths provided Plato with content for his ideas. By his dialogical method he sorted out this meaning, rather than simply creating it. Similarly, in philosophizing, the Christian thinkers returned to Platonic and Aristotelian themes with a new heart and mind, sensitized by their new redemptive and Trinitarian experience. The result was an inversion of the Aristotelian perspective, even by those who would be most Aristotelian in the technical implementation of their philosophy. For Aristotle, the point of initiation of knowledge was the senses, and his philosophy arose through his physics. It was built upon the requirements and implications of matter and change in the physical order. The human was seen to transcend the material, but was defined especially in relation to the physical order as care-taker of nature.

In contrast, the Trinitarian sense of what it means to be corresponds rather to the *noesis noeseos* or Life Divine to which Aristotle concluded at the very end of his *Metaphysics*. Indeed, he did not hesitate to call his metaphysics a theology, both because it alone treated God among its objects and because it was the type of knowledge of all things which befitted God above all others.[40] In this light, it might be said that the distinctive Christian metaphysical sense — as also the Hindu metaphysics of the *Vedanta Sutras* (see Chapter IV) and the Islamic mystic vision (see Chapter VII) — reflects the point to which Aristotle concluded, namely, the outer Transcendent, the Absolute, or Brahman, from which, in which and into which all is or exists.[41]

Yet it is important to note that this remains a philosophy, rather than a theology based on faith. For here the principles are not derived from revelation, but are established by the light of human reason. The work of revelation here is not to provide the premises for philosophical reasoning and discovery, but to provide a context in which this reasoning is evoked, encouraged and called to the high standards required if it is to contribute insight that is sure and universal in this global age.[42]

NOTES

1. Iqbal, *Reconstruction*, p. 4.
2. *Ibid.*, pp. 128-129, 142.
3. Jaeger, p. 10.
4. *Metaphysics*, 1, 1, 981-982.
5. Bernard Lonergan, *Method in Theology* (London: Darton, Longman and Todd, 1971), pp. 4-5.
6. *Ibid.*, pp. 6-13; "St. Thomas's Thought on *Gratia Operans*," *Theological Studies*, III (1942), 573-74.
7. McLean and Aspell, *Readings*, p. 31.
8. *Ibid.*
9. Anaximander, fragments, see McLean and Aspell, *Readings*, pp. 14-17; McLean and Aspell, *Ancient Western Philosophy*, pp. 22-28.
10. McLean and Aspell, *Ancient Western Philosophy*, ch.

III.
11. Dasgupta, I, 53, See Paul Deussen, *The Philosophy of the Upanishads* (New York: Dover, 1 966), pp. 182-95, 237-39.

12. Jaeger, pp. 24-36.

13. McLean and Aspell, *Readings*, p. 40, fr. 3.

14. W.K.C. Guthrie, *The Earlier PreSocratics and the Pythagoreans*, Vol. I of *A History of Greek Philosophy* (Cambridge: At the University Press, 1962), p. 41.

15. McLean and Aspell, *Readings*, p. 40, fr. 3.

16. *Ibid.*, p. 40, fr. 3 and 6.

17. *Ibid.*, pp. 42-43, fr. 8. See Guthrie, pp. 28-29.

18. Fragment 8; see Alexander P.D. Mourelatos, *The Route of Parmenides: A Study of Word, Images, and Argument in the Fragment* (New Haven: Yale, 1970).

19. *Metaphysics*, XII, 7, 1072 b 26-29.

20. McLean and Aspell, *Readings*, pp. 42-43, fr. 8.

21. Plato, *Sophist*, 259 A.

22. *Ibid.*, 248 E.

23. Plato, *Republic*, 509.

24. *Ibid.*, pp. 509-511.

25. *Noesis noeseos*: "Thought thinks itself as object in virtue of its participation in what is thought," *Metaphysics* XII, 1072 b 19-29.

26. *Ibid.*

27. Joseph Owens, *The Doctrine of Being, The Aristotelian Metaphysics: A Study in the Greek Background of Mediaeval Thought* (Toronto: PIMS, 1951).

28. A. Mansion, "Positions Maîtreses de la philosophie d'Aristote," in *Aristote et Saint Thomas d'Aquin* (Louvain: Université de Louvain, 1955), pp. 58-67.

29. Mulla Sadra, see Chapter VII below.

30. Iqbal, p. 4.

31. Plotinus, *Enneads*, II 5(25), ch. v.

32. Maurizio Flick and Zoltan Alszeghy, *Il Creatore, l'inizio della salvezza* (Firenze: Lib. Ed. Fiorentina, 1961), pp. 32-49.

33. Mortimer Alder, *The Idea of Freedom: A Dialectical Examination of the Conception of Freedom* (Garden City, NY: Doubleday, 1958), I, 609.

34. John I:1-5, 8.

35. Cornelio Fabro, *La nozione metafisica di partecipazione secondo S. Tommaso d'Aquino* (Torino: Societa Ed. Internazionale, 1950), pp. 75-122.

36. A Survey of a number of authors on this point is found in Robert Henle, *St. Thomas and Platonism* (Hague: Nijhoff, 1956), p. xviii. See also William D. Ross, *The Ideas of Plato* (Oxford: Oxford University Press, 1942), p. 226; Joseph Owens, *A History of Ancient Western Philosophy* (New York: Appleton-Century-Crofts, 1959), pp. 358-59.

37. Arthur Little, *The Platonic Heritage of Thomism* (Dublin: Golden Eagle Books, 1950), p. 14.

38. Aristotle, *Posterior Analytics*, 1, 2, 71 b-72 a.

39. *The Method and Division of the Sciences*, trans. by Armand Maurer (Toronto: The Pontifical Institute of Mediaeval Studies, 1953).

40. *Metaphysics*, I, 2.

41. *Vedanta Sutras*, I, 1, 2.

42. John Paul II, *Encyclical Letter: Faith and Reason*, Sept. 1998.

CHAPTER VI

SYSTEMATIC CHRISTIAN PHILOSOPHY AS A WAY TO GOD

The focus of Christian philosophy upon being as existence and hence as active, described in the previous chapter, had profound implications for the understanding of the relation of the human person to God, and first of all for the sense of the divine itself. In Plato's more passive vision the divine was less than such highest ideas as the One or the Good, which rather were passive objects of contemplation. Taking being in a more active sense allowed Aristotle to appreciate the supreme Being as divine life, that is, as thinking and precisely as thinking on thinking itself, that is, as subsistent thought, openness or lucidity.

Iqbal and the Islamic tradition rightly feared that if this notion were a product of human reasoning it would still be essentially limited and limiting: this is his incisive and trenchant critique of the cosmological and other modes of reasoning to God.[1] Certainly reasoning in terms of limited and limiting forms and categories would be subject to this critique. But as noted in the previous chapter, the process by which the subject of metaphysics, its internal principles and external causes are discovered is carried out not in terms of forms or of limited categories, but in terms of existence. This is affirmation without negation and hence without limitation.

Nevertheless, Iqbal makes a key contribution to any appropriate reading of a systematic Christian philosophy by reminding one that the notion of God is not a product of human reasoning. Rather, as seen above through the archeology of human knowledge, the Absolute is there as the center of human life from its earliest totemic beginnings; it flowers as humankind achieves a mythic mode of thought; and it is the very beginning of metaphysics as founded by Parmenides. According to Augustine's dialectic of love, it is not we who first loved God, but He who first loved us: from him come life and light and love.

From this it appears that the classical "five ways" to God have been largely misunderstood. They are not "proofs" for the existence of God, much less ways of constructing the reality of

God. Instead they are ways of binding all things back to God (*religio*, as one of the etymologies of 'religion'), whether considered in terms of their origin, level of being, goal, purpose or meaning. Despite his critique of the cosmological arguments, Iqbal seems to intuit this when he writes that their true significance will appear only "if we are able to show that the human situation is not final."[2]

In this light, one need not fear that an affirmation of man, whether by personal freedom or technological means, will be detrimental to religion; rather human life becomes the proclamation of God's wisdom, power, love and providence. On this basis, Thomas proceeds systematically to shed the requirement not only of an external agent intellect, but even of a special divine illumination for each act of reason, as well the notion of seeds of possibility for all new realizations. All of these were ways by which earlier Christian-Platonism had attempted to preserve a role for God in human progress. Instead, humans are seen as the sacrament of God, His sign and symbol, His creative vice-regents and hence as artists in, and of, this world. Therefore, Thomas does not hesitate to affirm of human beings whatever is required in order that, properly according to their own nature and in their own name, they be able to fulfill these roles in this world. This is the proper autonomy of humans in God; it is a way that truly leads home to God.

PARTICIPATION AND THE STRUCTURE OF A RELIGIOUS VISION

The existential sense of being and its openness to the infinite has allowed more recently for a renewed appreciation of Thomas's structure of participation by which human autonomy is an affirmation, rather than a derogation, of God. In any limited being, its essence or nature constitutes by definition a limited and limiting capacity for existence: by this the being is capable of this much existence, but of no more. Such an essence must then be distinct from existence because, of itself, existence bespeaks only affirmation, not negation or limitation.

But a being whose nature or essence is not existence, but only a capacity for existence, could not of itself or by its own nature justify its possession and exercise of existence. The Parmenidean principle of noncontradiction will not countenance existence coming from non-existence, for then being would be reducible to non-being or nothing. Such beings, then, are dependent precisely for their existence, that is, precisely as beings or existents.

This dependence, however, cannot be upon another limited being similarly composed of a distinct essence and existence, for such a being would be equally dependent, in turn. The multiplication of such dependencies, even infinitely, would but multiply, rather than answer, the question of how composite beings with a limiting essence nevertheless have existence. Hence, limited beings composed of existence and essence must depend upon another being for their existence, that is, must participate in another. That "other" must ultimately be radically different, that is, it must be precisely incomposite being whose essence or nature, rather than being distinct from and limiting its existence, is identically existence. This is Being Itself — the total infinite to which Iqbal refers as making possible finite being and thinking.

The incomposite Being is simple, the One *par excellence*; it is participated in by all multiple and differentiated beings for their existence. The One, however, does not in turn participate; it is the unlimited, self-sufficient, eternal and unchanging Being which Parmenides had shown to be required for reality. "Limited and composite beings are by nature relative to, participate in, and are caused by the unique simple and incomposite being which is Absolute, unparticipated and uncaused."[3]

This sense of participation makes it possible to speak of the nonreciprocal relation of finite or composite being to infinite or incomposite being and to identify the essentially caused character of the former.[4] This is a crucial step beyond the Platonic tradition which rightly can be criticized for failing to develop adequate tools for distinguishing humans from God. An existential metaphysics understands causality in terms of participation in the infinite. Hence, even while placing central emphasis upon union with the divine, its conceptual and ontological structures never lose sight of the distinction of the human from the divine. At the same time, through making this distinction it sees every aspect of the caused or created being as totally derivative from, and hence as expressing, the infinite. *Let man be man; indeed let all creatures be, for they glorify God, the Infinite and the All Mightily, the Munificent and the Merciful!*

For his sense of participation some early Church Fathers placed Plato among the prophets. The understanding of participation was clarified and enriched by Aristotle's sense of being as active, by the work of his great medieval Islamic commentators and by the Christian existential sense of being. The resulting metaphysics provides the systematic clarification needed by Iqbal's insights regarding religion for the increasingly complex structure of the physical and social environment in which we live. In the face of the dilemma of human *hubris* vs religious passivity in our days this provides indispensable help in responding to the needs of those devoted in faith. It can aid them to understand better the relation of their increasingly complex life to God and thereby assist them in living their faith in our times. In a word, it is a way to come home, and to be at home, religiously in our times.

THOMAS'S FIVE WAYS TO GOD

The Five Ways

Thomas Aquinas constructed his "five ways"[5] on this insight regarding the participation of limited beings in the absolute and unparticipated being. They have remained the classic expression of *a posteriori* ways to the Absolute.

He notes five things about the beings which we observe by our intellect as it works with our senses: (1) they undergo change, (2) they cause change, (3) they begin and cease to be, (4) they realize their being or goodness to greater and lesser degrees, and (5) they are oriented to goals beyond themselves. Each of these five factors manifests that these beings are limited and hence that each is a composite of an essence or nature which is a capacity for a corresponding and proportionate existence or act. This internal composition or dynamism shows that they are not self-sufficient, for essence as potential or capacity for existence cannot provide the actual existence itself. Hence, such beings must depend for their existence upon the One which is not composite and which therefore, as noted by Parmenides, is unchanging, unique and unlimited. That is, the many beings we encounter are predicated upon Being Itself *(Ipsum Esse)* which is simple, and which alone is absolute or self-sufficient. As absolute it is distinct from all else, which in turn can exist only by being related to or participating in that which is absolute or self-sufficient. This is the central structure of the reasoning of the classical "five ways".

But our concern here is not to suppose the existence of God to be unknown. As seen in the above chapters, from the original totemic times God has always been central to human consciousness. What is taking place in this very first step in Thomas's Summary of Theology (or *Summa Theologica*), is rather relating all, including humankind, back to God. Here we shall not look at the five ways as answers to an unreal doubt about whether God exists. Thomas was responding to the first scientific question for an Aristotelian science, namely, whether the subject of the science exists. In existential terms this is to ask whether this issue has meaning for life or how it relates to the clarification of the source, the inner character and the goal of human life.

Plato had been able to analyze this only externally in terms of the relation of the many to the one and on the basis of formal causality. Combining Aristotle's insight regarding internal structures with the Christian understanding of being as existence, Thomas was able to carry out an internal analysis. He was able to identify the internal structure constituted by the existence and essence of multiple beings which in turn manifests them to be participations, that is, effects by active or efficient causality of the unparticipated One.

In these terms the first three are ways in which changing, contingent beings are seen to be from God, to depend upon and to manifest his creative power. First, as caused they emerge into being; second, as causes they reflect in their power the creative force of the creator; third, as contingent they manifest in every facet of their existence the triumph of being over nothingness.

The fourth way points out that each level of these realizations of being, with their proper level of dignity and truth, goodness and beauty, manifests and proclaims the absolute goodness and beauty of the divine. This is the most mystical of the ways because it bespeaks not merely that all is from the divine, but that all beings manifest God, live in the divine — and especially that God lives in them. To perceive the beauty of a sunset is to see thereby something of the beauty of God. With this awareness, to see the face of another, whether in tears or in joy, is through them and indeed in them to see the face of God. This is the deep religious insight of a St. Francis in which all of nature is brother and sister because all bespeak the divine, or of Christ for whom to give a cup of water to the least of one's brethren is to give it to God.

The fifth way is especially dynamic in its awareness that life does not end in any finite reality, which is to say that there are no dead ends. Rather all things point ahead and relay our attention onward to God. We can love others and life itself fully and without limit, for all share in and lead toward the infinite, subsistant love from which we derive and toward which we are directed in all that we are and do. The life we live from God, in God and toward God is act, meaning and love without limit.

By means of the above structured and dynamic understanding of participation, Thomas Aquinas was able to philosophize life in the systematic structure of participation in the transcendent as coming from God, lived in God and leading toward God. Indeed, in the view of Cornelio Fabro, L.B. Geiger, Arthur Little[6] and others, this theme constituted the central discovery, the coordinating and fructifying principle of his entire systematic philosophy and theology. Here, we can identify but a few factors in order to illustrate the contribution of this *a priori* way to human awareness of God and to the sense of life with others in this world. We shall proceed according to the order of Thomas's five ways to God beginning from the first three as they build upon the origin of all finite beings from the infinite creator of all.

It will be noted that having carried out the *a posteriori* reasoning from effect to cause in order to relate all things to God enables one in turn to proceed in an *a priori* manner from cause to effect. Unfortunately, '*a priori*' has come to suggest arbitrariness, whereas etymologically it means proceeding on the basis of that which comes first and is most basic and hence most established, namely, proceeding from a cause to its effects. The importance of this second, *a priori*, phase for metaphysics cannot be over-emphasized, for only by understanding being on the basis of that which is Self-sufficient or Absolute and which transcends all else can we gain truly basic insight into being as such and hence into the limited, multiple, participating beings we are and among which we live. This was seen by Descartes, Spinoza, and Leibniz, all of whom developed works in metaphysics which proceeded from the absolute to the relative. Indeed they considered this synthetic procedure to be the proper method for metaphysics.

The realist character of Thomas's thought and his insistence upon the use of a scientific method for metaphysics led him to insist upon beginning this science *a posteriori* upon finite being as its subject. However, once the cause of that subject -- the Incomposite or Unparticipated Being -- was discovered all could be seen more deeply and more richly through the awareness of that Absolute on which all depends, and of all things precisely as dependent thereupon through the radical totality of the creative act. In this light the five ways open the way to a broad and deep range of *a priori* reflection and insight.

Implications of the First Three Ways

To begin with, note must be taken of the extent of the dependence of participated beings on unparticipated Being. A preliminary, but not provisional, instance of great importance for our theme is the dependent character of matter — which the Greeks had presupposed to be a given, unquestioned and, hence, unexplained. In this light action consisted in the transformation of matter, that is, in its successive shaping according to different forms. This process ultimately came full cycle and would begin once again. In this perspective, the individual had no further purpose or meaning than to continue the cycle; nothing was radically new, unique or hence personal.

Above, we saw that early Christian thought directed attention to matter and to its origin from God. *A priori* reflection in the light of this transcendent source and cause of all can provide further understanding. As simple and not composed of a distinct limiting essence and existence, the Absolute Being Itself is unlimited. Hence, no other reality can be equally original with it, for to have two such beings would mean that being would be had only partially by each. In that case, each would in fact be limited and composite; there would be no Absolute. But then, the question concerning the origin of limited or composite beings would have no answer: not in themselves and not in a simple, absolute and transcendent cause. There would remain only Parmenides's "all impossible way", in which being is non-being, an abyss not of being but of nothingness.

Since nothing can be equally original with the Absolute, for their whole reality all else must participate in the Absolute fullness of perfection. Each, to the full extent of its being, must derive from, and hence image in a partial manner, the One. While different from every other limited being, each one constitutes with the others an ever unfolding manifestation of Being itself.

Though there are more beings, however, there could never and need never be more of being than the One Absolute unlimited plenitude. The checks one writes do not multiply the money one possesses; nor does one lose knowledge in sharing it, but rather multiplies its instances. Thus, no matter how many participate in the One, it remains ever the Plenitude of Being and is in no sense diminished. The simple, incomposite being does not depend upon composite beings; on the contrary, composite beings depend entirely upon the incomposite One. But participations are not competitors, nor do they draw down the capital on which they depend; rather, others are cooperators and together all are able better to manifest the divine in this world. Human society is then not a distraction from God, but a means of His presence.

This participated and caused character of being applies to all limited realities and to the components thereof; hence, it applies also to matter whose proper reality is that of a relation of potency to form as its act, without which it could have neither meaning nor reality. As a constituent principle of the essences of physical beings, matter, too, must share in their reality and to that degree in their creation. Just as there can be no matter existing independently of form, neither can there be matter which, with that form, does not constitute an essence and participate to the full extent of its reality in the Absolute.

The causal activity of the divine in participation is creation from nothing. By this is not meant, of course, that there is no cause, for actively considered participation is causing. What is meant is that it involves only (a) the act which is the Absolute or transcendent, and (b) the effect as depending upon it, and by which the transcendent is designated as cause or creator. What is excluded is any independence or equally original existence of the effect either in its totality or in any of its principles, e.g. matter.[7] The full classical phrase is creation from nothing as regards the effect itself and any subject thereof (*creatio ex nihilo sui et subiecti*). Some, in China particularly, refer to the cause as outer transcendence.

In this total sense, then, the creative source transcends the created effect in every facet of its being. Conversely and correlatively, limited beings as participating all their being in the divine are constituted fully, with all their capacities for being and acting according to the full perfection of their nature. God's power is manifested not in making up for deficiencies in his creatures through causing their effects or supplementing their intellectual abilities as in, e.g., an Occasionalism, but through endowing his creatures with the ability to seek indissociably both their perfection and his glory to the full extent of their nature.

Recent phenomenological thought suggests new, less technical and perhaps more available, ways of thinking about how human life is, and must be, founded in the Transcendent. Maurice Nedoncelle[8] notes that my identity and relatedness to others are not something which I construct, but are possessed by me from the beginning of my life. All my actions are mine; they pertain to my identity which I was given and did not make or create.

By reflection, then, it is possible to trace back the characteristics of my life to gain some sense of the nature of the giver of that life. First, my life must be not from another individual who is contrary to me as one thing to another, for this could give me not my identity, but only something distinct and alien to me. Hence, this source of my being must be not another being of a limited and contrary nature, but a unique and limitless source able to be the origin of all individuals. Similarly, as I examine my relationships to others, I find that the deepest and most humane among them — friendship and marriage, for example — are not limited and measured, but precisely open beyond place or time, health or economic condition. In contrast to legal agreements, I make promises to friends which are not conditioned by time; the commitment in marriage is specific only in its rejections of all limiting conditions: "for richer or poorer, in sickness or health, till death do us part." This proclaims that the context for life together transcends all particularities of place and time.

Further, as I survey my life I see that it is ever open to new and innovative responses to others in the most concrete and seemingly repetitive circumstances of our daily life. What I eat for breakfast and those with whom I eat it may be identical, but breakfast is never the same. Our life is not lived according to a scientific formula with everlasting sameness, but is endlessly new and unfolding as we explore together the many ways of being concerned and being sorrowful, being amazed and being delighted.

This manifests that human life is lived in terms not of the limitations of concrete things or of abstract formulae and laws, but of an infinity of Being which transcends us in life and enables us truly to be free and creative. Though the person is not God, the phenomenologists point out that the properly human characteristics of conscious life manifest that it is lived in an order which derives from, and is directed toward, the living God.

Implications of the Fourth Way to God

Reflection on the fourth of Thomas's five ways to God, but now from an *a priori* perspective, suggests how this outer transcendent and absolutely perfect reality should be conceived. Were it to stand in opposition to man, were its action to be an intrusion upon human life, were its prerogatives to be at the expense of human perfection, then it would disrupt the Confucian vision of harmony and subvert its philosophy. But is this the case?

What would be the conditions for such a disruptive relationship? It would need to be not that of the good as perfecting or realizing the human, but as opposed to a humanity whose very nature had been corrupted and become evil. This view obtained only in the Reformation or antithetic phase of Christian theology which saw humanity not only as fallen, but corrupted in its very nature. The Judeo-Christian view, however, is clearly that of man created in the image of God, sharing and manifesting — if in a limited way — the divine perfection: "And God saw all the things that he had made, and they were very good."[9] To speak of man's nature as being corrupt can only be a theological metaphor reflecting the philosophical nominalism of the time, which in any case did not admit universal concepts or natures. In any proper philosophical sense a nature either contains all of its components or simply ceases to be that nature. A number three which loses one of its component units is not a corrupt number three, but no three at all; instead it has become a number two. However weakened by the abuse of sinfulness, like all natures, human nature remains good as a limited way of participating in, and manifesting, the absolute perfection of

God.

A disruptive relationship between outer and inner transcendence, between divine grace and self perfection, might arise also not in human nature but in the process of its development if this were to be conceived as other than a single process of self-realization. But again, that would appear to be a philosophical impossibility, for how could some alien intrusion be called self-development. In the long Catholic tradition — the Christian thesis and synthesis — just as human nature is not corrupted but has its perfection as a manner of participation in divine perfection, so does its development and self-perfection. God acts throughout this process. Just as in creation his action does not substitute for human substance, but makes it to be, so in acting in the process of human perfection He does not substitute for human activity, but capacitates the human work of self-perfection and self-realization.

In brief, God does not subvert human reality as free and self-responsible; indeed, it would be a contradiction if human perfection were not its own self-perfection. Rather, as the unique and unchanging Absolute Being, God stands definitively against non-being and imperfection, creates humans, makes them to be, and enables them to undertake their magnificent process of self-realization. It is life in Him that enables one to be in one's own human way.

Our difficulties in seeing this come from our tendency to view God as a human being and, hence, to introduce two similar operative agents in our self-realization. It is important that we distinguish the two and let God be God. The causality of his infinite nature is the creative action of making me and my activities simply to be, while I, in my limitation, can shape them according to this or that character and relationship. All is from God as first cause or creator; all is also from humans as second causes or causes of change. The two are not incompatible, much less are they conflictual; neither substitutes for the other. The late President John F. Kennedy said it well in his inaugural address: "In this world, God's work is man's own."

In this way, the Christian vision sees only God as absolutely perfect and, hence, self-sufficient. Humans are complete, but are not abandoned in their created nature. Their nature is to seek their self-realization in a process that responds to the power of the divine. By an absolute and self-sufficient power they are made to stand in their own right. Thus, one must not be manipulated to lesser purposes by any person or group. The Transcendent Creator has made humans to be fully human, autonomous and hence equal; their dignity and rights are firmly founded in this divine origin, which, in turn, they reflect. Thereby, all human persons are precious beyond question, and it is the duty of people acting in consort as society to protect that dignity and promote those rights, both individually and socially.

Implications of the Fifth Way to God

The fifth of Thomas's five ways to God, when subsequently reflected upon in an *a priori* manner, opens in a special way to a dialogue among religions by taking up the question of the goal of life and founding the sense of harmony by love. This does not set man as the ultimate goal in relation to which God is merely the source and support; rather God is one's ultimate end or goal. Aristotle articulated part of this vision in his treatment of human happiness or fulfillment at the beginning and end of his ethics. Happiness, he said, consists in contemplation as the highest realization of the highest human power (intellect) with regard to the highest reality, namely, life divine. This is not the abandonment, but the fulfillment of human life; it is the point at which the human person lives most fully.

To this, religion adds, beyond death, the goal of life with God that is no longer mediated through limited beings, but face to face. This does not negate the natural fulfillment of which Aristotle spoke, but carries it further by grace to an even more perfect realization in terms of the essence of divine life as an exchange of knowledge and love. Though this is made possible by a special divine grace, like life itself it cannot be given exteriorly, but must be lived as personal self-realization.[10]

In this context, one can see the true character of evil — or let evil be evil. It is not merely an unfortunate flaw in human perfection which a person comes to know and bear, but which is nobody else's business. If our life is lived in response to God's love and as a way toward reunion with our transcendent personal Source and Goal, to abandon goodness is to reject the divine gift and to refuse the divine rendezvous. It is a personal rejection whose significance goes beyond oneself to one's absolute Source and Goal. This is to extend the Confucian universe of the gentlemen, from what is fitting or ugly in relation to one's fellow humans, to that which is fitting vis a vis God as well. Further, this is not an affair between an individual alone and God for, as all are made in God's image, to do evil or refuse good to the least of our brothers is to do so to God himself. Hence, as the Chinese tradition always sensed, to disrupt the harmony of the community is to disrupt harmony with heaven.

Here, we find the source of the ultimate seriousness of human life: the depth of evil when committed; the urgency of response to need where we can help; and the sublime, indeed divine, beauty of the simplest life lived in harmony with nature, man and God. As above, this religious vision evolves and carries forward the realm of which Confucius spoke. It unpacks this, surrounds it with contextual principles, and opens it to its ultimate import in a sublime sense of the harmony he so richly valued.

A religious vision can provide as well a rich context for the sublime teaching of Confucius on love, to take the example of but one culture. It joins to the key principle of respect for one's father the commandment to love, honor and obey father and mother. It proposes a graded love with the strongest and most detailed obligations in relation to those to whom we are closest by consanguinity and community. It places upon this a divine seal by adding that one who claims to love God and yet does not love his neighbor is a liar,[11] that one who would bring offerings to the altar but is not reconciled with his brother must first become reconciled with his brother in order to be able to approach the altar of the Lord of Heaven.[12]

In some ways the religious message extends and intensifies the human vision. For it would speak not only of control, or of obedience of wife and children to husband and father, but would enjoin husbands to love their wives. It envisages these relations not merely as obligatory because they are imposed, but as imposed because they are freely and lovingly entered into. They are then not only obligations of justice, but implications of love. Finally, it does not leave all solely as the effect of the fallible will of a father, but puts this in the context of God as Father whose love and justice the human father is to imitate and to whom one has ultimate allegiance.

Indeed, this could imply even leaving father and mother in order to carry the love they first showed into a broader service of humankind. Such broadening of horizons relocates the issue of filial and unfilial behaviour in a richer and liberating context in which such aberrations as arbitrariness and self-centeredness on the part of parents can be transcended, and the essence of a child's love for them can more amply be fulfilled in family and in society at large.

This opens the possibility of advancing the humanist Confucian sense of harmony by not restricting it merely to the adhesion of all the individuals in a family or society to the will of their one father or governor, but by grounding this relation within a liberating and expanding relation to the Infinite One. Over time, the former, more restrictively human perspective seems to lend itself to an autocratic style. Historically this seems indeed to have taken place and could have many particular causes. For example, it seems well established that at times, for reasons of political stability, an autocratic sense of harmony was officially promoted — which, of course, at first blush seems an easier way to run a family or nation.

Indeed, some would argue that the original sense of Confucius was rather that of a dynamic cohesion and cooperation of multiple elements within an harmonious whole. This certainly should be revived, but to do so it is important to search for the principles which would found, maintain and protect such an integrative sense of harmony from reductivist tendencies. Here, the sense of participation can be particularly helpful. For, if all were to be conceived simply in terms of human beings without anything transcending the father or governor, it would fall simply to the will power of father or governor to establish order and all would veer toward autocracy. To avoid this and enable all to tend freely toward their perfection, both individually and as a social whole, it is important that they be able to conceive their life in relation to an open and unlimited Transcendent Good as Source and Goal of all. By this all are united, enlivened and cohesive in the exercise of their freedom. This is most significant for the transition to democratic modes of life and enables the sense of harmony to become the dynamic basis for civic responsibility and social cohesion.

THREE WAYS OF SPEAKING ABOUT GOD

In view of this totality of the dependence of participating beings upon the Absolute, it is apparent that any insight concerning the nature of the absolute would contribute a radical elucidation regarding realities which participate therein. In order to make its contribution to this understanding a systematic philosophy must first prepare the language it will employ. In particular, any implication of limitation in human thought or expression must be removed from language concerning the Absolute.

We saw in the previous chapter that being as the subject of the science of metaphysics expressed only differentiated or limited beings. We saw also that differentiated and composite beings were participations in unlimited and incomposite Being. This has crucial implications for extending analogously the notion of being. As the subject of the science of metaphysics, being had analogously but properly been said of the entire range of finite beings. Metaphysics stated the existence of each being according to its limiting or defining essence or nature, i.e., each being is or exists according to (or to the extent of) its own essence or nature. This had the form of a four term analogy of proper proportionality, a proportion of proportions: "the existence of A : the essence of A :: the existence of B : the essence of B." On the basis of the participation of such composite subjects in their incomposite or unlimited cause the analogous range of being can now be extended from finite to infinite being. This adds to the four terms above the proportion ":: the existence of God : the essence of God."

The causal relatedness of participated or finite effect to incomposite or infinite cause makes three essential contributions to this extension of the analogy of being to God. (a) It justifies the affirmation of the third proportion in the analogy, namely, the existence of the Absolute to the essence of the Absolute, because the being and intelligibility of limited beings (the first and second proportions) cannot be grounded in nothingness (nothing does nothing, as Parmenides notes), but only in Being Itself. (b) It constitutes the proportion of the first two proportions as limited beings to the infinite being expressed by the third proportion, for the effect as dependent on the cause must be similar thereto. (c) It founds the proportion in which Absolute Being is expressed (the existence of God to the essence of God) for it requires that the essence of the Absolute be identical with its existence rather than distinct from, and limiting, its existence. Thus, where being said of a finite being states existence according to its essence as a limited and hence unique instance of, e.g., human nature, being said of the Absolute in which it participates states the Unique Existence lived in its plenitude: the One God, Infinite, Eternal and Munificent.[13]

The above concerns the construction of analogy in a metaphysics whose subject is limited being, from which it moves to its infinite cause. Analogy is no less necessary as a metaphysics moves from the Absolute to the finite; otherwise, existence would be taken to mean only the Absolute and the Parmenidean rejection of differentiation would be its last, rather than its opening, word.

In both parts of metaphysics it must be remembered that thought is a human activity and its terminology a human creation. This does not mean that it is only about humans or other limited beings; in fact, it is characteristic of beings which know, as distinct from those which do not, that they can react on the basis of what things are in themselves or as object, rather than simply on the basis of their own subjective conditions. Nevertheless, the classic dictum that "whatever is received is received according to the mode of the receiver" applies also to knowledge. This is particularly significant when from our perspective as participated and related beings we speak of the Plenitude of Being that is Unparticipated and Absolute. For this reason along with the positive and analogous language mentioned above — the classical *via positiva* or *affirmativa* — there is a second or negative way of speaking — the classical *via negativa* — which denies of the Absolute that mode of expression which reflects the composite nature of humans who speak of God and the limitations of their cognitive capacities to know and to speak. In order to say that the Absolute or the Plenitude of being is good, or even simply that it is, we must use more than one term and unite these in a judgment. As composite, however, this cannot be the nature of that One, which the structure of participation showed to be precisely Incomposite. Therefore, it is absolutely necessary to deny that the composite character of our speech applies to the One.

This is not an alternate, but a concomitant, to the positive way; both must be used in every statement of Incomposite Being. About this we must be clear. One cannot deny the existence or goodness of the Unparticipated without rejecting the Absolute. On the contrary, one must follow the positive way and affirm that the Absolute exists, which is to say that existence in its original state is realized absolutely. What is denied in the negative way is simply that the absolute exists according to the composite mode which inevitably characterizes all human expressions of the Absolute.

Hence, the negative way does not mean that the Absolute does not exist, or even that it is not non-existent for that could reduce God to the minimal realization of existence. The negative way is not about the Absolute at all, but about the human mode of expressing it.

Going further, in the way of eminence — or *via eminentiae* — one combines the positive with the negative way to say that the Absolute realizes existence eminently, that is, in a mode which surpasses our ability to express. The function of the negative way is simply to keep open the vision of being. This initially was opened by "the negative judgment of separation" of being from any limitation; through this the subject of the science of metaphysics was obtained. This must be kept open for the eminent affirmation of Being Itself so that incomposite Being can manifest itself to the human mind despite the mind's restrictions. In turn, it enables humans to respond in positive terms which similarly are open and unfettered.[14]

LEARNING FROM GOD ABOUT HUMANITY

These reflections upon language provide direction for reflection upon the nature of the Plenitude of Being and Life. Aristotle in his *Metaphysics* spoke of the categories or divisions of being as basically different ways of being. He distinguished ten categories, of which one was substance, the others accidents or attributes of substance. Each substance differed from every other substance; the same was true of the attributes or accidents which divided being between themselves and in relation to substance. Aristotle's concern was to codify what Hindu philosophy would call the differentiated world of names and forms, intending thereby to lead the mind to the supreme instance of being, through relation to which, by a *pros hen* ("to that") analogy, all could be most profoundly unified and comprehended. In this categorical or predicamental sense attributes are by nature limited and differentiated. By their realization in the substance the individual develops or becomes more perfect, that is, participates more of being. There is, of course, no question of such categories being applied to the undifferentiated or Absolute.

There is, however, another sense of attribute, one that is transcendental rather than predicamental or categorical. Such attributes apply to all beings; they are the attributes of being as such. They are not really distinct one from another or from being; they do not add reality to being. Neither are they distinct by what is technically termed a major distinction of the mind as are genera and species, because that would imply some other real composition in being. Rather, each state explicates or "unfolds" the very reality of being, making explicit what was actually but only implicitly stated by the term "being" as that which is. It must be emphasized that they are not additions to being. They are not attributes which are beings, but characteristics of the reality of being as such, stating simply what it means to be. These attributes include unity as stressed by Parmenides and later Plotinus, truth which is found in Aristotle and Augustine, and the good which was central to the main body of Plato's work. They are reflected in the classic Hindu trilogy: *sat, cit, ananda* (existence, consciousness, bliss).

To these as modes of being there are two types of approach. These are not the *a posteriori* and the *a priori* approaches noted above, by which one proceeds along the way to and from God as transcendent. Rather they relate to God as immanent in creation, especially in the human person as his image. Here the two approaches are rather those of theory and practice. The first looks to the nature of the supreme Being, "the life divine" of Aristotle's *Metaphysics* and its attributes of unity, truth and goodness and learns thereby more of the character of finite beings in time. The other looks into the experience of these beings precisely as images of God, that is, as living their freedom in time and thereby constituting history. In this latter, more phenomenological approach one looks into the human consciousness to learn of the wonders of God and his manifestation. The former approach can be neatly structured and clear in its lines of reasoning, though, of course, inexhaustible in meaning. The latter is myriad in the diversity of human experience from which it derives. It calls for aesthetic unification in order to achieve a synthesis or unity, but it speaks immediately to our being and indeed to our personal and social life in time.

What follows will reflect this same order for each transcendental attribute, beginning with the systematic or theoretical approach for reasons of technical clarity and then following with more phenomenological notes in order to bring out the significance of the unity, truth and goodness of God for human life.

In order to develop a systematic list of such attributes, Thomas studied the different types of judgments of existence. If *absolute* or concerned with being itself a judgment can be affirmative: being is being; or negative: being is not shared with non-being, nor is it partially non-being, which, as Parmenides had noted, simply was not. This indivision of being is its unity or oneness: being as such is *one*.

In contrast, judgments of existence can also be *relative*, provided the relation be in terms of reality which is not in principle limited or limiting. For example, to define radio waves in terms of the limited reception of an AM radio would be to understate their extent. For this reason the relations of being must be stated in terms, not of limited physical life, but of the open and unlimited human consciousness or spirit: not of the potter, but of the poet. The relative judgments state the relation of being to spirit as open to all and every being, or to being as such. In relation to the intellect, being can be said to be, not concealed, but positively intelligible or *true*. Further, as the will is sensitive to the value of all being, in relation to will being is said to be desirable or *good*.[15]

As characteristics of being as such, unity, truth, and goodness state or unfold the reality of the incomposite, unparticipated or infinite Being in which they are found absolutely. To make progress in awareness of the absolutely One, True, and Good we may look phenomenologically into our experience of self-identity, knowing, and willing. In doing so, however, we must be sure to remove those elements of composition or potency which mark these spiritual acts as limited in their human realizations.

These notions are not strange to philosophy. As was seen above, Parmenides created metaphysics as a science in terms of Being as One. Aristotle's metaphysics not only culminated in divine life, but understood being entirely as a *pros hen* analogy or relation thereto.[16] Hegel would see theology as a symbolic form of philosophical truths which culminated in unity, truth and the good.

Moreover, religion is a human virtue, a mode of human action which conceives, unfolds, lives and celebrates the sense of life and meaning. Kant's thought provides a place for this at the very center of human freedom and, hence, of human life.

But in a religious vision being is primarily and in principle

- not multiple, limited and changing, but One, unlimited and

eternal;
- not material and potential, but spirit and fullness of Life;
- not obscure and obdurate, but Light and Truth; and
- not inert and subject to external movers, but creative Goodness, Freedom and Love.

This is the foundational Christian and indeed the general sense of being. The work of reason carried out by philosophy in such a culture would be sensitized to look for this — always by natural reason — in the human experience of being and to read human experience in this light. The human person is not, as in Aristotle, the servant of nature, but the image of God. Human life is understood then primarily not in terms of physical change, but of Divine light and love.

Divine light and love, however, are not distant and unreachable. Christ, like Confucius and others, laid down concrete patterns in which this has been lived and experienced by peoples through the centuries. They are classical instances of the traditions in which we are born and from which we receive our trove of self-understanding and our sensibility to others, our ability to conceive our world and to communicate with others in love and concern. Thus, our experience of life lived in these terms as persons and communities provides insight into these three characteristics or properties of being and of God, which in turn enable us better to shape our lives.

This may add something to the Encyclical *Faith and Reason*. In n. 46 it spoke of the relation of revelation and reason as a circle. One begins from revelation and ends up in theology as the deeper and more scientific understanding of revelation. Between these two poles, however, there is philosophy, carried out by the light of reason which works out its principles and draws its conclusions, both of which are universal in import. What is said here does not disagree and would want to stress the autonomy of the human person and the work of human reason. But here we would stress also the impact of the culture, and hence of the religious context, upon the work of reason. For philosophy done in a humanist and individualist culture justice is the supreme value and social ethics and personal moral growth are interpreted in its terms. However, where a religious sense is present and the family and community rather than only the self is the focus, the virtue of love comes forward and becomes the form of all the virtues. This is reflected to some degree in the Encyclical's adversion to the list of essential issues which would not be taken up in philosophy except for its religious context. Chapter X below will attempt to thematize this role of culture in order that it not remain merely contextual to philosophy, but rather contribute importantly to the meaning of philosophy.

If then, philosophy in the Christian context looks not to the material order, but to the divine as its paradigm of reality, in order to unpack the effect of the Christian sense of transcendence upon philosophy we would do well to examine more closely the distinctive characteristics of its divine paradigm. This suggests examining serially the enrichment that the Christian notion of the Trinity brings to the philosophical sense of being, articulated according to its properties of one, true and good. For this the Christian mysteries refer to corresponding divine Persons as source and goal.

We have seen that for the Graeco-Christian philosophical tradition the inner properties of being as such are unity, truth and goodness; and that for Hindu philosophy, the characteristics of the Absolute are expressed in the corresponding, but explicitly living, terms of existence (*sat*), consciousness (*cit*) and bliss (*ananda*). For the Christian, these are not simply characteristics of the divine, but persons related as Father, Son (Word) and Holy Spirit. To gain insight, then, into the impact of the Christian sense of the Transcendent upon the root sense of Being and the metaphysics of freedom, we shall look first to the richness of the unity of being as this appears to human reason in the Christian cultural context of the Transcendent as Father, or in its Hindu correlative as Existence (*sat*). Next, we shall look for the meaning of truth when considered by natural reason in cultures marked by a sense of the Divine Word as Logos and of the Transcendent as consciousness (*cit*). Finally, we will look to the sense of goodness when seen in the context of the Spirit of love proceeding from the Father and Son or in Hindu thought simply as bliss (*ananda*).[17]

Our goal here will not be to define these as properties of being, or *a fortiori* to develop a theology of the Trinity. It will be rather to sample some of the ways in which the Christian cultural context has made possible an enrichment and deepening of the properly philosophical insight into the properties of being and, hence, into the meaning of being both in itself and as lived by God and man. Further, because this religious vision of the Transcendent has been at the center of a people's self-understanding as they have faced the problems of living together in society, it relates as well to social life and the modes of living together in freedom.

Unity

1. *The Nature of Unity.* With the mind thus opened for Absolute Being and a method for allowing its life to be explicated through reflection, it is now possible to sample the nature of the insights which serial systematic reflection of this type can contribute to awareness of the Absolute and of our participation therein.

The first of these explicitations of the Plenitude of perfection is that which Parmenides had stated so forcefully, namely, unity or oneness. As Existence (*sat*) being is undivided, that is, it is in no way non-being: it stands against or out of nothingness (the *ex-sto* of existence). This much must be said of being as such, and hence of any being or any aspect of being. Through an analysis of the participated character of differentiated and composite beings, however, it was possible to open the mind to that Unparticipated Being from which all else derives, and to know that it is not composite but absolutely simple in its internal constitution.[18] As such it is unlimited in perfection and realizes the totality of the perfection of the act of to be; it is the All-perfect, the All-powerful. Further, it does this without division or differentiation, as metaphysics always has insisted. Boethius expressed this classically as perfect self-possession; in contrast to time, he defined eternity as "the perfect and simultaneous possession of limitless life."[19]

We have seen in totem and myth the unitive implications of this for one's relation to one's fellows and to nature. A systematic philosophy of participation develops this understanding by clarifying that the many participated beings are not simply divisions of place in what previously was undifferentiated, for that could mean a simple juxtaposition or contiguity of things. Nor is it merely the type of dependence that obtains between brothers in a family who remain ever related by consanguinity and origin. The formal effect of the participative, creative causality of Being Itself is the constitution of differentiated and participating beings. But this is not merely as individuals in a species, for then the concerns of the species would remain supreme and the individual person could be sacrificed thereto. Rather, the effect of participation as creation is the very being or existence which constitutes the human person indissociably as both unique in oneself and related to all others.

This creative causality continues to be exercised as long as the creatures continue to exist; this is called conservation. Thus, the unity of all participating beings is predicated, not upon a fact of the past, but upon their presently and actually participating in the existence or actuality of the life of the All-perfect. This is ever causally and creatively active in them to the full extent of their being. This is the deeper sense which occasionalism strives to appreciate, but, it would seem, without so adequate a sense of the autonomy of creatures and their proper causality.

2. *A Religious Phenomenology of Unity*. What was said above about matter being caused means that all reality whatsoever in, or of, being is the dynamic expression of that which in itself is simple. This is the "*discretio divina*" or divine dispersion of which Thomas speaks. It constitutes a plurality of participated beings related as contraries among themselves such that the being of one is not that of another. Hence, the two beings together express more of being than either one alone.

Nicholas of Cusa would take this as a principle and it is of the greatest import in our times not only of migration and dispersion of humankind, but of communication and immigration. This creates pluralist national and global societies in which diverse peoples must interact closely. Cusa would point out that their participated character does not constitute them as opposed to each other, but rather as mutually complimentary. If all are to be seen in terms of the whole, now referred to as a "global" perspective, then the "other" pertains to my meaning and intelligibility. Nevertheless, the participants do not constitute more of being than the Absolute itself, but only more beings, more instances of being.

To get our footing here, let us turn again to Parmenides's vision of the One as absolute and infinite in which we live and breathe and have our being. From the very beginnings of Greek philosophy, as the first metaphysician he recognized this unity as a first characteristic of being. In his Poem, he reasoned that in order to stand against the nonbeing or negation implied in the notions of begin ning, limitation or multiplicity, that is, in order simply to be rather than not be, being as such — and, hence, Being Itself — had to be one, eternal and unchanging. Practically all religions recognize these characteristics as belonging to the divine. With Parmenides, they recognize that what is problematic is not how God can be, for being does exist and in the final analysis must be self-sufficient: by definition there is no other reality or being upon which it could depend. What is problematic is rather how it is possible for finite or multiple beings to exist?[20]

Since finite or limited beings do, in fact, exist, their reality must be a participation in the infinite, eternal and unchanging One, the "external" transcendent which they reflect in every facet of their being. It is as sharing in this absolute nature that limited beings are not mere functions of other realities, but subsist in their own right. In making them to be as participations in Himself, the creator makes them to stand in, though not by, themselves, to have a proper identity which is unique and irreducible. This is the foundation of Boethius's classical definition of the person as a *subject* of a rational nature. Inasmuch as they reflect the divine, such beings are unique and unable to be assumed by some larger entity — even by the divine. Because they reflect the Absolute and Transcendent, they exist in their own right.

At the same time, because all limited beings are made to be by the same unique Transcendent Being, the very fact of their participated and individual uniqueness, rather than alienating them, relates them one to another. If to be is to exist in myself as a creature of God, it is identically to be related both to Him and to all other manifestations of His being. In the light of the Transcendent, being means to be radically myself and irreducible to nonbeing — whether this reduction be in the form of my own being, of subjection to another, or of merger as a mere member of a group. By the very same participation in the One divine source and goal of all, to be myself is equally and indissociably to be related to others. One is not compromised, but enhanced by the other; I achieve my highest identity in loving service of others in need.

This, in turn, founds the harmony of nature. It is the reason also, why to live in harmony with nature and other persons is to live fully. Within this harmony it implies, as Jefferson wrote in the "Declaration of Independence": "all men are endowed by their Cre ator with certain inalienable rights, among which are life, liberty and the pursuit of happiness." The task of the social order is not to diminish this or even to grant it, but to recognize, protect and promote it.

Truth

1. *The Nature of Truth.* The second characteristic of being is truth, which in Eastern thought is reflected in the term *cit*. As a characteristic of being as such and hence of any being, it explicates being as open to consciousness or able to be known by intellect. In positive terms being is intelligible, in negative terms it is unconcealed. This much can be known by reflection upon the ability of the intellect to make Parmenides's all englobing judgment: being is, non-being is not. Inasmuch as the intellect can make this judgment about being, being as such must be open to intellect or be intelligible. This is not an adjunct to, but formally includes, the unity of being. What is open to intellect or is intelligible cannot be other than or alongside being in its identity or unity, for then what would be known would not be being, but simply nothing. Truth is not another actuality than being in its unity or identity; it is expression and proclamation — the shout, as it were, of the triumph of being over nothingness.

Further, when this is reflected upon in terms of the participational structures identified above, it becomes evident that the Absolute, incomposite, simple act of existence in which all participate must in undifferentiated identity be at once: (a) agent or subject of intellection or consciousness, (b) power of consciousness, (c) act of consciousness, and (d) object of consciousness. This is but a further explicitation of what is meant by the unity which is the One; it constitutes a simple and subsistent act of knowledge or consciousness — it is Truth Itself.[21] As with *cit* in Eastern thought, it is consciousness without object[22] in the sense of anything distinct from it, on which it would depend and by which it would be determined. This means, not that it is without content or meaning, but that it is meaning itself.

Further, because it is totally self-conscious it perfectly comprehends the full range of the limited states of perfection or combinations of perfections according to which its essence can be imitated in participating beings. Socrates had intuited this pattern of ideas in his search for virtue and Plato recognized the prior ontological reality of ideas. Augustine located these in subsistent Truth. There, Thomas identified its character as exemplar cause after the pattern of which all things are created.[23] Interestingly, the most profound systematic comprehension of its constitution is had through the notion of measurement and the functions of being and non-being therein.[24] It would seem that this notion in some form entered the mind of the author of *Rg Veda*, X, 25, mantra 18, "Who with a cord has measured out the ends of the earth"; which some relate to the *Rg Veda* X 129, mantra 5, "A cord was extended across."[25]

In any case, the Unparticipated as Truth or total lucidity in which all participate for their being is the foundation of the intelligibility of the universe. It is the basis of the conviction that the path of intelligibility is the path of reality and *vice versa*. In that light the discovery of sense or meaning is not a mere intellectual pastime of solitary minds, but the way to share with others more deeply in the real. If so then the rule of reason, especially in the broad sense of wisdom when enriched but not abrogated by love, is the sole rule that is truly humane both in personal and in public life.

2. *A Religious Phenomenology of Truth*. Truth unfolds the unity of being. Unfortunately, too often unity has been seen in terms that are static, reductionist and even commercial. Property, for example, has been looked upon as the right to withhold possessions. Rights have been seen as licenses to turn inward along the lines of an all-consuming egoism of freedom as choice and in terms of my exclusive interests. In that light, my being comes to be looked upon as a possession to be acquired and conserved or, worse still, to be bartered for something of equal quantity or quality.

Were the sense of reality essentially material, the paradigm would be that of blind and senseless atoms colliding randomly and chaotically one with another. Then, the laws of conservation of energy and commercial exchange would dictate that we guard what we have, share it only when we can get equal return and exploit others to the degree possible. In this case, Hobbes's descriptions of man as wolf to man and as short, brutish and mean would not be far from the mark.

In contrast, a culture marked by a sense of outer

Transcendence is quite the opposite. The original and originating instance is being as pure knowledge or, better, Truth. As imminently one and simple, there is in us not so much division as unity between our capabilities and their actuation, between our minds and the ideals they generate. All is one: the infinite capacity is fully actual, the infinite power to know is one with its ideas or insights, the infinite knower is identically the known, i.e., infinite being: in a word, subject and object, mental capacity and mental output are identically the one act of being.

Such a Transcendent is then not so much all-knowing as wisdom or knowledge itself, and, to the degree that knowledge implies a process of achievement or a grasp of something other, it would be more appropriate to speak not of infinite knowledge, but of truth that is all-perfect or Truth Itself. Being is Truth in its prime instance, and, hence, also in each of its participations to the degree that they participate in the One, which is to say, to the full extent of their being.

Being and life then are not dark and hidden, mysterious and foreboding; on the contrary, what light is to our eye, being is to our spirit. Being makes sense to the mind, and, where sufficiently in act, it inevitably "sees" or knows. Primarily, it is subsistent knowledge and truth; by extension it is our limited participations thereof.

Also, as the word is to our tongue, being declares, expresses and proclaims itself; it is Word or Logos and participations thereof. A Christian culture is especially sensitive to this, for in Christian teaching the Word of God is a person and personal, the Son of the God the Father. Through this Word, all things were created. Having become incarnate as Christ, Jesus would say "Whoever has seen me has seen the Father":[26] if you really know me, you know also my Father[27] who spoke me. John, the author of the fourth gospel, said it classically: "That was the true light, which enlighteneth every man that cometh into this world."[28]

One cannot overstress the degree which philosophy, done in a religious context, is sensitized to the intelligibility or truth of being. It gives immediate and special resonance to Parmenides' opening statement upon initiating metaphysics: "Being is; nonbeing is not" and "It is the same thing to think and to be." All being is open, indeed is openness, to intellect; correlatively, what is radically closed to mind simply is not and cannot be.

In the context of the transcendent Truth itself, this resonates vibrantly. Philosophy moves confidently — if not always correctly — to overcome obscurity and fear; science races forward, confident that each step of insight constitutes solid progress in humankind's exploration of the universe; problems are not destructive dilemmas and permanent contradictions, but challenges to be solved, opportunities for new knowledge. The mind thrives in such a context; the creativity of the human genius is invigorated and moves forward.

Further, truth speaks itself as word; indeed it proclaims itself. To attempt to hide the truth would image Cronus in the ancient Greek myths who attempted to swallow his children rather than allow them to enter into the light. This is contrary to the nature of being and as violent as attempting to stop the ocean tide or to force a river to flow upstream; in the long run eventually it must be unsuccessful. Being is fundamentally truth and, hence, openness, manifestation and communication. This is the nature of reality itself and, hence, the key to the self-realization of both individuals and peoples.

In the image of the Son who as Word expresses all that the Father is, and like Logos as the first principle through whom all is created, being is open, expressive and creative. Just as a musician or poet unfolds the many potential meanings of a single theme, so being as truth unfolds its meaning and communicates itself to others. Here, the human intellect plays an essential role by conceiving new possibilities, planning new structures, and working out new paths for humankind in the pilgrimage of life with others. Justice, too, is implied in the sense of true judgments in the public forum about being. Such judgments must honor and express the sacredness of beings in their unity or self-identities and promote their mutual union one with another. This is the essence of the role of leadership in family, business and society.

It was the dark plot of Goebbels to harness the new 20th century technology of communication to a restrictive and hence false ideology in order to create the modern means for mind control. The philosopher's dream is rather that these means can be engaged by the free and enquiring mind in its fascination with truth, communication and cooperation. This is the key to the implementation of a modern democratic society.

Goodness

1. *The Nature of the Good.* The third characteristic of being is goodness, which in Eastern thought is reflected in the term *ananda*. This is a still more explicit affirmation of unity and truth, for what is and is able to be known can also be appreciated in its own perfection and as perfective of others. In this sense being relates to will as being desirable, that is, as good. More directly each being, in its unity as undivided with non-being, seeks and holds to its own being or perfection; in this sense being can be said to be love of its own perfection.

When the unparticipated Plenitude of Being, Unity, and Truth is considered in these terms it can be seen that this Absolute is Goodness Itself. As with Truth, it is the subsistent identity of (a) agent or subject, (b) power or will, (c) act, and (d) object of the act. Thus, the plenitude of perfection is subsistent Goodness or Love itself. This is not desire as would be the love of a perfection which is absent. Rather, it is a perfectly conscious identity with unlimited goodness;[29] hence, it is holiness. As the perfect possession of this goodness, it is also its enjoyment; that is, it is bliss or *ananda*.

In this explicitation of the unparticipated, incomposite Being there is also to be found the intelligibility of the creative or participative character of the Absolute. Note that what is sought is intelligibility, not necessity. From Plotinus through Spinoza to Hegel, philosophers sought for a necessary and hence necessitating understanding of the creative act itself. They succeeded only in generating a vision neither of human freedom nor of Absolute and Unconditioned being. For to attain such a goal they made the effect to be necessary rather than free, and the source to be dependent upon its effects for its perfection rather than self-sufficient. What should be sought is not a necessitating reason for the Absolute's creativity, but only intelligibility for actively participating or sharing its perfection.

We saw that Truth Itself comprehends the order of possible being, that is, all the ways in which the simple Plenitude of perfection can be imitated or shared by differentiated being. Subsistent Love, blissfully rejoicing in its goodness, perceives therein the idea of a possible universe, with all the ways it has of sharing in being, life and goodness. This provides the sufficient but non-compelling reason.

"It is a gift that deserves to be given." Its causality is predicated, not upon a need, a lack, or a desire in the All-perfect, but upon "the gracious will to share, chosen in perfect freedom."[30]

Participating beings are known and loved by the same act of Knowledge and Love by which the One knows and loves itself.[31] They do not measure Absolute Truth, but are known as sharing therein; neither are they loved as ends in themselves, but as ordered to Goodness or Love Itself. In the orders of both final and efficient causality creatures come to be on account of the Absolute Goodness; they are "ordered or directed to this goodness as to be received or participated in."[32] The life of each person is thus an echo of, or a participation in, Subsistent Love. If lived well each life should be in harmony with others and with nature, all of which are participations in that same Love. Even more, as an imitation of that Love by which one is loved, one can know that one's life is to be lived in terms of sharing with others, rather than of holding to oneself. This, rather than merely the avoidance of the suffering which would inevitably follow any opposite course, is both the reason and the means for avoiding *karma* or grasping. Finally, a philosophy of participation can aid one to understand that life lived in imitation of creative Love will bring oneself and others into that same Love which, having been the Alpha, must be also the Omega of all.

2. *A Religious Phenomenology of the Good.* Such goodness as the third property of being corresponds in the Christian Trinity to the Holy Spirit as the love of Father and Son. It expresses the conjunction and fulfillment of unity and truth in celebration of the perfection of being or, where imperfect, in the search for that perfection or fulfillment. Holiness is precisely this devoted holding by being to its perfection or goodness where possessed or its search when not yet attained.

Further, as Being Itself is absolute and eternally self-sufficient, and hence has no need for other beings, it creates not out of need, but out of love freely given. This transforms the understanding of human life, which can now be seen to be not merely freedom to choose, to gather and accumulate; or statically to maintain, repeat or conserve; nor even as with Kant the ability to do as we ought. Rather, it is freedom of self-determination, whereby we can "change our own character creatively by deciding for ourselves what we shall do or should become."[33] This may be closer to Confucius's original sense of harmony as a dynamic interrelation of multiple and changing units. If so, it would be also the role of peacemaker in the image of the "Prince of Peace."

Yves Simon summarizes some implications of this for human freedom. He points out that it is based, not in the indeterminism of freedom as mere choice, for that would face the will with the impossible task of deriving something from nothing. Rather, human freedom is the result of a supradeterminism.[34] That is, because the human intellect and will are open to the infinite One, the original Truth and Good, the human person through thought and will can respond to any limited participated good whatsoever, yet without being necessitated thereby. In this lies the essence of freedom: as liberated from determining powers, whether internal or external, the will is autonomous; at the same time it is positively oriented toward the good and its realization in all circumstances and in limitless ways. This is the positive attraction of beauty and harmony; it is the vital source for the human creativity of which Confucius spoke and about which Kant wrote in his *Critique of the Aesthetic Judgement*.

Still more dynamically, the originating Transcendent Spirit implies that being is transforming, innovating and creative. Received as gift, our life must in turn be passed on by sharing it with others in love. Even death — whether analogously through suffering in the image of the cross or physically at the end of one's days — does not overwhelm, but becomes a way to new life. The Apostle Paul expressed well the combination of irreducible confidence and indomitable hope implied by this sense of life lived in the context of the Absolute and Transcendent:

> We have this treasure in earthen vessels, to show that the transcendent power belongs to God and not to us. We are afflicted in every way, but not crushed; perplexed, but not driven to despair; persecuted, but not forsaken; struck down, but not destroyed; always carrying in the body the death of Jesus, so that the life of Jesus may also be manifested in our bodies (*II Cor.* 4:7-10).

A philosophy of the person as image of this transcendent divine principle, lived in a cultural context sensitized by the dynamic Trinitarian interrelations of persons, transforms the philosophical sense of the person in the world. One remains part of nature, but rather than being subject thereto as a mere producer or consumer, one is a creative and transforming center, responsible for the protection and promotion of nature. Similarly, one is by nature social and a part of society; but rather than being subject thereto as an object, one is its creative center and must be an integral part of all decision making.

The movements of freedom in this half century reflect the emergence of new understanding of human dignity, equality, and participation in the socio-political process. This heightened sense of the dignity of the person and the search for adequate foundations for democracy naturally have generated new interest in religion. There, in the image of the Trinity, the three characteristics of being stand out in human life. First, self-affirmation is no longer simply a choice of one or another type of object or action as a means to an end, but a radical self-affirmation within Existence Itself. Second, self-consciousness is no longer simply self-directed after the manner of Aristotle's absolute "knowing on knowing"; rather, the Absolute Truth knows all that it creates as being a reflection of its own being, truth and goodness. The participating instances of self-awareness image this by transcending themselves in relation to others. Finally, this new human freedom is an affirmation of existence as sharing in Love Itself, that is, in the creative and ultimately attractive divine life — or in Indian terms, "bliss" (*ananda*).

This new sense of being and freedom in the context of a culture marked by the Christian mysteries reflects the meaning of the Transcendent for man and of man. This culture is based in Christ's death and Resurrection to new life; hence, Christian baptism is a death to the slavery of selfishness and a rebirth to a new life of service and celebration with others. Being is a gift or divine grace, but no less a radically free option for life on our part.

Philosophically, this new life of freedom means, of course, combating evil in whatever form: hatred, injustice and prejudice — all are privations of the good that should be. However, the focus of being, seen from our path to the Transcendent is not upon negations, but upon giving birth to the goodness of being and bringing this to a level of human life marked by an enriched harmony of beauty and love.

In summarizing his exposition of the cosmology of the *Rg Veda*, Radhakrishnan concludes: "We see clearly that there is no basis for any conception of the unreality of the world in the hymns of the *Rg Veda*. The world is not a purposeless phantasm, but is just the evolution of God."[35] Above we have seen the way in which a systematic philosophy can analyze and develop further this theme. It elaborates the distinction of the composite and differentiated being from the incomposite and undifferentiated being, but it avoids duality inasmuch as the very being or existing of the composite beings which constitute the differentiated universe is nothing other than the participation — the sharing and manifesting — of That One. Further, it enters into the Absolute in order to learn more of that Wisdom and Love which is the Plenitude of perfection, unsublatable and creative.

CONCLUSION

By way of conclusion to this study of a systematic Christian philosophy as a way to God it may serve to remark briefly upon the reality of the participants, the nature of the cause, and the task for a systematic philosophy.

1. Thomas studied the reality of the differentiated universe in his *Summa contra Gentiles* written for missionaries to Islam. One such school of theology, the *Mutakallim* had attempted to affirm the power of the Absolute by holding the unsubstantiality of creatures. They claimed that creatures could not themselves cause, but were mere occasions for the creative action of the Absolute, indeed, that creatures ceased to exist at each moment and had continually to be recreated. Etienne Gilson points out that no point is argued by Thomas with more passion.[36] In the light of his participational insight the Absolute creator was not being affirmed, but denied, by the reduction or elimination of the reality or active power of its creatures. Thomas repeatedly returns to this theme in his chapters on "The True First Cause of the Distinction of Things" and "On the Opinion of Those Who Take Away Any Proper Actions from Natural Things."[37] It should be noted that in these chapters he is not arguing for the reality of multiplicity as a simple chaos of

different and clashing beings. What he is asserting is the reality of an ordered unity, the sharing of the One in a graded and interactive order of individuals, species, and genera. In other words, he is carrying forward Aristotle's view of a universe of beings which, acting according to their proper natures, imitate, each in its own manner, the unity and perfection of "That One" which is the plenitude of perfection or perfection itself.

Because causing is a sharing, not a loss, of perfection — as can be seen best in the work of the poet — the effect is some degree of likeness to the cause. Due to the essentially limited character of any one composite being, the divine intention to share limitless perfection provides sufficient intelligibility for the creation not of one only, but of a great multitude of beings, each of a different form from the other. Further, it explains why these beings should be not inert, but active; and how by their interaction they form an intensive unity which the more munificently shares in, and proclaims, the perfection and power of its source. By not only being, but sharing its being, creation manifests the power of its source; by its complex order creation manifests the wisdom of its origin; by the good of its order, which contributes to the well-being of all, it manifests the Love that is its source.[38]

2. This development of the systematic structure of the metaphysics of Thomas Aquinas generally has used not the term "God," but the terms "Absolute," "That One," and the like to state the Plenitude of being and perfection in which all participate. This was done in order both to illustrate and to test the conviction that the real content of a so-called "theistic metaphysics" is not incompatible with, but dependent upon and indeed coterminous with, the One that is articulated in terms of the Absolute. The oft supposed opposition between the so-called God of the philosophers and the God of revelation and scripture would appear to be predicated upon an inadequate understanding of either one or both terms.

Unfortunately, the term 'God' and the theism predicated thereupon are subject to the continual recurrence of the destructive anthropomorphic tendencies which had overtaken the Greek myth in the days of Xenophanes. A.C. Bose gives a more recent list of such tendencies in the introduction to his *Call of the Vedas*. A monotheistic God must, he thinks, be masculine, a father, patriarch and king, who lives in a particular place and is locked in combat with an anti-God.[39] This is reflected in the notion of divine action after the pattern of a despot, against which Spinoza wrote in his *Ethics*. All such notions imply limitation, for they situate the divine within a set of contrary notions each of which, being distinct from its contrary, implies limitation. Such limitations require the correction which is expressed by the notion of the Absolute articulated in a philosophy of participation as the incomposite and subsistent Plenitude of Being.

Conversely, the term 'absolute' also has its vicissitudes. In order to protect this from limitation, affirmations of its positive perfection are at times denied, leaving in the final analysis an impersonal essence expressed in double negatives ungrounded in positive affirmation. A systematic metaphysics of participation concludes instead to the Absolute as supreme, indeed, subsistent being, the plenitude of perfection.

We saw the purification of the transcendental characteristics of being by removing from them all elements of limitation such as seeing their constitution as a composite of a limiting essence with their existence. When conjoined with reasoning from participating beings to the Plenitude in which they share, this manifested the Absolute to be Unity, Truth, and Goodness. If being in whatever degree is unique, knowing, and loving, then being which is subsistent Unity, Knowledge, and Love must be personal above all.

It was seen also that unity, truth, or goodness are explications of what is actually but only implicitly stated by being. Hence, they carry no implication of limitation or contrariety. The same must be said of identity, knowledge, or love which are the characteristics of the person. They are as open as is the meaning of existence itself, which each of these affirms in a progressively more explicit manner. Consequently, as such, "person" is not a closed or contrary notion, but is open as is truth and love. The more perfect the person, the more it is open and sharing; the more personal the communication the more it is able to be shared without diminution of its source. Again our paradigm is God, the subsistent Person (which theology would elaborate as triune) who, without loss, is the sharing of love, truth, and being itself.

Of such being, Absolute and personal, the term God is appropriately predicated. Jaeger says of the pre-Socratics, "The predicate

God, or rather divine, is transferred from the traditional deities to the first principle of Being (at which they arrived by rational investigation), on the ground that the predicates usually attributed to the gods of Homer and Hesiod are inherent in that principle to a higher degree or can be assigned to it with greater certainty."[40] The same is true of the Absolute in the thought of Thomas at the juncture of the Platonic, Aristotelian, and Christian traditions.

This is not to say that humans have a comprehensive knowledge of God, or indeed of any existent; nor is it meant to imply that they can grasp the unique way in which God exists — the eminent and proper mode of deity. Neither of these is within human capabilities. But it does question the common assumption that there is an opposition, rather than a necessary identity, between the notion of the Absolute and that of the Personal God. In the systematic philosophy of Thomas they are identical and indispensable one to the other. Today, when our awareness of the meaning of person is subject equally to great threat and to development, this is perhaps the most creative element in the metaphysics of the religious traditions.

3. Taken together the two prior considerations generate a paradox for the human mind and suggest the importance of the work of philosophy. The first conclusion concerned the reality of the participated and differentiated universe, including humanity: both are from God as their origin and toward God as their goal. The second conclusion concerned the absolute character of God as the unparticipated, undifferentiated and incomposite. The conjunction of the two indicates that paradoxically both humans and their universe are directed toward that which definitively transcends them.

It is the task of a metaphysics of participation to resolve this paradox, not by eliminating the reality of either the composite or the incomposite, but by uniting them in their affirmation of being. Reality acts according to its nature and can share only what it is, for, as Parmenides notes, to derive being from non-being is an all impossible way.[41] Thus, the effect of the causality of the incomposite being, whose essence or nature is precisely existence or to be, is the existence or act of being of its creatures. In other words, it is precisely because of the definitive transcendence of the divine as the unique, subsistent Being that God is present to us in his very essence, causing by his power our being. In this light, two conclusions follow. Because our essence is distinct from our existence, as is the case for all composite beings, it can truly be said that God is more present to us than we are to ourselves. Further, because His immanence is in proportion, rather than in tension, with his transcendence, it is more proper to say, not that God is in us who participate in Him, but that we exist in God.

This vision has been the well-spring of the world's Scriptures. The Hebrew and Christian Scriptures express the transcendence in terms of heaven. The *Vedas* point especially to that which is within. Both say that God is beyond all and that one must lose oneself in order to find Him. As lived, it has been the basis of the great schools of asceticism, of Sufism and of the Yoga developed in India and greatly admired by those engaged in the spiritual quest the world over.[42]

This must stand also as a test for every philosopher, drawing one beyond the successes of one's system and urging one ever forward to more adequate awareness of the infinite correlation of Transcendence and Immanence. This is the eminently worthwhile task; it will ever challenge and elicit the combined efforts of mankind.

Dasgupta summarized the vision of the *Upanishads* as follows:

> In spite of regarding Brahman as the highest reality, they could not ignore the claims of the exterior world and had to accord a reality to it. The inconsistency of this reality of the phenomenal world with the ultimate and only reality of Brahman was attempted to be reconciled by holding that this world is not beside him but it has come out of him, it is maintained in him and it will return back to him.[43]

Every philosophical system must ask whether it or any other has succeeded in taking full account of, and giving definitive expression to, all the elements in that rich statement of the common patrimony of humankind. If the answer is "yes" then our philosophic work is completed. If not then in this age of science and technology, of rapid development of society and person, the philosophy department should be the most exciting place in the university. For it is there that one can reach most deeply into one's heritage to retrieve meaning long since forgotten. There also, and in concert with other metaphysical systems in the heritage of mankind, one is invited to evolve the more ample systematic vision of that participation in Plenitude required in our increasingly complex times for the communion of men in God.

NOTES

1. M. Iqbal, *Reconstruction of Religious Thought in Islam*, ed. M. Saeed Sheikh (Lahore, Pakistan: Iqbal Academy and Institute of Islamic Culture, 1989).

2. *Ibid.*, p. 32.

3. Fabro, *La nozione metafisica di partecipazione*, secondo S. Tommaso d'Aquino (Torino: Societa Ed. Internazionale, 1950).

4. *Ibid.*

5. Thomas Aquinas, *Summa theologica* (New York: Benziger, 1947), I, q. 2, aa. 2-3; *Summa contra Gentiles*, trans. by A. Regis (New York: Hanover House, 1955), II, 10-21.

6. See note 3 above.

7. *Summa contra Gentiles*, II, 16; *Summa Theologica*, I, qq. 11 and 14; *On the Power of God* (Westminster Md: Newman Press, 1952), q. 3, a. 1 ad 12; and *Truth*, trans. by R. W. Mulligan et al. (Chicago: Regnery, 1952-1954), q. 2, a. 5.

8. Maurice Nedoncelle, "Person and/or World as the Source of Religious Insight," in George F. McLean, ed., *Traces of God in a Secular Culture* (New York: Alba House, 1973), pp. 187-209.

9. *Genesis* I:31.

10. Gerald Stanley, "Contemplation as Fulfillment of the Human Person," in George F. McLean, ed., *Personalist Ethics and Human Subjectivity*, vol. II of *Ethics at the Crossroads* (Washington, D.C.: The Council for Research in Values and Philosophy, 1995), appendix.

11. *I John* 2-3.

12. Mt 5:20-37.

13. George F. McLean, "Symbol and Analogy: Tillich and Thomas," *Revue de l'Université d'Ottawa*, XXVIII (1958), 193-233, reprinted in *Paul Tillich in Catholic Thought*, T. O'Meara and D. Weisser, eds. (New York: Doubleday, 1969), pp. 195-240.

14. *Summa Theologica*, I, q. 13.

15. *Truth*, qq. 1 and 21.

16. Joseph Owens, *The Doctrine of Being in the Aristotelian Metaphysics: A Study in the Greek Background of Mediaeval Thought* (Toronto: PINS, 1951).

17. Raimundo Panikkar, *The Unknown Christ of Hinduism: Toward an Ecumenical Christophany* (New York: Orbis, 1981).

18. *Summa Theologica*, 1, qq. 3 and 11.

19. *De consolatione philosophiae*, trans. by H.R. James (New York: New University Library, 1906), 5, 6.

20. See Parmenides; see also Shankara, *Commentary on the Vedanta Sutras*, Introduction.

21. *Truth*, qq. 1-8; *Summa Theologica*, 1, qq. 14 and 16.

22. Keith, p. 437.

23. *Summa Theologica*, 1, q. 15.

24. T. Kondoleon, "Exemplarism," *New Catholic Encyclopedia*, V, 712-15. See also *On the Power of God*, q. 3, a. 16 ad 5 and *Summa Theologica*, 1, q. 15, a2.

25. A.A. MacDonell, *A Vedic Reader* (Oxford: At the Clarendon Press, 1917) p. 210.

26. John 14:1-12.

27. *Ibid.*

28. John I:9.

29. *Truth*, q. 21; *Summa Theologica*, 1, qq. 19 and 20, a.1.

30. John Wright, "Divine Knowledge and Human Freedom: The God Who Dialogues," *Theological Studies*, XXXVIII (1977), 455.

31. *Summa Contra Gentiles*, 1, 76.

32. Wright, p. 464.

33. Mortimer J. Adler, *The Idea of Freedom: A Dialectical Examination of the Conceptions of Freedom* (Garden City, N.Y.: Doubleday, 1958), I, 606.

34. Yves R. Simon, *Freedom of Choice*, P. Wolff, ed. (New York: Fordham Univ. Press, 1969), p. 106.

35. Radhakrishnan, I, 103.

36. E. Gilson, *Elements of Christian Philosophy* (Garden City, NJ: Doubleday, 1960), pp. 189-93.

37. *Summa Contra Gentiles*, II, 45 and III-I, 69.

38. *Ibid.*, III-I, 69, 16 and II, 45, 7-8.

39. Abinash Bose, *The Call of the Vedas* (Bombay: Bharatiya

Vidya Bhavan, 1970), pp. 19-21, 30.

    40. Jaeger, pp. 31, 203-206.

    41. McLean and Aspell, *Readings*, p. 40, frs, 2, 6, 7.

    42. Abhishiktananda, *Saccidānanda: A Christian Approach to Advaitic Experience* (Delhi: ISPCK, 1974), pp. 30-34, 64-65.

    43. Surendranath Dasgupta, *A History of Indian Philosophy* (Delhi: Motilal Banarsidass, 1975), I, 51.

CHAPTER VII

AL-GHAZĀLĪ AND MULLA SADRA:
Islamic Mystical and Existential Ways to God

We saw above the elaboration of the ways opened by Greek philosophy by the discover by the Christian Father of the existential character of being (Chapter V) and the systematic elaboration of this insight in the high Middle Ages by Thomas Aquinas (Chapter VI). Islam faced similar issues, which it resolved in its own way and with its special resources.

The Islamic figures, al-Farabi and Ibn Sina, who redeveloped the Greek philosophical tradition did not appear to provide adequately for the sense of human freedom and eschatology found in the *Qur'ān*. Hence, al-Ghazālī, as we shall see below, turned away from philosophy to follow the mystical Sufi way. Some have considered this to be the end of the Islamic philosophical tradition ignoring thereby the intensive philosophical tradition evolved in Persia and further east by such towering figures as Mulla Sadra. His work constitutes a veritable summa of that tradition. It is unified in terms of being understood not through essence, but through existence, albeit in a neo-Platonic rather than the Aristotelian pattern of Thomas Aquinas. Here we shall look at these two archetypic Islamic mystical and existential ways to God.

I. AL-GHAZĀLĪ'S MYSTICAL WAY TO GOD

To grasp the thought of al-Ghazālī we need to retrace our steps a bit at this point from the 13th to the 12th century, from Thomas Aquinas to al-Ghazālī. This is not a thematic reversal, however, for by that time the tradition of Greek philosophy had already been developed with outstanding success by such Islamic philosophers as al-Farabi, Avicenna and Averroes. Indeed these three provided a great deal of the Aristotelian interpretation on which Thomas and the later Scholastics were to build.

However, in the midst of what, in these terms, was great success, al-Ghazālī judged that a different way was needed. This was due in part to the limitations of the Greek mind, which Thomas too would need to combat in Paris where they reemerged in the form of the so-called Latin Averroism. More broadly, however, it reflected also the dissatisfaction with philosophy expressed by M. Iqbal in his *Reconstruction of Religious Thought*.

For Iqbal, making man at home in the world might be a proper task for "metaphysics . . . (as) a logically consistent view of the world with God as part of that view." But he sees another stage in which

> metaphysics is displaced by psychology, and religious life develops the ambition to come into direct contact with the ultimate reality. It is here that religion becomes a matter of personal assimilation of life and power; and the individual achieves a free personality, not by releasing himself from the fetters of the law, but by discovering the ultimate source of the law within the depths of his own consciousness.[1]

Iqbal would probably be very interested in recent developments in phenomenology. For him,

> the aspiration of religion soars higher than that of philosophy. Philosophy is an intellectual view of things; and as such, does not care to go beyond a concept which can reduce all the rich variety of experience to a system. It sees Reality from a distance as it were. Religion seeks a closer contact with Reality. The one is theory; the other is living experiences, association, intimacy. In order to achieve this intimacy thought must rise higher than itself, and find its fulfillment in an attitude of mind which religion describes as prayer — one of the last words on the lips of the Prophet of Islam.[2]

It was to this sensibility that al-Ghazālī turned his entire concentration. For a people to turn from the path of reason with its scientific capabilities to a mystical way, to choose the path of contemplation over that of reasoning, has great and lasting implications for the broad processes of modernization. Focused rather on pragmatic and utilitarian reason as an approach to life in this world, modernity has presented many challenges, not least to Islam in its fidelity to God above all else.

There can be little doubt, however, about the preeminence among the ways to God of al-Ghazālī's mystical approach. It points beyond science alone to the further reaches of the human spirit to which many other cultures only now are becoming sensitive. And it does this in ways that can contribute to the construction of a culture which goes beyond negative critique of the world to the positive and constructive thrust of the global.

To follow the history of the rich development of that long tradition is beyond the scope of this work. As our goal here is to identify the multiple ways to God it may be sufficient to focus on that fork in the road at which Islam took a decisive step toward a mystical path. In this chapter we shall see how al-Ghazālī describes it in his *al-Munqidh min al-dalāl* with special attention to the epistemological and metaphysical issues this involved.

THE CONTEXT

In order to understand a person's life usually it is helpful to know something of his or her social, political and cultural contexts. How important this is depends, on the one hand, upon theoretical considerations and, on the other hand, upon the person him or herself. The theoretical issue is the extent to which a person is to be understood in terms either of interiority or of openness and relation to others. Deep reflection suggests that the degree of one's interiority and reflective self-possession is the key to one's ability to relate to others with that free and passionate sense of justice which is the fruit of love.

This is important for a personal history. Without this balanced sense of the person, on the one hand, a life would be interpreted simply in terms of external events or of powerful political authorities, in relation to which the individual is but a marionette. Worse still, any claim to personal and free decision making would be interpreted as fraud or disobedience. On the other hand, that same life could be interpreted in a simply self-reflective manner, reducing it to egoistic self-seeking. This would miss the significance of personal and reli gious interiority for the life of society as a whole.

All of this is especially true in the concrete case of al-Ghazālī who lived at the center of an intensely religious culture, the understanding and development of which was his central concern and major accomplishment. D.B. MacDonald described him as "The greatest, certainly the most sympathetic figure in the history of Islam, and the only teacher of the later generations ever put by a Muslim on a level with the four great Imams." For W.M. Watt "al-Ghazālī has sometimes been claimed in both East and West as the greatest Muslim after Muhammad, and he is by no means unworthy of that dignity." To H.A.R. Gibb he was "a man who stands on a level with Augustine and Luther in religious insight and intellectual vigor."[3]

To see the socio-political, indeed the geo-cultural, context in its true perspective it is helpful to take up the suggestion of Marshal G. Hodgson, at the beginning of his *The Venture of Islam: Conscience and History in a World Civilization*.[4] He argues effectively that to understand not only Islam, but world, civilization it is necessary to break free from Eurocentrism. In the Middle Ages the central drama of world civilization was not being played out in the small kingdoms of Western and Southern Europe. Rather it consisted in the emergence of Islam in confrontation with Byzantium, and from the Nile to the Oxus, where the Irano-Semitic culture is found. In this context, the Roman Empire and Western Christianity shrink in relation to the importance of the emergence of Islam to the East.

Prior to al-Ghazālī Islam had undergone an explosive development. After the life of the Prophet Muhammad 570-632 A.D., it expanded with remarkable swiftness within 100 years across Africa to Spain in the West and far to the East. The unity of religious and social authority in Muhammad and in the Islamic community faced heavy challenges during the second century of Islam when the spiritual authority of the Caliph was submerged by the military, and hence political, power of the Sultans. The early orthodox Caliphate of 'Uthmân and others was succeeded by the Umayyad caliphate and this, in turn, by the 'Abbāsid caliphate. Al-Ghazālī lived during the later, declining period of this caliphate (1058-1111 A.D., or the years 450-505 A.H. counting from Muhammad's Hegira or trek from Mecca to Medinà).

The guard of the Abbāsid Caliphs, which was drawn from

foreign, especially Turkish, elements, assumed the real political power. They were replaced by the Persian Buwayhid from 945-1055, who were replaced in turn for a century by the Turkish Seljoukides, when the Caliph al-Qā'im, recognized Toghrul Beg as Sultan in Baghdad. This began a line which for a century would rule the vast expanse from the Mediterranean to Afghanistan.

During this time, which was that of al-Ghazālī, a strong attempt was underway by the Fatimides of Egypt to supplant the sunnite Abbāsid Caliphs in order to assume the religious and political leadership of all Islam. Claiming to be descendants of Ali the successor of Muhammad, and of Fatima his daughter, they brought together the Shi'ite Alides and conquered North Africa, with Cairo as their capital. Their intent was to dominate Iraq, Syria, Khorasan and the entire Abbāsid empire. To this end Hassan b Sabbāh, founder of *Batinism ta'limīte*, a new form of Ismaélism, sent emissaries against the sunnite Moslems.

Among these there were assassins whose most famous victims were Nizam al-Mulk, Wazir to Sultan Malikshāh, and his son, Fakhr al-Mulk. It had been the custom of the learned Nizam al-Mulk to have among his court a group of famous jurists and theologians. By teaching Shafé'ism and Ash'arism they provided a counterforce against the Shi'ism of the Fātimides in favor of the sunnite Abbasids and the Seljoukides. To this end al-Mulk founded many schools, led by that in Baghdad. It was precisely as director of this school that he appointed al-Ghazālī in 484/1091. In the religio-political complex of Islam at that time, this was the critical post.

LIFE OF Al-GHAZĀLĪ

The earliest biography of al-Ghazālī is by 'Abd al-Ghāfir al-Fārisī[5] who knew personally "Muhammad son of Muhammad son of Muhammad Abū Hāmid al-Ghazālī." Al-Ghazālī was born in Tūs (450/1058) and began his studies in *fiqh* (Islamic law) there in the school of Rādkāna. He then moved to Forjān under Abu'l-Qāsim al-Ismā'īli. Finally he became an outstanding student at Nîshāpūr under, among others, al-Juwayni, sunnite Imām al-Haramayn. His studies included law, jurisprudence, dialectics, religion and logic, reading works on *hikma* and *falāsifa*.

After some time he experienced a distaste for the abstract

sciences and turned toward the Sufi religious approach under Fāramdhī, (died 477), one of the most famous shaykhs of the time. Though he followed the religious practices of cult and ejaculatory prayer and overcame obstacles, he did not achieve the religious experiences he sought, so he returned to the abstract sciences.

In epistemology he held all proofs to be equally valid, which left him bemired in casuistry. This made him a brilliant dilettante, but without bases for certitude regarding the three great truths, namely, the existence of God, the last judgment, and prophecy. *Fiqh* does not justify these fundamental beliefs, but supposes them. Al-Ghazālī excelled in reasoning (*anzar*) and argumentation and early began to write his own works. But this dilettantism may have been the reason why his famous teacher, al-Juwayni, came to be somewhat put off by the brilliant but aggressive argumentation of his student.

Upon the deaths of Fāramdhī and of al-Juwayni in 478 his education was complete. He was the major heir to the cultural tradition of his native Khorāsān, which excelled in both thought and Sufi religious experience. Soon he joined Nizām al-Mulk at his 'Askar or military-political base. There he brought together in brilliant discussion the many visiting leading ulemas, imams and men of letters so that his fame spread widely. At 34 he was appointed by Nizām head of the Nizāmiyya School in Baghdad, which he led with great distinction for the four years, 484-488 (1091-1095).

At the beginning he was still the brilliant dilettante. Much later, from the position of a mature wisdom and holiness, he would apologize for the arrogance with which he pursued argumentation in that earlier, less mature period, when his search was motivated by the pursuit of honor and fame.

Fārisī reports that at the Nizāmiyya he undertook important study in three major directions. He researched the science of the roots or sources of jurisprudence (*'ilm al-usūl*); he redeveloped the school of Shāfi'ite jurisprudence; and he carried forward *al-khilāf* or comparative jurisprudence. On all of these he wrote works and acquired surpassing fame and an entourage.

This attention to sciences concerned with the concrete and the practical,[6] suggests Jabre, gave him the illusion of standing on solid ground and contributing to the realization and defence of a human-divine kingdom in this life. He had joined Nizām al-Mulk in his battle against the threat of *Ta'limism* as a new form of Shi'ite bātinism which stressed the essential importance of the teaching of the Immam. It was a different line of succession going back to very early Muslim times.

This effort received a shattering blow on 10 Ramadan 485/ 1092 when Nizām al-Mulk, Wazir or Prime minister of the Seljoukide Sultan and patron of al-Ghazālī, was assassinated by a young Bātinite, as would the son of Nizām, Fakhr al-Mulk, fifteen years later in 500/1107.

According to abū Bakr ibn'al-'Arabī it was early the next year (486/1093-1094) that al-Ghazālī underwent a definitive conversion to Sufism and turned from the sciences of things here below to those of the hidden, transcendent aspects of religion. The character and content of this conversion is the centerpiece of the *Munqidh*. It is no exaggeration to say that all else in the book was chosen and ordered precisely in order to explain that conversion and the new dimension of knowledge which was opened to him by the Way of the Sufis.

It is not possible to say what weight the political facts of his day, particularly the assassination of Nizām, had on the conversion of al-Ghazālī. He himself does not refer to them in the *Munqidh*. There he restricts himself to describing the different approaches to knowledge or religion proposed by others and his own thorough investigation and critique of them. By systematically excluding them he points to the Way of the Sufis as the sole remaining speculative alternative. Moreover, by distinguishing theory and practice he drew the implication that it was necessary to move beyond speculation to a higher level of experience which provides its own positive warranty.

Some would want to hold only to his own spiritual experience and suggest that the fear which he mentions at this time was not fear of a fate similar to that of Nizām, but a fear of God which is the beginning of wisdom.[7] This would seem to separate al-Ghazālī from the circumstances of his time in which — in view of the role of the conflict of sunnite vs shi'ite theology as the coordinating matrices of the conflicting temporal regimes — he was centrally engaged.

Further, this position violently separates soul from body to focus entirely upon the disincarnate mind. But it is no derogation of the soul and its spiritual journey to place it firmly in matter or body, time or history. That one learns true values by reflecting on the death of others or upon the circumstances which threaten one's life is as common an occurrence as taking part in a burial or even visiting a hospital. It is not surprising then that his earlier attempt to practice Sufism was taken up once again by al-Ghazālī and with renewed vigor. His sincerity in this is testified by the decade-long ascetic retreat which he would soon take up and which he would never really abandon.

In the *Munqidh* he writes at length on a long debate within himself about making a definitive break with his present life of honor and adulation by students and leaders. Did this begin from the death of Nizām or, as would seem more probable, had it begun before, been catalyzed by the death of Nizām, and come to a conclusive decision in 486 AH. If so was the subsequent time in Baghdad concerned only with tactics for carrying out his decision to leave his post there?

At any rate, in 488/1095 he left Baghdad as part of a plan to definitively abandon his post there and the country as a whole, while explaining only that he intended to make the pilgrimage to Mecca. He wandered as a hermit in Damascus, Jerusalem, Hebron (and possibly Alexandria) for nearly two years. During that time he made the 489/1095-1096, pilgrimage to Mecca. Ibn'al-'Arabī reports seeing him in Baghdad in Jumāda 489/1095-1096, engaged in teaching, investigating the doctrines of the philosophers and writing. If he is correct about that date, later that year al-Ghazālī made a definitive break from Baghdad. By 491, or 492/1094 at the latest, he returned to his home in Tūs where he lived a life of prayer, worship, meditation and study.

This retreat lasted some ten years when the son of Nizām al-Mulk, Fakhr al-Mulk, who was trying to lay down a firm line of defence against *Bātinism ta'limite*, summoned him to return once again to his earliest teaching post at Nîshāpur.

At this point, al-Ghazālī reports, he was coming to the conclusion that, due to the pervasive corruption in society, interior prayer was not enough; to it the work of teaching must be added. The invitation added an external impetus to his interior inclinations, and he took up his teaching once again in 499/1106. This was to be of short duration, for the following year Fakhr al-Mulk too was assassinated. Soon al-Ghazālī returned to his home in Tūs. There at the side of his house he built a school for teaching *fiqh*, which always had been his main area of teaching, as well as a Sufi monastery for those in search of prayer, spiritual learning and ascetic practice. Al-Ghazālī himself undertook for the first time intensive study of *hadīth* or the traditions regarding the prophet. He continued writing till his very last days and passed away on Monday 14 Jumāda II, 505/1111.

WORKS

The writings of al-Ghazālī, like that of many great thinkers of his day, are very vast, both in breadth and in overall length. A few notes on the categories of his works might convey some sense of their scope.[8]

1. *The Islamic Sciences of Fiqh and Kalām*: *fiqh* was the center of his teaching and some of his writing in this field remain classics to the present day. On Kalām his only work is *al-Iqtisād fi l-I'tiqād* (*The Golden Mean of Belief*), which is a fine summary of its main theological questions. He seemed to place little trust in Kalām or apologetic theology. Indeed, his very last work was *Iljām al-'Awāmm 'an al-khawd fi 'Ilm al-Kalām* (*Restricting the Masses from Engaging in the Science of Kalām*).

2. *Against Bātinism*: combatting Bātinism, especially the Ta'līmites, was a major political and cultural campaign of the time. al-Ghazālī played a central role in the intellectual dimension of this effort by his teaching and through a number of sharply written works.

3. *Philosophy*: al-Ghazālī speaks of the need to understand thoroughly the ideas of philosophy. In *Maqāsid al-Falāsifa* (*The Aims of the Philosophers — Intentiones Philosophorum*) he produced a classic summary of Greek logic, physics and metaphysics as presented by the Islamic philosophers of his day. The work was much used in the Middle Ages, especially in the West, as a definitive handbook of philosophy. However, al-Ghazālī's intent in the work was to lay the groundwork for the decisive attack on philosophy which he carried out in *Tahāfut al-Falāsifa* (*The Incoherence of the Philosophers; Destructio Philosophorum*). Despite Averroes's reply in *Tahāfut al-Tahāfut* some decades later, al-Ghazālī succeeded in marginalizing philosophy, especially in Sunnite Islam, and thereby terminating the tradition of Islamic work in Greek

philosophy.

The *Munqidh min al-Dālal*, the center of concern here, is a semi-autobiographical work. Through a tour of the intellectual horizons of the day, it leads the reader to Sufism as the only sure access to truth.

The title used here is a combination of two titles: *Munqidh Min al-Dalāl wa al-'mufsih 'an al-Ahwāl* (What Saves from Error and Displays the [Mystical] States [of the Soul]) and *al-Munqidh min al-Dalāl wa al-Muwassil ilā Dhi al-'Izza wu al-Jalāl* (What Saves from Error and Unites with the Possessor of Power and Glory).

4. *Spiritual Guidance*: The *Ihyā' 'Ulūm al Bin* (*The Revitalization of the Sciences of Religion*) is his great spiritual work. Where the *Munqidh* leads one to the Sufi Way, this work enters into detail in describing what is discovered as one proceeds along this Way — the savored experience itself, of course, remaining beyond words. The *Iyā* is composed of four parts, each having ten books. Part I begins with a book on knowledge which is followed by books on "The Five Pillars of Islam", i.e., the profession of belief, the canonical prayers, almsgiving, fasting and pilgrimage. Part II concerns 'ādāt, or ways of acting regarding food, marriage, etc. Part III treats *al-muhlikāt* (the things that lead to damnation). It begins with a psychological masterpiece on the mysteries of the heart and follows with books on ascetic practices for overcoming the appetites. Part IV concerns *al-munjiyāt* (the things that lead to salvation) and constitutes his spiritual masterpiece. It treats repentance, gratitude, fear, hope, poverty, love, openness to God, spiritual awareness, the review of conscience, meditation, death and the next life. All this is written with such great beauty that McCarthy cites an ancient author to the effect that "the *Ihyā* would supply for all Islamic literature if the latter were to be lost" for it conveys "all that is best and most appealing in Islam as a religion and as a 'revelation' of God's love for man and the heights attainable by man's love for God."[9]

ANALYSIS OF *AL-MUNQIDH MIN AL-DĀLAL*

The Work

Al-Ghazālī wrote the *Munqidh* between 499/1106 and 500/1107 in Nisphāpūr. He was 50 years old at the time and about to return to teaching. As a personal testimony it calls to mind Augustine's *Confessions*, Descartes's *Discourse on Method* and Newman's *Apologia pro vita sua*. Its complex intellectual structure and purpose makes it one of the most outstanding works in world literature. Al-Ghazālī states in the introduction that he wrote the work at the request of a brother in the faith who asked him "to reveal . . . the purpose of the sciences, the evil and the depths of the schools of thought." This could be a real account and/or a literary device; in any case, most agree that it was meant for a type of reader, not for only one individual. The work is intended to explain how he first established the bases and limits of reason, and later broke beyond reason to find the Way to definitive certitude and spiritual fulfillment. By a process of exclusion his review of the competencies and limits of kalām, of philosophy, and of the doctrine of the ta'limites led him to Sufism. There he found the Way which could take him to the prophetic light, beyond which "there was no other light on the face of the earth."[10]

Proximately, he was worried by the Bāinites who wished to propose, as an infallible Imam, the Fatimid Caliph of Cairo. Al-Ghazālī considered this prerogative to have belonged only to Muhammad himself. Like the Ash'ari facing the Mu'tazilites two centuries earlier, he was forced to rethink sunnite dogma for himself and his contemporaries, and thereby to renew the religious spirit. It was, moveover, a task which it had been prophesied would be needed at the beginning of each century.

To appreciate this project it may be helpful to look first at its structure, especially as analyzed by Farid Jabre,[11] and then to consider its meaning and accomplishment.

General Introduction

Al-Ghazālī notes that from his early youth, before the age of 20, he had been concerned with the problem of certitude and had examined critically all the roads leading not only to religious conviction, but even to nihilism. Rather than accept the easy but blind conformism of *taqlīd*, however, he attempted to seize the deep basic reality of things, especially of human nature itself as it opened to the divine. In this regard what he sought was certain knowledge, which he described as a state of soul so bound to, and satisfied by, its object that nothing could detach it therefrom.

The First Crisis

In search of this perfect certitude he turned first to sense knowledge, but soon recognized the illusions it generated. When he turned to reason and its first principles; however, he had difficulty distinguishing their certitude from that which he had experienced in dreams: indeed for the Sufis the whole of this life was a dream. After two months of despair with regard to knowledge he regained confidence in the directives of reason. This confidence, however, came not as a clear deduction from any methodical reasoning, but was seen as a light which God projected into his heart.

Evaluation of Other Ways

Long after — his education having been completed, and now at the head of the school at Baghdad — he returned once again to this issue of certitude. Now, however, it was not merely the general question of how certitude could be had in any reasoning; rather, it was how one could be bound irrevocably in blessed union with God. As truth was being sought by four different groups each proposing its own path, some time after 484/1091 and over a period of years at Baghdad, al-Ghazālī set about studying each in depth to see which provided the true Way to God.

1. *Kalām*: Through the Prophet, God revealed the body of true beliefs upon which depends human happiness in this life and the next. Because some deny this and attempt to disturb the faith of the believers, an apologetic approach (the *kalām*) was developed. This seeks to argue from premises which these unbelievers do admit in order to show the contradictions into which they are lead by their unbelief. *Kalām* is of little service, however, for it can serve only those with a strong sense of the first and necessary principles

of reason, and generally these persons limit their convictions solely to such principles. In time *kalām* broadened its concerns to search into the deep reality of things through the use of such philosophical categories as substance and accidents, but it could attain little sure knowledge.

2. *Falāsifa*: Thinking that this had never seriously been studied, in Baghdad al-Ghazālī spent two years reading the works of the Falāsifa and a third in organizing his thoughts. He divided the Falāsifa into three categories and quickly rejected the first two: the nihilists (*dahriyyūn*) or *Zanādiqa* who deny the existence of God, and the naturalists (*tabi-'iyyun*) who believe in a powerful and wise being, but reject life after death.

In contrast, he gave extensive attention to the third category, the theists (*ilāhiyyūn*), which include especially not only the Greek philosophers, Socrates, Plato and Aristotle, but the Islamic philosophers, Avicenna and al-Farabi. Al-Ghazālī does not propose rejecting all their positions: mathematics, logic, physics, politics and ethics could be accepted with care and prudence. The difficulties of the philosophers arose especially in the field of theodicy where they did not have success in furnishing the kinds of proofs demanded by their logic.

He warns against the dangers in either totally accepting or totally rejecting the philosophers, arguing strenuously for an open attitude to truth wherever it appears. Truth is not contaminated by being juxtaposed to errors, nor does it become false when included in books which contain errors on other matters. Thus, similarities between revealed truths in his works and elements in the works of some philosophers do not render the revealed matters any less true.

In sum, however, the skeptical attitude of his teacher, al-Juwayni reigns: *Falasafa* will not suffice because reason is unable to know the basic truths of things, especially (but not only) with regard to the spirit in man and its union with God.

3. *The Theory of Teaching*: A competing claimant to provide a sure way to God — and one most obtrusive in his day, even to the point of assassinations — was the company of those who claimed that such truth could not be approached by reason, but only through instruction by a teacher, particularly by the infallible Imam of the *shi'ites*. Al-Ghazālī proceeded to develop a clearer statement of their principles than could they themselves, but he did so in

order to refute them. He accepted the principles of the *ta'limites* regarding the need for a doctrine and for an infallible teacher, but turned this against them by pointing out that such a teacher was only Muhammad. More basically, however, he rejected the general skepticism regarding reason implicit in their argument and their reduction of faith to blind conformism.

With regard to the contingent social order al-Ghazālī considered error to be always possible, but not to have eternal implications. Where teaching has been received from an infallible, though now dead, teacher it should be followed; otherwise jurisprudential judgement (*ijtihād*) must suffice.

With regard to the fundamental truths of belief, these exist in the *Qur'ān* and the *Sunna* or community. As shown in his book, *The Just Balance*, these truths can be argued. But, as was true even with Muhammad's teaching, there is no guarantee that all persons will be convinced.

Al-Ghazālī argues that the *ta'limit* position is not consistent, for the authority of any text which would affirm the existence and infallibility of their Imam would need to be based on prophecy and certified by miracles. The appreciation and application of such certification, however, require precisely the kind of reasoning capability rejected by their position.

The Mystical Way of Sufism

By exclusion he then turned to the way of Sufism which he notes to be both a knowledge and, even more fundamentally, a practice which constitutes a yet deeper knowledge. As practice, its goal is detachment from all else for the purpose of attachment to God. He attained information and some understanding of Sufism by reading the works of Makki, Muhāsibi, Junayd, Shibli and Bistāmi. But he noted that the essence of Sufism was a matter not of knowledge, but of lived experience described as savoring the truth.

Hence he had to reorient himself from an outward search for objective truth to the realization of an inward state of soul: it was not a matter of knowing the definition of detachment, but of becoming detached step by step. This spiritual turn was for him a matter of great drama and pain. He had always held the three great truths: The Existence of God, Prophecy, and Resurrection on the Last Day, and had stoutly taught and defended them. But he notes with regret that he had done so with attachment to worldly honor, even to the point of treating others harshly. If, however, eternal happiness depended not on attachment but on detachment, then he had a crucial choice to make: to remain with all the attachments of his life as leader of the school in Baghdad or to break away.

The pressure of the growing awareness of this choice over a six months period beginning from Rajab 488 progressively paralysed him to a point where he could neither speak nor eat. Then, by God's help, he was able to make the break. For the rest of his life he led a life of prayer. He was a hermit for two years in Syria and Palestine; he notes especially his time in the minaret of the mosque in Damascus. Family cares recalled him once again to his home, which he left but briefly to teach at Nîshāpur. But with his progressive practice of the Sufi Way of self-denial, prayer and meditation, in Tūs the spirit of God entirely suffused his life.

He recounts the stages of the Sufi Way as the purification of the heart from all that is not God and total absorption in God through annihilation of Self. Each interior step of the heart is accompanied by a corresponding step of knowledge unveiling and contemplating the truth. These take one to a proximity with God, but this is not yet the state of inherence or true union. For that it is necessary to proceed by lived, even savored, experience on three levels: (1) knowledge by faith or belief based on the good opinion one has of one's spiritual masters or teachers; (2) indirect knowledge by verification with the help of reasoning; (3) direct knowledge by taste, which he describes as savored in order to insist upon the subjectivity of an interior appreciation of God as present beyond any objective, exterior knowledge.

These levels are permeated by the notion of prophecy; it is the Prophet who achieves most vividly the direct experience of God which is the goal of the Sufi Way. Hence, at this point in the *Munqidh* he undertakes a detailed progressive analysis of the nature of prophecy in order to be as clear as possible regarding the reality of the divine union which is both the Way and the truth, both knowledge and practice, and, beyond all, life divine.

The Nature of Prophecy: An Urgent Human Need

Here al-Ghazālī mounts a major effort to communicate to his readers/friend the character of the lived experience to which the Sufi Way leads. He begins with a detailed sequence of the development of the various senses, followed by the ability to discern things beyond the sense level at age seven, and then the ability to grasp abstract notions, i.e. things as necessary, possible or impossible. Finally, there opens the eye of prophecy which grasps a domain beyond reason. He exemplifies the transcendence of this world beyond that of reason by comparing the latter to the insensitivity of a blind person before colors or of reason before the world of dreams. This capacity of the human for trans-rational experience is a special gift of God.

He treats three questions regarding prophecy: its possibility, its existence and its realization in a particular person. First, its possibility is illustrated by knowledge of the laws of medicine and astrology which are known to be true but are not subject to rational deduction. Second, dreams testify to the fact of a realm of knowledge beyond reason. Third, prophetic knowledge exists in the experience which can be developed by following the Way of Sufism. Like knowledge of whether someone is authentically a doctor or jurist, recognition of the existence of prophecy in a particular person requires first some sense of the nature of prophecy. This can be had by meeting such persons and considering their teaching and actions. However, the life of the Prophet is its own best witness. More than external miracles, which upset the laws of nature, prophecy is itself a miracle which perfects nature beyond anything to which nature of itself could aspire.[12] It is then by being with Sufis that one comes to know that the higher experience has been attained by some, and thus that it does exist and can be attained by their Way.

Practical Problems and the Return to Teaching

The remainder of the work focuses on the practical problems or difficulties in bringing the Way into more general practice. In their substance humans are both body and spirit or heart. The latter is the proper place of knowledge of God, but like the body it too can die if it lacks knowledge of God or falls ill through disobedience to

Him. What is more, just as the body is healed by medical properties which the reason cannot understand, so the heart can be healed by practices of cult which only the higher experience of the prophet can appreciate.

Al-Ghazālī explained the nature of prophecy by leading the reader step by step toward experiences that transcend both the senses and reason. But in order to be attracted toward such a goal one needs to experience it in others. Here, the difficulty is precisely the bad examples of those supposedly learned persons who should be practicing it, or the defects of others who do attempt to practice the Way. The result is general tepidity.

Al-Ghazālī responded both in theory and in practice. Regarding theory or truth, to those whose tepidity is due to:

- *ta'līmism*, as a virus aggressively promoted in his day and proposing passive dependence on an infallible Imam, al-Ghazālī directs that they read his work: *The Just Balance*.

- the teaching of the *falāsifa*, who aggressively extend the realm of reason and reduce all else in the *Qur'ān* to mere allegory, al-Ghazālī directs that they review his teaching on prophecy as transcending the capacities of reason.

- the arguments of the libertines, al-Ghazālī directs that they read his work, *The Alchemy of Happiness*.

- the claim that prophecy is only for the common people, but not for those who can understand its contents and develop an empirical ethics (*hikma*) based on God, al-Ghazālī teaches that in fact they reject prophecy because they reduce what is distinctive about it, namely, its transcendence of reason, to the level of a sage usage of reason.

Moreover, al-Ghazālī is conscious that holiness as an inner reality can be betrayed above all from within. He recognizes that those who should exemplify the experiences achieved in the Way may be impeded in so doing by various temptations, and therefore generate scandal rather than being beacons for others. Al-Ghazālī attempts to protect against this by assuring: (1) that all have knowledge of the difference between good and evil and should not be misled by anyone who falls before temptations, which after all are experienced by everyone, and (2) that knowledge of the Way is itself a corrective for it directs one to repent and move on, not to remain in sin.

But al-Ghazālī had a practical response to make as well. Because tepidity seemed to be spreading he became convinced that a strenuous effort at education was needed. He made a last effort in that direction by accepting the invitation of the son of Nizām to take charge of the school at Nîshāpūr. When this approach was cut short by the assassination of his patron, he moved his effort to his home in Tūs, where he built a school and monastery to teach and promote the practice of Sufism.

MEANING OF THE *MUNQIDH*

The above analysis of the text has attempted closely to follow its structure. The text, however, is not simply autobiographical, but a somewhat stylized ordering of the elements of his life and hence of his Sufi experience. In this his goal, he says, is to respond to the question of the purpose of the related sacred sciences and the evil and depth of the pertinent schools of thought. Hence, in order further to unfold the import of the *Munqidh* it may help to add here some reflections upon the different philosophical issues involved.

Epistemology

The issue of knowledge[13] and its competencies is basic here, for his purpose is to show not only what reason can do in order progressively to lead toward the Way, but even more what reason cannot do in order, through contrast, to make manifest what is distinctive and indispensable in the mystical Way of the Sufis. Moreover, beyond the issue of the way to personal perfection, al-Ghazālī's understanding of knowledge was the key to his work on *The Incoherence of the Philosophers* (*Tahāfut al-Falāsifa*). This played a central role in the Islamic rejection of its own heritage of work on the Greek philosophers' classic elaboration of reason. In terms of present-day concerns, this may relate, on the one hand, to the troubled history of the relation of religion to the processes of modernization derived from the scientific elaboration of reason. On the other hand, it may relate also to the mystical direction of Islamic thought and its potential for contributing to the present renewal of the search for spiritual meaning in response to the loss of meaning in our increasingly rationalized society.[14]

To see how this can be so one should note with Farid Jabre that while the work was written toward the end of al-Ghazālī's life its literary point of view is rather that of the period of his leadership of the school at Baghdad. Particularly, it reflects the point at which he comes seriously to investigate the adequacy of the sciences and the schools of thought. From this point of view the work — and his life — clearly divide into two parts: the first is preliminary and is devoted to the basis for scientific reasoning, the second main section is devoted to questioning these bases with a view to showing the need, the nature and the goal of the Way of the Sufis.

Each phase is marked by a personal crisis, the first of which foreshadows the second. McCarthy downplays the first as the relatively universal hesitation of the late adolescent when forced to take up responsibility for his or her own capacity of knowledge.[15] In contrast, Jabre,[16] as it were, places a magnifying glass on this first crisis in order to uncover much more precisely the nature of the epistemology which al-Ghazālī developed for human reason. This would remain with him throughout his life and would be the point of reference against which he would delineate the further step to the mystical and the prophetic.

Moreover, because al-Ghazālī later notes that he never doubted the great truths of the faith, Jabre would distinguish this first crisis from Descartes' universal doubt and limit it to the motives of credibility of faith before the judgment of reason. But if Descartes could stress the importance of keeping one's fundamental beliefs even while applying the technique of his methodic doubt,[17] the young al-Ghazālī could claim to have done no less in his own general state of initial confusion.

Jabre would focus al-Ghazālī's early crisis on the rational means or motives which justify belief and considers that this defines all that follows. In contrast, al-Ghazālī himself seems there to describe a more general crisis regarding the validity of reason. This is but an introductory first step toward the general epistemological question which evolves later in the main body of the text. It is there that he treats the nature and ability of reason to achieve the real nature, or by spatial analogy, the deep reality (*haqīqa* or pulp) of things as opposed to merely their surface appearance.

To this spatial analogy of levels on the part of the object, there corresponds in al-Ghazālī's thought a parallel set of levels on the part of the self. The deepest level is the trans-rational goal of the Sufis, but this can be illumined through contrast to the more surface or preliminary levels, which are those of sense and reason that al-Ghazālī lists in his section on prophecy. Let us attempt a more precise delineation of his notion of reason. This could provide insight not only into his perception of the nature of the goal of the mystical Way, but also into the limitation of the sciences. In the *Tahāfut* this forces the break of the subsequent Islamic tradition from its earlier work in the Greek tradition.

In Aristotle's logic, which ruled his development of the structure of the sciences, all begins from first principles such as that of non-contradiction first sketched out by Parmenides. These have absolute and universal value from the beginning of the work of reason. In this light, by a process of induction from the particular to the universal, the natures of things are abstracted. With these the deductive syllogisms are constructed in the various sciences, each with their distinctive universal principles.

Jabre suggests that al-Ghazālī took only the form of such syllogistic reasoning (via the Arab *qiyas*), and into this poured a quite different content. This was not simply the result of induction from concrete sense experience, even in the cases of the positive sciences. For Ghazālī the intellect does see, but its objects are not simply human constructs. Absolute judgments regarding the necessary, the possible and the impossible are always present, but with regard to other judgments the human intellect is only a capacity. Hence, it needs to be enlightened by the *hikma*, of which the greatest is the word of God, especially the *Qur'ān* by which vision is accomplished.

What then of "the first principles"? For Ghazālī these are grasped directly in and for themselves; they have an unchangeable character which is imposed with necessity upon the mind. Their purpose is to prepare the mind by providing an anticipated experience of necessity, which truly belongs only to God and the truth of the Prophet. Despite even this, however, they could yet be considered a mirage or illusion, for their definitive truth is possessed only when they are envisaged in terms of, that is, in and by, Islam.

To understand this seeming affirmation and yet negation of

the competency of reason it is necessary to recall that epistemology is essentially dependent upon metaphysics for an understanding of the nature and origin of knowledge, since that too is a reality and subject to the laws of being. McCarthy points out that in his metaphysics Ghazālī was always a convinced occasionalist. God in creating nature and humankind remained the one truly Real Being and hence the source of all action. Humans may act, but the reality or being of the effect was the result of the activity not of man, but of God. For knowledge this means that man may think, but that the reality of knowledge and truth is the effect not of man, but of God.

An intermediate position was held by the Christian Platonists of the School of St. Augustine for whom a special light or illumination was needed in order to explain the universality and necessity of the human knowledge which man drew from particular and changing reality. In response to this position, it was the contribution of Thomas Aquinas to see that the power of God implied that His creatures be self-sufficient. This meant that in their own (created) right they possessed all the competencies needed in order to realize all the actions which were in accord with their nature.[18] This extended the power of God proportionately and by participation to all His work.

(This was an important corrective by Thomas to one of the main defects which Ghazālī found in Averroes. Ghazālī was concerned that too close a following of Aristotle led Averroes to attenuate the reality of the individual's spiritual soul and to an inadequate affirmation of the resurrection on the Last Day. This Ghazālī classified as heretical.)[19]

For Ghazālī the conviction that the realization of truth was the effect of God, not of man, meant that the first truths could be looked upon in two ways. If seen in relation to the truth about God and constituting part of knowledge about God, they received therefrom truly definitive power.

The first principles could, however, be looked upon in another way, namely, as principles for any reasoning to God, or indeed for any reasoning whatsoever. Such knowledge is not certain. This is expressed by the phrase "the equivalence of proofs" (*takāfu' al-adilla*) indicating that "falsehood on the part of a proof does not entail the falsity of the object it proves." It can apply either to the necessary principles and to all properly speculative knowledge or only to the latter, all which it blankets with doubt.

Up to 28 years of age, during the period when Ghazālī was introduced to philosophy, *kalām, fiqh* and all the sciences, his mind was molded according to this pattern by his teacher, Juwayni, who was among the initiators of this view, which Ibn Khaldūn considers the distinguishing doctrine between "the ancients" and "the moderns". It is not surprising then that Ghazālī would be the one to write the *Tahāfut al-Falāsifa* and thereby be the major figure in the discontinuation of the Islamic strain of Greek philosophy. Averroes's belated effort to answer in his *Tahafut al tahāfut* was destined beforehand to be ineffective, for no reasoned reply could be effective when reason was no longer held to provide knowledge that was certain.

The Metaphysics of Mysticism

Ghazālī's epistemology did not change in the second period of his life, beginning from the age of 34, when he was placed in charge of the Nizāmiyya School in Baghdad. Writing as he does from this epistemological perspective, Farid Jabre tends to downplay the philosophical significance of this second period.[20] He sees it as but a repetition of the first period, though now in psychological and phenomenal terms describing Ghazālī's lived experience of the limitation of reason. To McCarthy, however, it is just the opposite; having reduced Ghazālī's first crisis to being simply a universal experience of passing from adolescence, he places all the meaning in the second phase of his life,[21] which all agree to be the main focus of the *Munqidh*.

It is suggested here that the truth lies between these two positions.[22] That is, the main lines of his epistemology can indeed be traced in the earlier period, as Jabre has done so effectively. He is correct in observing that during that earlier period Ghazālī did not advance beyond the realm of reason and that it lacked definitive certainty. But if that be so, when in the second period he does actively apply himself to the Way that leads beyond reason, identifies its veracity, and then applies himself in a ten-year retreat to the assiduous practice of the Way from which results his *Ihya*, the landmark of Islamic spirituality, certainly something of the greatest moment has taken place. It is hardly a mere "répétition de la première

... sous un autre form,"[23] as Jabre claims. This failure to appreciate the distinctive reality of the achievement of the second phase of Ghazālī's life would seem to result from seeing it only in psychological terms as the flow of phenomena of a human order. Rather, appreciating it in the metaphysical terms, e.g., of a Heidegger, as the unveiling of Being Itself through the intentional life of *dasein*, or in properly mystical terms, McCarthy approaches with great respect, even awe, as before a sanctuary of the divine. This enables him to grasp the tremendous fascination of the religious event lived by Ghazālī and described in the main body of his text.[24]

If the *Munqidh* has a consistent message, it is that, at its highest, reason remains insufficient and that even in its efforts to defend religion in the *Kalām* it is weak and largely ineffectual.

One cannot come to the reality of the divine in the depth of the human heart by mere belief according to dogmatic formulas, for such formulas remain surface, brittle and subject to dissolution. The approach to the divine is rather by ascetic and ritual practices which progressively remove the chains that bind the heart so as to allow it to open before the corresponding unveiling of the divine. It is in this that one comes to certain knowledge (*yaqīn*), rising above religious conformism (*taqlīd*), through actively savoring the experience of God. Here, reason as prepared by the practices of cult and informed by meditation upon the prophetic teaching, has only to reflect upon itself as a concrete reality.

In contrast to the objective and relatively exterior stance of pure speculative reason which can lead only to *I'tiqad*, Ghazālī insists that in the mystical Way of the Sufis the divine is seized immediately and savored. He stresses thus the interiority and lived subjectivity of this process. This accords with his description of certainty as a state of soul so bound to, and satisfied by, its object that nothing could detach it. Even more, it is real union with God and definitive fulfillment, of which certainty is but a sign.

In this light it is possible to appreciate more deeply the meaning of the *Munqidh*. It is not only a gripping account of a psychological drama with deep sonorities of Ghazālī's life in Baghdad. His review of other ways, his discovery that all were wanting — philosophy, *kalām* and especially *taqlīd* — and his being led thereby to the Sufi Way of self-abnegation and union with God was not only the progression of the life of one person. Beyond this it is a descrip tion of the Way of continued emergence of the divine in time through prophecy and of the opening of hearts through the mystical path. It is truly an account of God-with-us, as this transforms human life and history.

One who appreciated the implications of this less thoroughly and less deeply than Ghazālī would have worked out some pragmatic compromise allowing him to stay in Baghdad — after all, as a newly spiritually sensitive director he would be better for the school than he had been when he acted too much on the basis of human reason and for the too human motives of fame and honor. It is a testimony to his sincerity and dedication that he could not act on the basis of any such compromise. In turn, this suggests responses to problems raised from a number of directions.

Ghazālī himself was conscious that some would suggest that he was being led by his ego to attempt to become the reformer of his century, according to the prophecy that each century would begin with a major reformer.[25] But if ever human reason could conceive such a hope it would certainly be based upon his position as director of the great Nizāmiyya school in Baghdad, not as a hermit enclosed in the minaret of the mosque at Damascus or in his hometown of Tūs.

Others would cite his phrase that all his prior life had been led by the search for fame, that his teaching "had not been directed towards God the Almighty alone . . . (but to) seek glory and renown."[26] Based on this they would question the sincerity of his conversion and hence of this account.[27] But the remark would be meaningless except in the context of conversion from such motivation.

Similarly, there are those who would question the sincerity of Descartes's references to God and in effect eviscerate Books III-V of his *Meditations* in order to protect the forced reductionism of their materialist reading of Books II and VI. In parallel manner, there are critics who, in order to protect their own overly literal and out-of-context reading of a very few lines, would reject the seriousness of Ghazālī's account of his conversion and by implication the authenticity of the whole teaching of his massive *Ihyā' 'Ulūm ad-Dīn*. But they must be guided by something other than Ghazālī's text or his life: their's is a hermeneutic not of his text but of their own suspicions.

Still others[28] would see his departure from Baghdad not in the spiritual terms in which he depicts it, but rather as the result of fear generated by the assassination of his sponsor, *Nizām al-Mulk*. Certainly, the Nizāmiyya school at Baghdad was the key intellectual battlefield and Ghazālī was its key figure. He does not hide the element of fear, which was not unnatural in the circumstances. But Ghazālī places it within the context of the much broader and deeper sweep of the challenge of conversion in his life. Undoubtedly, the assassination of the patron of his School was too great and threatening a happening to be ignored. But this account, written when he was an advanced Sufi, naturally describes all in terms of his awareness of the Providence of God, rather than as simply the machinations of mere humans. The description of his life is in terms of his search for the Way, and of what can be communicated of this that has meaning for a broad class of readers interested in the Way to truth. In these terms the assassinations and other turmoils of his particular time are of marginal importance.

It might be noted further that even late in his ten year period of retreat, when he was considering how to respond to the tepidity abroad in Islam, he considered it important to have an authoritative patron. This could be taken as an issue of protection, but it seems more probable that it was considered important as an element in the plan of Nizām to develop an alliance of faith and political power which could protect against Batinism and promote the Sunnite Islamic faith. The assassination of Nizām al-Mulk meant, of course, the sudden collapse of this worldly hope. The *Munqidh* then may not be adequate history. But the work has survived because it focused not upon surface events that happen only once, but upon what is essential in the human pilgrimage and gives it ultimate meaning.

One would hope then that he would have written much more extensively here about his lived experience of the Way during his retreat following his departure from Baghdad. But, of course, he has done this brilliantly and in the greatest detail in the 40 books of the *Ihyā*; it is there that one must turn for the enduring harvest of his life of faith.

THE IMPACT OF THE *MUNQIDH*: PAST AND PRESENT

For Islam the impact of the *Munqidh* was decisive, especially if one includes the pattern of work it reflects, including Ghazālī's decisive critique of philosophy in the *Tahāfut*, his description of the discovery of the mystical way though a critique of the sciences, including *kalām*, in the *Munqidh* itself, and the massively imposing *Ihyā* with its detailed exposition of the spiritual wisdom gained from his long Sufi retreat. It is not without reason that Ghazālī has been described as the greatest Muslim after Muhammad himself.

As the classical sciences of *kalām* and *fiqh* had come to appear respectively as too apologetic and too external, there was urgent need to renew access to the religious wellsprings of Islam. The obvious candidate for such an expedition was reason. This had been developed to a high state by the Greeks, whose major works had been translated into Arabic. It had been richly developed by such ingenious Islamic thinkers as al-Farabi, Ibn Sina (Avicena) and Ibn Rushd (Averroes). But was reason enough — particularly as developed in terms of a culture of the ancient Greek gods, rather than of the revelation of the One God? Three responses were possible.

The first, by Ibn Sina and Ibn Rushd, was that reason could be of great assistance in this effort to discover the religious meaning of life and to order all life in that light. Indeed, their great works illustrate this point so well that no external certification of their significance need be added to that which shines from within.

There is, however, a fatal weakness in human reason. As human it is limited and can never be adequate to the divine which transcends it. Yet, as reason it looks for universal principles and laws which order all and render all intelligible to a limited mind. This tension shows up most in the Platonic and neo-Platonic line of Greek reasoning upon which, especially, the Islamic philosophers drew. The result was a tendency to tailor such realities as the "assemblage" or "resurrection" of the body on the last day and the personal spiritual principle to categories which were not really adequate to the task. Ghazālī drew up a list of 20 such points, three of which he cites in the *Munqidh*. Ghazālī's judgment in the *Tahāfut* that this avenue was simply too dangerous to the integrity of revelation and should effectively be abandoned was accepted, despite the somewhat later protestations of Averroes.

The second was that of Ghazālī himself. In three years of work on the philosophers he mastered their work and indeed wrote one of the major summaries of their thought for his time, the *Maqāsid al-Falāsifa*. In the end he felt, nonetheless, that he needed to abandon that avenue as well as *Kalām* and, of course, the position of the *ta'līmites*; by exclusion he could see clearly that he must devote himself to the mystical Way of the Sufis. This led precisely beyond objective reason to an interior path of abnegation until his heart could open to a divine embrace so intimate and life-giving that it could actively be savored.

The impact upon Islam of this step, so effectively presented in the *Munqidh*, was of the highest order. Matching the turn away from Greek philosophy, there came a new appreciation of the spiritual and mystical dimension of Islam. However, while Ghazālī's work leaves no question about the need to go beyond the sciences in faith, it is not iconoclastic. That is, its objective is not to destroy these sciences or to impede people from their study. He is at pains to plead against this and to stress the need to look for truth everywhere, to accept it wherever it is found, and to recognize that it can be found even in the presence of error. Hence, upon discovering for himself the Sufi Way he remained ever the teacher of *fiqh*, and indeed returned to that work formally at the end of his life.

In assessing the impact of his life, then, it might better be seen not as an attack on the sacred sciences, but as aiding to overcome their arid scholasticism, as narrowing the gulf between them and the wellsprings of the spirit, and even as discovering ways to infuse this new life into the old sciences.

To this should be added then a corrective of the commonplace that Islamic scholarship ended with, and even by, Ghazālī. Though this may be true largely of the field of Greek philosophy, scholarship in Islam took on a new mode. Spiritually it became more deep and rich and corresponded more to the intensive faith of the people. Or perhaps this should be put the other way round, namely, that Ghazālī's strong religious mark on the subsequent cultural history of Islam, second only to Muhammad himself, reflects the pilgrimage made by Ghazālī and described in his *Munqidh*.

If so, this certainly is due in part to the fact that Ghazālī recognized, explored and effectively presented a dimension of Islam not previously given so great a place. Some, writing from the individualistic Anglo-Saxon perspective, refer to this as an individualization of the Islamic faith, but the closed, self-centered character of individualism hardly does justice to the Sufi Way through the self to the Infinite source and goal of all. By abnegation one truly dies to self in order to be opened to the transcendent. Hence it would seem more true to speak not of an individualization, but of a personalization of the life of faith. This would no longer be the affair only of great leaders — caliphs or sultans — but of the millions of persons who practiced this religion. And if these cultic practices are carried out in unison by large bodies of persons they are seen by Ghazālī as making the heart flexible and nimble for the Way which each must follow toward union with God. In other words, all was given new life by Ghazālī's work which described the Way to the divine Source and Goal of life. In turn this marks the character of each of the faithful and hence of the community of believers, namely, Islam as a whole.

There is, however, a possible third response to the relation of reason to this path of faith. We have seen the first response, that of Ibn Sina and Ibn Rushd, which gave primacy to reason in an attempt to reconcile it with faith. We saw also the second response, that of Ghazālī, which did not move against reason, but was concerned above all with how this needed to be transcended in the Way to God.

The third response comes not from Islam, but from Christianity. This honored the works of the Arabic philosophers, not least Ghazālī's *Maqāsid al-falāsifa*, which often rightly was taken as the most effective summary of the Greek tradition of philosophy for the times.

In the Christian medieval context there were both those who greatly admired this philosophy and others who, with Ghazālī, pointed to its defects with regard to the spiritual dimension of the person, resurrection, etc. It was the proper contribution of Thomas Aquinas during the following century to work out a resolution of these problems. He did so, neither by simply repeating Aristotle nor by abandoning his metaphysics, but by appreciating the deepened sense of being unveiled in a cultural context marked by faith. The creative work to heal the discrepancies between Greek philosophy and a faith-filled vision of life and meaning could be considered quite properly a continuation of the work of the Islamic philosophers.

On the one hand, the thrust of medieval Christian philosophers such as Aquinas was not to oppose Ghazālī, as had Ibn Rushd in his *Tahāfut al Tahāfut*, but to respond positively to his concerns for the literal integrity of the faith. With Ghazālī, they acknowledged the inadequacy of Greek thought for the vision of the human in this world and the next, which had emerged under the light of faith. But they then went about the creative and properly philosophical task of resolving these conflicts by developing philosophy itself. In this sense they moved philosophy forward into an era of faith, both Islamic and Christian.

On the other hand, with the philosophers, Thomas acknowledged the need to reconcile reason and faith, rather than simply to surpass reason. For though faith was more than reason, it did not contradict reason, but was aided by it. Thus, the work of Thomas included very detailed commentaries on the works of Aristotle. Aquinas' *Disputed Questions* and *Summa Theologiac* constitute also a detailed philosophy of the human person and an ethics.

While Thomas thus provided the context in which a spiritual theology could be constructed, it is notable that R. Garrigou-Lagrange, an eminent Thomist, in actually carrying out such a construction drew notably on the mystic experience of Theresa of Avila and John of the Cross.[29] This may suggest that this third alternative of Thomas Aquinas did not succeed in adequately integrating the first approach by objective reason with the second by mystical interiority, and that Ghazālī's work has a further major role to play in any such integration.

Nevertheless, this third response by Thomas Aquinas, by resolving the problems pointed out by Ghazālī in the first response by Ibn Sina and Ibn Rushd, made it possible to continue to mine the vein of Islamic-Greek philosophy with its emphasis on reason. This opened the way to the development of the sciences and their accompanying technology that have characterized the modern age. Indeed, to the degree that the modern developments of scientific thought are especially Platonic in character, they correspond more to the Platonic character of Islamic philosophy than to the ultimately Aristotelian character of Thomas's own thought.

Commonly it is noted, however, that in modern times attention to reason has degenerated into rationalism, accompanied by a desic cating lack of adequate attention to the life of the spirit. Indeed, the triumphs of rationalism in the 20th century have been characterized by an oppressive totalitarianism and a deadening consumerism. These deficiencies of rationalism call for Ghazālī's clear proclamation of the distinctive character of the spirit, and of the Way which leads thereto. They also call for Mulla Sadra's resumption of philosophy in terms not of form or essence, but precisely in terms of existence, about which below.

But healing our times must begin with the Spirit and the Way, for only in their higher light can we face the unfinished task of working out the relation of reason to the fullness of the human spirit. This suggests then that the goal of Ghazālī for our times would be that reason be inspired by, and directed to, life in the Spirit. This, in turn, would enable the progress of reason truly to serve men and women, not only as images, but indeed as intimates of God. This is the central message of Ghazālī's *Munqidh*, if not for his day, then certainly for ours. Perhaps not surprisingly then, at the end of this millennium it is precisely the message of the Encyclical of John Paul II, *Fides et Ratio*.[30] This is developed at length and in cooperation with Islam in the companion volumes to this one, namely, *Faith and Reason* and *Religion and the Relation between Cultures*.

II. MULLA SADRA'S PHILOSOPHY OF EXISTENCE: ISLAMIC AND CHRISTIAN CONTRIBUTIONS

Whereas al-Ghazālī had turned away from philosophy, Mulla Sadra went about correcting it. He criticized philosophy as having been focused upon essence and therefore missing the significance of freedom in the actual exercise of life. To grasp the contemporary significance of Mulla Sadra's existential philosophy it would help to begin with a review of the general crisis generated at this turn of the millennia by the reduction of reason to an interplay of clear but empty concepts. We live in our day Mulla Sadra's description of the meaninglessness of the pursuit of essence alone. The general response must be a revival of the sense of existence, first uncovered by the early Church Fathers.

Next, we shall study the reality and internal constitution of finite beings as existing in their own right in order to capture the significance of Mulla Sadra's existential philosophy for the proper autonomy of creatures.

Finally, in the light of the above, we shall review the role of existence in the medieval Islamic and Christian efforts to respond in philosophy to the requirements of eschatology for human persons who are real, free and responsible before God -- a matter of no less significance in social life today.

In sum, we shall move diachronically reviewing once again the earlier discovery of existence, through an understanding of the proper autonomy of beings as creatures of God, to the human person as free and responsible. Synchronically, it will move first from essence to existence, second from existence to the subsistence of finite beings, and third from subsistence to the human person as free, responsible and creative in the work of creation. Throughout we will look for ways in which insights by Christian Philosophers can cooperate and contribute to the effort of Mulla Sadra to develop an Islamic philosophy which can help in responding to revelation.

MULLA SADRA'S EXISTENTIAL RESPONSE TO THE CONTEMPORARY PHILOSOPHICAL CHALLENGE

a. Essence and the Crisis of Reason Today

In order to identify the crisis of reason in which we stand at this turn of the millennia, we need to review broadly the history of our era. The first millennium is justly seen as one in which human attention was focused upon God. It was the time of the Prophets Christ and Mohammed — "Peace be upon them both" — and much of humanity was fully absorbed in the assimilation of their message.

The second millennium is generally seen as focused upon human reason. Its first five hundred years were marked by the reintegration of Aristotelian reason within a religious context by such figures as Ibn Sina, Ibn Rushd and Thomas Aquinas. The second half of this millennium — from 1500 — was marked by a radicalization of reason. A certain Promethean *hubris* emerged that, as with the fallen Angel of Milton's *Paradise Lost*, humankind could save itself by its powers of scientific reason.

Previously, human reason had always attempted to draw on the fullness of human experience, to reflect the highest human and religious aspirations, and to build upon the accomplishment of earlier generations — philosophers had always sensed themselves as standing on the shoulders of their predecessors. Now, however, Francis Bacon directed that the idols which bore the content of the traditions be smashed; John Locke would erase all prior content of the mind in order to reduce it to a blank tablet; Rene Descartes would put all under doubt. What was sought was an aseptic laboratory in which could be constructed by technical reason alone a body of clear and distinct concepts, united by necessary links after a mathematical model, and universally applicable.

It was true that Descartes's intent in applying his doubt was to be able progressively to reintroduce the content of the mind, now on a clear and certain basis. But what was restored was not the rich breadth of human experience, but only what could be had with mathematical clarity and certitude. Thus, of the content of the senses which were bracketed by doubt in the first Meditation, only the quantitative and measurable were allowed back into his system. All the rest was left simply on a provisory status to the degree that it proved useful in avoiding what was physically harmful. By such abstractive processes human reason omitted existence, person, freedom, culture and creativity.

In this light even the goals of knowledge and of life were radically curtailed. For Aristotle, and even more for Christianity and Islam in the first 1500 years of this era, the goal had been contemplation of the magnificence and munificence of the highest being, God. For the Enlightenment, in contrast, it became control of nature and utility in the service of humankind. But even here, as the goals of human life were reduced to the material order, this became human service to the machine and to physical nature, economically conceived. This was the true enslavement of humankind.

Mulla Sadra, Muhammad ibn-Ibrāhīm Sadr al Dīn Shīrazi (1571/72-1640), a contemporary of Descartes (1596-1650), was trenchant in his description of the vacuity of essences when treated by reason in this reductive manner. Today, Giambattista Vico (1668-1744) is considered particularly clairvoyant for having predicted — 70 years after Mulla Sadra had done so — that the human race would be reduced by such abstractive reason to a race of brutes -- intellectual brutes, but brutes nonetheless.

By the beginning of the 20th century humanity felt itself poised by the power of science for the final push to create a human Utopia. This would be done not only by subduing and harnessing the physical powers of nature, but by transforming humankind through genetic and social engineering. Looking back from the present vantage point we find history to have proved quite the contrary.

First, the powers of science were diverted into two destructive World Wars and the development of nuclear weapons capable of extinguishing the entire human race.

Second, in philosophy Royce's ideals and idealism would give way to Dewey's pragmatic social goals which could be controlled and even produced by human effort. Or at least this was thought to be so until it came to be recognized that in positivist terms it was not possible to articulate such social goals. Positivism then succeeded pragmatism, but only to have to admit before long that its own controlling "principle of verifiability" (and then of "falsifiability") was not intelligible according to its own norms of meaning.

Third, with reason listening only to itself, religion was reduced to the service of man, rather than of God; it came to be seen as a superstructure built upon economic exploitation or even superstition. The religiously contextualized philosophical traditions were no longer understandable for they exceeded the reductionist terms of the modern Enlightenment; the great Hindu and Islamic traditions were dismissed as mystifications.

As a result, on one side of the Cold War, Marxism as a scientific history of social organization proved to be cruel and dehumanizing beyond belief until finally it imploded from its own internal weakness. The ideology on which meaning was conceived and life was lived in that half of the world was extinguished as if the sun went down never to rise again.

On the other side of the Cold War, the consumer society has shown itself incapable of generating meaningful life, but capable of exploiting everyone else. Most recently it has become manifest that its ideology of the totally free market is destructive of the weaker majority of the world.

Now we move through a period termed "postmodern", whose philosophy is in reality rather the final, critical period of modernity. Having become conscious of its own deadly propensities, rationalism responds in terms of its own tools of power and control, which for freedom can be only disastrous. Knowing that it must stop its own destructive path it proceeds blindly to destroy its own speculative foundations, all notions of coordinating structures and stages, and, of course, all practical or ethical norms. Everything must be trashed because the *hubris* of rationalism closes off any sense of the real root of its problem which Mulla Sadra and Vico had pointed this out at the beginning, namely, the reduction of being to essence and of life to concept. Today we witness reductive reason in a paroxysm of despair, like a scorpion in a circles of fire committing its own *auto da fe*.

In stark and concrete terms we live the effect of a loss of the sense of existence and the attempt to articulate and control all in the conceptual terms of essence.

b. The Roots of Mulla Sadra's Existential Response

Where can we go from here; where find an alternate way? Heidegger points out that each major step ahead implies a decision to develop one path which leaves alternate paths unexplored. Hence, the real step ahead consists in the step back (*Schritt zurück*) to that which thus far has been undeveloped. This suggests that in order to understand Mulla Sadra's penetrating and skillfully elaborated philosophy of existence it may help to review once again the sense of existence as it emerged initially among the Christian Church Fathers in the early centuries of this era.

Although Greek philosophy grew out of an intensive mythic sense of life in which all was a reflection of the will of the gods, it nonetheless presupposed matter always to have existed. As a result, attention and concern were focused upon the forms by which matter was determined to be of one type rather than of another. For Aristotle, this was the most manifest reality and his philosophizing began from there. By the end of his metaphysics he had come by a philosophical route to considerations of divine life as the principle of all.

Iqbal expresses the still deeper religious insight of Islam: "It is in fact the presence of the total infinite in the movement of knowledge that makes finite thinking possible." It is not we who discover God, but the being of God which enables us to think at all. Al-Ghazālī would abandon Ibn Sina's Islamic effort to develop the Greek philosophical tradition for lack of this awareness and Iqbal would criticize all efforts to reason to God on the same basis.[31]

I fear, however, that this response is too radical, for simply to reject the Greek pattern of reasoning to God is to lose the tools it provides for seeing the relation, or tieing back to God (re-tie or "*re-ligatio*" being an etymology of religion) each and every aspect of finite reality. This is the deeper and perduring significance of Thomas's "five ways" as they proceed in terms of efficient (Ways I-III), formal (Way IV) and final (Way V) causality.

This said, however, the challenge of Ghazālī and Iqbal remains, namely, is the human intellect sufficiently open to the divine in order for its work to be, not the creation of an idol in the place of God, but an opening to its own divine source, ground and goal? The Greek philosophical awareness of what it meant to be real would need considerable enrichment in order to be able to appreciate the foundational significance for human thought of its grounding in a fully transcendent and infinite Being.

It is possible to turn directly to revelation in the Holy Books which encourage one to look further into these issues. But if philosophy is to be a human endeavor with universal import then it cannot employ revelation as a premise. There are, however, two other approaches.

One approach is to do an archeology of knowledge, tracing it from its initial totemic form, through myth to philosophy. Such a study, carried out in the earlier chapters above, manifests human thought to have been deeply, richly and inherently religious from its origins.[32]

The other approach is to examine the point at which Greek thought encountered a culture shaped by revelation in order to see the development which took place in philosophical insight at that point. It was the early Christian Church Fathers developed an awareness of the meaning of being as existence. This consisted in transcending the Greek notion of being as form, which meant simply a certain differentiated type or kind, to an explicit awareness of the act of existence (*esse*) in terms of which being could be appreciated directly in its active and self-affirmative character. The precise basis for this step is difficult to identify in a conclusive manner, but some things are known.

The Greeks had considered matter (*hyle* -- the stuff of which things were made) -- to be eternal. Hence, no direct question arose concerning the existence or non-existence of things. As matter always had been, the only real questions for the Greeks concerned the shapes or forms under which it existed. Only at the conclusion of the Greek period did Plotinus (205-270 A.D.), rather than simply presupposing matter, attempt the first philosophical explanation of its origin. It was, he explained, the light from the One which, having been progressively attenuated as it emanated ever further from its source, finally turned to darkness.[33] The answer may not be satisfactory, but our interest lies in whence came this new sensitivity to reality which enabled him even to raise such a question. To relive this promises to enable one to recreate the original insight regarding existence.

It is known that shortly prior to Plotinus the Christian Fathers were aware of the need to explain the origin of matter. They explicitly opposed the Greek supposition of matter and affirmed that, like form, it too needed to be explained. The origin of both they traced to the Pantocrator; hence, the proper effect of creation was neither form nor matter, but the existence of beings so composed, or existence simply.[34]

Later, this would be the central insight also of Mulla Sadra. It is still being unfolded in the contemporary emergence of the existential sense of the human person. This directs the mind beyond form and species, that is beyond essence, and beyond place and time or any of the scientific categories. It centers instead upon the unique reality of each being, above all of the person as a participant in the creative power of God, as a being bursting into time who is and cannot be denied. It rejects the person being considered in any sense as nonbeing, or being treated as anything less than its full reality. The human person is a self, affirming its own unique existence, and irreducible to any specific group identity. It is an image of God for whom life is sacred and sanctifying, a child of God for whom to be is freely to dispose of the power of one's new and unique life in union with all humankind.

In sum, it was the unfolding by the Church Fathers of awareness of God and of his creation that made possible the discovery of existence which Mulla Sadra so brilliantly developed. This enabled him to articulate a line of causality deeper and more primary than the horizontal causality of motion between creatures, namely, to explore the vertical line of existence from God to creatures and their return to Him.[35] Mulla Sadra would develop this latter line with the philosophical tools he personally elaborated in a neo-Platonic vein as the flow of pure being.[36] For him the creative act of God and human actions were the same act.[37]

This, however, urges the question of the reality of the horizontal causal line, of the human and of one's interaction with other persons and with nature. Today these are the issues of social justice, the treatment of minorities, and the protection of the environment as special human concerns at this juncture. We shall look next for ways in which these concerns can be grounded ontologically and then finally for ways to implement the free and creative possibilities of humankind opened by Mulla Sadra. As the project is vast we must proceed here in somewhat summary fashion to suggest issues and sources which merit subsequent development.

THE EXISTENCE AND COMPOSITION OF FINITE BEINGS

If attention during the first millennium was focused upon God, it can be said that for the second millennium it has been focused upon this world, especially upon the human person. During the first millennium it was sufficient to see these in some relation to God, to show with Plato that unity did not preclude multiple beings provided they be seen precisely as related by participation to God.

The issue of this second millennium has been rather the existence of creatures — not by themselves, but in themselves. Since God exists, can there be room for the world, and particularly for truly free human beings? Here we shall look at two issues: (a) the subsistence of finite beings as existing in themselves, and (b) the internal constitution of such beings. The third issue, namely, the freedom and autonomy of the human person will be the subject of Part III. We shall treat each issue and its response in sequence; in fact, however, they constitute a cumulative problematic, just as their response also is cumulative.

a. Subsistence: the Existence of Finite Beings

In the first millennium of Christ and Mohammed as human attention was quite absorbed in assimilating their teaching about

God, the relative disappearance of the human was not considered to be a special problem, for humankind searched in God for its fulfillment. In the middle of this present millennium, however, attention shifted to the human. For some this was the person in search of God and for one's proper role in His creation. Increasingly, however, philosophers took a Promethean attitude. Today they will not be satisfied unless the legitimate human question in religion is recognized and receives an answer, namely, the issue of the status and role of creatures and of the human person in God's Providence.

Certainly, the path of being is the royal path for the human mind to develop its knowledge of, and response to, God. Parmenides had seen this immediately; it was the very first step in his initiation of the science of metaphysics in the West. As Mulla Sadra rightly pointed out, if this were a process of abstraction then the first principles would be empty.[38] If, however, they are statements of being and the mind proceeds according to the reality of existence then they articulate the Divine and its work.

In his Poem,[39] Parmenides noted that being as such is affirmation, and hence could not include its own negation: being is, non-being is not. Negation is essential to beginning and limitation, and hence to multiplicity and change; but being as such is affirmation and hence must be eternal, one and unchanging. Mulla Sadra agrees and thus sees being as absolute and noncomposite or simple, which is to say, that it is the unique and infinite Divine life.

Some would see Parmenides as denying all reality to limited, multiple or changing being. Nevertheless, the second part of this Poem is entirely concerned with such changing beings. How to reconcile the two — the unlimited and the limited, the infinite and the finite, eternity and time — was left to Plato. He responded by developing the structure of participation. But in his famous allegory of the cave this worked in a manner similar to light so that the multiple were but shadows or images (*mimesis*) of the One. Aristotle soon abandoned the use of the term "*mimesis*" for fear that it would not allow for an adequate appreciation of the active reality of limited beings, but reduce them to passive shadows.[40]

Earlier medieval Christian philosophy, working on a Platonic and neo-Platonic model, experienced difficulty in asserting the distinct activity of finite beings. While benefiting from the mystical potentialities of the vertical line of causality from God's existence, its Platonism left it poorly equipped to affirm the distinctive reality of the horizontal causal line between creatures. Hence, some form of divine supplement in the form of illumination or "seeds" was required as if creatures were not quite entitled to act — and by implication to be — in their own right.

Mulla Sadra shares this problem. His attempts to resolve it in a neo-Platonic, emanationist framework led him to statements which strongly suggest that if being is existence and not essence then not only is God all, but there is nothing other.[41] It is true, as Mulla Sadra points out, that God's existence is also consciousness, which develops a limitless number of existents according to multiple modes[42] as finite beings.[43] But when this route was classically developed by Shankara in the rich Hindu metaphysical tradition the reality of limited being seemed ultimately to be absorbed into God. In even closer parallel to Mulla Sadra, Ramanuja attempted to give more distinctive reality to limited beings by constituting them ultimately via attributes of God. All three would say that in the stage of reasoning (in contrast to that of intuition) the world is real. Fazlur Rahman noted that higher knowledge does not negate old knowledge, but puts it into perspective.[44] Yet there was always the still higher or deeper — and, in any case, truer — level of intuition in which the world and the individual could be called an illusion (*maya*) by Shankara and "perishing" by Mulla Sadra.[45]

For a distinctive step beyond the difficulties of this Platonic and neo-Platonic horizon one needs to turn to Aristotle who precisely went beyond Plato's more passive sense of beings as images or shadows remembering what had been passively observed and now remembered. For Aristotle the point of departure was being as changing and hence as active and dynamic. Beings were ultimately substances standing in their own right and all depended not on a passively contemplated One, but on a quintessentially active divine life as the act of "knowing on knowing".

Paul Tillich notes that because Platonic formalism does not adequately establish the distinctive reality of the world and human beings, while nominalism and positivism do not establish the reality of God, philosophizing in a religious context has gravitated naturally toward an Aristotelian realism in recognition of both God and world. This was precisely the step taken by Thomas Aquinas.

In going beyond the Platonic thought of the Patristic age, and adding to it Aristotle's scientific structures and active sense of being — now intensified in terms of existence — Thomas opened a new scientific philosophical age in which "theology", properly as a logos, could be born.

For Mulla Sadra, thinking Platonically, these categories remained a passive function of essence and hence were seen as existentially empty. In contrast Aquinas, thinking in an Aristotelian manner, took them actively and in relation to existence. Hence a substance is that to which it pertains precisely to exist in itself, and a being possessing or exercising such existence would be a subsistent being. For Capriolus, in contrast to Cajetan, the proportioned existence itself, and not a mode, is itself the principle of subsistence. This insight regarding being as act and active made it possible to receive more fully the revelation of God's creative act as making things themselves to exist (something that Mulla Sadra manifested himself most anxious to do through his critique of essence). Thomas's deployment of the Aristotelian category of substance in the existential context of creation makes it possible to appreciate the existence of finite beings as from, by, and for God, yet as lived by beings existing in themselves (*in se*).

b. The Internal Composition of Finite Beings

It is not sufficient, however, simply to leave subsistence as existence for of itself this would be the divine. Hence, in order for creatures not to be absorbed into God, which Fazlur Rahman sees as continually threatening the thought of Mulla Sadra, it is necessary to look into the constitution of beings which so exist. For lack of this the Mutakallimun were left with an occasionalism which carried a number of implications. There were no finite substances or beings which exist in themselves (*in-se*); instead all must be recreated at each moment. From this it follows also that human actions do not effect or cause things, but rather are the occasions upon which God brings things about as His effects. Fazlur Rahman insists that for Mulla Sadra this does not mean that only God causes, but that nothing causes without God.[46] However, he recognized that some expressions of Mulla Sadra seem to go beyond this and there my be some inconsistencies as he struggles with this point.

Further, while occasionalism is generally and correctly

considered a metaphysical position regarding the being of effects, it is not so readily recognized that it has powerful epistemological implications. In formal logic the syllogism is constructed of two premises, which in precise combination cause the conclusion; this is the very heart of logical reasoning. If, however, with occasionalism it is not finite beings, but God who causes effects, then the premises do not cause the conclusion. This results in what al-Ghazālī referred to as the "equivalence of proofs":[47] the premises may be wrong but the conclusion could be correct, for there is no necessary connection between them. In such a case, one could not avoid skepticism with regard to human reasoning.

Thomas agreed that God was indeed great, but not because he caused the finite effects of each human action, but rather because he caused finite beings who were themselves fully capable of carrying out all the actions and effects which corresponded to their nature. This is the proper autonomy of the human person; it is the implication of the participation of beings as act in Absolute Being as existence itself.

The reasoning of Aquinas a century after Ghazālī is indicative of what can be done with Mulla Sadra's insight of the centrality of existence. The discussion of being as existing had proceeded in al-Farabi and Ibn Sina to the point of distinguishing it from form, and relating it to essence as its principle of limitation and definition. But how these were related in a being, and indeed as constituting that being, was not understood. As Mulla Sadra would later argue, if existence was an accident in relation to essence then essence would need to exist in at least logical priority to existence -- which would be logically absurd.[48]

Based on his appreciation, like Mulla Sadra's, of being as existing, Aquinas reasoned as follows:

(a) as existence is quintessentially affirmation, where it is not infinite but limited (that is, where existence is not absolute, but in part negated) this must be due to something other than existence;

(b) that "other" could not be merely outside of being such as its efficient cause, for being must have in, and as, itself whatever is required in order that it be what it is (it must be undivided in itself); further

(c) as "inside being" this "other" would have to be; yet as

"other than existence" it could not be of itself; hence the "other" as principle of limitation would have to be made to be by existence, in relation to which it stands as potency;

(d) this "other" must be then a determined and limiting capacity for existence, that is, a capacity for "this much of existence and no more"; and finally

(e) existence being thus limited and graded, Fabro and Mulla Sadra would call this an intensive notion of being.[49]

On this basis Thomas expanded the meaning of Aristotle's act and potency from merely form and matter as the internal components of changing beings, to express the relation between the internal components of limited beings: existence as act and essence as potency. Neither existence nor essence are things or beings, but are rather internal principles of being. Existence is that by which a being is — which was Mulla Sadra's great insight. But essence is also necessary, for it is that by which a being is what it is — a limited and determined being distinct from all else.

Limited or finite beings are then composite beings. Their existence could not be self-explained, that is, explained by their essence, which in this regard is potency. It could be explained only by Being that is incomposite or simple. This is quite the essence of Mulla Sadra's metaphysics. The studies of Fabro on the history of the notion of participation show this to have been a personal discovery of Aquinas.[50] His essential formulation of the nature of multiple beings or of the finite order as participating in the absolute being of God was the relation of composite beings (beings composed of existence as act and essence as potency) to the incomposite, simple, and hence absolute Being.[51]

Fabro pointed out further that the inner constitution of being meant that beings were inherently analogous. Each finite being constitutes a proportion of proportions, that is, of its existence to its proper essence (the existence of being A is in proportion to the essence of being A, as the existence of being B is in proportion to the essence of being B. This analogy between finite beings enables one to appreciate the extension of language as one proceeds from the finite or composite beings as effects (where the essence and existence are really distinct principles of being) to the infinite, incomposite or simple being as cause (where essence and existence are not distinct, but one). Analogy, Fabro would conclude, is the language of Being;[52] Mulla Sadra would describe this as systematic ambiguity (Tashkik).[53]

THE EXISTING HUMAN BEING AS FREE, RESPONSIBLE AND CREATIVE

a. The Freedom and Responsibility of the Existing Human Being

Pope John Paul II in his recent Encyclical "Faith and Reason" suggests that the proper methodology for theology and philosophy is cyclical, that is: (a) to begin from revelation as received through the Prophets and Sacred Books which challenge one to develop fully and solidly the capabilities of the human mind, then (b) to proceed carefully, actively and creatively to the development of philosophy by the light of human reason, and finally (c) to return to revelation so that philosophy thus developed can contribute to the proper unfolding of revelation in history.[54]

The significance of revelation for philosophy becomes even more evident as one attempts to articulate philosophically a vision of the human person which can face the challenges of eschatology. This demands not only the full spiritual openness of the human to the Transcendent, but also, in view of personal resurrection and definitive judgment, an individual with personal freedom and responsibility subsisting in this world.

This challenge was central to the drama of the life of al-Ghazālī as he described it in his *Munqidh*. The spiritual nature of humankind was the crucial issue for al-Ghazālī and the one which moved him to break away from philosophy as developed by the great Islamic heirs of the Greek tradition, al-Farabi and Ibn Sina.

For Aristotle the discovery of form and matter as intrinsic principles of any changing being meant that the form was intimately, indeed totally, related to the matter it informed. But if so then how could this form be the source and foundation of spiritual activity? If matter was concrete and singular, how could the form of matter be a principle for the abstract and universal terms which were central to scientific thought or, even more, the principle for the free exercise of the human will?

Aristotle's solution, taken up by al-Farabi and Ibn Sina almost

1500 years latter, was that such terms must depend on a form which was separated from matter — an agent intellect existing separately which could be drawn upon by many persons. But as this would need to be also the principle of free human actions, it would then be difficult to assess personal responsibility. This, in turn, constituted a difficulty in interpreting the Scriptural passages regarding personal immortality and the last judgment. As a result the Greek oriented Islamic philosophers tended to interpret final judgment and eternal reward rather as allegorical than objective statements of the reality of human life.

Al-Ghazālī naturally drew back. All his instincts as a devoted servant of God told him "to take to the road,"[55] to escape this heretical attenuation of the faith regarding the meaning and exercise of human life. The result was his departure from Baghdad and from philosophy.

This was the crisis which Mulla Sadra would face later. Confronted with the restrictive confines of philosophy done in terms of essences or natures he would separate himself from such thinking at every turn and in every way. Al-Ghazālī could see that a separated agent intellect would not allow for personal freedom and responsibility. Mulla Sadra's interpretation of the agent intellect as a divine attribute[56] would appear to encounter similar difficulties, especially as to the personal nature of human freedom and its responsibility for evil.

Christian philosophy took the opposite path; reflecting its sense of the autonomy of creatures under God, it placed the agent intellect in the individual human person. But there it encountered Aristotle's original difficulty: if the soul was spiritual how could it also be the form of the body? In the Augustinian tradition up to Bonaventure this was resolved by positing multiple souls, but this created its own difficulties for the unity of the human person as identically bodily in nature and spiritual in dignity — something of great importance in our day.

In a manner analogous to his work on the inner constitution of finite beings described above, Thomas approached the issue of the spiritual nature of the human person, of human freedom and responsibility. He reasoned in the light of being as existence that:

- one being could have but one existence;
- one existence could have but one essence, and

- one essence could have but one form.

Hence, there could be but one form (or soul) in the human person, whose nature is then neither beastly, nor angelic, nor both, but properly and uniquely human.

This entails, in turn, that the human mind is not dependent on a separated intellect in order to form universal concepts. Rather, the human intellect itself has the capacity to abstract universal natures from concrete sensed objects. Thus the agent intellect which for the Greeks, as for the Islamic scholars of Greek philosophy, had been separated from the human person and shared by many was now seen to be an internal capacity proper to each person, who was free, responsible and subject to judgement and reward for his or her actions.

There are other implications of supreme importance for our present attempt to construct a world that is truly humane: the unique dignity and destiny of the human body; the properly sensual and engaged, yet transcendent character of human consciousness; the role of the human person as the Cusan point of unity of all creation; and the social character of human rights and their extension to the right to food, to work, to one's culture and religion, etc.

In sum, the participation that Plato saw only externally as between beings was now articulated in terms of the internal constitution of being. Finite beings and hence human persons could be seen as substances existing in their own right (*in se*), but not by themselves or absolutely (*a se*), as is God. As self-conscious and free, persons could act responsibly and hence be subject to final judgment, reward or punishment for lives lived well or ill. Their basic orientation as sharing in divine life is to the good and hence to resurrection and reward. This eschatology insisted upon by revelation and all who would be faithful thereto suggests as in need of further development any theory which would deny creative freedom or responsibility to persons and peoples, either as an ontological or as a socio-political reality.

Mulla Sadra recoiled from the effects in philosophy of treating essences alone, which would reduce being to essence. But he is in danger of falling into the opposite dilemma, namely, of making existence to be being. Though here he is on more solid ground--for this is true of God as simple, absolute and self-explanatory —

nonetheless, he is in danger of losing in the divine the reality of finite beings. As with the second half of the Poem of Parmenides and with Shankara, he goes about articulating brilliantly the dynamic process that does exist on this level, yet always he is dogged by his words that in a final sense this is nothing. (Fazlur Rahman notes the similar ambiguity between passages of Mulla Sadra in which the first principles bespeak the very reality and power of God, and other passages in which such principles are spurned as empty and vacuous.[57]) The significance of the work of Aquinas lies in the step he took toward resolving this central tension of being. To do so he developed the notion of subsistence in a philosophy of being as existence, rather than as essence, situating therein all required for the spiritual activity of human persons. As we shall see below, Mulla Sadra approached this rather in terms of process.

b. Human Cooperation in God's Creation

In the philosophy of this century the thought of Mulla Sadra is perhaps most reflected in that of M. Iqbal who wrote his thesis on Mulla Sadra and drew notably on Bergson and related thinkers, and in Alfred North Whitehead's process philosophy. It might be especially helpful to look at the concerns of the latter to uncover the special relevance of Mulla Sadra for our times.

Whitehead and the derivative school of philosophers share the concerns of many that a philosophy built in terms of substance would be limited and limiting. They fear that it would restrict the capabilities of humans to their generic and specific features, that all change could be understood only as accidental and hence superficial, and that human progress would then be considered marginal rather than central. Finally, they fear that God as absolute would not be able to take account of, or be affected by, the heroic struggle and real achievements of people. Hence, they think of being as process and of finite beings very much in Mulla Sadra's sense. The world is a process of derivation from God[58] similar to a "particular 'structure of events'. . . . Things are particular segments of this continuous process regarded as a particular 'event system' for purposes of description."[59]

Of course, an existential philosophy of being would respond that natures are markers of human dignity below which no one should be treated; that they are capabilities for conscious and free action according to the essence of each human person; that each concrete essence is unique, just as is each existence; and that the related actions as accidents are not merely external adjuncts, but make the whole person to be such. That is for example, they make the person, to be kind and loving or the opposite. This seems essential for the eschatological human destiny to judgment, resurrection and life in divine goodness.

Nevertheless, each age has its own proper concerns and unfolds its own particular dimension of the human mystery. Contemporary culture is marked by dynamic change which intensifies the search for identity and purpose. The process thought of Mulla Sadra brings great richness to this search:

- his philosophy of existence focuses attention on the concrete particular person;
- his integrating sense of finality as orientation to the Absolute Good gives a sense of purpose, for God's creative act is both efficient cause making us to be and final cause drawing us to him in love;[60]
- his dynamic movement-in-substance (*haraka fi'l-jawhar*)[61] enables an intense sense of development and progress; and
- his systematic ambiguity opens new horizons of diversity and unity in this age of cultural globalization.

All this must be harvested and applied in our present circumstances. However, my sense is that if we remain within the terms of scientific reasoning employed thus far we will fail to reap the rich harvest of needed insight that Mulla Sadra brings to our present task.

He points out rightly the limitations of conceptual reason and the need to move beyond this to intuition, but he sees this as otherworldly and characteristic rather of the Perfect Man. What is both needed and within reach is instead a new level of human consciousness while in this life, namely, an aesthetic awareness. In the structure of Kant's *Critiques* this comes third. It goes beyond science and the universal and necessary categories of the *Critique of Pure Reason*, and beyond the universal categorical imperative of the *Critique of Practical Reason*. Yet, aesthetic awareness does not leave these behind, but integrates both in the third *Critique of Aesthetic Judgment.* This is understanding in terms of beauty and the sublime which mark an eschatology.

The aesthetic is able to grasp the higher principles which in their simplicity do not abstract from, but contain the multiple in their uniqueness. Creative intuition appreciates the dynamic process, but does so from the point of view of its aspiration for a goal in which opposition and conflict are overcome by goodness and love. For Mulla Sadra this is a realization which is beyond this life; it is had through reunion with the Perfect Man, become an attribute of God. However, the final cause is not only the last in realization, but the first in exercise in as much as it mobilizes and coordinates all the rest. Hence, eschatology is not only a time after this life, but shapes our life process from the beginning. To appreciate this — which is to live life meaningfully and fully — calls for a mode of awareness that can appreciate the concrete particularity of acts of human freedom. It must do so in a way that stimulates, integrates and harmonizes them in intuitions united in terms of beauty and the sublime. To be lived consciously in time, eschatology requires an aesthetic mode of awareness. Read in these terms, Mulla Sadra's work on existence and process can be appreciated in its full inspiration. It states life with a holy awe, is buoyed up and drawn forward with confidence, and opens to that commitment of love from which peaceful progress proceeds. Deeply understood, his philosophy emerges as a work of the Spirit — of faith, hope and charity — which can turn hatred into love, conflict into peace, and death into eternal life.

NOTES

1. Iqbal, p. 180.
2. *Ibid.*, p. 62.
3. Richard Joseph McCarthy, *Freedom and Fulfillment* (Boston: Twayne, 1980), pp. xii-xiii and xlvi-xlvii.
4. (Chicago: The University of Chicago Press, 1974), 3 vols, especially the Introduction and General Prologue in Vol. I, pp. 30-99.
5. McCarthy, pp. xiv-xx.
6. Farid Jabre in al-Ghazālī, *Al-Munqidh min al-Dalāl (Erreur et Délivrance)* trans., intro., and notes par Farid Jabre

(Beyrouth: Commision Internationale pour la Tradūction des Chefs-d'Oeuvre, 1959), pp. 21-22.
7. McCarthy, pp. xxxv-xlii.
8. *Ibid.*, pp. xxi-xxiv; Jabre, p. 53.
9. *Ibid.*, pp. xxiii.
10. *Munqidh*, chapter 4.
11. Jabre, pp. 27-41.
12. Gerald Stanley, "Contemplation as Fulfillment of the Human Person", in George F. McLean, ed., *Personalist Ethics and Human Subjectivity*, Vol. II of *Ethics at the Crossroads* (Washington, D.C.: The Council for Research in Values and Philosophy, 1995), appendix.
13. Jabre, pp. 41-51.
14. V. Havel, "Address in Philadelphia", July 4, 1994 in *The Washington Post*, July 6, A 19.
15. McCarthy, pp. 121-122, nn. 43-44.
16. Jabre, pp. 41-47.
17. R. Descartes, *Discourse on Method*, III.
18. G. F. McLean, "Philosophic Continuity and Thomism" in *Teaching Thomism Today* (Washington: Catholic University, 1963), pp. 23-28.
19. *Munqidh*, chapter 2, part 2.
20. Jabre, p. 48.
21. McCarthy, p 121, n. 43.
22. Hodgson, vol. II, p. 186, n. 18, points insightfully in this direction noting that the philosophy/theology of Paul Tillich may be the best modern correspondent to the thought of Ghazālī on how "reason leads to the need for ultimate faith, but awaits revelation to carry it further. . . . (This) is not a matter of supplementing reason on its own level, but of complementing it in total experience."
23. Jabre, p. 48.
24. McCarthy, pp. lvi-lx.
25. *Ibid.*, pp. xxvi-xxix.
26. *Munqidh*, chap. 2, part 3.
27. 'Abd al-Dā 'im al-Baqarī, *I'tirāfāt al-Ghazālī, aw kayfa 'avrakla al-Ghazālī nafsahu* (The Confessions of al-Ghazālī) (Cairo: 1943). See McCarthy, pp. xxvi-xxix.
28. F. Jabre, *al-Munqidh*, pp. 22-23. See McCarthy's response, pp. xxxv-xlii.

29. R. Garrigou Lagrange, *Christian Perfection and Contemplation according to St. Thomas Aquinas and St. John of the Cross*, trans. M.T. Doyle (London: Herder, 1937); *The Three Ages of the Interior Life, Prelude to Eternal Life*, trans. M.T. Doyle (London: Herder: 1947).

30. John Paul II, *Fides et Ratio*, Sept. 14, 1998, http://www.vatican.va/holy_father/...c_15101998_fides-et-ratio_en.stml.

31. M. Iqbal, *Reconstruction of Religious Thought in Islam*.

32. There is a similarity here to social contract political theory which sees all in terms of a supposed original position, that is, a social contract hypothetically conceived. All such social theory is developed within the framework of that original contract. Our position differs, however, in that it proceeds not on an hypothesis, but by returning to the earliest character of human thought as anthropologically established.

33. Plotinus, *Enneads II*, 5 (25), ch.5.

34. Maurizio Flick and Zoltan Alszeghy, *Il Creatore, l'inizio della salvezza* (Firenze: Lib. Ed. Fiorentina, 1961), pp. 32-49; Mulla Sadra, *Livre des Penetrations Metaphysiques*, ed. H. Corbin (Teheran: Inst. Franco-Iranien, 1964), VII. (Henceforth *LP*.)

35. Fazlur Rahman, *The Philosophy of Mulla Sadra* (Albany: SUNY, 1975), pp. 74-75. (Henceforth *FR*.)

36. Mulla Sadra, *Asfar*, I, 2, pp. 320, 339-341; *FR* p. 89.

37. *FR*, p. 176.

38. *Asfar*, IV, 2, p. 115; I, 3, p. 429; *FR*, p. 238.

39. Parmenides, fragments in G. McLean and P. Aspell, *Readings in Ancient Western Philosophy* (New York: Appleton, Century, Crofts, 1970); Alexander P.D. Mourelatos, *The Route of Parmenides: A Study of Work, Images, and Argument in the Fragments* (New Haven: Yale, 1970). 40. *LP* VIII, n. 8.

41. *Asfar*, I, 2, pp. 308-318; *FR*, pp. 30-31.

42. Exploring the possibilities of consciousness, Paul Tillich suggested a reverse phenomenological approach proceeding through human concern to God as "Ultimate Concern." *Systematic Theology* (Chicago: Univ. of Chicago, 1951), vol. I; *The Courage to Be* (New Haven: Yale Univ. Press, 1952).

43. *Asfar*, IV, 2, p. 116; I, 3, p. 213; *FR*, p. 238.

44. Shankara, *Vedanta Sutras*, Introduction; *LP* VIII, n. 8; *Asfar*, I, 2, p. 292; *FR* p. 38.

45. "The relationship between theology and philosophy is best construed as a circle. Theology's source and starting point must always be the word of God revealed in history, while its final goal will be an understanding of that word which increases with each passing generation. Yet, since God's word is Truth (cf. Jn 17:17), the human search for truth — philosophy, pursued in keeping with its own rules — can only help to understand God's word better. It is not just a question of theological discourse using this or that concept or element of a philosophical construct; what matters most is that the believer's reason use its powers of reflection in the search for truth which moves from the word of God towards a better understanding of it. It is as if, moving between the twin poles of God's word and a better understanding of it, reason is offered guidance and is warned against paths which would lead it to stray from revealed Truth and to stray in the end from the truth pure and simple. Instead, reason is stirred to explore paths which of itself it would not even have suspected it could take. This circular relationship with the word of God leaves philosophy enriched, because reason discovers new and unsuspected horizons." John Paul II, *Encyclical Letter: Fides et Ratio*, n. 73.

46. Aristotle abandoned the use of mimesis after the very first books of his *Organon*, seemingly for fear that it did not assure the reality of finite things.

47. *FR*, p. 178.

48. G. McLean, Introduction to Al-Ghazālī, *Deliverance from Error and Mystical Union with the Almighty; Al-Munqidh min al- Dalal* (Washington: The Council for Research in Values and Philosophy, 1999), p. 50.

49. *LP* V; *FR*, pp. 32-33.

50. *Asfar*, I, 3, p. 83; *FR*, p. 114; C. Fabro, *Participation et causalite selon S. Thomas d'Aquin* (Louvain: Pub. Univ. de Louvain, 1961).

51. *Ibid.*; *La Nozione metafisica de partecipazione secondo S. Tommaso d'Aquino* (Torino: Societa Ed. Internazionale, 1950), 75-122.

52. *Ibid.*

53. *Ibid.*

54. Fazlur Rahman, "Sadra's Doctrine of Being and God-World Relationship" in *Essays in Islamic Philosophy and Science*, ed.

George Hourani (Albany: SUNY); *FR*, pp. 34-37.
55. Al-Ghazālī, *Deliverance from Error and Mystical Union with the Almighty*, III, p. 93.
56. *FR*, p. 77.
57. See note 8 above.
58. *FR*, p. 171.
59. *Ibid.*, pp 97-98.
60. *Asfar*, I, 2, pp. 263 and 273; *FR*, p. 80
61. *FR*, pp. 94-108.

PART III

CONTEMPORARY PHILOSOPHICAL WAYS TO GOD

CHAPTER VIII

HUMAN SUBJECTIVITY AND PERSONAL WAYS TO GOD

We began the last chapter with some passages from Iqbal which I would like to recall here for, as was noted there, the path to which he pointed was not only that taken by al-Ghazālī, but that which is opening now at this dawn of the new millenium. For Iqbal making man at home in the world might be a proper task for "metaphysics . . . (as) a logically consistent view of the world with God as part of that view." But he saw another stage in which

> metaphysics is displaced by psychology, and religious life develops the ambition to come into direct contact with the ultimate reality. It is here that religion becomes a matter of personal assimilation of life and power; and the individual achieves a free personality, not by releasing himself from the fetters of the law, but by discovering the ultimate source of the law within the depths of his own consciousness.[1]

In this light Iqbal would probably be very interested in recent developments in phenomenology which have been central to the recent discovery of human subjectivity as a new, vastly more fruitful interior dimension of reality. Iqbal notes that

> the aspiration of religion soars higher than that of philosophy. Philosophy is an intellectual view of things; and as such, does not care to go beyond a concept which can reduce all the rich variety of experience to a system. It sees Reality from a distance as it were. Religion seeks a closer contact with Reality. The one is theory; the other is living experiences, association, intimacy. In order to achieve this intimacy thought must rise higher than itself, and find its fulfillment in an attitude of mind which religion describes as prayer — one of the

last words on the lips of the Prophet of Islam.[2]

Hence the search into human subjectivity is really at the heart of Iqbal's concern for the reconstruction of religion. He brilliantly rearticulated the Islamic vision in terms of the vitalism of his time, which was but the beginning of this century's discovery and appreciation of human subjectivity. Hence, it is necessary to follow the emergence of this attention and to elaborate the possibilities of the phenomenology to which it led in order to extend Iqbal's work of religious reconstruction. This has the potentiality of enabling the human spirit to liberate itself from egoism, and to come finally home — this time not only to self, but to others and to God.

ANSELM AND THE INTERIOR WAY

This, of course, is not a new venture. Classically the path had been elaborated by Augustine in a tradition richly elaborated by St. Bonaventure in his *Itinerary of the Mind to God (Itinerarium mentis ad Deum)*. In this St. Anselm[3] played a special role.

To appreciate human subjectivity as a way to God it might help to situate it in relation to two landmarks, one medieval and the other modern. The first, Thomas Aquinas, working in the objectively oriented Aristotelian context, rejected the approach of Anselm as consisting in a process of the mind without necessary foundation in things themselves (ST I, 2, 1). In this perspective what was real was what existed outside or over against (ob-ject) the human mind, which could be a place of all kinds of fanciful, imaginary patterns of ideas. What that did not adequately appreciate was the importance of the creative work of the mind and the way it constituted the highest form of created and hence of limited existence.

That was to be appreciated only later and indeed would characterize the modern mind. Today we recognize that world power consists less in the physical resources of land and minerals than in information and technological capabilities. Philosophically, this emergent typically modern appreciation has been marked by Descartes as a defining figure of the philosophy of the age who not only emptied the mind until he identified as an Archimedean fulcrum an idea which could not be doubted, but moreover set about reconstructing the world exclusively in terms of what was clear and distinct to the human mind. All else was simply a matter of prudence. Later Immanuel Kant would proceed to show how the content of the mind and the ordered universe itself consisted not in what was there to be drawn into and informed by the human consciousness, but rather what was precisely the result of that process.

This chapter will focus on how this unfolded in recent existential and phenomenological philosophies. But it is the major thesis of this entire work that the awareness of God is not a later addition or superstructure of human knowledge, but that it is foundational to both being and consciousness. Hence, rather than simply adding the modern phenomenology of human consciousness over and above earlier, objective pathways it seems important to look back into the earlier classical philosophers such as St. Anselm to see if such insight is present and foundational there.

Anselm had written a long work, the *Monologion*, which developed a very extensive pattern of *a posteriori* reasoning from the various dimensions of the objective universe as effects to God as their cause. After having done this he was asked to write a brief work giving the jist of what he had written. Hence his *Proslogion* is a note on the conclusion of his *a posteriori* reasoning carried out in objective terms. He was intent on pointing out that God as thus known was not only the greatest of beings but existence itself. Existence pertained to the very essence of God and, as Iqbal would later affirm, this was the condition of possibility for all thinking and being.

His procedure was to note first that God is "a being than which nothing greater can be conceived." This could be either the conclusion of his *a posteriori* philosophical reasoning in the *Monologion* or an assertion of faith. Either way it is a matter of understanding and not just of will because even the unbeliever understands its meaning or nature.

But he goes further to affirm that this is not only a matter of understanding, but also of existence, because otherwise such a being with existence added would be even greater than "that greater than which nothing can be conceived" — an evident impossibility.

He reinforces this by a later note in which he distinguishes the term and its signification. Were one to use a term without its proper signification one could assert anything: that fire is water, that being is not being or that God does not exist. If, however, one takes thought seriously and holds to its signification then one cannot assert that God as "that greater than which nothing can be conceived" could not exist.

Hence he concludes, even if one were unwilling to believe that God exists it would be impossible for him to understand this to be true. As God is Being Itself it is impossible not only to have finite beings without him (the *a posteriori* reasoning), but for him not to be. This is inconceivable because impossible; it is the center of both thought and being.

THE RESURGENCE OF SUBJECTIVITY

At the beginning of this century, it had appeared that the rationalist project of stating all in clear and distinct objective terms was close to completion. This was to be achieved in either the empirical terms of the positivist tradition of sense knowledge or in the formal and essentialist terms of the Kantian intellectual tradition.[4] Whitehead writes that at the turn of the century, when with Bertrand Russell he went to the First World Congress of Philosophy in Paris, it seemed that, except for some details of application, the work of physics had been essentially completed. To the contrary, however, the very attempt to finalize scientific knowledge with its most evolved concepts made manifest the radical insufficiency of the objectivist approach and led to renewed appreciation of the importance of subjectivity.

Similarly, Wittgenstein began by writing his *Tractatus Logico-Philosophicus*[5] on the Lockean supposition that significant knowledge consisted in constructing a mental map corresponding point to point to the external world as perceived by sense experience. In such a project the spiritual element of understanding, i.e., the grasp of the relations between the points on this mental map and the external world was relegated to the margin as simply "unutterable." Later experience in teaching children, however, led Wittgenstein to the conclusion that this empirical mental mapping was simply not what was going on in human knowledge. In his *Blue and Brown Books*[6] and his subsequent *Philosophical Investigations*[7] Wittgenstein shifted human consciousness or intentionality, which previously had been relegated to the periphery, to the very the center of concern. The focus of his philosophy was no longer the positivist replication of the external world, but the human construction of language and of worlds of meaning.[8]

A similar process was underway in the Kantian camp. There Husserl's attempt to bracket all elements, in order to isolate pure essences for scientific knowledge, forced attention to the limitations of a pure essentialism and opened the way for his understudy, Martin Heidegger, to rediscover the existential and historical dimensions of reality in his *Being and Time*.[9] The religious implications of this new sensitivity would be articulated by Karl Rahner in his work, *Spirit in the World*, and by the Second Vatican Council in its Constitution, *The Church in the World*.[10]

For Heidegger the meaning of being and of life was unveiled and emerged — the two processes were identical — in conscious human life (*dasein*) lived through time and therefore through history. Thus human consciousness becomes the new focus of attention. The uncovering or bringing into light (the etymology of the term "phenomenology") of its unfolding patterns and interrelations would open a new era of human awareness. Epistemology and metaphysics would develop — and merge — in the very work of tracking the nature and direction of this process.

Thus, for Heidegger's successor, Hans-Georg Gadamer, the task becomes the uncovering of how human persons, emerging in the culture of a family, neighborhood and people, exercise their freedom and weave their cultural tradition. This is not history as a mere compilation of whatever humankind does or makes, but culture as the fabric of human symbols and interrelations by which a human group unveils being in its time. An account of this process of the development of culture as the basis for the realization of civil society today will be chapter IX of this work.

Iqbal provides needed direction here by pointing out that a religious outlook is not an external search for power and control susceptible to reduction to empirical investigation and pragmatic interpretation. Rather religion entails an inner attitude which takes us to the very roots of our being and even to its source.

These developments of the present century point us deeply into human subjectivity, but what ultimate meaning does this unveil for life? Could this new focus upon human subjectivity be but another chapter in *Paradise Lost* in which humankind attempts to seize its own destiny, and thereby to exclude God? Does interacting more consciously mean to attack others more devastatingly, killing not only bodies but spirits as well? Will the new awareness of cultures open new periods of persecution and cultural genocide? Very concretely, "Can we get along" as peoples, as cultures and as civilizations?

"Appreciation"[11] is a key element in Iqbal's thought regarding religion. It unites the elements of the previous chapters of this work regarding systematic philosophy, namely, existence, the subsistence of the human person and the causal participation of human life in the divine. It does so, however, not as effective, objective realities to be known, but as subjective realities to be lived and savored in a manner that is itself as religious as prayer and contemplation. This is the intent of a phenomenology in terms of the consciously lived appreciation of our life as gift. It leads one to the total absolute, now however not only as a condition of knowledge, but as the source and hence the goal of love. This can be seen through phenomenologies of "gift", homecoming, the I-thou relation and participation. We shall look at each of these in turn.

PHENOMENOLOGY OF "GIFT" AS A WAY TO GOD

One can begin with the person as a polyvalent unity operating on both the physical and non-physical or spiritual levels. Though the various sciences analyze distinct dimensions, the person is not a construct of independent components, but an identity: the physical and the psychic are dimensions of oneself and of no other. Further, this identity is not the result of one's personal development, but is had by one from his or her very beginning; it is a given for each person. Hence, while one can grow indefinitely, act endlessly, and do and make innumerable things, the growth and actions will be always one's own. I am the same given or person who perdures through all the stages of my growth.

This givenness appears also through reflection upon inter-personal relations. One does not properly create these, for they are possible only if one already has received one's being. Further, to open to others is a dynamism which pertains to one's very nature and which can be suppressed only at the price of deep psychological disturbance. Relatedness is given with one's nature; it is received as a promise and a task: it is one's destiny. One determines only the degree of one's presence to others.[12]

Unfortunately, this givenness is often taken in the sense of closure associated with the terms 'datum' or 'data', whether hypothetical or evidential. In the hypothetical sense, a given is a stipulation agreed upon by the relevant parties as the basis for a process of argumentation: "granted X, then Y". Such are the premises of an argument or the postulates in a mathematical demonstration. In the evidential sense, data are the direct and warranted observations of what actually is the case. In both these meanings the terms 'given' or 'data' direct the mind exclusively toward the future or consequent as one's only concern. Here the use of the past participle of the verb stem (*data*) closes off any search toward the past so that when one given is broken down by an analysis new givens appear. One never gets behind some hypothetical or evidential given.

This closure is done for good reason, but it leaves open a second — and for our purposes potentially important — sense of 'given'. This is expressed by the nominative form, '*donum*' or gift. In contrast to the other meanings, this points back, as it were, behind itself to its source in ways similar to the historians' use the term 'fact'. They note that a fact is not simply there; its meaning has been molded or made (*facta*) within the ongoing process of human life.[13] In this sense it points back to its origin and origination; this could be a road home.

However, this potentially rich return to the source was blocked at the beginning of the 19th century by a shift to an anthropocentric view. The universe of meaning was circumscribed by the human as a physical or temporal reality among other beings. There was not only, in Heidegger's terms, a forgetfulness of being, but a merciless campaign to control man by ridiculing or suppressing any and all attempts at deeper explorations of reality. From New York to Oxford, to Moscow to Beijing metaphysics became the pariah — which makes so telling the present reemergence of metaphysics as the center of human interest.

In the reductivist humanist horizon facts came to be seen especially as made by humans — conceived either as individuals in the liberal tradition, or as a class in the socialist tradition — to which correspond the ideals of progress and praxis, respectively. Because what was made by man could always be remade by him,[14] this turned aside a radical search into the character of life as gift. Attention remained only upon the future, understood simply in terms of the human and especially of what humans could do by their own, either individual or social, praxis.

There are reasons to suspect that this essentially humanist orientation is not enough for the dynamic sense of a cultural heritage and the creative sense of harmony as cooperation with others. Without underestimating how much has been accomplished in terms of progress and praxis, the world-wide contemporary phenomenon of alienation, not only between cultures but from one's own culture and people, suggests that something important has been forgotten.

First, as notes Iqbal, by including only what is "objective" and abstractively clear, these approaches begin by omitting that which can be had only in self-knowledge, namely, one's self-identity and all that is most distinctive and creative in a people's heritage. Focusing only upon the objective which is analytically clear and distinct to the mind of any and every individual renders alien the notes of personal identity, freedom and creativity, as well as integrity, wholeness and harmony. These characterize the more synthetic philosophical and religious traditions which are realized by self-knowledge, and evoked in deep interpersonal bonds,[15] under the personal guidance of a teacher, spiritual director or guru.[16]

Second, there is the too broadly experienced danger that in concrete affairs the concern to build the future in terms only of what has been conceived clearly and by all will be transformed, wittingly or unwittingly, into oppression of unique self-identity and destruction of integrative cultures both as civilizations and as centers of personal cultivation. Indeed, the complaints of cultural oppression heard from so many parts of the world lead one to doubt that the humanist notion of the self-given and its accompanying universalist ideals can transcend the dynamics of power and leave room for persons, especially for those of other cultures.

Finally, were the making implied in the derivation of the term 'fact' from 'facere' to be wholly reduced to 'self-making,' and were the 'given' to become only the 'self-given,' we would have stumbled finally upon what Parmenides termed "the all impossible way" of deriving what is from what is not.[17] Iqbal's essential insight — shared by the Hindu, Islamic and Judeo-Christian traditions — that all is grounded in the Absolute should guard against such self-defeating, stagnating and destructive self-centeredness.

It is time then to look again to the second meaning of 'given' and to follow the opening this provides toward the source implied in the notion of gift. Above, we noted that self-identity and interpersonal relatedness are gifts (*dona*). We shall now look further into this in order to see what it suggests regarding the dynamic openness required for cooperation between persons and cultures.

First, one notes that, as gift, the given has an essentially gratuitous character. It is true that at times the object or service given could be repaid in cash or in kind. As indicated by the root of the term 'commercial,' however, such a transaction would be based on some merit (*mereo*) on the part of the receiver. This would destroy its nature as gift precisely because the given would not be based primarily in the freedom of the giver.

The same appears from an analysis of an exchange of presents. Presents cease to be gifts to the degree that they are given only because of the requirements of the social situation or a claim implicit in what the receiver might earlier have given. Indeed, the sole way in which such presents can be redeemed as gifts is to make clear that their presentation is not something to which one feels obliged, but which one personally and freely wants to make. As such then, a gift is based precisely upon the freedom of the giver: it is gratuitous.

There is striking symmetry here with the 'given' in the above sense of hypothesis or evidence. There, in the line of hypothetical and evidential reasoning there was a first, namely, that which is not explained, but upon which explanation is founded. Here there is also a first upon which the reality of the gift is founded and which is not to be traced to another reality. This symmetry makes what is distinctive of the gift stand out, namely, that the giving is not traced back further precisely because it is free or gratuitous. Once again, our reflections lead us in the direction of that which is self-sufficient, absolute and transcendent as the sole adequate source of the gift of being. Phenomenological reflection leads us home to what Iqbal intuited, namely, that only a total Absolute makes possible anything finite, including knowledge and our very selves.

Further, as an absolute point of origin with its distinctive spontaneity and originality, the giving is non-reciprocal. To attempt to repay would be to destroy the gift as such. Indeed, there is no way in which this originating gratuity can be returned; we live in a graced condition. This appears in reflection upon one's culture. What we received from the authors of the *Vedas*, a Confucius or a Mohammed can in no way be returned. Nor is this simply a problem of distance in time, for neither is it possible to repay the life we have received from our parents, the health received from a doctor, the wisdom from a teacher, or simply the good example which can come from any quarter at any time. The non-reciprocal character of our life is not merely that of a part to the whole; it is that of a gift received to its source.[18]

The great traditions have insisted rightly both upon the oneness of the absolute reality and upon the lesser reality of the multiple: the multiple is not The Real, though neither is it totally non-reality. Anselm's elaboration of the notion of privation contains a complementary clarification of the gratuitous character of beings as given or gifted. He extended this notion of privation to the situation of creation in which the whole being is gifted. In this case, there is no prior subject to which something is due; hence, there is no ground for it or even any acceptance. Anselm expressed this radically non-reciprocal nature of the gift — its lack of prior conditions — through the notion of *absolute privation*.

It is *privation* and not merely negation, for negation simply is not and leads nowhere, whereas the gift is to be, and once given can be seen to be uniquely appropriate. It is *absolute privation*, however, for the foundation of creation is not at all on the part of the recipient since there is no prior subject to which creation is due. Rather, the basis or foundation of creation is entirely on the part of the source.[19]

To what does this gift correspond on the part of the source? In a certain parallel to the antinomies of Kant which show when reason has strayed beyond its bounds, many from Plotinus to Leibniz and beyond have sought knowledge, not only of the gift and its origin, but of why it had to be given. The more they succeeded the less room was left for freedom on the part of the person as a given or gift. Others attempted to understand freedom as a fall, only to find that what was thus understood was bereft of value and meaning and hence was of no significance to human life and its cultures. Rather, the radical non-reciprocity of human freedom must be rooted in an equally radical generosity on the part of its origin. No reason, either on the part of the given or on the part of its origin makes this gift necessary. The freedom of man is the reflection of the pure generosity by which it is given. If, in general, man is the image of God, then, in particular, human freedom is the image of God's love.

At this point philosophy begins to gain that intimacy which Iqbal sees as characterizing religion. The intellect takes on that union which is more characteristic of a mystical state. One appreciates one's freedom as given and responds spontaneously. This, in turn, enables one to respond freely in love to the love by which one's heart or very capacity for loving has been given. This, in turn, transforms it into generosity in the image of the outgoing love of one's creator. We begin to approach in awe the inner sanctuary of being, namely, the very center of what it means to be and find that this is preeminently the subjectivity that is love.

Yet in all this the metaphysics of existence keeps cause and effect distinct from one another. One is not absorbed into the divine love by which one is given, but instead is affirmed as being in one's own right and thereby as an outgoing, generous and loving source in this world.

Thus, religion as appreciation entails not withdrawal from the world, but its engagement and transformation. This appears from a continuation of the phenomenology of self or ego as gift, which implies in turn a correspondingly radical openness or generosity. As gift one is not something which is and then receives. It was an essential facet of Plato's response to the problems he had elaborated in the *Parmenides* that the multiple can exist only *as* participants of the good or one. Receiving is not something they *do*; it is what they *are*.[20] As such at the core of one's being one reflects the reality of the generosity in which one originates. Hence, understanding oneself as gift entails understanding oneself also as giving of oneself in openness to others.

MARTIN HEIDEGGER AND THE HOMEWARD PATH TO GOD

The nature of the insight which this way to God provides is richly articulated in terms of way, and specifically of journey and homecoming by Martin Heidegger. In these terms he infolds the working of the subjectivity of the poet as that in which the Holy, the Origin or the Ground is received and lived. Vensus George in his excellent work, *Authentic Human Destiny*,[21] describes this with such unique and penetrating insight in his analysis of Heidegger's work on Holderlin that he should be cited here at considerable length.

> It is Being which summons Dasein to his homeland. The summoning takes the form of Being manifesting itself to Dasein in its characteristics. Firstly, Being is Glad-some (*das Heitere*), which suggests the nuances of brightness of the light, serenity and gentle joy.[22] The Glad-some is the source of joy and so it is the most Joyous one (*das Freudigste*). The Glad-some, by sending rays of joy enlightens the homeland and makes it a welcome place for the homecoming Dasein. This, in turn, lights up the disposition of the home-comer to experience all that is noble in the homeland.[23] Secondly, Being presents itself as the Holy (*das Heilig*). By 'the Holy' Heidegger means neither God nor gods. 'The Holy' is the ultimate conserving power which guards beings in the integrity of their being. Being, as the Glad-some, is the Holy. The articulation of the Holy constitutes the primordial poem, which is seen as the 'thoughts' of Being-as-the-spirit.[24] Thirdly, Being shows itself as the Origin (*Ursprung*). Heidegger says: ". . . what is most proper and most precious in the homeland consists simply in the fact that it is this nearness to the Origin — and nothing besides. . . ."[25] Being, as the Origin, is best understood in the image of an overflowing and continuous source. It is Being, as source, that attracts the poet-wanderer to its nearness.[26] Finally, Being shines forth itself as the Ground (*Grund*). Though Being is a continuous source, and gives itself out, it retains itself as the source constantly. In other words, Being, while giving itself out, does not empty itself, but rather remains a steadfast and consistent source. It is, in

this sense of self-retaining and continuous source, that Being presents itself as the Ground.[27]

Thus, Being summons Dasein to its nearness by manifesting itself as the Glad-some, the most Joyous, the Holy, the Origin and the Ground. In Being's manifestation of its qualities begins Dasein's homecoming. Heidegger considers Dasein's homecoming in terms of poetry, viz., in terms of bringing into poetry the primordial poetic presencing of Being. Being addresses and hails itself as the primordial poem, to which the poet (Dasein) must give expression in words. Dasein's homeland is to be found in the very source that hails Dasein, viz., Being.[28] There are three moments or stages in the poet's homecoming.

The first moment depicts the poet's early days and his experience of the source. The poet, as a youth grows up in the realm of the source, without ever fully appreciating it. But, as his poetic spirit is 'open to the open', he has some (pre-ontological) awareness of Being. But this awareness is often obscured as the source manifests itself in finite beings. The more he aims at penetrating the mystery of the source that is manifested in beings, he gets lost in things, and Being, as it were, evades him. Because of the withdrawing nature of the source he is not able to hold off the difference between Being and beings.[29] In spite of this state of forgetfulness of Being, the poetic spirit (Being) keeps him oriented towards Being. The orientation towards the source evokes in the poet an awakening to go abroad to seek that which brings him closer to the source. Here, Heidegger compares the German poet, who is the master of form (clarity of exposition), but can be fully forgetful of the spirit, viz., fire, which is the characteristic of the Greek poet. The German poet can have fire, only if he has the courage to leave the homeland and make the journey abroad, so that in coming back after the journey he can dwell genuinely 'at home' near the source.[30] Such a journey abroad is an essential condition for the homecoming and becoming-at-home. Indeed, the journey from its first moment is a returning, as it is that which makes the poet experience what he really is, i.e., his poetic destiny.[31]

The second moment is the actual taking of the journey abroad. To experience the source, the poet must move with the stream, move down to the sea and experience the richness of the source.[32] To appreciate the native soil, as the homeland that is near to the source, the poet must make a voyage to the land of Greece,[33] and be burned by the fire of Being.[34] In the journey, the poet is constantly guided by Being. Every experience abroad reveals more and more of the home. Finally, ". . . the fire has let him experience that it itself must be brought back from abroad into the homeland in order that there this proper endowment, the facility for clear expression, can release its native powers in relation to the fire."[35] It, in turn, will help him to produce a poetry of proper depth.

The third moment is the poet's return to the homeland. It is the return to the homeland enriched by his experience abroad which brings the poet to maturity. It helps the poet to possess the homeland in a new and authentic way.[36] For example, the poet's voyage to Greece and being burned by the fire, which is characteristic of Greek poetry, helps him to understand the disciplined style and clarity of expression of German poetry in a new way, and this, in turn, would make him a mature poet.[37] Thus, the poet's homecoming helps him to understand his homeland in a new way. It is a moving into the nearness[38] and a following of the source.[39] But, the passage into the source is not such that we can dissolve the mystery dimension of the source or Being. The poet can never get at this fully. So Being, as mystery, has to be faced in reverential awe (*Scheu*).[40] Being, as Joyous, is experienced by the poet with joy (*Freude*).[41] Thus, the poet experiences Being by varying attunements. In the process he comes to the nearness of Being, and finds that therein lies his homeland. Being-at-home in his homeland, i.e., by his dwelling in the neighborhood of Being, the poet is able to sing or give expression, in poetry, to the Being-dimension of beings. It is the genuine homecoming and dwelling.

According to Heidegger, the following and drawing near to the source involved in homecoming, is not something accomplished once for all. It is Dasein's original experience of homecoming which is brought about by the summoning of Being. It is Dasein's original return to the source, i.e., Being. The process must continue as long as the poet remains a poet. It must be sustained and preserved by a continuous abiding in the nearness to the source, thereby making it a place of dwelling (*Wohnen*).[42] To quote Heidegger: "The one condition of becoming-at-home in his proper domain, ... [is that] the journey abroad has been fulfilled. But this fulfillment remains fulfillment only on the condition that what has been experienced ... is preserved."[43]

Poetic dwelling consists in the poet's continuous keeping of what he learned from the journey, viz., his awareness of the beginnings, the turning points and his original return. Besides, it involves a deeper appreciation of the Being's poetic presencing, as the Glad-some, the Joyous, the Holy, the Source and the Ground, which has in the first place made the original homecoming possible. In other words, poetic dwelling involves a re-collecting poetically upon 'what-is-past'. Such a poetic dwelling is not a mere remembering of 'what-is-past' as past, but, rather, it, besides effectively bringing to memory 'what-is-past', makes the original homecoming a 'still-to-come' experience in the future and a present experience of giving utterance to the original experience in the form of poetry. Thus, poetic dwelling, by which Dasein continues to dwell in the nearness of Being is temporal and it has the dimensions of recalling the past, coming to the future and rendering the present, in relation to the original homecoming. We could elaborate the poetic dwelling in these aspects of temporality, viz., the past, the future and the present.

The past, viz., the original homecoming, which was Being's poetic presencing, is that on which the poet must poetically dwell. The past, in question, is not a mere memory of what has happened once and been forgotten, but it is such that it has an influence on the poet. Thus, the past, still, is a 'having been'. The past, as 'having been' is real to the poet now, as it was for him when he first experienced.[44] The poetic dwelling on the past as 'having been' on the part of the poet is a greeting or hailing (*Gruessen*)[45] of Being for its poetic presencing. It involves a certain docility and self-surrender on the part of the hailer (the poet) to the hailed (Being). In doing so, the hailer allows the hailed, by his openness to be hailed, to shine forth in a way that is proper to the hailed. The hailed accepts the hail of the hailer and, in turn, hails the hailer.[46] Thus, in the reciprocal haling of Being and the poet (Dasein), the original homecoming is re-lived and thereby preserved. Heidegger remarks on this point as follows: "The heavenly fire (Being) imposes itself on him (the poet) who hails it . . . as thought and abides near him as that which comes-to-presence in . . . what-is-past (the original experience of homecoming)."[47]

Ways to God 305

The Holy or the Hailed is also the poet's future, because by his poetic destiny, the poet must bring forth in words the original poetic presencing of the Holy.[48] The Holy comes to the poet as a primordial poem, before his poetizing. The poet must bring the primordial poem into words. Thus, for the poet to dwell poetically upon 'what-is-past', i.e., upon the primordial poetic presencing of Being (original homecoming), is to dwell upon 'what-is-coming' to him in the future, as by his poetic dwelling the poet experiences again and preserves the Holy as given in 'what-is-past'. Dwelling upon 'what-is-coming' is conversely to dwell upon 'what-is-past'. In other words, the poet dwells upon the Holy that is given in the past as 'having been' (the past) and as 'that-which-is-coming' (the future). Thus, in the Holy, the past and the future are unified.[49]

When the Holy gives itself as the primordial poem and continues to come (future) to the poet, who has been hailed by the Holy itself by its original poetic presencing (past), the task of the poet is to render present (present) the Holy in the words of his poetry. The poet does this, insofar as he poetically dwells, by being at home near the source. The present dimension of the poetic dwelling consists fundamentally in that the poet learns to use his native propensity for poetry, viz. the ability for clear expression, and organization of the poetry, with an authentic freedom of the spirit. In the initial stage of poetic presencing the poet, though close to the source, neither knew the source clearly, nor was he aware of his inner propensity for poetry. But the original homecoming liberates him, and lets him know and dwell in the homeland, i.e., nearness to Being, besides letting him know his native ability for poetry in a new way. Thus, now, the poet knowing the source and the homeland, dwells in it poetically, and gives authentic expression to his experience of the source and the homeland, facilitated by his new awareness of his native ability for poetry. It happens only as a result of the poet's experience of the original homecoming. To quote Heidegger: the poet "exercises (his) native endowment, the clarity of expression, 'freely' only then, when what is clear in his utterance is permeated by the open experience of that which is exposed."[50]

Thus, original poetic presencing of Being, i.e., the original homecoming of the poet is preserved and sustained as an ever-present dwelling in the nearness of being by poetic-dwelling. It involves: a re-calling it as an experience of the hailing of Being in the past; a waiting on it as an experience in which the Holy (Being) continues to come to the poet in the future; and as an experiencing of the Holy in the here and now, to which the poet gives the fullest expression in the present in poetry by using his inner ability for poetic utterance in an authentic freedom of the spirit. From what we have said, it could be concluded that the original presencing of Being in the primordial poem is preserved and sustained in the poetry or in the poetic word of the poet. William J. Richardson speaks of the poetic word of the poet as ". . . a word of 'hailing' inasmuch as it greets what is past; at the same time, it is a 'prophetic' word, inasmuch as it articulates what is coming; both for the same reason because it seeks to utter past and future in their original correlation, the holy as such. Such a word can be uttered only if the poet has learned to use his native talent with a freedom that is genuine."[51]

Heidegger, thus, speaks of the attainment of dwelling in the nearness of Being, in terms of poetizing, both on the part of Being and that of Dasein (poet). Dasein is a dweller in the neighborhood of Being when he experiences giving of Being in poetic presencing and preserves it by poetic dwelling, by giving expression to his experience of Being in poetry. By using the image of poetic giving, poetic receiving and poetry, Heidegger drives home the point that Dasein's dwelling in the nearness of Being is brought about by a reciprocal interaction of Being and Dasein.

MARTIN BUBER: 'I AND THOU' AS A TEST OF AUTHENTICITY

But if the action of Dasein — the human person as conscious and exercising one's subjectivity — is essential to one's way to God then the attitude of the person becomes essential to this manifestation of God and its reception. In other words, a prayerful human subjectivity becomes essential to the reality of the divine self-revelation to, and through, the human person. Thereby there begins to emerge why and how God's interchange with humanity is a matter of freedom which God, even in his omnipotent love, cannot and would not change.

Martin Buber (1878-1965) indicates this in a type of cautionary note or *via negativa*. Buber had developed Husserl's phenomenological insights in terms of relations, noting that these may be either I-it or I-thou. The former is impersonal, and in it the I is a thing; the latter is personal, and in it the I is a person. In view of this distinction, speaking thus of Max Scheler, he states an important caution relevant to considering any concrete reality a revelation of God:

> A modern philosopher supposes that every man believes of necessity either in God or in "idols" which is to say, some finite good such as his nation, his art, power, knowledge, the acquisition of money, the "ever-repeated triumph with women" — some good that has become an absolute value for him, taking its place between him and God; and if only one proves to man the conditionality of the good, thus "smashing" the idol, then the diverted religious act will all by itself return to its proper object.[52]

Buber objects that this presupposes that the relation of man to finite goods is the same as that of man to God, and that revelation is simply a matter of substituting the proper for the improper object. In fact, he notes, the relation to a "particular something" which has come to replace eternity as the supreme point in one's values is directed to the experience and use of an "It". This can be healed only by a change, not merely of the goal, but of the nature of the relation from "I-it" to "I-thou".

> If one serves a people in a fire kindled by immeasurable fate — if one is willing to devote oneself to it, one means God. But if the nation is for him an idol to which he desires to subjugate everything because in its image he extols his own — do you fancy that you only have to spoil the nation for him and he will then see the truth.[53]

Many intellectuals in Germany had once looked to National Socialism as the coming divine revelation, only to have had to oppose it with heroism when the real nature of Naziism became manifest. If one is concerned that all things participate in, and proclaim, the glory of God, however, it is not sufficient to say that such faith had been an authentic contact with the unconditional itself, and that only its concrete expression proved deficient. If it is the life of God which is being shared, then its implications for peace in unity, for justice in truth, for love in goodness, are not incidental, but substantive to the participation. Thus the concerns for the quality of life today — not only as an effect of industrial development, but as the personal character of society — are central.

GABRIEL MARCEL: PARTICIPATION AS COMMUNION WITH GOD

As Buber pointed out, what is important here is not only the object of the concern, even if that be the quality of life what is; what is the truly fundamental is the character of the human subjectivity, of the concern for the quality of life. In this light the work of the playwright-philosopher, Gabriel Marcel (1889-1973), is of particular significance to our project.[54]

A New Level of Reflection

Marcel's attention is directed first to the quality of contemporary life and its effect upon the person's self-understanding. What he finds is ominous. Economic and political structures interpret the entirety of human meaning and value simply in function of a rationalized system of production. Marcel points out, as Carnap eagerly insisted, that our being as persons is ignored by the modern scientific world-view. This focuses upon the surface; it understands man in terms of operational or functional relations; intentionally, it ignores the person's interior being or autonomous center.[55] Marcel called this attention to the surface, that is, to empirical detail only, primary reflection; it is objective, universal, analytic and verifiable.

Personally, it had always been clear to Marcel that the fragmentary and partial data of the senses were inadequate. At first, however, he attempted to pass beyond this by means of abstraction to an Hegelian Absolute Knowledge or Bradlean Absolute Experience as self-sufficient, concrete, and more genuine than sense experience. From the beginning and throughout his life Marcel was in profound agreement with Bradley's affirmation in *Appearance and Reality* of an original and immediate awareness of the One on the level of feeling.[56] In science analytic reason fragments this unity in order to reunify it in a conscious manner. Science, however, can never fully realize this goal, and it remains for metaphysics to recapture unity on the level of thought.

On further reflection, however — similar to Plato's enrichment of, rather than revolt against, Parmenides — he noted that the Absolutes of Hegel and Bradley allowed no place for the human thinking by which they were recognized and even demanded.[57] They were abstractions. By this he did not mean that they were not real, for they were requirements of human thought. He meant rather that they needed to be opened to the reality of the person who is the subject of that thought.

This enabled Marcel not only to understand more deeply the dilemma which modern rationalism has constructed for man, but to derive some orientation for its resolution. On the one hand, when understood by idealism as the supreme principle of meaning and creativity, the self is "transcendentalized" as the universal and unifying principle. As a result, the portrait of the individual self which is dialectically derived therefrom by pure thought is too flattering; it is the human being as it should be, not as it is.[58] On the other hand and paradoxically, because the person is seen only as a limitation of the Absolute Essence, one is devalued before this Unity.[59] To the incursions of pragmatic functionalism, mentioned above, this adds the totalitarian and no less pragmatic oppressions by the dialectical rationalisms of both of the political right and left.

The threat, however, is not only from without. The gravest danger in philosophy is that if its vision is not sufficiently open, it will result in people devaluing themselves. The idealist position, wrote Marcel, "that each one of us is perfectly alone in life and that isolation is, as it were, the price paid for freedom . . . obstructs communication with other people by preventing him from even imagining them in their concrete reality."[60]

From all that has been said in the above chapters, one can suspect that so strong a stricture upon idealism from one who remains thoroughly committed to its major concern for a conscious and absolute Unity bespeaks the development of an added level of awareness This is concerned, as he says, "with other people . . . in their concrete reality." It is the essence of the very general contemporary revolt against the essential as abstract and impersonal, and in favor of the existential as concrete and personal. This is a dimension of meaning with which any contemporary philosophy must grapple, for, like the knowledge of good and evil, it enables what previously had been seen only in its positive meaning to be appreciated in its ambiguity. For example, Marcel even urges that in the context of a Bradlean idealism self-consciousness had seemed to have only unlimited positive meaning. Now, however, far from being an illuminating principle as traditional philosophy has held, this very idealism is seen to shut the human person in upon him- or herself and thus result in opacity rather than enlightenment.[61] If man cannot do without that light, however, the question now is how the ambiguity can be clarified and the negative side surmounted so that the light might once again illumine the person's path or way to God.

Conversely, if self-consciousness is understood concretely, that is, as being realized in the body, in the world, and especially in relation with other persons, there is a striking parallel to the growth in self-awareness implied by the personal and free response to the redemptive invitation. In Chapter V, we saw how that made it possible for the awareness of being to develop from form to existence which, in turn, made possible the Christian synthesis of the Platonic and Aristotelian visions. It will be important now to see what Marcel's existential awareness of the concrete will contribute to an understanding of plenitude and participation and what this will imply for the meaning of the person in society.

To take account of the concrete person, Marcel sees the need for a new type of reflection. Unlike first reflection this does not abstract and universalize; it does not seek information about an object or treat it simply as an instance of a specific type. Rather it is concerned with the full concrete reality of being, with what Marcel calls their ontological weight.[62] This is being taken not as a noun but as a verb, with all the act that implies. Whereas first reflection was an attempt to obtain complete and fixed data which will enable anyone to carry out an exhaustive analysis of an object, second reflection concerns this personal reality of the subject in its ontological weight as self-affirmation which is not subject to exhaustive analysis.

Second reflection, as phenomenological method, has a further implication for Marcel. If the one to whom we relate must not be reduced to an object, neither must we ourselves be omitted from the concrete reality of this encounter. On entering personal relations we are not abstract and inert as measuring rods, but concrete and active as selves.[63] Here, there can never be the Cartesian ideal of a perfect problem analogous to mathematics.

Marcel's main effort was to carry out second reflection upon the inter-personal "I-thou" relation and upon such of its characteristics as hope and courage. His objective was not to reason to the active reality of Being Itself, but to allow its plenitude, its Infinite and Absolute character to reveal itself to us through participation. This converges with, and explains, the principle which we drew from Paul Ricoeur and applied in Chapter II above, namely, that the fundamental existential unity is both affective and cognitive and is to be found in the feeling of kinship between men lived in the unity of family and of society.

The Promise

One of Marcel's reflections might help to trace the main lines of his thought; it is his reflection upon creative fidelity, elaborated in his book by the same title.[64] Step by step its reflection upon personal experience reveals the character both of personal participation and of the Absolute Plenitude which is its precondition. Typically, it is carried out in terms, not merely of two persons in general for that would be an abstraction, but, for example, of Arthur and Agnes. Further, the circumstances also are concrete, as in a play. At no point in the phenomenological reflection on these acts will there be a process of universalization; the reflection will move rather by convergence of the concrete details of what actually occurs. It is in this existential convergence or synderesis that the ontological weight or true meaning of life and its preconditions will be revealed.

For example, Agnes is visited by Arthur when she is teaching in a distant village, and Arthur promises to return in a few days; or in a moment of exaltation Arthur asks Agnes to marry him, promising to love her always. Marcel would note that Arthur's promises are not the factual statements that he is visiting Agnes or does love her; they state that he *will* visit her and *will* love her always. What is important here is that such promises, while concrete, are not conditioned upon the particular circumstances of their time and place. Such conditions in their partial, conflicting, and incoherent nature are treated as negligible. Rather, he promises to love her, as it were, despite them — no matter what![65]

Moreover, this ability to make such promises, to commit oneself definitively and in terms which are not able to be characterized in objectively verifiable conditions, is not incidental to human life. It is the very alternative to anarchy in human relations and hence is a condition of possibility for a life that is human. The extent of this unconditional character increases as one moves from matters which are less, to those which are more, personal: from a bank loan in which one binds oneself, no matter what the circumstances, to repay at a certain time a definite amount; through an oath of office by which one binds oneself, whatever be the circumstances and for the full duration of one's term of office, to fulfill the duties of a particular role as specified by law; to the marriage promise to love made precisely "for richer or poorer, in sickness or in health, till death do us part," and open to the totally pervasive care and concern that is love. In explicit negative terms this mutual commitment of

Arthur and Agnes rejected any merely empirical, objective, abstractive, or partial understanding of their life with one another; it was a total commitment precisely because made despite all the unforeseeable and changeable circumstances. Positively, they promised to love and cherish each other till death did them part.

The radical totality in this mutual act of freedom by Arthur and Agnes manifests a transcendent Presence, for this totality can be understood only through its direction to being fully, and basically to the fullness of being which is Being Itself. This is the condition of possibility for their life together being not a mere succession of separate and dissociable actions, but a continuous and unified whole. Due to this their fidelity to each other is not static, inert or immobilizing, but active and creative.[66] Formal correspondence to abstract laws which are clear, distinct and univocous for all will be necessary, of course, but not sufficient. Rather, their life will constitute an actively developing recognition of a living, personal and transcendent ontological Presence. This can never be grasped; it can even be forgotten or betrayed. Nevertheless, it is continually evoked as that in terms of which each moment of fidelity is lived; it is the living fullness of truth and love of which all that is true and good in person's lives are participations.

Participation, then, does not imply that one's life is set and predetermined as a part of the whole. The transcendence of this Presence enables one's life to be spontaneous and yet in its freedom to be united with others. We are not an assemblage of isolated individuals playing prefixed roles which, in a Bradlean manner, are designed to coincide. We are ever new creations shaping our lives in active communion as in an orchestra, that is, in the act of living with others.[67] Other persons are neighbors who stand before one not as objects to be dealt with, but as selves to be greeted. Together persons form a fraternity or community built not upon a deadening equality resentful of difference, but upon a common sonship. This is lived by a diversity of persons, but as children of the one God and hence as brothers one to another. The success of one enriches and ennobles the others; the sufferings and sorrows of each are matters of common concern.

When Arthur and Agnes said "for richer or poorer, in sickness and health", they did not become indifferent to each other's concerns. On the contrary, for Arthur the past and future concerns of Agnes took on an ultimate meaning which they could never have for Agnes herself. Arthur is passionately, unconditionally concerned for Agnes if she is even moderately sick, as is Agnes for Arthur and for her child, Mary. This is a concern which a doctor, nurse, or other professionally involved person can seldom, if ever, share. It manifests that abiding Presence which transcends all the differentiated conditions of name and form and in which, through participation, our lives have their ontological weight: their real meaning for ourselves, and their communion with others.

This is more than a mere relation of given individuals, even one that is stable and lasting. More properly it is a communion, for in this each finds his or her being and freedom.[68]

> This tie not only does not fetter him, but frees him from himself. . . . Each one of us tends to become a prisoner of himself not only in his material interests, his passions, or simply his prejudices, but still more essentially in the predisposition which inclines him to be centered on himself and to view everything from his own perspective.[69]

The more intense the recognition and response to others the more one breaks away from this self-centeredness and the greater the intimation of the suprapersonal "real and *pleromic* unity where we will be all in all."[70] From this comes hope, not as a series of particular claims to be achieved by our efforts, but as a relaxation, a humility, and a patience which enables us to see things whole and to respond with total love, dedication and perseverance.

Is the "pleroma," or Plenitude in which all participate personal? If by personal is meant someone related as a contrary to others, then this would not apply; it should be called, not impersonal, but suprapersonal. Thus, in his *Metaphysical Journal* he refers to God as the "Absolute Thou" which is not an object, a "he".[71]

IMPLICATIONS

The first two parts of this volume concerned ages long past when communication between continents was, at best, little and slow. This is no longer the case and we are in the process of forming a global culture. Some, using only first reflection, would predicate this upon a process of abstraction which would discount the distinctive human creativity which has created our cultures in order to find a least common denominator consisting in a crude form of utilitarianism. This would devalue our cultural pluralism; we would all be the poorer. Chapter II recalled Heidegger's notion of retrieve, namely, that the more significant progress is to be made not in simply continuing incrementally along the path long tread, but in taking up an alternate path which had not yet been explored. This suggests a more comprehensive model for the manner in which shared problems can generate culturally diversified responses.

It was noted in Chapter III that a transformation takes place when a need arises, that to respond to that need we must reach back to retrieve from our foundational wisdom, and that the new equilibrium will be a synthesis of this rediscovery with the structured content of the prior stage of development. In the present situation of highly developed media of communication there is no reason to believe that the needs will arise separately in the East and the West, the North and the South — quite the contrary. In the West the combined development of science and technology channeled thought too exclusively into first reflection, restricted to the empirical at the expense of secondary or self-reflection. This has generated an experience of alienation and created a need to rediscover the person and God, as was described above.

What is now being communicated most actively from West to East, and North to South is: (a) the scientific world-view, which educational systems are extensively involved in disseminating, and (b) related industrial and technological means, which both the public and private sectors are fully engaged in developing. To this should be added the implied threats to the person as these attitudes are applied in the areas of commerce and public administration.

It is not surprising then to find arising throughout the world a similar set of needs gravitating around the understanding, protection, and promotion of the person in private and social life. This is manifested in the combined search by both older and younger generations more adequately to realize civil rights and a greater sensitivity to disadvantaged minorities, to women, to the ecology and especially to cultures. On the part of the young, especially, this is manifested negatively in their heightened skepticism regarding past social structures, and positively in their insistence upon a more active role in the decisions by which they are affected.

If the problems are common, however, the response should be distinctive to the several cultures. It should not take the nihilist path of rejecting one's cultural foundations or the alienating path of substituting another's. Rather, it should consist in a creative transformation of one's heritage. As seen above, this will require reaching back to one's roots to find elements not previously developed. For a detailed and controlled effort it will require also the systematic and hermeneutic philosophic tools developed thusfar, especially in one's own and perhaps also in other traditions.

This raises three questions: First, what is the condition of these tools? Second, how can they develop the heritage of wisdom regarding the divine and human participation therein to aid people in finding their way in this period of intensive development? Third, what implications does the new interpersonal sensitivity have for the philosopher's effort?

Co-operating systems. Regarding the condition of the tools for systematic philosophy, Dasgupta's *History of Indian Philosophy* and most other studies of Indian philosophy present philosophical systems in parallel fashion, distinct and almost separate one from another, much as did Madhva in his *Sarva-darsana-samgraha* in the thirteenth century. Dasgupta notes that "As a system passed on it had to meet unexpected troublesome criticisms for which it was not in the least prepared. Its adherents had therefore to use all their ingenuity and subtlety in support of their own positions, and to discover the defects of the rival schools that attacked them."[72] The same has been true in other regions of the world.

What might now be accomplished in philosophy for humankind if the new spirit blowing across the land meant that after 1500 or even 2500 years it were possible to draw upon the combined wisdom of these carefully developed systems. By this I do not mean simply an impoverishing compromise based upon a least common denominator, but a combination of resources which would realize more perfectly the distinctive contributions of each. In Chapter V above, we saw the elaboration by Thomas in the Middle Ages, at a new level of awareness, of a creative synthesis of Plato's insight regarding participation in the One with Aristotle's scientific concern for the reality of the physical order. This suggests some questions for philosophers today.

First, is there implicit in the contemporary concern for both the physical development of the world's resources and the preservation of the environment a newly developing awareness of reality? If so, could this enable the attention of a Madhva and a Carnap to the diversity of the world to be seen as complimentary rather than as contradictory to the principles of unity and meaning as found in Shankara and Heidegger.[73] Would not some causal participational model help in making it possible to understand and articulate, not only how the universe founds its reality in the One, but how the One proclaims its reality by sharing it with multiple beings as universe?

Second, is there in the contemporary reaffirmation of freedom democratically shared among men an implicit deepening in awareness of personal affirmation which might enable us to draw out the deeper truth of the thought of Ramanuja and Shankara if seen as complementary rather than as mutually exclusive? Ramanuja's notion of attributes which qualify, and in that sense limit, the divine would need to be corrected in the light of Shankara's clear proclamation of the Absolute's unity and Plenitude of perfection: Parmenides will always have said the most important word![74] But in order to take account of the person it is important to trace participation to its source as unfolded through some sequential pattern of unity, truth and goodness. As transcendental each would be open and unlimited in its affirmation of being; hence, they would not qualify or limit the divine which they progressively explicate. This might help, not only to ground persons in the One, but to articulate the life of the Absolute, and to uncover the meaning of that life for social cohesion, justice and progress in our increasingly complex societies.

Such a system could be extended further. It is said that Shankara was not interested in developing a logic because systems of logic were already at hand. The same might be said of systems combining the elements for an understanding of the material or physical universe. Such systems become logicisms or materialisms only when not employed within a larger and more integrating vision. Aristotle's system of the sciences is an example of one way in which each body of knowledge can make its proper contribution to a philosophy which integrates them in an understanding of all things. In this each part is related to the highest knowledge which is absolute consciousness, by whose attractiveness all is moved in the physical and ethical orders. A coordination of the combined philosophical resources today might prove to be no less impressive, nor less needed in order to face the problems of contemporary life.

Participation and Technology. The implications of the contemporary awareness of the person must be carried beyond the interaction between humans, however. One of the major factors in the contemporary problematic is the development of scientific and technological capabilities which threaten to depersonalize their creators. It is not enough to decry these capabilities, for they have shaped the present world in which we live and we cannot now survive without them. Nor is the problem immediately resolved by noting that humans carry out their inventive role as participations in the divine fullness of being, for this could still be a depersonalization if human intellection were merely to be implementing a preformed plan within the limitations of predefined categories. In a merely mechanical, imitative process there would be none of the creativity of freedom now experienced in the capacity to promote nature. There would be no recognition of the fact that nature is not an exteriorly imposed limit or even simple material for human creative activity.

But in this the roots of the real dilemma begin to appear. It is not simply a question of whether the person has either absolute freedom in his or her actions in the sense of an absolute indeterminacy (and empty gratuitousness), or a structured relationship to an ordered and determined body of nature. This dilemma can be overcome by the appreciation of both humanity and nature as dependent upon the Divine. As expressions of the same perfection they complement rather than exclude each other, so that human freedom can express itself in nature.

The real question is whether and how this order of nature actually relates to the area of freedom one has in the divine, and hence to what degree one can exercise a creative freedom in imaging the divine in the technological area. Solving this problem points to the basis of the human understanding of nature. Progress can be made on this problem by reflecting upon the nature of God Himself as absolute and perfect, as being in His simplicity the plenitude of all perfection. This combination of the infinity of perfection with the unity of the Divine is most important for our problem, because it means that there is no perfection, actual or conceivable, which is not included in the simple unity which is the Divine itself. The vast possibilities which open before man in this technological culture, the new usages for matter and new forms of material and social development which are conceivable by the limitless capacity of the mind—all are included within the unity of the infinite simplicity.

Having neither past nor future, the eternal holds all this in perfect possession.[75] The term 'possession' is, however, capable of still further meaning. The Aristotelian conception of knowledge has always identified knowing with unity, rather than with the dichotomy of subject and object. This is reflected in Thomas Aquinas for whom God as Truth itself is the perfection of divine Unity. As unlimited perfection, he is unlimited intelligibility; further, as unlimited act he is also unlimited knowing. The identification of both intelligibility and knowing constitutes in a most perfect way truth itself.[76]

This identification of the source of all being with an unlimited simple and absolute truth is the guarantee, the inspiration and the challenge of the person in this technological age. It is the guarantee because it assures that no structure or category which expresses a limited degree of perfection or of being can ever be identified with truth itself or can ever stand as a limit to human striving toward further perfection. Thus, if the forms of nature are increasingly relativized and transcended, it is not a movement towards irrationality or arbitrariness, but rather towards a new, more complete and more profound manifestation of Truth Itself. Striving towards further self realization, humanity is always striving towards a new participation in the infinite perfection of the Divine. In doing this rationally, it is participating in the knowledge had by the ultimate exemplar cause, according to which God understands the ways in which His absolute perfection is imitable in an unlimited number of ways.[77] Thus, one can draw a parallel between the Divine Word as containing the intelligible perfection of all creatures and the human artisan who contains in his or her mind the plans for that which he or she will produce.[78]

There is here also a source of inspiration, for since the principle of this knowledge is the divine infinity itself, there is no limit to the amount of perfection which can be conceived. Finally, since this knowledge of the good in conjunction with the will is the principle of love, neither is there any limit to the impetus to progress through the creative intellectualization of nature which is characteristic of our technological culture.

From this there follow the true dimensions of the present challenge for philosophy in an increasingly technological, industrialized and scientific culture, as well as an indication of the full dimensions of the task which lies before it. It is not sufficient to define this in terms of conquering matter as an evil opponent, or simply of improving it as a means to our ends. Rather, what is called for is the appreciation that our technological activities give glory to God by participating in the creative intellectual work of His creation. In this one is subordinate to God in one's being and intellectual work, but is responsible and creative on the pattern of the Divine intellect. In a less perfect manner, through a continued actualization of one's intellectual capacities, one proceeds to develop ever new ways in which the plenitude of perfection can be participated in the present circumstances of nature. This is to participate in the divine light, carrying that into the midst of nature. Thus, one's task is never simply one's own because it opens onto a truth — and hence onto a meaning and value — which transcends all else and ultimately is absolute in itself.

There are dangers here that one will not look high enough, that one may look upon nature only as a limit or as mere indeterminacy manifesting nothing. In that case, one would be driven back upon oneself where, finding nothing absolute and final, one would dash the great promise of technology on the rocks of materialism, pessimism, and atheism. The only protection against this is truth itself. In these times of intensive development, humankind must look above itself in active contemplation which includes the full notion of communion with the Divine as the source and goal of intellectual endeavors. There one finds both the source of the meaning and beauty already created and the inspiration to work with nature so that it might respond more fully to human needs.

Philosophizing and Communion. Finally, as personal, one must not only be free oneself and exercise one's high priesthood in relation to nature, but must also commune with other person's. Above we saw Marcel's concern that Idealism, especially in its British form, contained a danger of closure upon the self. This is a special problem today due to the convergence of a number of factors: the increasing demands placed upon resources by the extended longevity and hence rising number of people, the increasing pressure placed upon persons by the technological and industrial coordination of their work, and the increasing human expectations due to the development of both personal self-awareness and communication. All of these combine to underline the importance of the concern for others which was reflected above in a number of the indices of the contemporary mind.

In the light of such factors philosophers must continually reassess the adequacy of their work. Buddhism's ideal of the Bodhisattva is classical in this context. Like the extension of the cycles of rebirths of the *jivanmukta*, it provides an important pointer, but may not take sufficient account of the newly developing personal and interpersonal awareness. The classical Christian notion of participation understood as sharing in existence and hence in Being itself is an essential contribution, for it enables us to be more fully aware of the reality of persons, of the transcendent importance of the life they lead and of the sufferings they undergo. It implies as well an appreciation of a brotherhood and sisterhood between humans as children of the same Father.

The contemporary awareness of persons goes further, however. As articulated by Buber and Marcel, persons now understand themselves precisely in relation to other free persons: the personal I is discovered in my "I-thou" relations. This evolves the notion of participation in the Absolute in at least three ways. First, I-thou relations require and participate in an I-Thou relation. Second, the I-Thou relation is achieved in I-thou relations. Third, living is not only sharing in God and returning to Him, but sharing His truth and goodness with our neighbors. The latter is not merely an implication of the former; it is the present human mode of its realization

Liberation or salvation is then not something we achieve by ourselves and then put off in order to help others. Particularly today, our truly personal acts — those with full ontological weight — are lived above all in communion with others. There is here the basis for a social philosophy in the Ghandian spirit. But one would not be true to that spirit if one were to see in it merely an ethics, for it is not only a question of what we should do; more fundamentally it is a question of metaphysics, of what we are and how we can live this more fully.

Marcel joins the great tradition of Eastern philosophy when he says that basically the answer to this question requires overcoming the tendency to center upon ourselves. His antidote may point the way to a contemporary road of liberation. This is to oppose centering upon oneself by opening to others in loving service. Our communion with our brother is our participation in Divine Presence, the Plenitude of Being in which we live

Even this, however, must be tested to be sure that we do not look to others only for what we can receive from them and thus remain ultimately closed upon ourselves. This is corrected by assuring that we are conscious of others as persons, as free centers, for whose good we are concerned. There is a test for this; it lies in our response to those who have nothing to give but their suffering. That can serve as a criterion for the authenticity of a contemporary philosophy of participation in the fullness of being. Beyond deductive certitude, a new measure has been added by which we can judge our work in philosophy. It is our concern, not only to understand emancipation or realize it in our lives, but to bring the good news to the poor.

NOTES

1. Iqbal, pp. 62, 180.
2. *Ibid.*, p. 62.
3. Anselm, *Proslogion*, in *St. Anselm*, tr. by S.N. Deane (La Salle, III, 1903).
4. See Chapter III above.
5. Tr. C.K. Ogden (London: Methuen, 1981).
6. (New York: Harper and Row).
7. Tr. G.E.M. Anscombe (Oxford: Blackwell, 1958).
8. Brian Wicker, *Culture and Theology* (London: Sheed and Ward, 1966), pp. 68-88.
9. (New York: Harper and Row, 1962).
10. *Documents of Vatican II*, ed. W. Abbott (New York: New

Century, 1974).

11. Iqbal, p. 77.

12. Maurice Nedoncelle, "Person and/or World as the Source of Religious Insight" in G. McLean, ed., *Traces of God in a Secular Culture* (New York: Alba House, 1973), pp. 187-210.

13. Kenneth L. Schmitz, *The Gift: Creation* (Milwaukee: Marquette Univ. Press, 1982), pp. 34-42. I am particularly indebted to this very thoughtful work for its suggestions. I draw here also upon my "Chinese-Western Cultural Interchange in the Future" delivered at the International Symposium on Chinese- Western Cultural Interchange in Commemoration of the 400th Anniversary of the Arrival of Matteo Ricci, S.J., in China (Taiwan: Fu Jen Univ., 1983), pp. 457-72.

14. Karl Marx, *Theses on Feuerbach*, nos. 6-8 in F. Engels, *Ludwig Feuerbach and the Outcome of Classical German Philosophy* (New York: International Publishers, 1934), pp. 82-84. Schmitz, *ibid.*

15. A. S. Cua, *Dimensions of Moral Creativity: Paradigms, Principles and Ideals* (University Park, PA: Pennsylvania State Univ. Press, 1978), chaps. III-V.

16. W. Cenkner, *The Hindu Personality in Education: Tagore, Gandhi and Aurobindo* (Delhi: South Asia Books, 1976).

17. Parmenides, *Fragment* 2.

18. Schmitz, pp. 44-56.

19. Anselm, *Monologium*, cc. 8-9 in *Anselm of Canterbury*, eds. J. Hopkins and H. W. Richardson (Toronto: E. Mellen, 1975), I, pp. 15-18. See Schmitz, pp. 30-34.

20. R. E. Allen, "Participation and Predication in Plato's Middle Dialogues" in his *Studies in Plato's Metaphysics* (London: Routledge, Keegan Paul, 1965), pp. 43-60.

21. (Washington, D.C.: The Council for Research in Values and Philosophy, 1998).

22. Cf. *HD*, p. 18.; *EB*, p. 247. In this text, '*das Heitere*' is translated as the 'serene', which is one of the nuances contained in the German term, but William J. Richardson, *Heidegger: Through Phenomenology to Thought*, translates it as the 'Glad-some' (The Hague, M. Nijhoff, 1974), p. 444, fn. 8.

23. Cf. *HD*, pp. 14, 18.; *EB*, pp. 247-248.

24. Cf. *HD*, pp. 17, 18, 86, 108, 116.

25. *HD*, p. 23.; William J. Richardson, p. 445.
26. Cf. *HD*, pp. 88, 125, 138.
27. Cf. *ibid.*, pp. 75, 138.
28. Cf. *ibid.*, p. 23.
29. Cf. *ibid.*, pp. 87-89.
30. Cf. *ibid.*, pp. 83-84, 89.
31. Cf. *ibid.*, pp. 79, 87.
32. Cf. *ibid.*, pp. 137-138.
33. Cf. *ibid.*, pp. 78-79.
34. Cf. *ibid.*, p. 90.
35. *Ibid.*, p. 89.; William J. Richardson, p. 451.
36. Cf. *HD*, p. 89.
37. Cf. *ibid.*, pp. 14, 109.
38. Cf. *ibid.*, p. 113.
39. Cf. *ibid.*, p. 138.
40. Cf. *ibid.*, p. 124.
41. Cf. *ibid.*, pp. 24-25
42. Cf. *ibid.*, pp. 137-139.
43. *Ibid.*, p. 121.; William J. Richardson, p. 453.
44. Cf. *HD*, pp. 79-80, 110.
45. Cf. *ibid.*, p. 91.
46. Cf. *ibid.*, p. 92.
47. *Ibid.*, p. 110.; William J. Richardson, p. 454.
48. Cf. *HD*, p. 98.
49. Cf. *ibid.*, pp. 107-108.
50. *Ibid.*, p. 111.; Cf. also *ibid.*, p. 112.
51. William J. Richardson, p. 457.
52. *I and Thou*, trans., W. Kaufmann (Edinburgh Clark, 1970), p. 153.
53. *Ibid.*, p. 154. See also Rollo May, *Paulus: Reminiscences of a Friendship* (London: Collins, 1974), chap. v.
54. *The Existential Background of Human Dignity* (Cambridge: Harvard University Press, 1963). In this series of lectures delivered late in his life, G. Marcel surveys and evaluates the development of his thought. This will be the principle source here for interpreting the main emphases of his philosophy.
55. Rudolf Carnap *et al, Wissenschafttliche Weltaufassung der Wiener Kriesi*, chaps. ii-iv, trans. by A. Blumberg in J. Mann and G. Kreyche, eds., *Perspectives on Reality* (New York:

Harcourt, Brace and World, 1966), pp. 483-494. See also G. Marcel, *The Philosophy of Existence,* trans. by M. Hariri (New York: Philosophical Library, 1949), pp. 1-30: B.F. Skinner, *Beyond Freedom and Destiny* (New York: Knopf, 1971), pp. 25 and 197.
   56. *Existential Background,* p. 21.
   57. *Ibid.,* p. 22.
   58. *Ibid,* p, 96.
   59. *Ibid.*
   60. *Ibid.,* pp. 33-34.
   61. *Ibid.*
   62. *Ibid.,* p. 79.
   63. *Ibid.,* pp. 40-42.
   64. Trans. by R. Rosthal (New York, 1964).
   65. *Existential Background,* pp. 65, 72. and 74.
   66. *Ibid.*
   67. *Ibid.,* p. 78.
   68. *Ibid.,* p. 88.
   69. *Ibid.,* p, 147.
   70. *Ibid.,* p. 141.
   71. Trans. by B. Wall (Chicago, 1952), p. 281.
   72. Dasgupta, 1, 64.
   73. Vensus George, *Authentic Human Destiny: The Paths of Shankara and Heidegger* (III B. 1; Washington, D.C.: The Council for Research in Values and Philosophy, 1998); Bede Griffiths, *Vedanta and Christian Faith* (Dehra Dun: Jyoti Sahi), p. 24,
   74. *Ibid.,* pp. 20-24.
   75. *Summa theologica* I, q. 28, a. 3.
   76. *Truth,* q. 8, a. 6.
   77. *Ibid.,* q. 2, a. 9 and q. 7, a 8 ad 2.
   78. *Summa contra Gentiles,* IV, 3.

CHAPTER IX

CULTURAL TRADITIONS AND CIVIL SOCIETY AS SOCIAL WAYS TO GOD

The emerging appreciation of subjectivity has opened new appreciation of the nature of freedom as lived in a cultural tradition and in the structures of civil society. This chapter follows upon Chapter VIII to unfold the import of this appreciation of subjectivity for social life. If freedom is the properly human exercise of life and being, if the pattern of values and virtues as it constitutes a cultural tradition is the form of that freedom as lived by a people, and if civil society is the structure through which this is exercised, then the exercise of freedom in the formation of a culture and civil society will constitute the pilgrimage of a people. In what sense is this a way to God?

To examine this in detail the present chapter will begin with an analysis of levels of freedom. It will relate them to the structure of the critiques of Kant in order to follow the epistemology each entails and to open the way to freedom as the human exercise of existence, the metaphysical center of human life. Second, on this basis it will turn to the constitution of a culture not as an empirical object of anthropological codification, but as the corporate exercise of the freedom of a people. Third, in order to engage this issue existentially, the chapter will then turn to civil society as the new emergence of freedom in these post totalitarian times.

This brings us to the challenge of our times, namely, whether a people can truly govern itself through the exercise of freedom. That is, can the cultural traditions of a people which are constituted of its cumulative freedom hold sufficient authority or directive power to bring together a diversified civil society in its own governance. This is, in a way, a translation of Kant's requirement of the autonomy rather than heteronomy, but here the autonomy being sought is not that of a secular rebellion against God, but the proper autonomy to the human person as a creature of God described in the Part II, which indeed was a systematic elaboration of the archaic religious roots identified in Part I.

LEVELS OF INSIGHT AND LEVELS OF FREEDOM

If freedom is the responsible exercise of our life then it can be understood how the search for freedom is central to our life as persons and peoples. But the term is used so broadly and with so many meaning that it can both lead and mislead. It seems important then to sort out the various meanings of freedom.

After surveying carefully the history of ideas Mortimer Adler and his team, in *The Idea of Freedom: A Dialectic Examination of the Conceptions of Freedom* (Garden City: Doubleday, 1958), outlined a number of levels of freedom: circumstantial freedom of self-realization as a choice of whatever I want among objects; acquired freedom of self-perfection as the ability to choose as we ought; and natural freedom of self determination by which we responsibly create ourselves and our world.

Empirical Freedom of Choice

At the beginning of the modern stirrings for democracy John Locke perceived a crucial condition for a liberal democracy. If decisions were to be made not by the king but by the people, the basis for these decisions had to be equally available to all. To achieve this Locke proposed that we suppose the mind to be a blanc paper void of characters and ideas, and then follow the way in which it comes to be furnished. To keep this public he insisted that it be done exclusively via experience, that is, either by sensation or by reflection upon the mind's work on the materials derived from the senses.[1] Proceeding on these suppositions as if they were real limitations of knowledge, David Hume concluded that all objects of knowledge which are not formal tautologies must be matters of fact. Such "matters of fact" are neither the existence or actuality of a thing nor its essence, but simply the determination of one from a pair of sensible contraries, e.g., white rather than black, sweet rather than sour.[2]

The restrictions implicit in this appear starkly in Rudolf Carnap's "Vienna Manifesto" which shrinks the scope of meaningful knowledge and significant discourse to describing "some state of affairs" in terms of empirical "sets of facts." This excludes speech about wholes, God, the unconscious or *entelechies*; the grounds of meaning, indeed all that transcends the immediate content of sense experience are excluded.[3]

The socio-political structures which have emerged from this model of Locke have contributed much, but a number of indices suggest that he and others have tried too hard to work out their model on a solely empirical or forensic basis. For in such terms it is not possible to speak of appropriate or inappropriate goals or even to evaluate choices in relation to self-fulfillment. The only concern is the ability to choose among a set of contraries by brute, changeable and even arbitrary will power, and whether circumstances will allow me to carry out that choice. Such choices, of course, may not only differ from, but even contradict the immediate and long range objectives of other persons. This will require compromises in the sense of Hobbes; John Rawls will even work out a formal set of such compromises.[4]

Through it all, however, the basic concern remains the ability to do as one pleases: "being able to act or not act, according as we shall choose or will".[5] Its orientation is external. In practice as regards oneself, over time this comes to constitute a black-hole of [self-centered] consumption of physical goods in which both nature and the person are consumed. This is the essence of consumerism; it shrinks the very notion of freedom to competitiveness in the pursuit of material wealth.

Freedom in this sense remains basically Hobbes' principle of conflict; it is the liberal ideology built upon the conception of human nature as corrupted, of man as wolf, and of life as conflict. Hopefully this will be exercised in an "enlightened" manner, but in this total inversion of human meaning and dignity laws and rights can be only external remedies. By doing violence to man's naturally violent tendencies, they attempt to attenuate to the minimal degree necessary one's free and self-centered choice's and hence the supposed basic viciousness of human life. There must be a better understandings of human freedom and indeed these emerge as soon as one looks beyond external objects to the interior nature and the existence of the human subject and of all reality.

Formal Freedom to Choose as One Ought

For Kant the heteronomous, external and empiricist orientation character of the above disqualifies it from being moral at all, much less from constituting human freedom. In his first *Critique of Pure Reason* Kant had studied the role of the mind in the scientific constitution of the universe. He reasoned that because our sense experience was always limited and partial, the universality and necessity of the laws of science must come from the human mind. This was an essential turning point for it directed attention to the role of the human spirit and especially to the reproductive imagination in constituting the universe in which we live and move.

But this is not the realm of freedom for if the forms and categories with which we work are from our mind, how we construct with them is not left to our discretion. The imagination must bring together the multiple elements of sense intuition in a unity or order capable of being informed by the concepts or categories of the intellect with a view to constituting the necessary and universal judgments of science. The subject's imagination here is active but not free, for it is ruled by the categories integral to the necessary and universal judgements of the sciences. In these terms the human mind remains merely an instrument of physical progress and a function of matter.

However, in his second *Critique*, that of *Practical Reason*, beyond the set of universal, necessary and ultimately material relations, Kant points to the reality of human responsibility. This is the reality of freedom or spirit which characterizes and distinguishes the person. In its terms he recasts the whole notion of physical law as moral rule. If freedom is not to be chaotic and randomly destructive, it must be ruled or under law. To be free is to be able to will as I ought, i.e., in conformity with moral law.

Yet in order to be free the moral act must be autonomous. Hence, my maxim must be something which as a moral agent I — and no other — give to myself. Finally, though I am free because I am the lawmaker, my exercise of this power cannot be arbitrary if the moral order must be universal.

On this basis, a new level of freedom emerges. It is not merely self-centered whimsy in response to circumstantial stimuli; nor is it a despotic exercise of power or the work of the clever self-serving eye of Plato's rogue. Rather, it is the highest reality in all creation. To will as I ought is wise and caring power, open to all and bent upon the realization of "the glorious ideal of a universal realm of ends-in-themselves". In sum, it is free men living together in righteous harmony. This is what we are really about; it is our glory — and our burden.

Unfortunately, for Kant this glorious ideal remained on the formal plane; it was a matter of essence rather than of existence. It was intended as a guiding principle, a critical norm to evaluate the success or failure of the human endeavor — but it was not the human endeavor itself. For failure to appreciate this, much work for human rights remains at a level of abstraction which provides only minimal requirements. It might found processes of legal redress, but stops short of — and may even distract from and thus impede — positive engagement in the real process of constructing the world in which we live: witness the long paralysis of Europe and the world in the face of the Jugoslav dissolution of the moral and hence legal foundations for life in our times.

This second level of freedom makes an essential contribution to human life; we must not forget it nor must we ever do less. But it does not give us the way in which we as unique people in this unique time and space face our concrete problems. We need common guides, but our challenge is to act concretely. Can philosophy, without becoming politics or other processes of social action, consider and contribute to the actual process of human existence as we shape and implement our lives in freedom?

When the contemporary mind proceeds beyond objective and formal natures to become more deeply conscious of human subjectivity, and of existence precisely as emerging from and through human self-awareness, then the most profound changes must take place. The old order built on objective structures and norms would no longer be adequate; structures would crumble and a new era would dawn. This is indeed the juncture at which we now stand.

Existential Freedom of Self-determination and Self-Constitution

Progress in being human corresponds to the deepening of one's sense of being, beyond Platonic forms and structures, essences and laws, to act as uncovered by Aristotle and especially to existence as it emerges in Christian philosophy through the Patristic and Middle Ages. More recently this sensibility to existence has emerged anew through the employment of a phenomenological method for focusing upon intentionality and the self-awareness of the human person in time (*dasein*). This opens to the third level of freedom stated above, namely, that of deciding for oneself in virtue of the power "inherent in human nature to change one's own character creatively and to determine what one shall be or shall become." This is the most radical freedom, namely, our natural freedom of self-determination.

This basically is self-affirmation in terms of our teleological orientation toward perfection or full realization, which we will see to be the very root of the development of values, of virtues and hence of cultural traditions. It implies seeking perfection when it is absent and enjoying or celebrating it when attained. In this sense, it is that stability in one's orientation to the good which classically has been termed holiness and anchors such great traditions of the world as the Hindu and Taoist, Islamic and or the Judeo-Christian. One might say that this is life as practiced archetypically by the saints and holy men, but it would be more correct to say that it is because they lived in such a manner that they are called holy.

In his third *Critique*, Kant suggests an important insight regarding how this might form a creative force for confronting present problems and hence for passing on the tradition in a transforming manner. He sees that if the free person of the second critique were to be surrounded by the necessitarian universe of the first critique, then one's freedom would be entrapped and entombed within one's mind, while one's external actions would be necessary and necessitated. If there is to be room for human freedom in a cosmos in which one can make use of necessary laws, indeed if science is to contribute to the exercise of human freedom, then nature too must be understood as directed toward a goal and must manifest throughout a teleology within which free human purpose can be integrated. In these terms, even in its necessary and universal laws, nature is no longer alien to freedom; rather it expresses divine freedom and is conciliable with human freedom.

This makes possible the exercise of freedom, but our issue is how this freedom is exercised in a way that creates diverse cultures as ways to God, i.e., how can a free person relate to an order of nature and to structures of society in a way that is neither necessitated nor necessitating, but free and creative? In the "Critique of the Aesthetic Judgment," Kant points out that in working toward an integrating unity the imagination is not confined by the necessi tating structures of categories and concepts as in the first *Critique*, or the regulating ideal of the second *Critique*. Returning to the order of essences would lose the uniqueness of the self and its freedom. Rather, the imagination ranges freely over the full sweep of reality in all its dimensions to see where relatedness and purposiveness can emerge. This ordering and reordering by the imagination can bring about numberless unities or patterns of actions and natures. Unrestricted by any *a priori* categories, it can integrate necessary dialectical patterns within its own free and creative productions and include scientific universals within its unique concrete harmonies. This is the proper and creative work of the human person in this world.

In order for human freedom to be sensitive to the entirety of this all-encompassing harmony, in the final analysis our conscious attention must be directed not merely to universal and necessary physical or social structures, nor even to beauty and ugliness either in their concrete empirical realizations or in their Platonic ideals. Rather, our focus must be upon the integrating images of pleasure or displeasure, enjoyment or revulsion, generated deep within our person by these images as we attempt to shape our world according to the relation of our will to the good and hence to realize the good for our times.

In fact, however, this is still a matter of forms and categories, rather than of existence. Further it is a matter of the human person in him or herself. What is possible, however, in the light of Part I and II of this work is to read this in terms of existence rather than of essence Chapter V and VI above make it also a matter of relation to the creation and the living of His grace in time. In this light the aesthetic enables one to follow the free exercise of existence in a human life. At this point then the third level of freedom becomes truly the work of God with us.

In this manner human freedom becomes at once the goal, the creative source, the manifestation, the evaluation and the arbiter of all that imaginatively we can propose. It is *goal*, namely to realize life as rational and free in this world; it is *creative source* for through the imagination freedom unfolds the endless possibilities for human expression; it is *manifestation* because it presents these to our consciousness in ways appropriate to our capabilities for knowledge of limited realities and relates these to the circumstances of our life; it is *criterion* because its response manifests a possible mode of action to be variously desirable or not in terms of a total personal response of pleasure or displeasure, enjoyment or revulsion; and it is *arbiter* because it provides the basis upon which our freedom chooses to affirm or reject, realize or avoid this mode of self-realization.

Thus, freedom in this third, existential sense emerges as the dynamic center of our life. It is the spectroscope and kaleidoscope through which is processed the basic thrust toward perfection upon which, as we shall see, culture as the pattern of public life is based and by which its orders of preference are set. The philosophical and religious traditions it creates become the keys to the dynamics of human life. Hence the possibilities of peace within a nation and cooperation between peoples must depend fundamentally on the potentialities of creative freedom for overcoming the proclivities of the first level of freedom for confrontation and violent competition, for surmounting the general criteria of the second level of freedom, and for setting in motion positive processes of concrete peaceful and harmonious collaboration.

CULTURAL TRADITION AS CUMULATIVE FREEDOM

It is not sufficient, however, to consider only the freedom of single actions for that could leave a human, and *a fortiori* a social, life chaotic and inconsistent. Hence, it is necessary to see how the exercise of freedom is oriented and enabled over time by persons and peoples.

Value

The drama of this free self-determination, and hence the development of persons and of civil society, is a most fundamental matter, namely, that of being as affirmation and definitive stance against non-being. The account of this and its implication was the work of Parmenides, the very first metaphysician. Identically this is the relation to the good in search of which we live, survive and thrive. The good is manifest in experience as the object of desire, namely, as that which is sought when absent. Basically, it is what completes life; it is the "per-fect", understood in its etymological sense as that which is completed or realized through and through.

Hence, once achieved, it is no longer desired or sought, but enjoyed. This is reflected in the manner in which each thing, even a stone, retains the being or reality it has and resists reduction to non-being or nothing. The most that we can do is to change or transform a thing into something else; we cannot annihilate it. Similarly, a plant or tree, given the right conditions, grows to full stature and fruition. Finally, an animal protects its life — fiercely, if necessary — and seeks out the food needed for its strength. Food, in turn, as capable of contributing to an animal's realization or perfection, is for the animal an auxiliary good or means.

In this manner, things as good, that is, as actually realizing some degree of perfection and able to contribute to the well-being of others, are the bases for an interlocking set of relations. As these relations are based upon both the actual perfection things possess and the potential perfection to which they are thereby directed, the good is perfection both as attracting when it has not yet been attained and as constituting one's fulfillment upon its achievement. Goods, then, are not arbitrary or simply a matter of wishful thinking; they are rather the full development of things and all that contributes thereto. In this ontological or objective sense, all beings are good to the extent that they exist and can contribute to the perfection of others.

The moral good is a more narrow field, for it concerns only one's free and responsible actions. This has the objective reality of the ontological good noted above, for it concerns real actions which stand in distinctive relation to our own perfection and to that of others — and, indeed, to the physical universe and to God as well. Hence, many possible patterns of actions could be objectively right because they promote the good of those involved, while others, precisely as inconsistent with the real good of persons or things, are objectively disordered or misordered. This constitutes the objective basis for the ethical good or bad.

Nevertheless, because the realm of objective relations is almost numberless, whereas our actions are single, it is necessary not only to choose in general between the good and the bad, but in each case to choose which of the often innumerable possibilities one will render concrete.

However broad or limited the options, as responsible and moral an act is essentially dependent upon its being willed by a sub ject. Therefore, in order to follow the emergence of the field of concrete moral action, it is not sufficient to examine only the objective aspect, namely, the nature of the things involved. In addition, one must consider the action in relation to the subject, namely, to the person who, in the context of his/her society and culture, appreciates and values the good of this action, chooses it over its alternatives, and eventually wills its actualization.

The term 'value' here is of special note. It was derived from the economic sphere where it meant the amount of a commodity sufficient to attain a certain worth. This is reflected also in the term 'axiology' whose root means "weighing as much" or "worth as much." It requires an objective content — the good must truly "weigh in" and make a real difference; but the term 'value' expresses this good especially as related to wills which actually acknowledge it as a good and as desirable.[6] Thus, different individuals or groups of persons and at different periods have distinct sets of values. A people or community is sensitive to, and prizes, a distinct set of goods or, more likely, it establishes a distinctive ranking in the degree to which it prizes various goods. By so doing, it delineates among limitless objective goods a certain pattern of values which in a more stable fashion mirrors the corporate free choices of that people.

This constitutes the basic topology of a culture; as repeatedly reaffirmed through time, it builds a tradition or heritage about which we shall speak below. It constitutes, as well, the prime pattern and gradation of goods or values which persons experience from their earliest years and in terms of which they interpret their developing relations. Young persons peer out at the world through lenses formed, as it were, by their family and culture and configured according to the pattern of choices made by that community throughout its history — often in its most trying circumstances. Like a pair of glasses it does not create the object; but it focuses attention upon certain goods involved rather than upon others. This becomes the basic orienting factor for the affective and emotional life described by the Scotts, Adam Ferguson and Adam Smith, as the heart of civil society. In time, it encourages and reinforces certain patterns of action which, in turn, reinforce the pattern of values.

Through this process a group constitutes the concerns in terms of which it struggles to advance or at least to perdure, mourns its failures, and celebrates its successes. This is a person's or people's world of hopes and fears, in terms of which, as Plato wrote in the *Laches*, their lives have moral meaning.[7] It is varied according to the many concerns and the groups which coalesce around them. As these are interlocking and interdependent a pattern of social goals and concerns develops which guides action. In turn, corresponding capacities for action or virtue are developed.

Indeed, Aristotle takes this up at the very beginning of his ethics. In order to make sense of the practical dimension of our life it is necessary to identify the good or value toward which one directs one's life or which one finds satisfying. This he terms happiness and then proceeds systematically to see which goal can be truly satisfying. His test is not passed by physical goods or honors, but by that which corresponds to, and fulfills, our highest capacity, that is, contemplation of the highest being or divine life.[8]

But what is the relation of this approach from below, as it were, to religion as seen from above, that is, from the point of view of revelation and grace which point to a more perfect goal and fulfillment? Thomas Aquinas' effort in his *Summa contra Gentiles*, analyzed by G. Stanley,[9] is to show the way in which this latter sense of religion is not a contradiction or substitution of the former, but rather its more perfect fulfillment than is possible by human powers alone. In eschatology the vision of God is not a negation of the contemplation of divine life of which Aristotle spoke, but its fulfillment in a way that exceeds human hopes.

Virtues

Martin Heidegger describes a process by which the self emerges as a person in the field of moral action. It consists in transcending oneself or breaking beyond mere self-concern and projecting outward as a being whose very nature is to share with others for whom one cares and about whom one is concerned. In this process, one identifies new purposes or goals for the sake of which action is to be undertaken. In relation to these goals, certain combinations of possibilities, with their natures and norms, take on particular importance and begin thereby to enter into the makeup of one's world of meaning.[10] Freedom then becomes more than mere spontaneity, more than choice, and more even than self-determination in the sense of determining oneself to act as described above. It shapes — the phenomenologist would say even that it constitutes — one's world as the ambit of human decisions and dynamic action. This is the making of the complex social ordering of social groups which constitutes civil society.

This process of deliberate choice and decision transcends the somatic and psychic dynamisms. Whereas the somatic dimension is extensively reactive, the psychic dynamisms of affectivity or appetite are fundamentally oriented to the good and positively attracted by a set of values. These, in turn, evoke an active response from the emotions in the context of responsible freedom. But it is in the dimension of responsibility that one encounters the properly moral and social dimension of life. For, in order to live with others, one must be able to know, to choose and finally to realize what is truly conducive to one's good and to that of others. Thus, persons and groups must be able to judge the true value of what is to be chosen, that is, its objective worth, both in itself and in relation to others. This is moral truth: the judgment regarding whether the act makes the person and society good in the sense of bringing authentic individual and social fulfillment, or the contrary.

In this, deliberation and voluntary choice are required in order to exercise proper self-awareness and self-governance. By determining to follow this judgment one is able to overcome determination by stimuli and even by culturally ingrained values and to turn these, instead, into openings for free action in concert with others in order to shape my community as well as my physical surroundings. This can be for good or for ill, depending on the character of my actions. By definition, only morally good actions contribute to personal and social fulfillment, that is, to the development and perfection of persons with others in community.

It is the function of conscience, as one's moral judgment, to identify this character of moral good in action. Hence, moral freedom consists in the ability to follow one's conscience. This work of conscience is not a merely theoretical judgment, but the exercise of self-possession and self-determination in one's actions. Here, reference to moral truth constitutes one's sense of duty, for the action that is judged to be truly good is experienced also as that which I ought to do.

When this is exercised or lived, patterns of action develop which are habitual in the sense of being repeated. These are the modes of activity with which we are familiar; in their exercise, along with the coordinated natural dynamisms they require, we are practiced; and with practice comes facility and spontaneity. Such patterns constitute the basic, continuing and pervasive shaping influence of our life. For this reason, they have been considered classically to be the basic indicators of what our life as a whole will add up to, or, as is often said, "amount to". Since Socrates, the technical term for these especially developed capabilities has been 'virtues' or special strengths.

But, if the ability to follow one's conscience and, hence, to develop one's set of virtues must be established through the interior dynamisms of the person, it must be protected and promoted by the related physical and social realities. This is a basic right of the person — perhaps *the* basic human and social right — because only thus can one transcend one's conditions and strive for fulfillment. Its protection and promotion must be a basic concern of any order which would be democratic and directed to the good of its people.

But this is only a right to one's conscience; religion goes further in that it looks to divine grace for help. Some virtues are the result not only of human practice, but of divine action. In other words the perspective shifts from the secondary causality of the human creature to the primary casualty of the divine existence itself. Its effect is created existence with its truth, justice and faith; love that expresses the goodness of the creation; and ecstasy in response to the sublime beauty of the divine.

Cultural Tradition

Together, these values and virtues of a people set the pattern of social life through which freedom is developed and exercised. This is called a "culture". On the one hand, the term is derived from the Latin word for tilling or cultivating the land. Cicero and other Latin authors used it for the cultivation of the soul or mind (*cultura animi*), for just as even good land, when left without cultivation, will produce only disordered vegetation of little value, so the human spirit will not achieve its proper results unless trained or educated.[11] This sense of culture corresponds most closely to the Greek term for education (*paideia*) as the development of character, taste and judgment, and to the German term "formation"

(*Bildung*).[12]

Here, the focus is upon the creative capacity of the spirit of a people and their ability to work as artists, not only in the restricted sense of producing purely aesthetic objects, but in the more involved sense of shaping all dimensions of life, material and spiritual, economic and political. The result is a whole life, characterized by unity and truth, goodness and beauty, and, thereby, sharing deeply in meaning and value. The capacity for this cannot be taught, although it may be enhanced by education; more recent phenomenological and hermeneutic inquiries suggest that, at its base, culture is a renewal, a reliving of origins in an attitude of profound appreciation.[13] This leads us beyond self and other, beyond identity and diversity, in order to comprehend both.

On the other hand, "culture" can be traced to the term *civis* (citizen, civil society and civilization).[14] This reflects the need for a person to belong to a social group or community in order for the human spirit to produce its proper results. By bringing to the person the resources of the tradition, the *tradita* or past wisdom produced by the human spirit, the community facilitates comprehension. By enriching the mind with examples of values which have been identified in the past, it teaches and inspires one to produce something analogous. For G.F. Klemm, this more objective sense of culture is composite in character.[15] E.B. Tyler defined this classically for the social sciences as "that complex whole which includes knowledge, belief, art, morals, law, customs and any other capabilities and habits required by man as a member of society."[16]

In contrast, Clifford Geertz came to focus on the meaning of all this for a people and on how a people's intentional action went about shaping its world. Thus he contrasts the analysis of culture to an experimental science in search of law, seeing it rather as an interpretative science in search of meaning.[17] What is sought is the import of artifacts and actions, that is, whether "it is, ridicule or challenge, irony or anger, snobbery or pride, that, in their occurrence and through their agency, is getting said."[18] For this there is need to be aware "of the imaginative universe within which their acts are signs."[19] In this light, Geertz defines culture rather as "an historically transmitted pattern of meanings embodied in symbols, a system of intended conceptions expressed in symbolic forms by means of which men communicate, perpetuate and develop their knowledge about and attitudes toward life."[20]

Each particular complex whole or culture is specific to a particular people; a person who shares in this is a *civis* or citizen and belongs to a civilization. For the more restricted Greek world in which this term was developed, others (aliens) were those who did not speak the Greek tongue; they were "barbaroi", for their speech sounded like mere babel. Though at first this meant simply non-Greek, its negative manner of expression easily lent itself to, perhaps reflected, and certainly favored, a negative axiological connotation; indeed, this soon became the primary meaning of the word 'barbarian'. By reverse implication, it attached to the term 'civilization' an exclusivist connotation, such that the cultural identity of peoples began to imply not only the pattern of gracious symbols by which one encounters and engages in shared life projects with other persons and peoples, but cultural alienation between peoples. Today, as communication increases and more widely differentiated peoples enter into ever greater interaction and mutual dependence, we reap a bitter harvest of this negative connotation. The development of a less exclusivist sense of culture and civilization must be a priority task.

The development of values and virtues and their integration as a culture of any depth or richness takes time, and hence depends upon the experience and creativity of many generations. The culture which is handed on, or *tradita*, comes to be called a cultural tradition; as such it reflects the cumulative achievement of a people in discovering, mirroring and transmitting the deepest meanings of life. This is tradition in its synchronic sense as a body of wisdom.

This sense of tradition is very vivid in premodern and village communities. It would appear to be much less so in modern urban centers, undoubtedly in part due to the difficulty in forming active community life in large urban centers. However, the cumulative process of transmitting, adjusting and applying the values of a culture through time is not only heritage or what is received, but new creation as this is passed on in new ways. Attending to tradition, taken in this active sense, allows us not only to uncover the permanent and universal truths which Socrates sought, but to perceive the importance of values we receive from the tradition and to mobilize our own life project actively toward the future.

The Genesis of Tradition in Community

Because tradition has sometimes been interpreted as a threat to the personal and social freedom essential to a democracy, it is important to see how a cultural tradition is generated by the free and responsible life of the members of a concerned community or civil society and enables succeeding generations to realize their life with freedom and creativity. This will be considered with special attention to ways to God and to religious traditions as lived in religious communities and their former role in enlivening and supporting persons and groups on their way to God.

Autogenesis is no more characteristic of the birth of knowledge than it is of persons. One's consciousness emerges, not with self, but in relation to others. In the womb, the first awareness is that of the heart beat of one's mother. Upon birth, one enters a family in whose familiar relations one is at peace and able to grow. It is from one's family and in one's earliest weeks and months that one does or does not develop the basic attitudes of trust and confidence which undergird or undermine one's capacities for subsequent social relations. There one encounters care and concern for others independently of what they do for us and acquires the language and symbol system in terms of which to conceptualize, communicate and understand.[21] Just as a person is born into a family on which he or she depends absolutely for life, sustenance, protection and promotion, so one's understanding develops in community. As persons we emerge by birth into a family and neighborhood from which we learn and in harmony with which we thrive.

Similarly, through the various steps of one's development, as one's circle of community expands through neighborhood, school, work and recreation, one comes to learn and to share personally and passionately an interpretation of reality and a pattern of value responses. The phenomenologist sees this life in the varied civil society as the new source for wisdom. Hence, rather than turning away from daily life in order to contemplate abstract and disembodied ideas, the place to discover meaning is in life as lived in the family and in the progressively wider social circles into which one enters.

If it were merely a matter of community, however, all might be limited to the present, with no place for tradition as that which is "passed on" from one generation to the next. In fact, the process of trial and error, of continual correction and addition in relation to a people's evolving sense of human dignity and purpose, constitutes a type of learning and testing laboratory for successive generations. In this laboratory of history, the strengths of various insights and behavior patterns can be identified and reinforced, while deficiencies are progressively corrected or eliminated. Horizontally, we learn from experience what promotes and what destroys life and, accordingly, make pragmatic adjustments.

But even this language remains too abstract, too limited to method or technique, too unidimensional. While tradition can be described in general and at a distance in terms of feed-back mechanisms and might seem merely to concern how to cope in daily life, what is being spoken about are free acts that are expressive of passionate human commitment and personal sacrifice in responding to concrete danger, building and rebuilding family alliances and constructing and defending one's nation. Moreover, this wisdom is not a matter of mere tactical adjustments to temporary concerns; it concerns rather the meaning we are able to envision for life and which we desire to achieve through all such adjustments over a period of generations, i.e., what is truly worth striving for and the pattern of social interaction in which this can be lived richly. The result of this extended process of learning and commitment constitutes our awareness of the bases for the decisions of which history is constituted.

This points us beyond the horizontal plane of the various ages of history and directs our attention vertically to its ground and, hence, to the bases of the values which humankind in its varied circumstances seeks to realize.[22] It is here that one searches for the absolute ground of meaning and value of which Iqbal wrote. Without that all is ultimately relative to only an interlocking network of consumption, then dissatisfaction and finally ennui.

The impact of the convergence of cumulative experience and reflection is heightened by its gradual elaboration in ritual and music, and its imaginative configuration in such great epics as the *Mahabharata* and in dance. All conspire to constitute a culture which, like a giant telecommunications dish, shapes, intensifies and extends the range and penetration of our personal sensitivity, free decision and mutual concern.

Tradition, then, is not, as in history, simply everything that ever happened, whether good or bad. It is rather what appears significant for human life: it is what has been seen through time and human experience to be deeply true and necessary for human life. It contains the values to which our forebears first freely gave their passionate commitment in specific historical circumstances and then constantly reviewed, rectified and progressively passed on generation after generation. The content of a tradition, expressed in works of literature and all the many facets of a culture, emerges progressively as something upon which character and community can be built. It constitutes a rich source from which multiple themes can be drawn, provided it be accepted and embraced, affirmed and cultivated.

Hence, it is not because of personal inertia on our part or arbitrary will on the part of our forbears that our culture provides a model and exemplar. On the contrary, the importance of tradition derives from both the cooperative character of the learning by which wisdom is drawn from experience and the cumulative free acts of commitment and sacrifice which have defined, defended and passed on through time the corporate life of the community.[23]

Ultimately, it bears to us the divine gifts of life, meaning and love, and provides a way both back to their origin and forward to their goal, their *Alpha* and *Omega*.

Reason and Hermeneutics

As the recognition of the value of tradition would appear to constitute a special problem for heirs of the Enlightenment, it may be helpful to reflect briefly on why this is so. Enlightenment rationalism idealizes clarity and distinctness of ideas both in themselves and in their interconnection; as such, it divorces them from their concrete existential and temporal significance. Such an ideal of human knowledge, it is proposed, could be achieved either, as with Descartes, through an intellect working by itself from an intellectually perceived Archimedean principle or, as with Locke and Carnap, through the senses drawing their ideas exclusively from experience and combining them in myriad tautological transformations.[24] In either case, the result is a-temporal and consequently non-historical knowledge.

Two attempts to break out of this have proven ultimately unsuccessful. One might be termed historist and relativist. In order to recognize historical sequence while retaining the ideal of clarity and distinctness, attempted to attain detailed knowledge of each period, relativizing everything to its point in time and placing historicity ultimately at the service of the rationalist ideal. The other, the Romantics, ultimately adhered to the same revolutionary enlightenment ideal even in appearing to oppose it, for, in turning to the past and to myths, they too sought clear and distinct knowledge of a static human nature. Tradition thus became traditionalism, for all was included in the original state of nature and our only way of obtaining a firm grounding for human life was simply to return thereto.

In the rationalist view, in contrast, any meaning not clearly and distinctly perceived was an idol to be smashed (Bacon), an idea to be bracketed by doubt (Descartes), or something to be wiped clean from the slate of the mind as irrational and coercive (Locke and Hume). Any judgment — even if provisional — made before all had been examined and its clarity and distinctness established would be a dangerous imposition by the will.

This points toward the importance of civil society for realizing human life in a manner that reflects and ultimately leads toward the divine. First the enlightenment ideal of absolute knowledge of oneself or of others, simply and without condition, is not possible, for the knower is always conditioned according to his or her position in time and space and in relation to others. But neither would such knowledge be of ultimate interest, for human knowledge, like human beings, develops in time and with others.[25] This does not exclude projects of universal and necessary scientific knowledge, but it does identify these precisely as limited and specialized. They make important but specific, rather than all-controlling, contributions. Hence, other modes of knowledge are required in order to take account of the ongoing and varied life of human freedom and its creative results. Further, this is not a solitary, but a group matter. Hence society, especially civil society, becomes the focus for the appreciation and evaluation of things and for the responses which build our world.

Secondly, according to Descartes,[26] reason is had by all and completely. Therefore, authority could be only an entitlement of some to decide issues by an application of their will, rather than according to an authentic understanding of the truth or justice of an issue. This would be "hastiness" according to Descartes's fourth *Meditation*. Further, the limited number of people in authority means that the vision of which they dispose would be limited by restricted or even individual interests. Finally, as one decision constitutes a precedent for those to follow, authority must become fundamentally bankrupt and hence corruptive.[27]

In this manner, the choice of clarity as an ideal, first by Plato and then by Descartes, has generated an exclusivist mind-set ruled by a reductivist mechanism. It is not only that what is not clear is put aside as irrelevant. Even more, the dynamism whereby we reflect the love by which we have been made and respond to it with openness and generosity comes to be seen in a negative light as cognitively blind, while freedom appears in a negative light as affectively arbitrary. The only way these could achieve a redeeming clarity for the human mind is to be reduced to the unambiguous and simplest visceral violence of Hobbes's struggle for survival, that is, by being reduced to the animal level where, precisely, human freedom is dispensed with.

In this light, too, there has been a tendency to isolate public authority from the shared moral sense of community. This, in turn, compromises the moral quality of government, which needs to include and be addressed by those who comprehend and share in the social good which government is to address. This we shall see is civil society.

If the cumulative experience of humankind in living together in peace is to make a contribution to the development of modern life, then, it will be necessary to return human knowledge to the ongoing lived process of humane discovery and choice in society. This, in turn, takes place within the broad project of human interaction and an active process of reception by one generation of the learning of its predecessors. The emerging consciousness of the importance of this effort has led to broadening the task of hermeneutics from the study of ancient, often biblical, texts to a more inclusive attention to the integral meaning of cultures. There it has found, not a mere animal search for survival, but a sense of human dignity which, by transcending survival needs enables human creativity in society and encourages a search for ever higher levels of human life leading ultimately to God.

The reference to the god, Hermes, in the term "hermeneutics" suggests something of the depth of the meaning which is sought throughout human life and its implication for the world of values. The message borne by Hermes is not merely an abstract mathematical formula or a methodological prescription devoid of human meaning and value. Instead, it is the limitless wisdom regarding the source of all and hence its reality and value. Hesiod had appealed for this in the introduction to his *Theogony*: "Hail, children of Zeus! Grant lovely song and celebrate the holy race of the deathless gods who are forever. . . . Tell how at the first gods and earth came to be."[28]

Similarly, Aristotle indicated concern for values and virtues in describing his science of wisdom as "knowing to what end each thing must be done; . . . this end is the good of that thing, and, in general, the supreme good in the whole of nature." Such a science will be most divine, for: "(1) God is thought to be among the causes of all things and to be a first principle, and (2) such a science either God alone can have, or God above all others. All the sciences, indeed, are more necessary than this, but none is better."[29] Rather than evaluating all in terms of reductivist clarity and considering things in a horizontal perspective that is only temporal and totally changing — with an implied relativization of all — hermeneutics or interpretation opens also to a vertical vision of what is highest and deepest in life, most real in itself and most lasting through time. This is the eternal or divine in both being and value, which is the key to mobilizing and orienting the life of society in time.

In this light one is able to understand better the character of religious communities which come together under the inspiration of the Prophets and great examples of the religious life as lived existentially: a Buddha, a Christ or a Muhammad — paradigmatic individuals in A. Cua's term. Each set a distinctive pattern of values and virtues which has been lived through history and unfolded by a community of persons who have attempted singly and together to live the multiple modes of this example. This we will see is a seminal source of the groupings which below will be termed civil society.

At the same time, while still echoing Socrates by searching for the permanent structures of complex entities and the stable laws of change, in redirecting attention to being in time, contemporary attention is open to the essentially temporal character of mankind and, hence, to the uniqueness of each decision, whether individual or corporate. Thus, hermeneutics attends to the task of translation or interpretation, stressing the presentation to those receiving a message, their historical situation and, hence, the historical character of human life. It directs attention not merely to the pursuit of general truths, but to those to whom truth is expressed, namely, persons in the concrete circumstances of their cultures as these have developed through the history of human interaction with nature, with other human beings and with God. It is this human history as heritage and tradition which sets the circumstances in which one perceives the values presented in the tradition and mobilizes his or her own project toward the future.

CIVIL SOCIETY

The Greek Tradition

There is another question here. If cultures as human are a work of freedom, this is not exercised by isolated individuals, but by persons in relation one to another, as was stressed by Buber and Marcel in Chapter VIII above. As an essential character of human life this relationship cannot be random in sequence with each act negating the others. This would neutralize and destroy human existence, which by nature must be affirmative and cohesive. Ethics and politics, first authored by Aristotle, are the classical disciplines in which this is analyzed; more recently it has come to be identified as civil society.

This essentially is the question of how human beings can establish a social unity which promotes, rather than subverts, the unique dignity and self-realization of all who are its members. This remains the basic issue to our day. It could be expected that whoever would open the way to resolving this issue would be the father of the Greek, and hence the Western, tradition in philosophy. This proved to be Plato and Aristotle.

Plato opened the way to taking up the reality of the many members of society and their unity through his notion of participation. This envisaged the many as having their reality from, expressing, and ultimately being directed toward the one. This breakthrough was foundational for all of Western philosophy. Plato's sense of participation was expressed in the long Platonic tradition through the imagery of light coming from a simple exalted source, but shining down in ever-expanding, if diminished, ranks. In his famous allegory of the cave in the *Republic*[30] Plato described the preparation of leaders as one of liberation from the darkness of the cave in order to ascend to the light and then, returning to the cave, to govern in an enlightened manner. This was not a role, but the center of one's reality. Hegel's work reflects this Platonic sense of the citizen.[31] It is, in sum, living in, with and for one's people — an overall life entirely dedicated to the public good.

There was, however, a weakness which showed up in his description of the ideal state in his *Laws* (in some contrast to his *Republic*). In response to the chaotic situation of his times, Socrates had sought a pattern of virtues which could provide real guidance in the actual situations of human action. Plato, seeking greater clarity in their regard, reduced them to ideal forms in relation to which the many individual instances were but passive formal images. This made room for diversity between different forms, but left the many instances of any one form as basically identical — just as all number threes are the same among themselves and in relation to threeness itself. As a result, the ideal state he described in the *Laws* had a shocking absence of any sense of the uniqueness of human beings. It reduced social life to a communal form in which all was determined by, and for, the state.

To the degree possible, and in terms of the sense of reality had at the time, this image of society was corrected by Plato's pupil, Aristotle, who first mapped out the field of philosophy as a science and a wisdom. It is here that we shall attempt to advance our eidetic reduction of the notion of civil society and to observe the contribution that philosophy can make to the development of that notion.

With regard to civil society Aristotle took three preliminary steps. Speaking thematically, rather than chronologically, he first developed the science of logic in order to make it possible to control the steps of the mind in extended and complex reasoning. The result was the first elaboration of the structure of scientific knowledge in both the theoretical and the practical orders. Second, he proceeded actually to design the sciences for the first time. He developed

Physics as an appreciation of the active character of physical reality, and by implication of all being. In his *de Anima*, the science of living beings, he identified intelligence and freedom as the distinctive characteristics of human life. These not only found the proper dignity of individual human beings, but imply a civic union of communication and cooperation between persons. The practical creative work of developing and directing these cooperative unions is the topic of ethics and politics as sciences of the practical order.

In the practical order of making and doing, the principles of scientific understanding lie not in the object but in the subject — the agent or artist. Aristotle's *The Nichomachean Ethics* begins with the observation that every action aims at an end, and that the end sought by all is happiness or the good life. *Politics* as a science consists of the study of the search for the good life as a goal not only of an individuals, but of the whole integrated society. What must be understood here and expressed in language is the goal, meaning and modes of the realization of life in community. Phenomenology has been developed precisely as a mode of access to this interior life of meaning. This is not external to personal and social life, but its very essence as the human good. Hence Manfried Riedel suggests that, if reached by a process of eidetic reduction after the manner of Husserl,[32] the language of Aristotle's politics can unveil the real meaning of civil society.

Generally, this is aided by Aristotle himself who begins most of his works with a description of how the matter in question has appeared historically through time, thereby gradually delineating the field whose scientific principles and structure he will seek to determine in the process of establishing the science of that field. Here Aristotle begins his politics not historically but thematically, delineating the elements in which political life consists.[33] Both approaches bring us to the same point, namely, that to be political means to govern and be governed as a member of a community.

Governance and Community

Most properly the political bespeaks governance or directive action toward the goal. Significantly, this is expressed by the term *arché* which originally means beginning, origin or first source. Secondly, this is extended to governance in the sense of sover eignty, that is, of directing oneself and others toward a good or a goal, while not being necessitated by other persons or things. *Arché* is the point of beginning or origin of social action; as such it bespeaks responsibility for the overall enterprise. This exercise of freedom by individuals and groups in originating responsible action is characteristically human. Though most actions of humans at the different inorganic and organic levels can be performed by other physical realities, it is precisely as these actions are exercised under the aegis of freedom that they become properly human acts. This issue of corporate directive freedom — its nature and range — is then the decisive issue today. How this is needed and how it effectively can be exercised is the heart of the issue of civil society.

There is a second dimension to the issue of governance in Aristotle. It is indicated in what many have seen as a correction of his evaluation of types of governance. His first classification of modes of government was drawn up in terms of the quantity of those who shared in ruling. When ruling is seen as a search for material possessions or property, the best form of government would be an *oligarchy* or rule by the few. For generally only a few are rich and they could afford to give more concern to the public weal rather than only to personal enrichment. Democracy, in contrast, is rule by the masses who are poor and thus to be expected to more concerned for their personal gain.[34] Aristotle needed to improve on this basically quantitative division founded empirically on the changing distribution of property, for conceptually there could be a society in which the majority is rich. Hence, he chose instead a normative criterion, namely, whether governance is exercised in terms of a search, not for goods chosen by a few out of self-interest, but for the common good in which all can participate.[35] In this light governance has its meaning as a species of a broader reality, namely, the community (*koinonia*) which comes together for its end, namely, happiness or the good life of the whole. Community supposes the free persons of which it is composed; formally it expresses their conscious and free union with a view to a common end, namely, the shared good they seek.

The polis is then a species of community. It is a group, which as human and hence free and self-responsible, comes together in governance to guide efforts toward the achievement of the good life. Community and governance are not the same or tautological, but they go together, for persons are united as a community by their common orientation to the same end, and as free they rightly guide or govern themselves toward that end. In this way Aristotle identifies the central nature of the socio-political order as that of a *koinōnia politika* or "civil society".

Civil society then has three elements. First, there is governance: *arché*, the beginning of action or the taking of initiative toward an end; this is an exercise of human freedom. But as this pertains to persons in their various groups and subgroups there are two other elements, namely, communication or solidarity with other members of the groups and the participation or subsidiarity of these groups or communities within the whole. In their search for the goal or end, that is, for the common good, the participants form communities marked by solidarity and interrelated in subsidiarity. Thus to understand a civil society we must seek to uncover the solidarity and subsidiarity of the community as its members participate in the governance of life toward the common good.

Solidarity. Through time societies have manifested an increasing diversity of parts; this constitutes their proper richness and strength. As the parts differ one from another, this increase is numerical, thereby bringing quantitative advantage as with an army. But it is even more important that the parts differ in kind so that each brings a distinctive concern and capability to the common task. Further, differing between themselves, one member is able to give and the other to receive in multiple and interrelated active and receptive modes. This means that the members of a society not only live alongside one another, but that their shared effort to realize the good life thrives through their mutual interaction.

Aristotle develops this theme richly in chapter 6 "On Friendship" in Book IX of his *Nicomachean Ethics*, stressing a theme which will reemerge later, namely, that the members of a civil society need to be of one mind and one heart. Toward the end of that chapter he evolves the importance of this for the common weal.[36]

Such solidarity of the members of society is one of its essential component characteristics. Plato would use the terms *methexis* and *mimesis* or participation for this. But Aristotle feared that if the individual were seen as but another instance of a specific type, or as but an image of the primary form, individuals would lose their reality. So he soon ceased to use this term; the term 'solidarity' which recognizes the distinctive reality of the parts seems to reflect better his thought.

In the human body, where there is but one substantial form, the many parts exist for the whole and the actions of the parts are actions of the whole (it is not my legs and feet which walk; I walk by my legs and feet). Society also has many parts and their differentiation and mutuality pertains to the good of the whole. But in contrast to the body, the members of a community have their own proper form, finality and operation. Hence, their unity is an accidental one of order, that is, in terms of the relation or order of their capabilities and actions to the perfection of the body politic or civil society and the realization of its common good.

Aristotle does not hesitate to state strongly the dependence of the individual on the community in order to live a truly human life, concluding that the state is a creation of nature prior to the individual.[37] Nevertheless, inasmuch as the parts are realities in their own right, outside of any orientation to the common good of the whole, society ultimately is for its parts: the society is for its members, not the contrary.

Subsidiarity.[38] But there is more than solidarity to the constitution of a civil society. Community in general is constituted through the cooperation of many for the common goal or good, but the good or goal of a community can be extremely rich and textured. It can concern nourishment, health maintenance, environmental soundness; it includes education both informal and formal, both basic and advanced, initial and retraining; it extends to nutrition, culture, recreation, etc. — all the endless manners in which human beings fulfill their needs and capacities and seek "the good life". As each of these can and must be sought and shared through the cooperation of many, each is the basis of a group or subgroup in a vastly varied community.

When, however, one adds the elements of governance (*arché*), that is, the element of freedom determining what will be done and how the goal will be sought, then the dimension of subsidiarity emerges into view. Were we talking about things rather then people it would be possible to envisage a technology of mass production automatically moving and directing all the components automatically toward the final product. Where, however, we are concerned with a community and hence with the composite exercise of the freedom of the persons and groups which constitute its membership, then it is crucial that this not be substituted for by a command from outside or from above. Rather, governance in the community initiating and directing action toward the common end must be exercised in a cumulative manner beginning from the primary or basic group, the family, in relation to its common good, and moving up to the broader concerns or goals of more inclusive groups considered both quantitatively (neighborhood, city, nation, etc.), and qualitatively (education, health, religion) according to the hierarchy of goods which are their concerns.

Aristotle recognizes the many communities as parts of the political order when he treats justice and friendship, inasmuch as this seeks not particular advantage but that of the whole.[39] Justice here, as distributive, is not arithmetic but proportionate to those involved according to the consideration and respect that is due to each.[40] In his concern for the stability of the state in the *Politics* he stresses the need for a structured diversity. Groups such as the family and village differ qualitatively from the state. It is necessary to recognize this and promote them as such for the vitality of the whole.

The synergetic ordering of these groups, considered both quantitatively and qualitatively, and the realization of their varied needs and potentials is the stuff of the governance of civil society. The condition for success in this is that the freedom and hence responsible participation of all be actively present and promoted at each level. Thus, proper responsibility on the family level must not be taken away by the city, nor that of the city by the state. Rather the higher units either in the sense of larger numbers or more important order of goods must exercise their governance precisely in order to promote the full and self-responsible action of the lower units and in the process enable them to achieve goals which acting alone they could not realize. Throughout, the concern is to maximize their participation in governance, that is, the exercise of freedom by the members of the community, thereby enabling them to live more fully as persons and groups so that the entire society flourishes. This is termed subsidiarity.

Thus, through considering phenomenologically Aristotle's analysis of the creative activity of persons striving consciously and freely toward their goals, it is possible to articulate the nature and constituent elements of civil society as a conscious goal of persons and peoples. It is a realm of persons in groups or community solidarities which, through a structure of subsidiarity, participate in self-governance.

This reflects also the main axes of the unfolding of the social process in Greece, namely:

(a) from the Platonic stress upon unity in relation to which the many are but repetitions, to the Aristotelian development of diversity as necessary for the unfolding and actualization of unity;

(b) from emphasis upon governance by authority located at the highest and most remote levels, to participation in the exercise of governance by persons and groups at every level and in relation to matters with which they are engaged and responsible; and

(c) from attention to one's own interests, to attention to the common good of the whole.

Progress along these axes will be the key to efforts to develop civil society and will provide guidance for efforts to promote a proper functioning of social life. This, in turn, is the concrete social manner in which people live their lives together as their ways to God.

Indeed, it is when considered in terms of what has been done in the previous chapters about ways to God that these elements of arché, solidarity and subsidiarity come most alive. We saw how human freedom was above all the privileged reflection in time of the absolute eternal being and its creative freedom. It is as participating in absolute freedom that the human person is inviolable and in oneself, never to be reduced to a means to another's ends.

What is more, this is shared most deeply with other humans to constitute a solidarity which goes beyond utilitarian arrangements or social contracts. This, of course, is ideally the essence of a religious community, but it is as well the deep motivation of the multiple coming togethers in groups in all fields that constitute a civil society. Paul Tillich will elaborate this in the following chapter.

These converge in the motion of subsidiarity where the pattern of groups and the higher decision making bodies are in principle to promote, rather than suppress, the smaller groups. Hence, it is no accident that when the European Union needed a way of understanding a union which would promote, rather than absorb its members it took up the notion of subsidiarity, theretofore a characteristic element of Catholic social thought.

CULTURAL TRADITION AND GOVERNANCE IN CIVIL SOCIETY

If, however, one can look to tradition in order to find general inspiration for life, will this be sufficient for civil society which must have not only a certain tenor or quality of life, but governance as well? In the past the solution has been to centralize authority which then became autocratic and voluntaristic. Under the cover of efficiency and equality this ruled by general decrees and subverted the rich differentiation of solidarity and subsidiarity essential to civil society. If the exercise of freedom as governance was a way to God it was the way of the ruler, not of the ruled; this way to God could be autocratic and elite, not democratic and popular. Is it possible for tradition as cumulative freedom to bear sufficient authority to provide, as an alternate, coordinated governance through freedom itself as this is exercised popularly in the various groups which people form for the realization of their lives.

In "The Idea of Confucian Tradition",[41] A. S. Cua traces the attention in Anglo-Saxon ethics and theory regarding moral traditions employing Ludwig Wittgenstein's development of the notion of "forms of life" in his *Philosophical Investigations*.[42] He notes its implicit presence in J. Rawls's relation of the sense of justice to one's history and traditions,[43] though formal attention to the role of tradition in ethics is found rather in A. MacIntyre's *After Virtue*.[44] Its sociological role in providing regularities in social life had been observed earlier by Karl Popper.[45] In the German tradition, in *Truth and Method*, Hans Georg Gadamer undertook, on the basis of the work of Martin Heidegger, to reconstruct the notion of a cultural heritage or tradition.

Perhaps the greatest point of tension between a sense of one's heritage and the Enlightenment spirit relates to authority. Is it possible to recognize authority on the part of a tradition which perdures, while still asserting human freedom through time? Could it be that a cultural tradition, rather than being the negation of freedom and, hence, antithetic to democracy, is its cumulative expression, the reflection of our corporate access to the bases of all meaning, and even the positive condition for the discovery and realization of needed new developments?

One of the most important characteristics of human persons and societies is their capability for development and growth. One is born with open and unlimited powers for knowledge and for love. Life consists in developing, deploying and exercising these capabilities. Given the communitary character of human growth and learning, dependence upon others is not unnatural — quite the contrary. Within, as well as beyond, our social group we depend upon other persons according as they possess abilities which we, as individuals and communities, need for our growth, self-realization and fulfillment.

This dependence is not primarily one of obedience to the will of others, but is based upon their comparative excellence in some dimension — whether this be the doctor's professional skill in healing or the wise person's insight and judgment in matters where profound understanding is required. The preeminence of wise persons in the community is not something they usurp or with which they are arbitrarily endowed; it is based rather upon their abilities as these are reasonably and freely acknowledged by others.

Further, this is not a matter of universal law imposed from above and uniformly repeated in univocal terms. Rather it is a matter of corporate learning developed by the components of a civil society each with its own special concerns and each related to the other in a pattern of subsidiarity.

All of these — the role of the community in learning, the contribution of extended historical experience regarding the horizontal and vertical axes of life and meaning, and the grounding of dependence in competency — combine to endow tradition with authority for subsequent ages. This is varied according to the different components of tradition and their interrelation.

There are reasons to believe, moreover, that tradition is not a passive storehouse of materials simply waiting upon the inquirer, but that its content of authentic wisdom plays a normative role for life in subsequent ages. On the one hand, without such a normative referent, prudence would be as relativistic and ineffective as muscular action without a skeletal substructure. Life would be merely a matter of compromise and accommodation on any terms, with no sense of the value either of what was being compromised or of that for which it was compromised. On the other hand, were the normative factor to reside simply in a transcendental or abstract vision the result would be devoid of existential content.

The fact that humans, no matter how different in culture, do not remain indifferent before the flow of events, but dispute — even bitterly — the direction of change appropriate for their community reflects that every humanism is committed actively to the realization of some common — if general — sense of perfection. Without this, even conflict would be impossible for there would be no intersection of the divergent positions and, hence, no debate or conflict.

Through history, communities discover vision which both transcends time and directs our life in all times, past, present and future. The content of that vision is a set of values which, by their fullness and harmony of measure, point the way to mature and perfect human formation and, thereby, orient life.[46] Such a vision is historical because it arises in the life of a people in time. It is also normative, because it provides a basis upon which past historical ages, present options and future possibilities are judged; it presents an appropriate way of preserving that life through time. What begins to emerge is Heidegger's insight regarding Being and its characteristics of unity, truth and justice, goodness and love. These are not simply empty ideals, but the ground, hidden or veiled, as it were, and erupting into time through the conscious personal and group life of free human beings in history. Seen in this light, the process of human search, discussion and decision — today called democracy — becomes more than a method for managing human affairs; more substantively, it is the mode of the emergence of being in time.

One's cultural heritage or tradition constitutes a specification of the general sense of being or perfection, but not as if this were chronologically distant in the past and, therefore, in need of being drawn forward by some artificial contrivance. Rather, being and its values live and act in the lives of all whom they inspire and judge. In its synchronic form, through time, tradition is the timeless dimension of history. Rather than reconstructing it, we belong to it — just as it belongs to us. Traditions then are, in effect, the ultimate communities of human striving, for human life and understanding are implemented, not by isolated individual acts of subjectivity — which Gadamer describes as flickerings in the closed circuits or personal consciousness[47] — but by our situatedness in a tradition. By fusing both past and present, tradition enables the component groupings of civil society to determine the specific direction of their lives and to mobilize the consensus and mutual commitments of which true and progressive community is built.[48]

Conversely, it is this sense of the good or of value, which emerges through the concrete, lived experience of a people throughout its history and constitutes its cultural heritage, which enables society, in turn, to evaluate its life in order to pursue its true good and to avoid what is socially destructive. In the absence of tradition, present events would be simply facts to be succeeded by counter-facts. The succeeding waves of such disjointed happenings would constitute a history written in terms of violence. This, in turn, could be restrained only by some utopian abstraction built upon the reductivist limitations of modern rationalism. Such elimination of all expressions of democratic freedoms is the archetypal modern nightmare, *1984*.

All of that stands in stark contrast to one's heritage or tradition as the rich cumulative expression of meaning evolved by a people through the ages to a point of normative and classical perfection. Exemplified architecturally in a Parthenon or a Taj Mahal, it is embodied personally in a Confucius or Ghandhi, a Bolivar or Lincoln, a Martin Luther King or a Mother Theresa. Variously termed "charismatic personalities" (Shils),[49] "paradigmatic individuals" (Cua)[50] or characters who meld role and personality in providing a cultural or moral ideal (MacIntyre),[51] they supersede mere historical facts. As concrete universals, they express in the varied patterns of civil society that harmony and fullness of perfection which is at once classical and historical, ideal and personal, uplifting and dynamizing — in a word, liberating.

Nor is it accidental that as examples the founders of the great religious traditions come most spontaneously to mind. It is not, of course, that people cannot or do not form the component groups of civil society on the basis of their concrete concerns for education, ecology or life. But their motivation in this as fully human goes beyond pragmatic, external goals to the internal social commitment which in most cultures is religiously based.

THE RECONSTRUCTION OF SOCIAL LIFE AS RELIGIOUS ACTION

Tradition and Its Application: Renewal in Civil Society

Anton T. Cua[52] traces to Vico[53] attention to the unreflective cognitive consensus on common needs and to Shaftesbury[54] the affective sense of common partnership with others that this entails. The result is the synchronic constitution of a community of memory whose members revere and commemorate the same saints and personages who have sacrificed to build or exemplify the community's self image. This results in a community of vision or self-understanding, as well as of hope and expectation. A cultural tradition, in this sense, is the context of the conscious life and striving of a person and of the communities of which one is a member; it is life in its fullest meaning, as past and future, ground and aspiration.

In this light, Cua notes that in his *Great Learning* Chu Hsi stresses the importance of investigating the principles at great length until one achieves "a wide and far-reaching penetration (*kuan-t'ung*)." Read as *Kuan-chuan*, this suggests an aesthetic grasp of the unique interconnection of the various components of the *tao* as the unique unifying perspective of the culture. This is not only a contemplative understanding, however, but implies active engagement in the conduct of life. If this be varied by subgroups structured in the patterns of solidarity and subsidiarity of civil society then the accumulation of cooperate life experience, lived according to *li* or ritual propriety and *i* or sense of rightness, emerges from the life of a people as a whole. "For the adherents of the Confucian tradition, the tradition is an object of affection and reverence, largely because the tradition is perceived as an embodiment of wisdom (*chih*), which for Chu Hsi is a repository of insights available for personal and interpersonal appropriation, for coping with present problems and changing circumstances."[55]

The truly important battle at the present time is, then, not between, on the one hand, a chaotic liberalism in which the abstract laws of the marketplace dictate and at the lives of persons, peoples and nations or, on the other hand, a depersonalizing sense of community in which the dignity of the person is suppressed for an equally abstract utopia. A victory of either would spell disaster. The central battle is, rather, to enable peoples to draw on their heritage, constituted of personal and social assessments and free decisions, and elaborated through the ages by the varied communities as they work out their response to their concrete circumstances. That these circumstances are often shifting and difficult in the extreme is important, but it is of definite importance that a people's response be truly their own in all their variety and of their society with all its interrelated sub-units. That is, that it be part of their history, of the way they have chosen to order and pattern their social life, and in these terms to shape their free response to the good. This is the character of authority exercised in and by a civil society. It reflects, and indeed is, the freedom being exercised by a people in all the varied groupings in which they have chosen to live and to act.

A first requisite for this is a dimension of transcendence. If what we find in the empirical world or even in ourselves is all that there is, if this be the extent of being, then our life cannot consist in more than rearranging the elements at our disposition — newness could only be of an accidental character. It is, however, the decisive reality of our life that it is lived in a transcendent context which goes beyond anything finite and indeed is inexhaustible by anything finite. Hence we are always drawn forward and called to radical newness. A tradition then is not a matter of the past, but of new applications. As reflecting the infinite creator and goal this is the decisively religious characteristic of human life.

As an active process tradition transforms what is received, lives it in a creative manner and passes it on as a leaven for the future. Let us turn then from the cumulative meaning and value in tradition, its synchronic aspect, to its diachronic or particular meaning for each new time, receiving from the past, ordering the present and constructing the future. This is a matter, first of all, of taking time seriously, that is, of recognizing that reality includes authentic novelty. This contrasts to the perspective of Plato for whom the real is the ideal and unchangeable forms or ideas transcending matter and time, of which physical things and temporal events are but shadows. It also goes beyond rationalism's search for clear and distinct knowledge of eternal and simple natures and their relations in terms of which all might be controlled, as well as beyond romanticism's attention to a primordial unchanging nature hidden in the dimly sensed past. *A fortiori*, it goes beyond method alone without content.

In contrast to all these, the notion of application[56] is based upon an awareness that "reality is temporal and unfolding". This means that tradition, with its inherent authority or normative force, achieves its perfection in the temporal unfolding of reality. Secondly, it shows human persons and social groups, not as detached intellects, but as incarnate and hence enabled by, and formative of, their changing social universe. Thirdly, in the area of socio-political values and action, it expresses directly the striving of persons and groups to realize their lives and the development of this striving into attitudes (*hexis*) and institutions. Hence, as distinct from the physical order, human action is a situation neither of law nor of lawlessness, but of human and, therefore, developing institutions and attitudes. These do not determine and hence destroy human freedom, but regulate and promote its exercise.[57] This is the heart of civil society for it shows how community and governance can come together.

Certain broad guidelines for the area of ethics and politics serve in the application of tradition as a guide for historical practice and vice-versa. The concrete exercise of human freedom as unique personal decisions made with others in the process of their social life through time constitutes a distinctive and on-going process. Historicity means that responses to the good are made always in concrete and ever-changing circumstances. Hence, the general principles of ethics and politics as a philosophic science of action cannot be purely theoretical knowledge or a simple accounting from the past. Instead, they must help people consciously exercise their freedom in concrete historical circumstances and groups which change and are renewed.

Here, an important distinction must be made from *techné* where action is governed by an idea as an exemplary cause that is fully determined and known by objective theoretical knowledge (*epistéme*). As in the case of an architect's blueprints, skill, such as that of the engineer, consists in knowing how to act according to that idea or plan. When it cannot be carried out perfectly, some parts of it simply are omitted in the execution. In contrast, civil

Ways to God 363

society and its ethics and politics, though similar in the possession of a practical guide and its application to a particular task, differ in important ways. First, by shared action toward a common goal subjects and especially societies themselves are as much constituted as they produce an object: if agents are differentiated by their action, societies are formed or destroyed by their inner interaction. Hence, moral knowledge, as an understanding of the appropriateness of human action, cannot be fully determined independently of the societies in their situation and in action.

Secondly, adaptation by societies and social groups in their application of the law does not diminish, but rather corrects and perfects the law. In relation to a world which is less ordered, the laws, rules and regulations of groups are imperfect for they cannot contain in any explicit manner the adequate response to the concrete possibilities which arise in history. It is precisely here that the creative freedom of a people is located. It does not consist in arbitrariness, for Kant is right in saying that without law freedom has no meaning. Nor does it consist in an automatic response determined by the historical situation, for then determinism and relativism would compete for the crown in undermining human freedom. Freedom consists, rather, in shaping the present according to the sense of what is just and good which we have from our cultural tradition. This we do in a way which manifests and indeed creates for the first time more of what justice and goodness mean.

The law then is not diminished by distinctive and discrete application to the varied parts of a complex civil society, but corrected and enriched. *Epoché* and equity do not diminish, but perfect the law; without them the law would be simply a mechanical replication, doing the work not of justice, but of injustice. Ethics, politics and especially aesthetics which takes account of the unique is then not only knowledge of what is right in general, but the search for what is right for this group or sub-group with its goal and in its situation. Adaptation of the means by the social group, whether occupational, religious or ethnic, is then not a matter of mere expediency. Rather, it is the essence of the search for a more perfect application of a law or tradition in the given situation and therefore the fulfillment of moral knowledge.[58]

It is important to note that this rule of the concrete (of what the situation is asking of us) is not known by sense knowledge, which simply registers a set of concrete facts on the horizontal level. In order to know what is morally required, the situation must be understood in the light of what is right, that is, in the light of what has been discovered vertically through tradition with its normative character about appropriate human action. Only in this light can moral consciousness as the work of intellect (*nous*), rather than of sensation, go about its job of choosing the right means.

Therefore, to proceed simply in reaction to concrete injustices, rather than in the light of one's tradition, is ultimately destructive. It inverts the order just mentioned and results in manipulation of our hopes for the good. Destructive or repressive structures would lead us to the use of correspondingly evil means, suited only to producing evil results. The true response to evil can be worked out only in terms of the good as the highest discovery by a people, passed on in tradition and applied by it in each time and place.

The importance of application implies a central role for the virtue of prudence (*phronesis*) or thoughtful reflection which enables one to discover the appropriate means for the circumstances. This must include, also, the virtue of sagacity (*sunesis*), that is, of understanding or concern for the other. For what is required as a guide for the agent is not only the technical knowledge of an abstract ideal, but knowledge that takes account of the agent in relation to other persons. One can assess the situation adequately only inasmuch as one, in a sense, undergoes the situation with the affected parties, living and suffering with them. Aristotle rightly describes as "terrible" the one who is capable of manipulating the situation, but is without orientation towards moral ends and without concern for the good of others in their concrete situations.

In sum, application is not a subsequent or accidental part of understanding, added on after perfect understanding has been achieved; rather it co-determines this understanding from the beginning. Moral consciousness must seek to understand the good, not as an ideal to be known and then applied, but rather through discerning the good for concrete peoples in their relations with others.

Cua finds similar notions in the distinctions of Chu Hsi in the neo-Confucian tradition regarding the diachronic sense of *tao* as residing between the substantial (*t'i*) and the operational (*yung*), the stable basic or latent schemata and its operational sense in changing circumstances (*fei*). Hsün Tzu distinguishes the constant (*ch'ang*) and the changing (*pien*), and Mencius the constant rule (*ching*) and the sliding scale (*ch'üuan*). Use of the latter as an exercise of moral discretion based on *li* is essential for moral life due to the imperfections of our knowledge and the urgent complexity of life. In these circumstances, to hold to a static mean would undermine the realization of the holistic goal of the *tao*.

Creativity in the application of the tradition in the concrete circumstances of life thus becomes essential. In this context Cua cites J. Pelican's deft aphorism: "Tradition is the living faith of the dead, traditionalism is the dead faith of the living."[59]

The Metaphysical and Religious Roots

The notion of application can help in sorting out the human dilemma between an absolutism insensitive to persons in their concrete circumstances and a relativism which leaves the person subject to expediency in public and private life. Indeed, the very statement of the dilemma reflects the deleterious aspect of the Platonic view of ideas. He was right to ground changing and historical being in the unchanging and eternal. This had been Parmenides's first insight in metaphysics and has been richly developed in relation to human action through the medievals' notion of an eternal law in the divine mind.

But it seems inappropriate to speak directly in these terms regarding human life, for in all things individual human persons and humankind as a whole are subject to time, growth and development. As we become increasingly conscious of this, the personal character even of our abstract ideals becomes manifest and their adapted application in time can be seen, not as their rejection, but as their perfection. In this, justice loses none of its force as an absolute requirement of human action. Rather, the concrete modes of its application in particular circumstances add to what might have been articulated in merely abstract and universal terms. A hermeneutic approach directs attention precisely to these unfoldings of the meaning of abstract principles through time. This is not an abandonment of absolutes, but a recognition of the human condition and of the way in which this continually and, in endlessly marvelous manners, unfolds the ultimate richness of the source and principle of social life.

For Confucius, the aesthetic vision is integrated in drama, of which dance is one moment. In the actual performance of *li* (ritual or liturgy), there is a combination of poetry, liturgical action and music. Confucius saw that in the poem our spirit can rise and stand in reality to achieve complete transcendence in the ecstasy of the spirit. This gives access in aesthetic terms to a source, not only of inspiration, but of vision that both draws one to aspire to greater perfection and opens the way for creative thought regarding ways in which this can be achieved (see Chapter III).

Some suggest, however, that Confucius may have looked upon aesthetics more as a matter of appreciation and conservation, rather than as original, creative and free expression. This suggests that, in the works of Confucius, there are resources important for developing a modern vision which were unmined by Confucius himself and his schools.

If so what should be the attitude of a philosopher in our day to this mode of aesthetics? If it be itself appreciative and conservative, is one who interprets it subject to the same approach and limited to the same content, or can interpretation legitimately open up new meaning in old texts? In other words, must ancient texts be read only with an ancient outlook? Indeed, is it even possible today to have an authentically ancient outlook — to see with eyes long closed — or does the attempt to do so require so much make-believe as to be in effect impossible? Even if one were to succeed in reconstituting the past, would one be faithful to the text which was written as a vital expression of the process of life, or would one instead be rendering lifeless a living text[60] (not unlike the biologist who makes a slide of once living tissue)?

It would seem, therefore, that our goal should be not simply to reiterate ancient times in reading ancient texts, but to recognize that we come to them from new times, with new horizons and new questions. We should allow them to speak anew to us; in so doing, the texts and philosophies are living rather than dead—and, therefore, more true. Texts read in this sense are part of living tradition in which is situated our struggle to face the problems of life and build a future worthy of those who follow.

Some would fear that to give such importance to the horizon of the reader of a text might constitute a relativism and lose the permanent significance of the insights of the author. But this would seem to reflect a material and mechanical model ruled by successive discrete moments of time in which universality is a function only of abstraction. This leaves what is universally applicable as relatively vacuous and reduces one to pragmatism as one's only response to concrete and changing circumstances.

Here, the real issue regards one's metaphysics: what is the nature of being, what does it mean to be? If the answer, as the Confucian sense of community would be the first to suggest, is not that reality is reductively matter trapped in time but at least the human spirit living through time, then to look for meaning in terms of the reaches of the spirit across time is not to lose but to find meaning. This is the sense of being emerging through the consciousness of Heidegger's person as *dasein*. Being is not merely what was, but what blossoms ever fresh in the human heart. In the same way, philosophy in reading ancient texts is not archeology but, like every human act, a creative unfolding of being in time. This creative freedom is the essential characteristic of the person.[61]

Moreover, it is precisely as this is seen in the context of an understanding of being as infinite and transcending that we are opened beyond ourselves and even beyond the present state of society. We are moved thereby to pursue the realization in time of a social life reflecting the Unity, Truth and Goodness of the divine in which being is founded and life consists. In this lies stimulation for progress and hope for success.

What, then, should we conclude regarding the root of the actuality, the good or the perfection of reality which mankind has discovered, in which we have been raised, which gives us dominion over our actions, and which enables us to be free and creative? Does it come from God or from man, from eternity or from history? Chakravarti Rajagopalachari of Madras answered:

> Whether the epics and songs of a nation spring from the faith and ideas of the common folk, or whether a nation's faith and ideas are produced by its literature is a question which one is free to answer as one likes. . . . Did clouds rise from the sea or was the sea filled by waters from the sky? All such inquiries take us to the feet of God transcending speech and thought.[62]

DEMOCRACY AND RELIGIOUS PLURALISM

Democracy as Dialogue of Cultural Traditions

Thus far, we have treated the character and importance of tradition as bearing the long experience of persons interacting with their world, with other persons and with God. It is made up not only of chronological facts, but of insights regarding human perfection and its foundations which have been forged by human efforts in concrete circumstances, e.g., the Greek notion of democracy and the enlightenment notions of equality and freedom. By their internal value, these stand as normative of the aspirations of a people.

Secondly, we have seen the implication of historicity for novelty within the context of tradition, namely, that the continually unfolding circumstances of historical development not merely extend or repeat what went before, but constitute an emerging manifestation of the dynamic character of being that is articulated by the art, religion, literature and political structures of a cultural tradition.

It remains for us now to treat the third element in this study of tradition, namely, the hermeneutic method. Synchronically, how can the infinite and eternal perfection of God be participated in by persons and peoples joined into the many groupings of a civil society. Diachronically, how can earlier sources which express the great achievements of human awareness be understood or unfolded in a way that is relevant, indicative and directive of our life in present circumstances? In a word, how can we interpret or draw out the significance of tradition for present action?

Interpretation of a Cultural Tradition. If we take time and culture seriously, then we must recognize that we are situated in a particular culture and at a particular time. All that can be seen from this vantage point constitutes one's horizon. This would be lifeless and dead, determined rather than free, if our vantage point were to be fixed by its circumstances and closed. Hence we need to meet other minds and hearts not simply to add information incrementally, but to be challenged in our basic assumptions and enabled thereby to delve more deeply into our tradition and draw forth deeper and more pervasive truth. How can this be done?

First of all, it is necessary to note that only a unity of meaning, that is, an identity, is intelligible.[63] Just as it is not possible to understand a number five if we include only four units rather than five, no act of understanding is possible unless it is directed to an identity or whole of meaning. This brings us to the classic issue of the hermeneutic circle in which knowledge of the whole depends upon knowledge of the parts, and vice versa. How can this work for, rather than against, the development of social life?

The experience of reading a text might be suggestive. As we read we construe the meaning of a sentence before grasping all its individual parts. What we construe is dependent upon our expectation of the meaning of the sentence, which we derived from its first words, the prior context, or more likely, from a combination of the two. In turn, our expectation or construal of the meaning of the text is adjusted according to the requirements of its various parts as we proceed to read through the parts of the sentence, the paragraph, etc., continually reassessing the whole in terms of the parts and the parts in terms of the whole. This basically circular movement continues until all appears to fit and to be clear.

Similarly, in regard to our cultural tradition and values, we develop a prior conception of its content. This anticipation of meaning is not simply of the tradition as an objective past or fixed content to which we come; it is rather what we produce as we participate in the evolution of the tradition and, thereby, further determine ourselves. This is a creative stance reflecting the content, not only of the past, but of the time in which I stand and of the life project in which I am engaged. It is a creative unveiling of the content of the tradition as this comes progressively and historically into the present and through the present, passes into the future.

In this light, time is not a barrier, separation or abyss, but rather a bridge and opportunity for the process of understanding, a fertile ground filled with experience, custom and tradition. The importance of the historical distance it provides is not that it enables the subjective reality of persons to disappear so that the objectivity of the situation can emerge. On the contrary, it makes possible a more complete meaning of the tradition, less by removing falsifying factors than by opening new sources of self-understanding which reveal in the tradition unsuspected implications and even new dimensions of meaning.[64]

Tradition and Discovery: Openness to Being Questioned. Of course, not all our acts of understanding about the meaning of a text from another culture, a dimension of a shared tradition, a set of goals or a plan for future action are sufficient. Hence, it becomes particularly important that they not be adhered to fixedly, but be put at risk in dialogue with others.

In this, the basic elements remain the substances or persons which Aristotle described in terms of autonomy and, by implication, of identity. Hermeneutics would expand this to reflect as well the historical and hermeneutic situation of each person in the dialogue, that is, their horizon or particular possibility for understanding. As an horizon is all that can be seen from one's vantage point(s), in dialogue with others it is necessary to be aware of our horizon, as well as that of others. For it is precisely when our initial projection of their meaning will not bear up under the progressive dialogue that we are required to make needed adjustments in our projection of their meaning.

This enables one to adjust one's prior understanding not only of the horizon of the other with whom one is in dialogue, but especially of one's own horizon. Hence, one need not fear being trapped; horizons are vantage points of a mind which in principle is open and mobile, capable of being aware of its own limits and of transcending them through acknowledging the horizons of others. The flow of history implies that we are not bound by our horizons, but move in and out of them. It is in making us aware of our horizons that hermeneutic consciousness accomplishes our liberation.[65]

For this, we must maintain a questioning attitude. Rather than simply following through with our previous ideas until a change is forced upon us, we must remain sensitive to new meanings in true openness. This is neither neutrality as regards the meaning of the tradition, nor an extinction of passionate concerns regarding action towards the future. Rather, being aware of our own biases or prejudices and adjusting them in dialogue with others implies rejecting what impedes our understanding of others or of traditions. Our attitude in approaching dialogue must be one of willingness continually to revise our initial projection or expectation of meaning.

The way out of the hermeneutic circle is then not by ignoring or denying our horizons and initial judgments or prejudices, but by recognizing them as inevitable and making them work for us in drawing out, not the meaning of the text for its author,[66] but its application for the present. Through this process of application we serve as midwife for culture as historical or tradition, enabling it to give birth to the future.[67]

The logical structure of this process is the exchange of question and answer. A question is required in order to determine just what issue we are engaging — whether it is this issue or that — so that we might give direction to our attention. Without this, no meaningful answer can be given or received. As a question, however, it requires that the answer not be settled or determined. In sum, progress or discovery requires an openness which is not simple indeterminacy, but a question which gives specific direction to our attention and enables us to consider significant evidence.

If discovery depends upon the question, then the art of discovery is the art of questioning. Consequently, in working in conjunction with others, the heart of the democratic process is not to suppress, but to reinforce and unfold the questions of others. To the degree that these probabilities are built up and intensified they can serve as a searchlight. This is the opposite of both opinion which tends to suppress questions, and of arguing which searches out the weakness in the other's positions. Instead, in democracy, understood as conversation and dialogue directed toward governance, one enters upon a mutual search to maximize the possibilities of the question, even by speaking at cross purposes, for it is by mutually eliminating errors and working out a common meaning that we discover truth.[68]

In this there appears the importance of interreligious dialogue. Rather than being merely an external act of mutual acknowledgement, in view of what has been said above it is a true requisite if our cultures are to be open and developing. As religion is the basic conscious recognition of the transcendent horizon which invites progress, interchange between religions is essential in order that this relation of cultures to their infinite source and goal remain open and be renewed, rather than the religious experience of peoples closing in upon itself. As will be seen below in the present context of globalization such interchange is the only alternative to the much feared conflict of civilizations predicted by S. Huntington.

Religious Pluralism and Progress

Further, it should not be presupposed that a text, such as a tradition, law or constitution, will hold the answer to but one question or can have but one horizon which must be identified by the reader. On the contrary, the full horizon of the author(s) is never available to the reader, nor can it be expected that there is but one question to which a tradition or document holds an answer. The sense of texts reaches beyond what their authors intended because the dynamic character of being as it emerges in time means that the horizon is never fixed but is continually opening. This constitutes the effective historical element in understanding a text or a tradition. At each step new dimensions of its potentialities open to understanding, so that the meaning of a text or tradition lives with the consciousness and hence the horizons — not of its author — but of people in dialogue with others through time and history. This is the essence of democracy as a process. It is the process of broadening horizons, through fusion with the horizons of others in dialogue, that makes it possible to receive from one's cultural tradition and its values answers which are ever new.[69]

In this, one's personal attitudes and interests remain important. If our interest in developing new horizons is simply the promotion of our own understanding then we could be interested solely in achieving knowledge, and thereby in domination over others. This would lock one into an absoluteness of one's prejudices; being fixed or closed in the past, they would disallow new life in the present. In this manner, powerful new insights can become with time deadening pre-judgments which suppress freedom.

One fears that this could be the final impact of Samuel Huntington's *Clash of Civilizations*. He sees civilizations as grounded in religions and develops at length the reason for his expectation that these will become ever more influential as time progresses. Unfortunately he sees all identities as essentially self-centered and conflictual.

In contrast, an attitude of authentic religion as well as of democratic openness appreciates the nature of one's own finiteness. On this basis, it both respects the past and is open to discerning the future. Such openness is a matter, not merely of new information, but of recognizing the historical nature of man and his basis in an

Absolute that transcends and grounds time. This enables us to escape what had deceived us and held us captive and to learn deeply from new experiences.[70]

This suggests that democratic openness does not consist in surveying others objectively, obeying them in a slavish and unquestioning manner or simply juxtaposing their ideas and traditions to our own. Rather, it is directed primarily to ourselves, for our ability to listen to others is correlatively our ability to assimilate the implications of their answers for delving more deeply into the meaning of our own traditions and drawing out new and even more rich insights. In other words, it is an acknowledgement that our cultural heritage has something new to say to us.

The characteristic hermeneutic attitude of effective historical consciousness is, then, not methodological sureness, readiness for new compromises or new techniques of social organization, for these are subject to social critique and manipulation on the horizontal level. Instead, it is readiness to draw out in democratic dialogue new meaning from a common tradition.[71] Seen in these terms our heritage of culture and values is not closed or dead, but, through a democratic life, remains ever new by becoming even more inclusive and more rich.

This takes us beyond the rigid rationalism of the civil society of the later Enlightenment and the too fluid moral sentiment of the earlier enlightenment. It enables us to respond to the emerging sense of the identity of peoples and to protect and promote this in a civil society marked by solidarity and subsidiarity.

In this as a social work one guiding principle is to maintain a harmony or social equilibrium through time. In addition the notion of application allows the tradition to provide resources and guidance in facing new issues and in developing new responses to changing times. With rising numbers and expectations, economic development becomes an urgent need. But its very success could turn into defeat if this is not oriented and applied with a pervasive but subtle and adaptive human governance sensitive to all forms of human comity. This is required orienting all suavely to the social good in which the goal of civil society consists.

This will require new advances in science and economics, in education and psychology, in the humanities and social services, that is, across the full range of social life. All these dimensions, and many more, must spring to new life, but in a basic convergence and harmony. The values and virtues emerging from a religiously grounded tradition applied in a freedom exercised in solidarity and subsidiarity can provide needed guidance along new and ever evolving paths. In this way the life of civil society can constitute a new birth of freedom.

SOCIAL INTERCHANGE AS THANKSGIVING TO GOD

Thus far we have articulated the cultural tradition as emerging from human experience and creativity in the exercise of human life, both personally and in the social groups which constitute a civil society. We have seen also how the force of this reflects its foundation in the Absolute unity, truth and love of the divine in time. This can be articulated also by extending the phenomenological analysis of gift begun in Chapter VIII above.

That sense of gift may make it possible to extend the notions of duty and harmony beyond concern for the well-being of myself and those with whom I share, and whose well-being is then in a sense my own. The good is not only what contributes to my perfection, for I am not the center of meaning. Rather, being as received is essentially out-going.

This has two important implications for our topic. Where the Greek focus upon their own heritage had led to depreciating others as barbarians, the sense of oneself and of one's culture as radically given or gifted provides a basic corrective. Knowing and valuing oneself and one's culture as gifts implies more than merely reciprocating what the other does for me. It means, first, that others and their culture are to be respected simply because they too have been given or gifted by the one Transcendent source. This is an essential step which Gandhi, in calling outcasts by the name "harijans" or "children of God," urged us to take beyond the sense of pride or isolation in which we would see others in pejorative terms.

But mere respect is not enough. The fact that I and another — my people or culture and another — originate from, share in and proclaim the same "total absolute", especially as this creates not out of need but out of love, implies that the relation between cultures as integrating modes of human life is in principle one of comple mentarity and out reach. Hence, interchange as the effort to live this complementarity is far from being hopeless. In the pressing needs of our times only an intensification of bonds of cooperation between peoples can make available the needed immense stores of human experience and creativity. The positive virtue of love is our real basis for hope.

A second principle of interchange is to be found in the participated — the radically given or gifted — character of one's being. One does not first exist and then receive, but one's very existence is a received existence or gift. To attempt to give back this gift, as in an exchange of presents, would be at once hopelessly too much and too little. On the one hand, to attempt to return in strict equivalence would be too much, for it is our very self that we have received as gift. On the other hand, to think merely in terms of reciprocity would be to fall essentially short of my nature as one that is given, for to make a merely equivalent return would be to remain centered upon oneself where one would cleverly trap, and then entomb, the creative power of being.

Rather, looking back one can see the futility of giving back, and in this find the fundamental importance of passing on the gift in the spirit in which it has been received. One's nature as given calls for a creative generosity which reflects that of its source. Truly appropriate generosity lies in continuing the giving of which I have received. This means shaping one's cultural tradition creatively in response to the present needs not only of ourselves but of others, and cooperating with the creative gifts at the heart of other cultures so that they may be fully lived and shared.

This religious vision requires a vast expansion or breaking out of oneself as the only center of one's concern. It means becoming appreciative and effectively concerned with the good of others and of other groups, with the promotion and vital growth of the next generation and those to follow. This is the motivation to engage with others in the creation of a civil society and to contribute thereby to the good of the whole. Indeed it means advancing Iqbal's insight regarding religious thought a step further to a total harmony of man and nature which reflects the total absolute as the condition of possibility of all.

CONCLUSION: THE RELIGIOUS RECONSTRUCTION OF LIFE IN OUR TIMES

The implications of such generosity are broad and at times surprisingly personal. First, true openness to others cannot be based upon a depreciation of oneself or of one's own culture. Without appreciating one's worth there would be nothing to share and no way to help, nor even the possibility of enjoying the good of the other. Further, cultural interchange enables one to see that elements of one's life, which in isolation may have seemed to be merely local customs and purely repetitive in character, more fundamentally are modes in which one lives basic and essential human values. In meeting others and other cultures, one discovers the deeper meaning in one's own everyday life.

One does more than discover, however. One recognizes that in these transcendental values of life — truth and freedom, love and beauty — one participates in the dynamism of one's origin and hence must share these values in turn. More exactly, one comes to realize that real reception of these transcendental gifts lies in sharing them in loving concern in order that others may realize them as well. This means passing on one's own heritage not by replicating it in others, but by promoting what others and subsequent generations would freely become.

Finally, that other cultures are quintessentially products of self-cultivation by other spirits as free and creative images of their divine source implies the need to open one's horizons beyond one's own self-concerns to the ambit of the freedom of others. This involves promoting the development of other free and creative centers and cultures which, precisely as such, are not in one's own possession or under one's own control. One lives then no longer in terms merely of oneself or of things that one can make or manage, but in terms of an interchange between free persons and people's of different cultures. Personal responsibility is no longer merely individual decision making or for individual good. Effectively realized, the resulting interaction and mutual fecundation reaches out beyond oneself and one's own culture to reflect ever more perfectly the glory of the one source and goal of all.[72]

This calls for a truly shared effort in which all respond fully, not only to majority or even common needs, but to the particular needs of each. This broad sense of tolerance and loving outreach even in the midst of tensions is the fruit of Iqbal's religious attitude of appreciation as mediated through a phenomenology of gift. It has been described by Pope John Paul II as a state in which violence cedes to peaceful transformation, and conflict to pardon and reconciliation; where power is made reasonable by persuasion, and justice finally is implemented through love.[73]

There is an image for this in the Book of Isaias. It is that of the many nations, each proceeding along its own way marked by its own culture, and all converging toward the Holy Mountain in which God will become All in all.[74]

NOTES

1. John Locke, *An Essay Concerning Human Understanding* (New York: Dover, 1959), Book II, chap. I, vol. I, 121-124.

2. David Hume, *An Enquiry Concerning Human Understanding* (Chicago: Regnery, 1960).

3. R. Carnap, *Vienna Manifesto*, trans. A. Blumberg in G. Kreyche and J. Mann, *Perspectives on Reality* (New York: Harcourt, Brace and World, 1966), p. 485.

4. *The Theory of Justice* (Cambridge: Harvard University Press, 1971).

5. M. Adler, *The Idea of Freedom: A Dialectical Examination of the Conceptions of Freedom* (Garden City, NJ: Doubleday, 1958), I, 62.

6. Ivor Leclerc, "The Metaphysics of the Good," *Review of Metaphysics*, 35 (1981), 3-5.

7. *Laches*, 198-201.

8. *Nichomachean Ethics*, VII, 9, 1159b25-1160a30.

9. Gerald F. Stanley, "Contemplation as Fulfillment of the Human Person," in *Personalist Ethics and Human Subjectivity*, vol. II of *Ethics at the Crossroads*, George F. McLean, ed (Washington: The Council for Research in Values and Philosophy, 1996), pp. 365-420.

9. J.L. Mehta, *Martin Heidegger: The Way and the Vision* (Honolulu: University of Hawaii Press, 1976), pp. 90-91.

10. V. Mathieu, "Cultura" in *Enciclopedia Filosofica*

(Firenze: Sansoni, 1967), II, 207-210; and Raymond Williams, "Culture and Civilization," *Encyclopedia of Philosophy* (New York: Macmillan, 1967), II, 273-276, and *Culture and Society* (London, 1958).

12. Tonnelat, "Kultur" in *Civilisation, le mot et l'idée* (Paris: Centre International de Synthese), II.

13. V. Mathieu, *ibid.*

14. V. Mathieu, "Civilta," *ibid.*, I, 1437-1439.

15. G.F. Klemm, *Allgemein Culturgeschicht der Menschheit* (Leipzig, 1843-1852), x.

16. E.B. Tylor, *Primitive Culture* (London, 1871), VII, p. 7.

17. Clifford Geertz, *The Interpretation of Cultures* (London: Hutchinson, 1973), p. 5.

18. *Ibid.*, p. 10.

19. *Ibid.*, p. 13.

20. *Ibid.*, p. 85.

21. John Caputo, "A Phenomenology of Moral Sensibility: Moral Emotion," in George F. McLean, Frederick Ellrod, eds., *Philosophical Foundations for Moral Education and Character Development: Act and Agent* (Washington: The Council for Research in Values and Philosophy, 1992), pp. 199-222.

22. Gadamer, pp. 245-53.

23. *Ibid.* Gadamer emphasizes knowledge as the basis of tradition in contrast to those who would see it pejoratively as the result of arbitrary will. It is important to add to knowledge the free acts which, e.g., give birth to a nation and shape the attitudes and values of successive generations. As an example one might cite the continuing impact had by the Magna Carta through the Declaration of Independence upon life in North America, or of the Declaration of the Rights of Man in the national life of so many countries.

24. R. Carnap.

25. H. G. Gadamer, *Truth and Method* (New York: Crossroads, 1975), pp. 305-310.

26. R. Descartes, *Discourse on Method*, I.

27. Gadamer, pp. 240, 246-247.

28. Hesiod, *Theogony* trans. H.G. Everland-White (Loeb Classical Lib.; Cambridge, Mass.: Harvard Univ. Press, 1964), p. 85.

29. Aristotle, *Metaphysics*, I, 2.

30. *Republic* VI, 509-527.
31. Cfr. *Hegel's Philosophy of Right*, trans. T.M. Knox (Oxford: Oxford University Press, 1958), nn. 183-187, pp. 123-124.
32. Manfred Riedel, "In Search of a Civil Union: The Political Theme of European Democracy and its Primordial Foundation in Greek Philosophy," *Graduate Faculty Philosophy Journal*, 10 (1983), 101-102.
33. *Politics*, I, 1, 1252a22.
34. *Ibid.*, III, 7.
35. *Ibid.*, III, 8.
36. *Nichomachean Ethics*, IX, 6, 1167b13.
37. *Politics*, I, 2, 1253a20-37.
38. John Movone, "The Division of Parts of Society According to Plato and Aristotle," *Philosophical Studies*, 6 (1956), 113-122.
39. *Nichomachean Ethics*, VII, 9, 1159b25-1160a30.
40. *Ibid.*, V, 3.
41. *The Review of Metaphysics*, XLV (June, 1992).
42. (New York: Macmillan, 1965).
43. *A Theory of Justice* (Cambridge: Harvard University of Press, 1971) and especially *Political Liberalism*.
44. (Notre Dame University Press, 1981).
45. "Toward a Rational Theory of Tradition," in K. Popper, *Conjectures and Refutation: The Growth of Scientific Knowledge* (London: Routledge and Keegan Paul, 1963), p. 123.
46. *Ibid.*, p. 254.
47. *Ibid.*, p. 245.
48. *Ibid.*, p. 258.
49. Edward Shils, *Tradition* (Chicago: University of Chicago Press, 1981), 12-13.
50. *Dimensions of Moral Creativity: Paradigms, Principles and Ideals* (University Park: Pennsylvania State University Press, 1978).
51. *After Virtue*, 29-30.
52. "The Idea of Confucian Tradition," *The Review of Metaphysics*, XLV (1992), 803-840.
53. Giambattista Vico, *The New Science*, trans. T. Bergin and M Fisch (Ithica: Cornell Univ. Press, 1988).
54. *Characteristics of Men, Manners, Opinions, Times*, ed. Robertson (Indianapolis: Bobbs-Merrill, 1964), Vol. I, p. 72.

55. "Confucian Tradition" and "Hsun Tsu and the Unity of Virtues," *Journal of Chinese Philosophy*, 14 (1978), 92-94.
56. Gadamer, pp. 281-286.
57. *Ibid.*, pp. 278-279.
58. *Ibid.*, pp. 281-286.
59. Jaroslav Pelican, *Vindication of Tradition* (New Haven: Yale University Press, 1984), p. 65.
60. B. Tatar, *Interpretation and the Problem of the Intention of the Author: H.-G. Gadamer vs E.D. Hirsch* (Washington: The Council for Research in Values and Philosophy, 1998).
61. Musa Dibadj, *The Authenticity of the Text in Hermeneutics* (Washington: The Council for Research in Values and Philosophy, 1998).
62. *Ramayana* (Bombay: Bharatiya Vidya Bhavan, 1976), p. 312.
63. Gadamer, p. 262.
64. *Ibid.*, pp. 263-64.
65. *Ibid.*, pp. 235-242, 267-271.
66. B. Tatar.
67. Gadamer, pp. 235-332.
68. *Ibid.*, pp. 225-332.
69. *Ibid.*, pp. 336-340.
70. *Ibid.*, pp. 327-324.
71. *Ibid.*, pp. 324-325.
72. Schmitz, pp. 84-86.
73. John Paul II, "Address at Puebla," *Origins*, VIII (n.34, 1979), I, 4 and II, 41-46.
74. *Isaias* 27:13.

CHAPTER X

THE DIALECTIC OF GOOD AND EVIL:
"Ultimate Concern" and History
as a Way to God

It has been no small tragedy of the last half of the 20th century that the new sensitivity to the personal character of life has been turned inward, rather than outward. The appreciation of one's freedom and dignity should be the basis for new and richer relations to others. As based in the Absolute, freedom and respect between persons and peoples should be intensified and take on an even sacred and inviolable character. It is truly tragic then if freedom is misinterpreted in terms of one's self alone in contrast to others, which results in a renewed and more terrible egoism with its derivatives, social oppression and conflicts. This indeed may be happening as reflected in the increasing chauvinism, intolerance and even genocide connected with the rising tide of immigrants and refugees.

In this humankind, and indeed Providence itself, confronts its greatest challenge today. The issue starkly put is whether good or evil shall prevail, whether God's love is to be frustrated in our times by human evil, whether human life is to be lived in terms of the Fall or the Resurrection. The thought of Paul Tillich can help us to find our way here, for he lived through the period of the two world wars, confronted the depths of evil opened by Hitler's Naziism in his own country, and was central to articulating the vision of resurrection and renewal in the period of reconstruction that followed World War II.

While preparing for his doctorate in philosophy (1911) and his licentiate in theology (1912), he drew less upon traditional Protestant thought in the Calvinistic and Lutheran tradition, than upon a philosophical combination of ethical humanism and dialectical idealism.

The ethical humanism was that of Ritschl and Troeltsch who had accepted Kant's location of the religious question in the realm of the will and practical reason, rather than in that of the intellect and pure reason. On this basis, religious issues were to be understood according to a religious and ethical personality considered ideal according to the culture of the time.

The dialectical idealism was especially that of F.W. Schelling, whose collected works Tillich early read in their entirety and wrote upon for his degrees in philosophy and theology. In their light, he deepened his appreciation of the divine presence in all things in history, which in terms of the structures of the dialectic can be seen as the dynamic expression of the divine. This appreciation of the progressive and developing manifestation of the divine in and through culture stood at the center of Tillich's teaching in the philosophy of religion and culture and in theology at the Universities of Berlin, Marburg, and Frankfort during the 1920's.

This was, as well, the root of his adherence to religious socialism, according to which the defeat of Germany at the conclusion of the First World War had cleared away all that was opposed to, or substituted for, God. This prepared the *Kairos* or moment of time when the divine would be manifested once again, now not in the Church, but in the people. The weakness of this view lay in its repetition of a well known phenomenon extending back to the Fall of the Angels, namely, the creature's refusal to recognize any source of life beyond its own. Its implicit premise was that man, not God, must save man; a little beyond this lay the definitive temptation, namely, to think that man must become God.

With such a god, human life sinks progressively to an ever more inhuman condition. Thus, the high hopes were shattered in the early 1930's as the socialist ideal took the concrete form of the National Socialist (Nazi) Party. Where the nation, race and people were put in the place of God, what had been looked to as a new manifestation of the divine became its ultimate denial. This echoed the experience repeated through history, namely, that man cannot save himself. Inevitably, reductive humanisms, man-made utopias, projects to control human history in terms however scientific, all enclose and then repress the dynamic openness of human freedom: life turns into death.

It is of the greatest interest to compare the response to defeat as described here, namely, the attempt to create a man-made utopia or super race, with that described at length in the work, *Polish Values*, edited by Leon Dyczewski (Washington: The Council for Research in Values and Philosophy, 1999). In post world War I

Germany the effect was a short lived burst of lightening violence — truly a "bilitz krieg" — which in 10 years created untold catastrophe and died. The effect of defeat and the partitions in 19th centuries Poland, in contrast, was poetic sublimation. Thereby the cause of justice for Poland became the cause of justice for all humankind: "for our freedom and yours;" the suffering of Poland became a reliving of the Cross of Christ in time. Despite the partitions the Polish nation did not die; through the Nazi invasion it survived; against the Communist oppression it rose nonviolently and in solidarity it put an end to the Soviet Empire. Indeed, this prefigures the content of the present chapter, stated long ago by Boethius in his *Consolations of Philosophy*, to wit, that evil is made to bear witness to the power of the good. In the Christian traditions, through death comes resurrection and new life: the Fall was a happy fault for it opened the way to God.

As Nazism manifested its true nature, Paul Tillich could not but strongly reject it in his public speeches in Germany, with the result that he was dismissed from the University of Frankfurt when Hitler came to power. Looking back to that time, Tillich sees the developments which bound together the two World Wars as more than merely personal or even national. They spelled the end of ethical humanism. "Neo-Protestantism is dead in Europe. All groups, whether Lutheran, Reformed, or Barthian, consider the last 200 years of Protestant Theology essentially erroneous. The year 1933 finished the period of theological liberalism stemming from Schleiermacher, Ritschl, and Troeltsch."[1]

In personal terms, this disillusionment led him to consider becoming a Catholic as the only alternative to "national heathenism." Instead, he came under the influence of Karl Barth's neo-orthodoxy because of its affirmation of God as transcendent. For Tillich, however, this did not mean that culture and history were not significant. The devastating history of the first half of this century confirmed for Tillich the acid existential criticism of meaning developed by Kierkegaard, Nietzsche, and Marx. But whereas the historical dialectic had seen God as manifested positively through history, now, when history comes to appear as meaningless, the contemporary religious problem becomes how God is manifested through, and in, the very meaninglessness of history itself.

It is a measure of the penetrating character of this reading by

Tillich of the religious problem of this century that it proved relevant not only to the harsh totalitarianisms of Europe, but to the liberal context of North America as well. There, upon his arrival in 1933, he found an analogous crisis. During the deceptive prosperity of the 1920's, there had been a certain religious parallel to the German situation. The search for God was substituted gradually by the impression that the natural progress of the era itself was God or his definitive manifestation. This was especially marked in the Social Gospel Movement which, under the influence of the pragmatism of John Dewey, had become a relativistic ethical humanism. It reduced the task of theology to generating convictions which need not be Christian or even concerned with God, as long as they were pragmatically efficient and apologetically defensible.[2] The economic depression in 1929 gave the lie to this direction of religious thought. Human progress then halted and the issue became that of adversity and how it was to be faced.

In America as well as in Europe it was no longer possible to identify God as the next stage of progress. Rather, God had to be found in the negation of values emanating in ever widening circles from the initial economic collapse. To this, the religious perspective which Tillich had begun to elaborate proved particularly relevant. The Neo-Naturalists had already begun to recall men from mere humanism to a theocentric philosophy of religion. But, unsatisfied with a God understood as a process wholly immanent in the universe, the evolution which Tillich's thought underwent in the early 1930s allowed him to stress the transcendent character of the divine and the essential implications of this for the reformation and redemption of culture.

THE PHILOSOPHICAL QUESTION

Paul Tillich laid the groundwork for such an analysis of sociocultural life by recognizing some basic dualities. If we are not trapped in a complete solipsism, then, on the level of thought, we must distinguish subject and object, the one who thinks and what is thought about, and, on the level of being, we must distinguish self and world. Neither idealism nor materialism have been successful in reducing one to the other; both subject and object must be recognized, and the success of a philosophy of life lies in its ability to reconcile the two. The self is indivisible in itself and distinct from all else; it is unique, unrepeatable, irreplaceable and unexchangeable. But if, on the one hand, the self is considered without its polar element of world with which to situate the individual and orient one's life, then all becomes isolated and arbitrary; there can be no meaningful participation of knower and known; actions become random and willful. If, on the other hand, the social unity is taken as an end in itself without regard for the individual, its goals are eviscerated and it itself becomes vicious. Reconciling both self and world is the key to human success or failure.

The life of philosophy, as of man himself, is the work of identifying these polar elements (thesis), seeing how, by their falling apart, life becomes destructive (antithesis), and how they can be reconciled (synthesis). In religious terms, the thesis is the Paradise of basic nature, the antithesis is the Fall into sin and death, and the synthesis is the Resurrection and new life. In terms of metaphysics, the three are successively the stage of essence or nature, of existence, and of their reconciliation in a dynamic harmony of being.

Concretely this was exemplified in the experience of Martin Luther King who wrote his Ph.D. on the dialectic of Tillich. For King the thesis was the reality of his people in the broader community; the antithesis was the breakdown of this structure veering into the polarities of racism; the synthesis would be overcoming these polarities and the resurrection of his people. It was not incidental that "We shall overcome" was his by-word.

In terms of the dialectic, Paul Tillich was able to analyze the crises through which he had passed in Germany and into which he entered in America, and to draw out the characteristics which must pertain to any body of contemporary religious thought. As religious, it would have to understand the presence of God in all things and their relation to Him. In contrast to the naturalists and humanists, his strong appreciation of the need for a transcendent dimension which inspires and empowers man excludes philosophy from being an adequate statement of religious thought. If, however, the transcendent be considered an answer, it is the answer to a question constituted by the crisis which is the present existential situation. The analysis of this crisis and the identification of this question of the ultimate is the proper task of philosophy. Theology cannot become imperial, for it exists in a situation of co-relation with philosophy precisely as the answer to philosophy's most profound questions of being and meaning.[3]

This reflects Tillich's own experience, which is archetypical for that of the 20th century. West and East, North and South, people have experienced significant disillusionment in their efforts to create a human paradise. Previous hopes and commitments have been shattered by the course of events; the critiques of Solzhenitsyn strike home both in societies where abundance has generated a hedonism which atrophies the spirit and in societies where inability to produce bespeaks long distortion and suppression of this same spirit. As with Tillich's experience of National Socialism, we face a situation in which the previous contexts of meaning have crumbled. This is especially true since the collapse in 1989 of Marxism, the ideology in which half of the people of the world interpreted life and meaning. Since that time this experience of the collapse of meaning has been articulated generally by postmodernism.

Certainly, this is not the time to attempt to construct a new ideology. Instead, the example of Tillich suggests that we can learn from disillusionment itself as the major experience of the present. By asking what is thereby made manifest to human awareness, we may be able to open to deeper and more solid foundations upon which social life can be reconstructed.

This can be seen also as a matter of transcending the previous human horizons of subject and object. As noted by Kant in his *Foundations of the Metaphysics of Morals*, such objective patterns of cause and effect allow for scientific precision and technical manipulation, but once established as a total horizon they become reductionist and repressive of the human spirit. More recent theory shows that, unless this horizon is transcended, any critique merely rearranges the dilemma in a cognitive loop which has no exit. Liberation inevitably becomes oppression once again and people have neither hope nor salvation. What is required is a way of transcending this horizon to a meta-critique which opens a new, deeper and more true way to view life. Tillich's reworking of the dialectic suggests how this can occur and opens a new and liberating insight concerning the ground of being which is present to our consciousness as our ultimate concern. His dialectic shows how this relates to the experience of meaninglessness and thereby plays a truly redemptive role, enabling humankind once again to be creative in facing the problems of its actual historical circumstances.

Paul Tillich was much concerned with the relation between subject and object both in its contemporary modality and in its fundamental nature. There has been a general consensus that the great tragedy of recent times has been the subjection of the person to the objects one produces, reducing oneself to the state of an impersonal object.[4] Below, we will be able to follow more closely the analysis of this contemporary situation. Tillich sees this self-object relation as the basic ontological structure of the self-world relation because it is the presupposition of ontological investigation, without itself being able to be deduced from any prior unity. Idealism has been no more successful in deriving the object from the subject than earlier naturalisms had been in reducing the subject to the state of a physical object. The polarity of the self-world or subject-object structure, then, "cannot be derived. It must be accepted."[5]

The polar relation of these elements assumes varied nuances according to the nature of the reality under consideration. This provides a very sensitive norm for evaluating any system of thought, for the strength and weaknesses of a philosophy will appear clearly from the degree of its success in reconciling the twin poles of subject and object in its own area. Tillich applies this norm in the form of the polar notions of individualization and participation to various types of religious thought.[6] Following his evaluation will provide us with insight into the requirements for authentic religion and will reveal the way in which he transforms the elements of classical Christian thought in the constructions of his own contemporary religious philosophy.

While neither polar notion can be fully realized without the other, individualization will be analyzed first. This element is implied in the constitution of every being as a self and points to the fact that it is particular and indivisible. As particular, the self maintains an identity separate from all else and opposite to anything to which it might be related. As indivisible it maintains its identity by retaining the integrity of its own self center, much as a mathematical point resists partition.[7] One can hear the traditional definition of the person in these notions which Tillich does not fail to extend to the temporal order, making self-affirmation something unique, unrepeatable and irreplaceable. The infinite value of every human person is a consequence of this "ontological self-affirmation as an indivisible, unexchangeable self."[8]

While this individuality is an indispensable element in reality, it is a grave error to consider it without its polar element, namely, participation. An exclusive insistence on the particular and the unrepeatable brings with it a nominalistic breakdown in the philosophy of essence.[9] This breakdown, in turn, becomes the source of a number of philosophical positions which have greatly influenced religious ideas. Some of the more important nominalist consequences are that "only the individual has ontological reality,"[10] that the divine will is random, and that finite beings are radically contingent.

For lack of any natural order, the epistemological expression of this nominalistic ontology is referred to by Max Scheler as controlling knowledge, by which the object must be transformed into a completely conditioned and calculable "thing" to be studied with detached analysis by empirical methods. The determination of ethical ends is outside the competency of this knowledge which restricts itself to the consideration of means and receives its ends from such nonrational sources as positive tradition or arbitrary decision. Such nominalistic results derive from the development of individuation without its polar element of participation.

The insufficiency of this thought is realized by Tillich. He considers pure nominalism to be untenable because its radical individualism renders impossible the mutual participation of the knower and the known.[11] Thus, the various forms of liberalism which have emphasized individuality almost exclusively have tended by that very fact to cut themselves off from all meaningful contact with the divine. A mitigated, but none the less dangerous, form of this is to make of God an object for us as subjects. Though logical predication cannot avoid doing this, it is necessary to reject its implied ontological negation of God's holiness and his reduction to being simply an object beside oneself as subject, merely one being among others.[12]

At no time, however, has the exaggerated stress on individualization appeared to be as problematic as in the context of modern meaninglessness after neo-Protestantism. Built upon biblical criticism and the Ritschlian theological synthesis of modern naturalism and historicism, neo-Protestantism was shattered in its social foundations by Marx, in its moral grounds by Nietzsche and in its religious basis by Kierkegaard.[13] The social crises of this century shattered even the structures with which man had attempted to reconstruct these foundations.

The question became no longer which values are true, but "the whole system of values and meanings in which one lived."[14] The traditional issues of individual sin and forgiveness lost their meaning because what had come into question was the very possibility of meaning itself. The challenge facing humankind then became that of finding the divine through nonbeing in its most radical form, namely, the anxiety of doubt and meaninglessness.

Despite this history of its exaggerations, however, individualization remains indispensable in providing the terms of the relation of man to God. But, in order for this relationship to be positive, the corresponding element of participation must also be present. Participation points to "an element of identity in that which is different or of a togetherness of that which is separated, whether it is the identity of the same enterprise, or the identity of the same universal or of the same whole of which one is a part, in each case participation implies identity."[15]

The task of participation is twofold. First, it gives meaning and content to the individual, keeping it from being an empty form. Further, it is an essential perfection, and, hence, proportionate to the being and its act. Thus, when the individual has the character of a person, participation achieves the perfect form of communion. Second, participation provides the real basis for unity with God by expressing the presence of the divine. No religion can be without this without ceasing to be a religion and being reduced to a secular movement of political, educational or scientific activism,[16] for it is the very relationship to the divine which is the essence of religion that is expressed by the notion of participation.

Tragically, however, this factor of participation turns into oppression — and this is the burden of the second phase or antithesis in his dialectic — when it is understood entirely in terms of relations between self-centered and limited persons as things. Then the unity between persons can be the product only of the imposition by one person upon another or of some even less personal group or structure upon others. In the personal experience of Tillich, it was precisely National Socialism which had to be transcended, but other forms of forced and unilateral emphasis upon social participation have also marked the 20th century.

The grounds for this tragic polarization of individualization and participation is laid in Tillich's *thesis*; its tragic mode appears as the *antithesis*; his *synthesis* of the two points the way to reconstruction as true resurrection.

THE THESIS

The original and varied elements which Paul Tillich intends to integrate in his philosophy enter his thought after the manner of the state of paradise in the biblical creation story. This is taken, however, in a new sense, for "the doctrine of creation is not the story of an event which took place 'once upon a time,' but the basic description of the relation between God and the world."[17] This includes what can be known of God, the production of His finite effects *ex nihilo*, and the response of man from his present situation of meaninglessness. Tillich expresses the dynamic interrelationship of these in terms of an existential dialectic which considers the problems and contradictions of present day existence at a depth at which the ontological principles of essence and existence and the epistemological principles of subject and object can be correlated.

> A complete discussion of the relation of essence to existence is identical with the entire theological system. The distinction between essence and existence, which, religiously speaking, is the distinction between the created and the actual world, is the backbone of the whole body of theological thought. It must be elaborated in every part of the theological system.[18]

The Polarity of Subject and Object

It was observed at the beginning that Tillich insists on the polarity of subject and object as the point of departure for his analysis of reality because both are presupposed for the ontological question. But, if they provide his point of departure in a first approach to the reality of essence or essence of reality, he leaves no doubt that he shares the modern concern to proceed to a point of identity where the alienation of subject and object is overcome. This is the result of the observation that persons have been reduced to the status of things by allowing themselves to be subjected to the objects they produce.[19] The strongest statement of this situation was made by Nietzsche, but the best may be Marx's description of the reduction of the worker to a commodity. Reality must not be simply identified with objective being; one must participate in some deeper principle or lose one's value and individuality. To identify reality with subjective being or consciousness, however, would be equally insufficient, for the subject is determined by its contrast with object. Consequently, what is sought is a level of reality which is beyond this dichotomy of subject and object, grounding and unifying the value of both.

The need for a point of identity and its function is better appreciated as one proceeds beyond the subject-object relationship to the investigation of either knowledge or being. "This point of procedure in every analysis of experience and every concept of a system of reality must be the point where subject and object are at one and the same place."[20] Thus, the analysis of experience directs one's attention to the logos which is the element of form, of meaning and of structure. In the knowing subject or self, the logos is called subjective reason and makes self a centered structure. Correspondingly, in the known object or world, it is called objective reason and makes world a structured whole.

Though there is nothing beyond the logos structure of being,[21] it is possible to conceive the relation between the rational structures of mind and reality in a number of ways. Four of these possibilities are represented by realism, idealism, pluralism and monism, but what is most striking is that all philosophers have held an identity or at least an analogy between the logos of the mind and that of the world.[22] Successful scientific planning and prediction provide continual pragmatic proof of this identity.

The philosophical mind, however, is not satisfied with the mere affirmation, or even the confirmation of the fact. There arises the problem of why there should be this correspondence of the logos in the subject with that of reality as a whole. This can be solved only if the logos is primarily the structure of the one principle of all, that is, of divine life, as well as the principle of its self-manifestation. Then it is the medium of creation, bridging "between the silent abyss of being and the fullness of concrete individualized, self-related be ings."[23] The identity or analogy of the rational structures of mind and of reality will follow from the fact that both have been mediated through the same identical divine logos.

In this way, "reason in both its objective and subjective structures points to something which appears in these structures but which transcends them in power and meaning."[24] Logos becomes the point of identity between God, self and world. Of these three, the logos of God is central and is participated in by self and world as they acquire their being. Thus, the logos of reason gives us a first introduction to the concept Tillich has of God overcoming the separation of subject and object to provide a deeper synthesis of the reality of both.

The Divine

This conclusion of the analysis of experience has definite implications for an analysis of being, because the identity is not merely an external similarity of two things to a third with no basis in the things themselves. The point of identification of subject and object is the divine, which is found within beings. The term "Being itself"[25] is the only nonsymbolic expression of the divine (though in relation to our consciousness this is termed the "ultimate concern"). God is within beings as their power of being — as an analytic dimension in the structure of reality.[26] As such, he is:

- the "substance", appearing in every rational structure;
- the creative "ground" in every rational creation;
- the "abyss", unable to be exhausted by any creation or totality of creations; and
- the "infinite potentiality of being and meaning", pouring himself into the rational structures of mind and reality to actualize and transform them.[27]

God is, then, the ground not only of truth, but of being as well; indeed, the divine is able to be the ground of truth precisely inasmuch as it is the ground of being.

These ideas have a long history in the human mind. In the distant past the *Upanishads* viewed the Brahman-atman both cosmically as the all-inclusive, unconditioned ground of the universe from which conditioned beings emanate, and acosmically as the reality of which the universe is but an appearance. The absolute is the "not this, not this" (*neti neti*), "the Real of the real" (*styasya satyam*).[28] A similar line of thought can be traced through Plato and Augustine to the medieval Franciscans and Nicholas of Cusa. Tillich is fond of relating his thought to these classical sources.

The proximate referent of his thought in positing this ontological principle of identity beyond subject and object is Schelling. At the very first, Schelling agreed with Fichte in making the "Absolute Ego" of consciousness the ultimate principle and reality. It is this consciousness which dialectically "becomes" the world of nature. But, on further consideration, Schelling failed to see the particular connection between the infinite Ego and the finite object. For this reason, he moved the "Absolute Ego" from the conscious side of the dichotomy to a central, neutral position between and prior to both objectivity and subjectivity. Thus, the Absolute is called not "Ego," but "the Unconditional" and "Identity",[29] and the idealism is no longer subjective, but ontological. Tillich readily accepted this insight of the early Schelling and, therefore, traced his own line of thought in between, but distinct from both the subjective idealism of Fichte and the objective realism of Hobbes. What is important is that neither side of the polarity be eliminated, both must be maintained. For this, there is required an Unconditional as the ground equally of subject and object.[30]

Two important specifications must be added to this notion of a divine depth dimension beyond subject and object. One regards the incapacity of limited beings to exhaust or even adequately to represent the divine: this implies the radical uniqueness of the divine. The other concerns the way God is manifested in the essence of finite beings: this points to the way they participate in the divine.

Transcendence

The first of these specifications, which Tillich is careful to make concerning this point of identity of subject and object, is that it cannot be grasped exhaustively by mind nor replicated completely by things, that is, that it is gnostically incomprehensible and ontologically inexhaustible, with the former reflecting the latter. "This power of being is the *prius* which precedes all special contents logically and ontologically."[31] It is not even identified with the totality of things. For this reason, the divine is termed the "abyss", because it cannot be exhausted in any creation or totality of creations.[32]

> Human intuition of the divine always has distinguished between the abyss of the divine (the element of power) and the fullness of its content (the element of meaning), between the divine depth and the divine *logos*. The first principle is the basis of Godhead, that which makes God to be God. It is the root of his majesty, the unapproachable intensity of his being, the inexhaustible ground of being in which everything has its origin. It is the power of being infinitely resisting nonbeing, giving the power of being to everything that is.[33]

This position of the divine as the inexhaustible depth dimension of reality is the basis of the distinction and individualization of God in relation to creatures. As infinite being and truth, the divine is beyond the separation of subject and object, self and world, and makes possible, in principle, a deeper realization of both. In the realm of being, it implies what Tillich calls the Protestant principle, namely, the protest against any thing being raised to the position of the divine. In his own experience, it extended particularly to the state, for he had to extricate himself from the terrible power of National Socialism's claim to a totalism which by definition left no room for human freedom. This protest extends as well to any creation of the church, including the biblical writings which must not be identified with the divine ground in any way.[34] No bearer of the holy may be permitted to claim absolute status for itself.

In the order of knowledge, the inexhaustible character of the divine implies that, if man is to proceed beyond finite realities to an awareness of what is truly divine, he must leave behind the rational categories of technical reason, for such categories limit the infinite. They make God an object, "a" being among others, rather than Being Itself. For this reason, God cannot be conceptualized.[35] To say that God is the depth of reason is to refuse to make him another field of reason. In fact, he precedes the structures of reason and gives them their inexhaustible quality precisely because he never can be adequately contained in them. Schelling has termed the divine the *Unvordenkliche*, because it is "that before which thinking cannot penetrate."[36] It was the error of idealism to think that this could ever be completely reduced to rational forms.

Tillich is protected from this error by his basic ontological image of the various levels of reality. "There are levels of reality of great difference, and . . . these different levels demand different approaches and different languages."[37] The divine is the deepest of these levels and consequently must be known and expressed in a manner quite different from that of ordinary knowledge and discourse. It is to this same fact that Tillich is referring when he introduces the dialectical relationship between these levels and speaks of the divine as the *prius*. This suggests that it will be necessary to proceed beyond conceptualization to an intuitive, personal awareness of the divine.

This will be described below, but one thing is already clear. Since the categories are the basis for the objective element in knowledge and the means by which it is made equally available to the many minds, intuitive awareness will have to be subjective and individual.

Participation

The other specification made by Tillich concerning the depth dimension regards its manifestation in the essences of finite beings. The notion of essence is found in some form in practically all philosophers, but classically in Plato and Aristotle. Plato attempted to solve the problem of unity and separation in knowledge by the myth of the original union of the soul with the essences or ideas. Recollection and reunion take place later and in varying degrees. Tillich stresses that, in Plato, the unity of soul and ideas is never completely destroyed. Although the particular object is strange as such, it contains essential structures "with which the cognitive subject is essentially united and which it can remember."[38]

Aristotle retains the notion of essence as providing the power of being: essence is the quality and structure in which being participates. But this is still potential, whereas the real is actual. Tillich accepts the Aristotelian position in these general terms and then uses it in order to develop his conception of creation. The divine was described above as the inexhaustible; in order for this to be creative an element of meaning and structure must be added. This is the second divine principle, the *logos*, which makes the divine distinguishable, definite and finite. The third principle is the Spirit "in whom God ʾgoes out from' himself; the Spirit proceeds from the divine ground. He gives actuality to that which is potential in the divine ground. . . . The finite is posited as finite within the process of the divine life, but it is reunited with the infinite within the same process."[39]

A second approach to the thesis of Tillich's dialectic is phenomenological. This approach notes that we are never indifferent to things, simply recording the situation as does a light or sound meter. Rather, we judge the situation and react according as it reflects or falls away from what it should be. This fact makes manifest essence or logos in its normative sense. It is the way things should be, the norm of their perfection. Our response to essence is the heart of our efforts to protect and promote life; it is in this that we are basically and passionately engaged. Hence, by looking into our heart and identifying basic interests and concerns — our ultimate concern — we discover the most basic reality at this stage of the dialectic.

In these terms, Tillich expresses the positive side of the dialectical relationship of the essences of finite beings to the divine. He shows how these essences can contain, without exhausting, the power of being, for God remains this power. As exclusively positive, these might be said to express only the first elements of creation, that they remain, as it were, in a state of dreaming innocence within the divine life from which they must awaken to actualize and realize themselves.[40] Creation is fulfilled in the self-realization by which the limited beings leave the ground of being to "stand upon" it. Whatever we shall say in the negative or antithetic section below about this moment of separation, the element of essence is never completely lost, for "if it were lost, mind as well as reality would have been destroyed in the very moment of their coming into existence."[41] It is the retention of this positive element of essence that provides the radical foundation for participation by limited beings in the divine and their capacity for pointing to the infinite power of being and depth of reason. As mentioned in the first section, such participation in the divine being and some awareness thereof is an absolute prerequisite for any religion.

In this first or positive stage of Tillich's dialectic, by placing the divine as the point of identity beyond both subject and object, he has introduced both elements according to which he evaluated previous religious philosophies. The element of participation so necessary for any religion has appeared and, along with it, the element of individuation. We must now look at Tillich's attempt in the second or negative stage of his dialectic to see both of these in existential dissolution through a unilateral process of individualization. It will remain for the third phase of the dialectic, the synthesis, to develop a contemporary understanding of the restoration of person and society as free participations in the divine. This would open a way to God which integrates the hopes of creation as well as the weakness of creatures. It would do so in terms not merely of personal, but of social life as well.

THE ANTITHESIS

Non Being

Tillich turns to the second phase of his dialectic in order to analyze the basic infinite-finite structure as a form not only of individualization, but, as we shall see, of estrangement. Its contemporary nature lies in its particular relation to nonbeing. Nonbeing is had in God, where it dialectically drives being out of its seclusion to make God living. But in God it is dialectically overcome, thus placing being itself beyond the polarity of the finite and the infinite negation of the finite.[42] In beings less than God this nonbeing is not overcome. The classical statement, *creatio ex nihilo*, means that the creature, which along with its participation in being has its "heritage of Being", also "must take over what might be called 'the heritage of nonbeing',"[43] "Every finite being which" participates in the power of being is 'mixed' with nonbeing; it is being in the process of coming from and going toward nonbeing."[44]

The radical realism of this view contrasts starkly with all social utopias. Not only are utopias man-made and hence subject to objectifying the subject, but they fail adequately to recognize the essential character of the nonbeing in human life. This cannot be encountered and overcome unless it is first recognized, and it is characteristic of the dialectic of Tillich, in contrast to that of Hegel and the utopic goal of Marx, that nonbeing pertains to the human condition, indeed even to the divine. To deny it is to be subject to it; whereas to recognize it first and then reconcile it is the path of liberation. The second stage of Tillich's dialectic, the antithesis, is this recognition.

It is to be noted that when Descartes wished to drive home his highly intellectual analysis of the self he followed up with the imaginative example of the ball of wax. Tillich draws on the biblical myth of the Fall to do the same for his notion of nonbeing, thereby enabling one to see its concrete meaning in the struggle to realize human freedom. The example of Martin Luther King above serves the same purpose and moreover illustrates the existential import of the dialectic being delineated here.

Tillich shuns the Hegelian understanding of the antithesis as nonbeing dialectically expressing being, for then existence would be simply a step in the expression of essence. In contrast, profound observation of the modern world, especially of the cataclysm of the First World War, forced home the point that reality is also the contradiction of essence. Some such distinction of essence and existence is presupposed by any philosophy which considers the ideal as against the real, truth against error or good against evil.[45]

This has been expressed by the concept of estrangement taken from Hegel's earlier philosophy and applied to the individual by Kierkegaard, to society by Marx, and to life, as such, by Schopenhauer and Nietzsche. In fact, since the later period of Schelling, it has been commonplace for a whole series of philosophers and artists to describe the world as one of fragments, a disrupted unity. This implies that individualization has become excessive and has led to the loneliness of man before his fellow men and before God. This, in turn, drives one into inner experience where one is still further isolated from one's world.[46] The presupposition of this tragic nature of man is his transcendent Fall.[47]

The Fall

How is this Fall, with its existential estrangement, to be understood? First, its possibility is traced to finite human freedom. In this state in which finite man is excluded from the infinity to which he belongs, freedom gives him the capacity to contradict himself and his essential nature. Furthermore, the fact that he is aware of this finitude, of the threat from nonbeing, adds the note of anxiety to freedom, producing a drive toward the transition into existence. Rooted in his finitude and expressed in his anxiety, once this freedom is aroused, one experiences the threat either of not actualizing one's potencies and thus not fulfilling oneself, or of actualizing them, knowing that one will not choose according to the norms and values in which one's essential nature expresses itself.[48] In either case one is bound to lose oneself and one's freedom.

The finite nature of one's freedom implies an opposite pole, called destiny, which applies even to the freedom of self-contradiction. Freedom "is possible only within the context of the universal transition from essence to existence" and every isolated act is embedded in the universal destiny of existence.[49] This means that the estrangement of man from his essential nature has two characteristics, the one tragic coming from destiny, the other moral (guilt) coming from freedom. Of itself, destiny connotes universality for the Fall is the presupposition of existence, and there is no existence before or without it.[50] Hence, everything that exists participates in the Fall with its twin character of tragedy and guilt. This applies to every person, every human act, and every part of nature as well.

The conciliation of the absolute universality of the Fall with the freedom it presupposes is one of those problems which are never really solved, because it is part of the human condition which it enlightens. The extension of guilt to nature is reinforced by evolutionary theories and depth psychology, but how the inevitability and the freedom of estrangement are to be reconciled remains an enigma. In one statement, Tillich affirms the necessity of something in finite freedom for which we are responsible and which makes the Fall unavoidable. In another work, he considers estrangement to be an original fact with "the character of a leap and not of structural necessity."[51] Despite these difficulties, in explaining how human estrangement is free, Tillich clearly presents it as the ontological realization of the Fall of mankind.

Anxiety

This negative phase in the dialectic is mediated to the level of consciousness by the general, and presently acute, phenomenon of anxiety which arises from the nonbeing in finite reality. "The first statement about the nature of anxiety is this: anxiety is the state in which a being is aware of its possible nonbeing."[52] It is, in fact, the expression of finitude from the inside. As such, it is not a mere psychological quality but an ontological one, present wherever finitude and its threat of nonbeing are found. Anxiety is then simply inescapable for finite beings. Were it a particular object, it might be feared directly, attacked and overcome. But as

> nothingness is not an 'object' there is no way for the finite to overcome nonbeing. Thus anxiety lies within man at all times. This omnipresent ontological anxiety can be aroused at any time even without a situation of fear, for the emotional element is but an indication of the perverse manner in which finite being is penetrated by the threat of absolute separation from its positive element of infinity, that is, with the threat of annihilating nothingness.[53]

The nonbeing of finitude and estrangement is present on each level of being and in three ways: ontic, spiritual and moral. This produces three corresponding types of anxiety. Ontic anxiety is the awareness that our basic self-affirmation as beings is threatened proximately by fate, the decided contingency of our position, and ultimately by death. Spiritual anxiety is the awareness of the emptiness of the concrete content of our particular beliefs and, even more, of the loss of a spiritual center of meaning resulting in ultimate meaninglessness in which "not even the meaningfulness of a serious question of meaning is left for him."[54] Moral anxiety is the awareness that in virtue of that very freedom by which one is human one continually chooses against the fulfillment of one's destiny and the actualization of one's essential nature, thus adding the element of guilt.[55]

All three elements of anxiety — death, meaninglessness and guilt — combine to produce despair, the ultimate or "boundary" situation. One element or another may stand out more clearly for various people or in various situations, but all three are inescapably present. It is guilt that seals Sartre's *No Exit*, for if there were but the nonbeing of death and meaninglessness, man could affirm both his ontic and his spiritual meaning by his own act of voluntary death. But guilt makes all this impossible. "Guilt and condemnation are qualitatively, not quantitatively, infinite."[56] They point to the dimension of the ultimate and the unconditional from which we have become estranged through our own responsible actions. In this way, Tillich's contemporary understanding of the situation of loneliness and despair is ultimately pervaded by a sense of guilt.

Nonbeing extends beyond being to knowledge. After recognizing that existence is both the appearance and the contradiction of essence, he adds that "our thinking is a part of our existence and shares the fate that human existence contradicts its true nature."[57] Reason is effected by the nonbeing of finitude and estrangement. Under the conditions of existence, it is torn by internal conflicts and estranged from its depth and ground.

Another note of the existential situation of knowledge is its inclusion of actualized freedom. This not only separates thought and being, but holds them apart. There results a special kind of truth, one which is attained, not in an absolute standpoint at the end of history, but in the situation of the knower: subjectivity becomes the hallmark of truth. Its contemporary tragic character is due to the fact that it results from separation and despair. "Truth is just that subjectivity which does not disregard its despair, its exclusion from the objective world of essence, but which holds to it passionately."[58]

Throughout this negative stage of the dialectic, there remains the original positive element, the bond to the divine. "Man is never cut off from the ground of being, not even in the state of condemnation,"[59] for really to lose the foundation of one's being would be utter annihilation. This essential insight of Hegel regarding sublation[60] would appear to have been tragically omitted by Marx who, in his concern for social transformation, understood all in terms of technical reason focused upon negation. But, if what is negated is the power of being upon which a human life and a people's culture have been based, then the possibilities of reconstruction are radically undermined and left without foundation. With no source of meaning, life not only loses meaning, but is condemned to remain thus. Neither negation nor negation of negation will suffice. The tragedy which Tillich brings to light is that, despite the presence of the power of being, in this state of existence man does not actualize, but contradicts the essential manifestation of his divine ground.

This is more than individualization; it is the tragically guilty estrangement of being and knowing from the divine, and from ourselves as images of the divine. Thus, Tillich's systematic analysis of the predicament of modern man manifests the true dimensions of the exaggeration of individualization experienced as a sense of loneliness and expressed theologically as the Fall of man. It does this in the contemporary context of meaninglessness by questioning not only the supports of the previous generations, but the very meaning of support. If this questioning be sufficiently radical, it may open the way to a rediscovery of the basis not only for a reordering, but for radical reconstruction.

THE SYNTHESIS

The first stage of Tillich's existential dialectic had presented the essential or potential state of finite reality in union with the divine. The second or negative moment of this dialectic placed individualization in its present context of meaninglessness. This is a powerful and profound expression of the difficulty in actualizing human dignity, which is identically the element of union or participation in the divine that is the essence of religion. Let us see how the third stage attempts to provide this element in a contemporary fashion.

Revelation

Since existential separation and disruption leave one opaque to the divine, Tillich will not allow the divine to be derived from an analysis of human experience: man cannot save himself.[61] If God is to be the answer to the existential question of man, he must come "to human existence from beyond it";[62] the divine depth must break through in particular things and particular circumstances. This is the phenomenon of revelation in which the essential power of natural objects is delivered from the bondage of its existential contradiction, so that the finite thing or situation participates in the power of the ultimate.

In this way, revelation provides more than a mere representation of the divine; it opens levels of mind and of reality hidden till now and produces the experience of the divine which is the most profound of these levels. The appearance of the divine varies according to the particular situation. Experienced in correlation with the threat of nonbeing, God has the form of the "infinite power of being resisting nonbeing," that is, he is Being Itself. As the answer to the question in the form of anxiety, God is "the ground of courage."[63] Each is a form of the particular participation in the divine which takes place in this situation. As this same participation is the basis for symbols of the divine, these differ in mode and duration depending upon the situation.

For a better understanding of the contemporary nature of Tillich's religious philosophy it is necessary to investigate further his development of the situation of revelation in the context of meaninglessness. As cognitive, this encounter includes two elements: one is objective and termed a miracle or sign-event; the other is subjective and named ecstasy and inspiration. The objective and the subjective are so strictly correlated that one cannot be had without the other: revelation is the truth only for the one who is grasped by the divine presence.[64]

Miracle does not mean a supernatural interference with the natural structure of events. To make this clear Tillich prefers the term 'sign-event', as signifying that which produces numinous astonishment in Rudolph Otto's sense of that which is connected with the presence of the divine. Such a sign-event can be realized in the context of meaninglessness because it presupposes the stigma of nonbeing, the disruptive tensions driving toward one's complete annihilation. In particular situations, this stigma becomes evident and manifests the negative side of the mystery of God, the abyss. However, such situations also imply the positive side of the mystery of God, for their very reality manifests the divine ground and power of being over which nonbeing is not completely victorious.

This explains the characteristics which Tillich attributes to a miracle. He speaks of a miracle as "an event which is astonishing, unusual, shaking, without contradicting the rational structure of reality; ... an event which points to the mystery of being, expressing its relation to us in a definite way; . . . an occurrence which is received as a sign-event in an ecstatic experience."[65] The subjective element pertains to the very nature of a miracle. Thus, even a person who later learns about the sign-event must share in the ecstasy if he is to have more than a report about the belief of another. An objective miracle would be a contradiction in terms.

This subjective element of "standing outside one's self" is the etymology of the term "ecstasy". It indicates a state in which the mind transcends its ordinary situation, its subject-object structure. Miracle was seen to be negatively dependent on the stigma of nonbeing. In the mind, what corresponded to this stigma was the shock of nonbeing, the anxiety of death, meaninglessness and guilt. These tend to disrupt the normal balance of the mind, to shake it in its structure and to force it to its boundaries where it openly faces nonbeing. There it is thrown back upon itself.

This might be useful in the interpretation of the history of the last century. For in facing the structural contradictions of his time, Marx took just this route. Seeing them as a call to man to save himself, he turned against all else as an opiate, and thereby opened the way for a new radicalization of the conflict of subject and object. Once objectified in one's work, now one would be totally objectified by society; family bonds would be intentionally subverted; and the sense of personal dignity would be annihilated before the state which would be all.

Tillich's dialectic points to the fact that, when forced to its extreme situation, to the very limit of human possibilities, the mind experiences an all pervading "no." There, face to face with the meaninglessness and despair which one must recognize if one is serious about anything at all, one is grasped by mystery. To acknowledge meaninglessness even in an act of despair is itself a meaningful act, for it could be done only on the power of the being it negates.[66] In this way, the reality of a transcending power is manifested within one.

In a radically contemporary mode, this is the expression within human consciousness of the classical theme of the non-ultimacy of that which is limited and contingent. Anything perceived as object opposed to subject must be limited and not all-sufficient; but this very perception bespeaks as its basis that which is self-sufficient and absolute.

This is not natural revelation whereby reason grasps God whenever it wills. Tillich takes an extra step, noting that the object-subject dichotomy which characterized the human mind enables it to recognize its contradictions, but not to resolve them. Natural knowledge of self and world can lead to the question of the ground of being and reason, but, as estranged in the state of existence, it cannot answer the question. For this God must grasp the human person;[67] this is revelation. The power of being is present in the affirmation of meaninglessness and in the affirmation of ourselves as facing meaninglessness; it affirms itself in a person in spite of nonbeing.[68]

Ecstasy and Ultimate Concern

In true ecstasy, one receives ultimate power by the presence of the ultimate which breaks through the contradictions of existence where and when it will. It is God who determines the circumstances and the degree in which he will be participated. The effect of this work and its sign is love, for, when the contradictions of the state of existence are overcome so that they are no longer the ultimate horizon, reunion and social healing, cooperation and creativity become possible.

Dr. Tillich calls the cognitive aspect of ecstasy inspiration. In what concerns the divine, he replaces the word knowledge by awareness. This is not concerned with new objects, which would invade reason with a strange body of knowledge that could not be assimilated, and, hence, would destroy its rational structure. Rather, that which is opened to man is a new dimension of being participated in by all while still retaining its transcendence.

It matters little that the contemporary situation of skepticism and meaninglessness has removed all possibility of content for this act. What is important is that we have been grasped by that which answers the ultimate question of our very being, our unconditional and ultimate concern. This indeed, is Tillich's phenomenological description of God. "Only certain is the ultimacy as ultimacy."[69] The ultimate concern provides the place at which the faith by which there is belief (*fides qua creditur*) and the faith that is believed (*fides quae creditur*) are identified.

It is here that the difference between subject and object disap pears. The source of our faith is present as both subject and object in a way that is beyond both of them. The absence of this dichotomy is the reason why, as noted, Tillich refuses to speak of knowledge here and uses instead the term 'awareness'. He compares it to the mystic's notion of the knowledge God has of Himself, the truth itself of St. Augustine.[70] It is absolutely certain, but the identity of subject and object means that it is also absolutely personal. Consequently, this experience of the ultimate cannot be directly received from others:[71] revelation is something which we ourselves must live.

Ultimate Concern

In this experience, it is necessary to distinguish the point of immediate awareness from its breadth of content. The point of awareness is expressed in what Tillich refers to as the ontological principle: "Man is immediately aware of something unconditional which is the *prius* of the interaction and separation of both subject and object, both theoretically and practically."[72] He has no doubt about the certainty of this point, although nonsymbolically he can say only that this is being itself. However, in revelation he has experienced not only its reality but its relation to him.[73] He expresses the combination of these in the metaphorical terms of ground and abyss of being, of the power of being, and of ultimate and unconditional concern.

Generally, this point is experienced in a special situation and in a special form; the ultimate concern is made concrete in some one thing. It may, for instance, be the nation, a god or the God of the Bible. This concrete content of our act of belief differs from ultimacy as ultimacy which is not immediately evident. Since it remains within the subject-object dichotomy, its acceptance as ultimate requires an act of courage and venturing faith. The certainty we have about the breadth of concrete content is then only conditional.[74] Should time reveal this content to be finite, our faith will still have been an authentic contact with the unconditional itself, only the concrete expression will have been deficient.[75] Here it is important to keep in mind Buber's caution in the previous chapter with regard to the thought of Max Scheler. Is it enough to change the object; is indeed the act of concern the same if the object is different? Or is a concern that is essentially relational in an I-thou rather than an I-it manner not differentiated in quality by its object?

Tillich sees two correlated elements in one's act of faith. One is that of certainty concerning one's own being as related to something ultimate and unconditional. The other is that of risk, of surrendering to a concern which is not really ultimate and may be destructive if taken as if it were. The risk arises necessarily in the state of existence where both reason and objects are not only finite, but separated from their ground. This places an element of doubt in faith which is neither of the methodological variety found in the scientist, nor of the transitory type often had by the skeptic. Rather, the doubt of faith is existential, an awareness of the lasting element of insecurity. Nevertheless, this doubt can be accepted and overcome in spite of itself by an act of courage which affirms the reality of God. Faith remains the one state of ultimate concern, but, as such, it subsumes certainty concerning both the unconditional and existential doubt.[76]

Can a system with such uncertainty concerning concrete realities still be called a realism? Tillich believes that it can, but only if it is specified as a belief-full or self-transcending realism. In this, the really real — the ground and power of everything real — is grasped in and through a concrete historical situation. Hence, the value of the present moment which has become transparent for its ground is, paradoxically, both all and nothing. In itself, it is not infinite and "the more it is seen in the light of the ultimate power, the more it appears as questionable and void of lasting significance."[77] The appearance of self-subsistence gradually melts away. But, by this very fact, the ground and power of the present reality becomes evident. The concrete situation becomes *theonomous* and the infinite depth and eternal significance of the present is revealed in an *ecstatic* experience.

It would be a mistake, however, to think of this as something other-worldly, strange or uncomfortable. It is *ec-static* in the sense of going beyond the usual surface observations and calculations of our initial impressions and scientific calculations, but what it reveals is the profundity of our unity with colleagues, neighbors and, indeed, with all humankind. Rather, then, than generating a sense of estrangement, its sign is the way in which it enables one to see others as friends and to live comfortably with them. As ethnic and cultural differences emerge, along with the freedom of each people to be themselves, this work of the Spirit which is characteristic of Tillich's dialectic comes to be seen in its radical importance for social life.

THEOLOGICAL IMPLICATIONS

In Tillich's method it is philosophy that asks the questions, but for the reasons given above the answer must come from beyond humankind, and hence must be theological. Up to this point, the positive exposition of Tillich's thought could have been developed without special relation to Christianity. However, he sees in his system the need for a central manifestation of God both to serve as a point of over-all unity and to conquer definitively the contradictions of existence. It is here that Tillich introduces Christ as the final revelation. We shall review briefly this major part of his system (volumes two and three of his three volume *Systematic Theology*) in order philosophically to indicate the direction taken by his thought as it enters the properly theological realm.

Definitive Revelation

Since reason remains finite and retains its state of existence even after receiving revelation, new difficulties continue to arise. The human tendency to oppose subject and object and to reduce subjects to objects with all its corrosive, repressive and dehumanizing effects was broken in its final power and the conflicts of reason were replaced by reconciliation once the human person's total structure was grasped by its ultimate concern and opened to the ground of being. Still, as old habits die hard their corruptive effects, though conquered, are not removed.[78] Hence, they are able to rise again and attack even the elements of revelation. The bearers of revelation can be mistaken for the ultimate itself, thereby making even faith idolatrous. Furthermore, the emergence of the subject-object horizon to dominance can lead to a loss of the ecstatic, transcending power of reason. In this case, reason forgets that it is but an instrument for awareness of the ultimate and tends itself to become an ultimate.

Fortunately, these distortions of faith and reason can be

definitively conquered; the means of this victory is called final revelation. It has various criteria, but all are bound up with the qualities which a revelation must have if it is to be the ultimate solution to the conflicts of our finitude in the state of estrangement.

The criterion on the part of the miracle is the power of final revelation for "negating itself without losing itself."[79] Definitive revelation must overcome the danger of substituting itself for the ultimate by sacrificing itself. This is Christ on the cross, perfectly united with God, who, in the surrender of all the finite perfection by which he could be a bearer of revelation, becomes completely transparent to the mystery he reveals. Thus, he becomes a bearer which merely points and can never be raised to ultimacy. This is the perfect fulfillment of the very essence of the sign-event concept.

In turn, Tillich sees Christianity receiving an unconditional and universal claim from that to which it witnesses, without Christianity as such being either final or universal. On the part of reason, another criterion of this special revelation is its capacity to overcome the conflicts in reason between autonomy and heteronomy, absolutism and relativism, emotionalism and formalism. The success of Christ in solving these conflicts provides a continuous pragmatic manifestation of Christ as the final revelation.[80]

The need for a definitive and incorruptible manifestation of the ground of being is responded to by final revelation which, as such, is not only the criterion, but the fulfillment of other revelations.[81] This becomes the "center, aim and origin of the revelatory events" which preceded and surrounded it. The preparatory revelations mediated through nature, men and events are called universal revelation, though they occur only in special, concrete circumstances. They have the function of preparing both the question and the symbols without which the answer provided by final revelation could neither be received nor understood.[82] But, with the advent of final revelation, preparatory revelation ceases, and the period of receiving revelation begins. The people (*ecclesia* or Church) become the bearer of the original fact of Christ; they continue the process of reception, interpretation and actualization. This combines the certainty of its basis in the ultimate with the risk of faith, for its belief that it cannot be surpassed by a new original revelation is the other side of its belief that revelation has the power of reformation within itself.[83]

Taking this risk with courage, final revelation is the definitive point where the estrangement of essential and existential being is overcome, where finitude is reunited with infinity, man with God, anxiety with courage and mortality with eternity. This is the eschatological reunion of essence and existence, foreshadowed and momentarily grasped in universal preparatory relations. It is definitively established by this final revelation in which Christ becomes the "new being" and God becomes incarnate.[84] This is "realized eschatology," but it has happened only in principle, that is, in power and as a beginning. "Those who participate in him participate in the 'new being,' though under the condition of man's existential predicament and, therefore, only fragmentarily and by anticipation."[85]

Social Implications

In this context, morality cannot remain the empty or arbitrary self-affirmation of a spiritual being. Its ultimate impulse and final aim is the expression of the transcendent ground of being, but its particular contents, being received from the culture, remain preliminary and relative. In this way, one's actions, like one's being, should be provisional manifestations of the divine depth dimension.

In its expression of the fragmentary nature of reality, this view includes the objectivity of positivism without its refusal to penetrate into the nature of existence. In expanding one's horizons beyond the physical, it integrates also the subjectivity of idealism without remaining trapped in a realm of essences.[86] Both insights are synthesized and transcended in a new ontological mysticism. This is not the classical mysticism which disregarded the cosmos for a direct union with a transcendent absolute. Instead, it points by faith to the unfathomable character of the ground of being and to the depth of life as prior to, and condition of, both subject and object. By restoring the element of participation in the divine, this goes to the heart of religion.

Tillich sees two reasons for considering this mysticism to be post-Reformation. One is the refusal of such a mysticism to elevate anything finite to the position of the divine. The other is its search for the essence of objectivity in the depth of subjectivity, approaching God through the soul.[87] Since this approach is made in the context of total meaninglessness which has characterized this end of the modern period, it is not only contemporary but opens to new hope for the new millennium.

In this study, we have examined the historical context of the thought of Paul Tillich, the philosophical problem this generated, the resulting elaboration of the dialectic, and its theological implications. The great popularity of his work during the period of reconstruction following World War II suggests that his experience and philosophical development might be helpful for many today in analogous circumstances of nation building and rebuilding.

One instance might be illustrative. As noted above, Martin Luther King wrote his doctoral dissertation on the dialectic of Tillich. When doing so, he saw love as the foundational transforming power at work in the heart, but considered it only a personal pilgrimage of the individual soul. Later, he wrote that he did not consider this to be a matter of social import. This changed upon visiting India when he came to see with the eyes of Gandhi that the Christian doctrine of love was indeed "one of the most potent weapons available to oppressed people in their struggle for freedom." Nevertheless, until he faced the struggle for racial dignity in Montgomery this insight remained only at the intellectual level of understanding. It was in the actual borderline circumstances of the struggle for freedom, when he was forced to the limits of meaning by the threat of nonbeing, that his intellectual insight was transformed into a commitment to a way of life.[88]

This is suggestive for philosophers in our times. Aristotle spoke of philosophy as being undertaken in leisure, after one has taken care of the necessities of life. The examples of Tillich and King suggest that Marx was correct in saying that in our times philosophy can, and, indeed, often must be done on another more realistic and historical basis. It was in facing the destructive power of the modern totalitarian state that Tillich found the need to transcend technical reason and to go beneath structures to the very ground of being. Through experiencing directly the negativity of an exploitive system in the form of bombings, fire hoses and vicious dogs, Martin Luther King was able to uncover and give voice to the power to overcome, and thereby lead his people to new dignity and freedom.

It is an ancient Indian proverb that when the pupil is ready the teacher will arrive. The examples of Tillich and King suggest that the condition for receiving the power to be may be the very quandaries and dilemmas of change when old structures by their inadequacies contradict life. If so, Tillich's dialectic points out how the more disastrous those structures are manifested to be — that is, through their very negativity — the more a new level of being can be received, life can be transformed and the human spirit can experience resurrection and new life.

NOTES

1. "The Present Theological Situation in the Light of the Continental European Development," *Theology Today*, VI (1949), 299.

2. H. S. Smith, "Christian Education" in *Protestant Thought in the Twentieth Century, Whence and Whither?* (New York: Macmillan, 1951), pp. 110-11.

3. Paul Tillich, *Systematic Theology* (Chicago: Univ. of Chicago Press, 1951), I, 18-28 and 59-66.

4. Paul Tillich, *Theology of Culture* (New York: Oxford University Press, 1959), pp. 91-94.

5. *Systematic Theology* (Chicago: University of Chicago Press, 1951), I, p. 174. Cf. "Participation and Knowledge, Problems of an Ontology of Cognition," *Sociologica*, Vol. I of *Frankfurter Beiträge zur Soziologie*, ed. Theodor W. Adorno and Walter Dirks (Stuttgart: Europäische Verlagsanstalt, 1955), p. 201. "Being, insofar as it is an object of asking presupposes the subject-object structure of reality."

6. This is developed at length in Paul Tillich, *The Courage to Be*, Terry Lectures (New Haven, Yale University Press, 1952).

7. *Systematic Theology*, I, pp. 170, 174-75. Cf. "Participation and Knowledge," *loc. cit.*, pp. 201.

8. *The Courage to Be*, p. 87.

9. *Ibid.*, p. 129.

10. *Systemic Theology*, I, pp. 73, 97, 177.

11. *Systematic Theology*, I, p. 177.

12. *Ibid.*, pp. 172-73 & 272.

13. "The Present Theological Situation in the Light of the Continental European Development," *Theology Today*, VI (1949), 299-302.

14. *The Courage to Be*, pp. 142, 152-53.

15. "Participation and Knowledge," *loc. cit.*, pp. 201-202. He terms the system which stresses participation a 'mystical realism'.

16. "The Permanent Significance of the Catholic Church for Protestantism," *Protestant Digest*, III (1941), 25-29.

17. *Systematic Theology*, I, p. 252.

18. *Ibid.*, p. 204.

19. *Theology of Culture*, pp. 91-94.

20. *The Interpretation of History*, trans. Part I N.A. Rasetzki, Parts II, III & IV Elsa L. Talmey (New York: Charles Scribner's Sons, 1936), p. 60.

21. *Systematic Theology*, I, pp. 156, 171-72, 279.

22. *Ibid.*, pp. 23, 75-76.

23. *Ibid.*, p. 158.

24. *Ibid.*, p. 79.

25. *Ibid.*, pp. 238-39. Cf. "Reply to Interpretation and Criticism," in *The Theology of Paul Tillich*, Vol. I of *The Library of Living Theology*, ed. Charles W. Kegley, and Robert W. Bretall (New York: Macmillan Co., 1956), p. 335.) To this single nonsymbolic expression of the divine he has added severe limitations.

26. *Systematic Theology*, I, p. 207.

27. *Ibid.*, p. 79.

28. *Brhadaranyaka-Upanishad*, II. i. 20, and IV. ii. 4, cited by T.N.P. Mahadevan, "The Upanishads," in *History of Philosophy, Eastern and Western*, ed. Sarvepalli Radhakrishnan (London: George Allen & Unwin, 1952), I, pp. 623-63.

29. *Theology of Culture*, p. 92.

30. *Systematic Theology*, I, p. 171.

31. *Theology of Culture*, p. 25.

32. "Symbol and Knowledge: a Response," *Journal of Liberal Religion*, II (1941), 203. Cf. *Systematic Theology*, II, p. 6.

33. *Ibid.*, I, pp. 250-51.

34. *Ibid.*, pp. 37, 227.

35. *The Courage to Be*, pp. 184-85.

36. *The Protestant Era*, trans. James Luther Adams (Chicago: Univ. of Chicago Press, 1948), p. 76.

37. "Religious Symbols and our Knowledge of God," *The Christian Scholar*, XXXVIII (1955), 192.

38. *Systematic Theology*, I, 94-99.

39. *Ibid.*, p. 251.
40. *Ibid.*, pp. 238, 255.
41. *Ibid.*, p. 83; Cf. "A Reinterpretation of the Doctrine of Incarnation," *Church Quarterly Review*, CXLVII (1949), 141.
42. *Systematic Theology*, I, pp. 179-80 & 188-91. Böhme's *Urgrund* and Schelling's "first potency" are examples of dialectical nonbeing in God.
43. *Ibid.*, p. 253.
44. *Ibid.*, p. 189.
45. *Ibid.*, pp. 202-203.
46. *Theology of Culture*, pp. 104-105.
47. *Systematic Theology*, II, 24-25, 45. Cf. *The Interpretation of History*, pp. 60-65.
48. "The Conception of Man in Existential Philosophy," *Journal of Religion*, XIX (July, 1939), p. 208. Cf. *Systematic Theology*, II, pp. 31-35.
49. *Ibid.*, pp. 32 and 38.
50. "A Reinterpretation of the Doctrine of Incarnation," *loc. cit.*, p. 142.
51. *Systematic Theology*, II, pp. 44.
52. *The Courage to Be*, p. 35. Cf. *Systematic Theology*, I, pp. 191-92
53. "The Conception of Man in Existential Philosophy," *loc. cit.*, pp. 211-14.
54. *The Courage to Be*, p. 48. Cf. *Systematic Theology*, I, p. 189; II, p. 74.
55. "Freedom in the Period of Transformation," in *Freedom: Its Meaning*, ed. Ruth Nanda Anshen (New York: Harcourt, Brace, 1940), pp. 123-24, 131-32.
56. *The Courage to Be*, p. 54.
57. *The Interpretation of History*, p. 61.
58. *Ibid.*, pp. 63-64.
59. *Systematic Theology*, II, p. 78.
60. "To sublate, and the sublated (that which exists ideally as a moment), constitute one of the most important notions in philosophy. It is a fundamental determination which repeatedly occurs throughout the whole of philosophy, the meaning of which is to be clearly grasped and especially distinguished from nothing. Nothing is immediate; what is sublated, on the other hand, is the

result of mediation; it is a non-being but as a result which has its origin in a being. It still has, therefore, in itself the determinateness from which it originates." G.F. Hegel, *Science of Logic,* trans. A.V. Miller (Atlantic Highlands, N.J.: Humanities Press, 1969), pp. 106-107.

61. This, he says, would be the humanistic-naturalistic or the dualistic approach to God.

62. *Systematic Theology,* I, pp. 64-65.

63. *Ibid.,* p. 61.

64. *Ibid.,* p. 111. Cf. "What is Divine Revelation," *The Witness,* XXVI (1943), 8-9.

65. *Systematic Theology,* I, p. 117.

66. *The Courage to Be,* p. 176. Despair supposes something positive. "The negative 'lives' by the positive which it negates." *Love, Power, and Justice: Ontological Analysis and Ethical Applications* (New York: Oxford University Press, 1954), pp. 38-39.

67. *The Protestant Era,* pp. 79-80. Cf. *Systematic Theology,* I, pp. 114-20.

68. *Christianity and the Problem of Existence* (Washington: Henderson Services, 1951), pp. 30-31.

69. *Dynamics of Faith,* Vol. X of *World Perspectives,* ed. Ruth Nanda Anshen (New York: Harper & Brothers, 1957), 17.

70. *Ibid.,* pp. 8-11.

71. "The Problem of Theological Method," *Journal of Religion,* XXVII (1947), 22-23.

72. "The Two Types of Philosophy of Religion," *Union Seminary Quarterly Review,* I (1946), 10.

73. *Systematic Theology,* I, p. 109.

74. "The Problem of the Theological Method," *loc. cit.,* pp. 22-23.

75. *Dynamics of Faith,* p. 18.

76. *Ibid.*

77. *The Protestant Era,* p. 18.

78. *Dynamics of Faith,* p. 79.

79. *Systematic Theology,* I, pp. 133-35.

80. *Ibid.,* pp. 147-54; *Dynamics of Faith,* pp. 78-79.

81. *Systematic Theology,* I, pp. 132-33.

82. *Ibid.,* pp. 138-39.

83. *Ibid.*, pp. 143-44.
84. "A Reinterpretation of the Doctrine of Incarnation," *loc. cit.*, pp. 144-45.
85. *Systematic Theology*, II, p. 118.
86. *Ibid.*, I, p. 236; *The Protestant Era*, pp. 66-68, 76-77, 217.
87. *Ibid.*, pp. 69-73; *Theology and Culture*, p. 107.
88. Martin Luther King, *Strength to Love* (London: Holder and Stoughton, 1964), pp. 149-50.

APPENDIX I

THE STRUCTURE OF DEVELOPMENT

BY JEAN PIAGET

Chapter I on the method used in constructing this analysis of ways to God draws extensively on the analysis of the cognitive development of the child by Jean Piaget. It seems helpful in this appendix to provide greater detail on this analysis and to do so largely in the words of Piaget himself.

As described by him in "The Mental Development of the Child," *Six Psychological Studies*, trans. A. Tenzer (New York: Vintage Book, 1967), ch. I, to which the page numbers below refer.

The following passages by Piaget sketch the main lines of this synthetic presentation of the development of the child as taking place in all four components of personality: cognitive, affective, behavioral and physiological. Here the sequence of the development is described separately in each of the four components. It is further enlightening to see how the development at one level in any of the four enables and is enabled by corresponding developments in the other four components on this level and how together they lead to the development of the next higher level.

COGNITIVE

(a) *Sense perceptions* in infancy (years 1-2) proceed according to the construction of four practical or action categories: object, space, causality and time, corresponding to "the substantial permanence attributed to sensory pictures. It is believed that what is seen corresponds to 'something' which continues to exist even when one does not perceive it." (p. 13) (Piaget here reflects the rationalist supposition focused upon mind and Locke's position that what we know are ideas, which progressively we relate to existing realities outside the mind. A more realist position would recognize the whole process in more existential terms of engagement in reality so that ideas are not means first known in themselves, through the intermediary of which we come to know objects, but rather media in which, as in a mirror, the object itself is known.)

(b) *Intuitive over-all pictures, concrete and non reversible* in early childhood (years 2-7) are characteristic of children's games of 'make-believe' or hide-and-seek:

> Symbolic play is not an attempt by the subject to submit to reality but rather a deforming assimilation of reality to the self. . . . Its function is to satisfy the self by transforming what is real into what is desired. Child in playing with dolls makes his own life as he would like it to be. He lives all his pleasures, resolves all his conflicts. Above all, he compensates for and completes reality by means of a fiction (p. 23).

(c) *Abstract intellectual concepts*, reversible for concrete things, of middle childhood (years 7-12).

> The real reason children at this age [begins to be able to] recognize the conservation of substance or weight is not identity (the small child is just as capable of seeing that "nothing has been added or taken away" as the older child), but the [newly developed] possibility of a rigorous return to the point of departure . . . operations that result in a correction of perceptual intuition — which is always a victim of illusions of the moment — and which "decenters" egocentricity so as to transform relationships into a coherent system of objective, permanent relations (p. 46).

In contrast below seven years of age children are able to dissociate a whole into its parts, but are then

> unable to compare one of the parts with the whole, which they have mentally destroyed; they can compare only . . . two parts. By contrast, at about seven years this difficulty attenuates and the whole can be compared to one of its parts, each part from then on being conceived as a true part of the whole

(a part equals the whole minus the other parts, by virtue of the inverse operation). . . .

Concepts and relations cannot be constructed in isolation but from the outset constitute organized sets in which all the elements are interdependent and in equilibrium. This structure, proper to mental assimilation of an operational order, assures the mind of an equilibrium considerably superior to that of intuitive or egocentric assimilation. The attained reversibility is a manifestation of a permanent equilibrium between the assimilation of things to the mind and the accommodation of the mind to things. Thus when the mind goes beyond its immediate point of view in order to "group" relations, it attains a state of coherence and noncontradiction paralleled by cooperation on the social plane. . . . In both cases the self is subordinated to the laws of reciprocity (p. 53-54).

(d) *Formal thought* with abstract hypothetico-deductive constructions in adolescence (years 12-). Here the child not only applies operations to objects, but

must also "reflect" these operations in the absence of objects which are replaced by pure propositions. The "reflection" is thought raised to the second power. Concrete thinking is the representation of a possible action, and formal thinking is the representation of a representation of possible action. . . . Formal operations provide thinking with an entirely new ability that detaches and liberates thinking from concrete reality and permits it to build its own reflections and theories. With the advent of formal intelligence, thinking takes wings (p. 63).

AFFECTIVE

This shows the following development:

(a) *instincts* mark infancy (1-2):

The evolution of affectivity during the first two years corresponds fairly closely to the evolution of motor and cognitive functions. There is a constant parallel between the affective and intellectual life throughout childhood and adolescence. This statement will seem surprising only if one attempts to dichotomize the life of the mind into emotions and thoughts. But nothing could be more false or superficial. In reality, the element to which we must constantly turn in the analysis of mental life is "behavior" itself, conceived, as we have tried to point out briefly in our introduction, as a re-establishment or strengthening of equilibrium. All behavior presupposes instruments and a technique: movements and intelligence. But all behavior also implies motives and final values (goals): the sentiments. Thus affectivity and intelligence are indissociable and constitute the two complementary aspects of all human behavior.

This being so, it is clear that during the initial stage of reflex techniques there are corresponding elementary instinctive stirrings linked with nutrition as well as the kind of affective reflexes that constitute the primary emotions. . . .

At the second stage (percepts and habits), as well as at the beginnings of sensorimotor intelligence, there is a corresponding series of elementary emotions or affective percepts linked to the modalities of activity itself: the agreeable or the disagreeable, pleasure and pain, etc., as well as the first realizations of success and failure. The fact that these affective states depend on action per se and not as yet on awareness of relationships with other people, this level of affectivity attests to a kind of general egocentricity. . . .

With the development of intelligence, however, and with the ensuing elaboration of an external universe and especially with the construction of the schema of the "object," a third level of affectivity appears. It is epitomized, in the language of psychoanalysis, by the "object choice," i.e., by the objectivation of the emotions and by their projection onto activities other than those of the self alone. . . .

When "objects" become detached more and more distinctly from the global and undifferentiated configuration of primitive actions and precepts and become objects conceived as external to the self and independent of it, the situation becomes completely transformed. On the one hand, in close correlation with the construction of the object, awareness of "self" begins to be affirmed by means of the internal pole of reality, as opposed to the external or objective pole. On the other hand, objects are conceived by analogy with this self as active, alive, and conscious. This is particularly so with exceptionally unpredictable and interesting objects-people.

The elementary feelings of joy and sadness, of success and failure, etc., are now experienced as a function of this objectification of things and of people, from which interpersonal feelings will develop. The affective "object choice" which psychoanalysis contrasts with narcissism is thus correlated with the intellectual construction of the object, just as narcissism correlated with lack of differentiation between the external world and the self. This "object choice" is first of all vested in the person of the mother, then (both negatively and positively) of the father and other relatives. This is the beginning of the sympathies and antipathies that will develop to such an extent in the course of the ensuing period (pp. 15-17).

(b) *Stably organized interpersonal emotions* (affections, sympathies and antipathies) in early childhood (2-7) linked to the socialization of action, e.g., obedience without reasoning in relation to the authority figure:

> the appearance of intuitive moral sentiments as a by-product of the relationships between adults and children; and the regulation of interests and values, linked to intuitive thought in general (p. 34).

(c) *Will* for moral and social choices in middle childhood (7-12) which thus are not simply determined by the circumstances:

> A new feeling, which arises as a function of cooperation among children and which social life engenders, consists essentially of mutual respect. There is mutual respect when two individuals attribute to each other equivalent personal value and do not confine themselves to evaluating each other's specific actions. . . .
>
> [This entails that] the new rule can become 'true' if each child adopts it; a true rule is merely the expression of a mutual agreement. The older child says that all rules of the game are rooted in a sort of contract among the players. Here we see mutual respect at work. The rule is no longer respected as the product of an external will but as the result of an explicit or tacit accord. For this reason the rule is truly respected in practice and not just in its verbal formulations. It is obligatory to the extent that the individual consents autonomously to the agreement on which the rule is based.
>
> That is why mutual respect entails a whole series of moral feelings unknown beforehand: honesty among players, which prohibits cheating not just because cheating is "forbidden," but because it violates the agreement among individuals who

esteem one another; camaraderie; fair play; etc. It is only at this age that the child starts to comprehend the implications of lying, and it is understandable from the foregoing that deceit among friends is considered more serious than lying to adults. . . .

The mutual respect that gradually becomes differentiated from unilateral respect leads to a new organization of moral values. Its principal characteristic is that it imputes relative autonomy to the moral conscience of individuals. From this point of view the moral of cooperation can be considered as a higher form of equilibrium than the moral of simple submission.

[Finally, the] will appears when there is a conflict of tendencies or tensions when, for example, one oscillates between a tempting pleasure and a duty. Then what does will consist of? In such a conflict, there is always an inferior tendency that, in and of itself, is stronger (the desire for pleasure, in this example) and a superior tendency that is momentarily weaker (the duty). The act of will does not consist of following the inferior and stronger tendency; on the contrary, one would then speak of a failure of will or "lack of will power." Will power involves reinforcing the superior but weaker tendency so as to make it triumph" (pp. 55-59).

(d) *The auto-incarnation of ideals* in adolescence (12-):

Personality formation begins in middle to late childhood (eight to twelve years) with the autonomous organization of rules and values, and the affirmation of will with respect to the regulation and hierarchical organization of moral tendencies. But there is more to the person than these factors alone. These factors are integrated with the self into a unique system to which all the separate parts are subordinated. There is then a 'personal' system in the dual sense that it is peculiar to a given individual and implies autonomous coordination.

Now this personal system cannot be constructed prior to adolescence, because it presupposes the formal thought and reflexive constructions. . . . personality implies a kind of decentering of the self which becomes part of a cooperative plan which subordinates itself to autonomous and freely constructed discipline. It follows that disequilibrium will recenter the self on itself, so that oscillations between the personality and the self are possible at all levels. . . . The adolescent makes a pact with his God, promising to serve him without return, but, by the same token, he counts on playing a decisive role in the cause he has undertaken to defend.

We see, then, how the adolescent goes about injecting himself into adult society. He does so by means of projects, life plans, theoretical systems, and ideas of political or social reform. In short, he does so by means of thinking and almost, one might say, by imagination— so far does this hypothetico-deductive thinking sometimes depart from reality. . . .

True adaptation to society comes automatically when the adolescent reformer attempts to put his ideas to work. Just as experience reconciles formal thought with the reality of things, so does effective and enduring work undertaken in concrete and well-defined situations, cure all dreams. . . . The metaphysics peculiar to the adolescent, as well as his passions and his megalomania, are thus real preparations for personal creativity, and examples of genius show that there is always continuity between the formation of personality, as of eleven to twelve years, and the subsequent work of the man. (pp. 65-69)

THE BEHAVIORAL

This entails a progression of motor habits, to socialization of behavior on the basis of such intuitive moral values as equality and fairness, to distributive justice and cooperation according to the needs of others, to action and even to sacrifice for an ideal.

(a) *Motor habits* (years 1-2). During the first two years the construction of the categories of the object: space, causality, and time, all "refer to purely practical or action categories and not as yet to ideas or thinking."

(b) *Socialization of behavior* on the basis of such intuitive moral values as equality and fairness in early childhood (yrs. 2-7):

> With the appearance of language, behavior is profoundly modified both affectively and intellectually. In addition to real or material actions the child learns to master during this period, as he did during the preceding period, he now becomes able, thanks to language, to reconstitute his past actions as a form of recapitulation and to anticipate his future actions through verbal representation.
>
> This has three consequences essential to mental development: (1) the possibility of verbal exchange with other persons, which heralds the socialization of action; (2) the internalization of words, i.e., the appearance of thought itself, supported by internal language and a system of signs; (3) last and most important the internalization of action as such which from now on, rather than being purely perceptual and motor as it has been heretofore, can represent itself intuitively by means of pictures and "mental experiments."

. . .

With the appearance of language, the young child must cope not only with the physical universe, as was the case earlier on, but also with two new and closely allied worlds: the social world and the world of inner representations. It should be recalled that with respect to material objects or bodies, the infant started with an egocentric attitude, in which the incorporation of objects into his own activity prevailed over accommodation (remodification of behavior as a result of experience). Thereafter, he gradually proceeds to situate himself in an objective universe (in which assimilation to the subject and accommodation to the real world become harmonized). Similarly, the young child at first reacts to social relations and to emergent thinking with unconscious egocentricity, which perpetuates the egocentricity of infancy. This egocentricity is then progressively given up, according to the laws of equilibration. These laws, however, are transposed to a higher level of functioning as a function of the need to cope with new realities. Throughout early childhood, therefore, one observes a partial repetition, on new behavioral planes, of the evolution already accomplished by the infant on the elementary plane of practical adaptations.

. . .

The most obvious result of the appearance of language is to permit verbal exchange and continuous communication among individuals. No doubt these interpersonal relations germinate as of the second half of the first year, thanks to imitation, since imitation is closely linked to sensorimotor development. There are no specific techniques of imitation. The infant learns to imitate gradually. At first, he copies gestures he can already execute spontaneously by watching the movements of the body and particularly the hands of other persons.

As his capacity for sensorimotor imitation increases, he is able to copy the movements of others with increasing precision, provided these movements are within his repertoire of behavior. Ultimately, the child reproduces new, more complex movements.

For example it is more difficult for him to copy movements having to do with the parts of his body not visible to him, such as the face and the head. The imitation of sounds follows a similar course, and when sounds are associated with specific actions they result in the acquisition of language itself (elementary word-phrases, then substantives and differentiated verbs, and finally sentences as such). Until a definite form of language is acquired, interpersonal relations are limited to the imitation of corporal and other external gestures and to a global affective relationship without differentiated communication. With language, by contrast, the inner life itself can be communicated. In fact, thought becomes conscious to the degree to which the child is able to communicate it.

. . .

An examination of the spontaneous language of children and their behavior in collective games shows, therefore, that early social behavior remains midway along the road between egocentrism and true socialization. Rather than extricating himself from his own point of view in order to coordinate it with the viewpoints of others, the child still remains unconsciously centered on himself. This egocentricity vis-a-vis the social group reproduces and prolongs the egocentricity we have already noted in the infant vis-a-vis the physical universe. In both cases there is a lack of differentiation between the self and external reality, which at this stage is represented by other individuals and no longer simply by objects. In both cases this initial confusion results in the primacy of the child's own point of view.

The psychological and, *a fortiori*, material constraint exercised by the adult on the child by no means precludes this egocentricity in the small child's relationship to the adult. While submitting to the adult and seeing him as highly superior to himself, the small child frequently reduces the adult to his own scale, just as certain naive believers do with respect to divinity. This results in a compromise between his own point of view and that of the superior being, rather than in a well-differentiated coordination between the two (pp. 17-21).

(c) *Distributive justice*, according to the needs of others and cooperation in middle childhood (yrs. 7-12):

progress in two directions: individual concentration when the subject is working by himself and effective collaboration in the group. These two aspects of the behavior that starts at around seven years are in reality complementary and derive from the same sources. They are, in fact, so intimately linked that one is hard put to say whether the child has become capable of a certain degree of reflection because he has learned to cooperate with others or vice versa.

. . .

True discussions are now possible in that the children show comprehension with respect to the other's point of view and a search for justification or proof with respect to their own statements. Explanations between children develop on the plane of thought and not just on the level of material action. "Egocentric" language disappears almost entirety, and the grammatical structure of the child's spontaneous statements attests to his need for a connection between ideas and logical justification.

. . .

there is a noticeable change in social attitudes after the age of seven, as can be seen in games involving rules.

. . .

Closely connected with this progress of social behavior, there are transformations of individual action which appear to be both the causes and the effects of this progress. The essence of these transformations is that the child becomes capable of at least rudimentary reflection. Instead of the impulsive behavior of the small child, accompanied by unquestioned beliefs and intellectual egocentricity, the child of seven or eight thinks before acting and thus begins to conquer the difficult process of reflection. Reflection is nothing other than intimate deliberation, that is to say, a discussion which is conducted with oneself just as it might be conducted with real interlocutors or opponents.

One could then say that reflection is internalized social discussion (just as thought itself presupposes internalized language). This view is in accordance with the general rule that one always ends by applying to oneself behavior acquired from others. Contrariwise, socialized discussion might also be described as externalized reflection. Since all human conduct is both social and individual, this problem, like all analogous questions, comes back to whether the chicken appears before the egg or the egg before the chicken.

The important point is that, in both respects, the child of seven years begins to be liberated from his social and intellectual egocentricity and becomes capable of new coordination which will be of the utmost importance in the development of intelligence and affectivity.

With respect to intelligence, we are now dealing with the beginnings of the construction of logic itself. Logic constitutes the system of relationships which permit the coordination of points of view corresponding to different individuals, as well as those which correspond to the successive percepts or intuitions of the same individual.

With respect to affectivity, the same system of social and individual coordination engenders a morality of cooperation and personal autonomy in contrast to the intuitive heteronomous morality of the small child. This new system of values represents, in the affective sphere, the equivalent of logic in the realm of intelligence. The mental instruments which will facilitate logical and moral coordination are the operation of logic in the field of intelligence and the will in the field of affectivity (pp. 39-41).

(d) *Action and even sacrifice for an ideal* (years 12-) (joining the affective adolescent development described above):

The adolescent goes about injecting himself into adult society. He does so by means of projects, life plans, theoretical systems, and ideas of political or social reform. In short, he does so by means of thinking and almost, one might say, by imagination— so far does this hypothetico-deductive thinking sometimes depart from reality.

. . .

In the adolescent's social life, as in other areas, there is an initial phase of "holding back" (Charlotte Buhler's [1931] negative phase) and a positive phase. During the first phase, the adolescent frequently appears asocial and practically asociable. Nothing, however, could be less true, since he is constantly meditating about society. The society that interests him is the society he wants to reform; he has nothing but disdain or disinterest for the real society he condemns. Furthermore, adolescent sociability develops through the young person's interactions with other adolescents.

. . .

True adaptation to society comes automatically when the adolescent reformer attempts to put his ideas to work. Just as experience reconciles formal thought with the reality of things, so does effective and enduring work undertaken in concrete and well-defined situations, cure all dreams. One should not be disquieted by the extravagance and disequilibrium of the better part of adolescence. If specialized studies are not enough, once the last crises of adaptation have been surmounted, professional work definitively restores equilibrium and thus definitively marks the advent of adulthood.

In general, individuals who, between the ages of fifteen and seventeen, never constructed systems in which their life plans formed part of a vast dream of reform or who, at first contact with the material world, sacrificed their chimeric ideals to new adult interests, are not the most productive. The metaphysics peculiar to the adolescent, as well as his passions and his megalomania, are thus real preparations for personal creativity, and examples of genius show that there is always continuity between the formation of personality, as of eleven to twelve years, and the subsequent work of the man (pp. 67-69).

CONCLUSION

basic unity of the processes which, from the construction of the practical universe by infantile sensorimotor intelligence, lead to the reconstruction of the world by the hypothetico-deductive thinking of the adolescent, via the knowledge of the concrete world derived from the system of operations of middle childhood.

We have seen how these successive constructions always involve a decentering of the initial egocentric point of view in order to place it in an ever-broader coordination of relations and concepts, so that each new terminal grouping further integrates the subject's activity by adapting it to an ever-widening reality.

Parallel to this intellectual elaboration, we have seen affectivity gradually disengaging itself from the self in order to submit, thanks to the reciprocity and coordination of values, to the laws of cooperation.

Of course, affectivity is always the incentive for the actions that ensue at each new stage of this progressive ascent, since affectivity assigns value to activities and distributes energy to them. But affectivity is nothing without intelligence. Intelligence furnishes affectivity with its means and clarifies its ends.

It is erroneous and mythical to attribute the causes of development to great ancestral tendencies as though activities and biological growth were by nature foreign to reason. In reality, the most profound tendency of all human activity is progression toward equilibrium. Reason, which expresses the highest forms of equilibrium, reunites intelligence and affectivity" (pp. 69-70).

APPENDIX II

MORAL DEVELOPMENT AT DIFFERENT AGE LEVELS:
Where They Are — Where They Can Go — What Adults Can Do

Margaret Gorman, Boston College

PRESCHOOL CHILDREN (3-6 years)	WHERE THEY ARE	WHERE THEY CAN GO	WHAT ADULTS CAN DO
ENVIRONMENT (world of things and others) Family, Primal others, siblings, None, (Transcendent Reality-God)	**VITAL** - increasing mobility - horizontal - standing - moving **COGNITIVE:** **Intellectual:** -sensory-motor-fantasy - Good is what significant others reward me for - Bad is what significant others punish me for **Self-Concept:** - significant others give me a sense of GOOD ME and BAD ME - sense of self derived from action and others - sees self as hardly separate from others **View of Others:** - cannot see others' point of view; egocentric - parallel play; egocentric **View of Transcendent** - God seen as human and angry like me - intuitive-projective **SELF** - I am what Hope I have and give - I am what I can WILL freely - I am what I can imagine I will be ---> EXPANDING ENVIRONMENT	- developing body skills to master environment - concrete-operational-heteronomous - Good is what the group says is good - Bad is what the group does not approve - I am what I think my friends think of me - I am what I think I look like - I can be separate from my parents - beginning of role-taking perspective - see others as different - respect differences - cooperative team play - chum relationships from external likenesses - God seen through stories and moral heroes and heroines literally understood - mythic-literal - first sense of God as Other, life with meaning - I am what I can learn to make - I am what I am competent to do - moving to practice of lived faith and shared beliefs - family, peers, classmates, those like us, neighborhood	- unconditional acceptance and understanding - give support but let children work on - limits set - guiding but not prohibiting movement - asks questions so they can see consequences and feelings of others - help them to learn the rules and see rules enable them to be more free - allow for reality testing - give ideals and be models - help them to see that to fail or make a mistake does not mean they are failures - give opportunities for success - help them to see team play as cooperative, not competitive - help them be aware of others' feelings and point of view - help them work together to help others - give stories of heroes, heroines, ideals, visions and dreams - As a free response of the child, adults cannot directly make child become hopeful, willing and imagining, but only help indirectly by creating conditions - help them develop groups and teams based on fairness, respect, care - provide an environment of fairness, respect and care

ELEMENTARY SCHOOL CHILDREN (6-13 years)	WHERE THEY ARE	WHERE THEY CAN GO	WHAT ADULTS CAN DO
ENVIRONMENT World of things and others: family, school ethnic groups, television	**VITAL:** ·developing bodily skills to begin to master the environment **COGNITIVE** **Intellectual:** ·concrete operational; need for clarity and certainty. ·what is good is what is rewarded or what the "in" group does	·beginnings of genitality ·beginning to be an adult physically ·growing stronger and more skillful ·formal operations-abstract thinking ability to formulate alternate solutions ·what is good is what the group does in order to function as group with other groups	·allow them to fail and to profit from their mistakes ·help them to accept failure as part of being human ·help them to be critical of group and T.V. standards ·give more role-taking experiences of groups unlike theirs ·help them see need for rules ·give rule-making opportunities ·give opportunities to help others
Peer culture, Transcendent reality: God or meaningful order	**Self-concept:** ·external view of self-physical aspects ·not yet introspective ·egocentric but uninterested in the inner world ·stable view of self ·self-esteem satisfactory but largely derived from adults	·awareness of inner world of thought, feelings; transition-outer to inner world ·awareness of peers evaluating self ·"truth" about self comes more from within or from best friends ·decline in respect for parents' view of self	·affirm qualities of honesty and courage ·help to make transition from family to larger group ·affirm "group" group identity
	View of Others: ·cannot yet perceive how others perceive one-self ·excludes others not in "in group" ·others require some sacrifice of one's needs and desires ·beginnings of mutuality	·more openness to groups not theirs ·more shared, mutual friendships ·greater awareness of others' feelings and needs ·moving from gang membership based on "fun" to community membership based on goals	·expose them to "good" chums ·be models of sound friendship ·help them develop groups with goals beyond their own needs (refugees, elderly, etc.)
	View of Transcendent: ·mythic literal; love of stories of heroines; myths understood literally ·little sense of belonging to a believing community	·synthetic-conventional ·strong sense of group supporting self with common, unquestioned beliefs about life's meaning and purpose	·provide a community which, while clear in its vision and moral ideals, is still open to respect for those of different beliefs and ideals ·exposure to other cultures
	SELF ·I am what I can learn to make work ·I am what I am competent to do ·I can perform limited rituals in a community of shared beliefs and moral directives	·I can have the courage to risk leaving behind the world of childhood and open myself to adult experience ·I can risk leaving my childhood dependency on a God ·to develop a sense of agency in relation to God	·help them go from concern for doing to concern for being. Give experiences of and reflection on success in order to transcend technique and be genuinely creative
	⟶ EXPANDING ENVIRONMENT	to larger groups based not on similarity and relationships but on similar ideals, visions, isms, likes, dislikes	·provide an environment supportive but firm in moral ideals ·models living up to ideals and affirmed and rewarded

ADOLESCENTS	WHERE THEY ARE	WHERE THEY CAN GO	WHAT ADULTS CAN DO
(13-17 years)	**VITAL:** -beginnings of genitality -beginning to be adult physically -growing stronger and more skillful	-growing capacity for genitality -skills developed -abundant energy	-allow growth to take place -no condemnation of impulses themselves -but setting limits on inappropriate behavior
ENVIRONMENT Family, peers, neighborhood, school, teen-agers, those like me	**COGNITIVE** **Intellectual:** -formal operations enable adolescents to construct hypotheses on how the world works -adolescent egocentricity: "I see the world as it is." -sees limits of parental dictates and values -immersed in groups standards and feelings -GOOD is what the GROUP dictates or what feels good	-awareness and acceptance of ambiguity -awareness of need for systematic statement of moral principles and the enforcement of justice to protect rights of all concerned -awareness of need for legal system with clarity and authority based on more than group consensus	-allow greater participation in rule-making and enforcement -foster experiences that reveal need for systematic legal system in order to live in society
	Self-concept: -self-concept disturbance -uncomfortable awareness of what others think about self -locus of self-knowledge shifts to within -truth about self now vested in best friends, not in parents -individuation and freedom important -"I am not a child but I do not know who I am"	-I am still a satellite of parents -going from mere negation of what parents desire for them (individuation) -to a more conscious choice of identity (autonomy) -from "I am not a child" to "I will be who I choose to be"	-recognize that the negation of the parents is only temporary -allow distance but give support and connectedness
	View of others: -while separating from parents, needs to belong with others -can only say: "I am like my friends" -cannot yet say: "I am doing what I choose" -hunger for group participation	-from dependence either on parents or on peers -to self-chosen values and goals -greater awareness that others see the world and me not as I do -greater mutuality-not needing the other to confirm identity	-more questions to reveal others' feelings and viewpoints -more exposure to different groups and cultures -reflection on their viewpoints and feelings -deepen and broaden relationships
	View of Transcendent: -concern about stories of God's love for me -moving to synthetic-conventional -unquestioning acceptance of group creeds, rituals, norms	-to individuative-reflexive or transition -greater awareness of vision and rationality behind creeds, group values and history -to lead to an informed commitment	-support and understand questioning & rebellion as part of the growing process and a "natural prerequisite" to adult commitment and fidelity -indicate one's own commitment in the face of ambiguity
	SELF: -I can risk leaving behind the world of childhood and open myself to adult experience	-I can be faithful or not be faithful to my promises and/or commitments -I can be an adult in my relationships with others and with God	-be models of commitment and trustworthiness; give opportunities for commitment; reflect on the effects of lack of fidelity -show great respect for the growing self
	----------> EXPANDING ENVIRONMENT	-wider environment of history. There are persons, and nations not like me with diverse, even conflicting values	-help them develop tolerance and acceptance of other environments -capacity and willingness to critique own environment

YOUTH (18-25 years of age)

ENVIRONMENT: "my group" • TV ads • competitive society • stifle

	WHERE THEY ARE	WHERE THEY CAN GO	WHAT ADULTS CAN DO
VITAL	- a more secure sense of genitality - more focused use of energy	- to a capacity of mutual genitality - to a wiser use of energy	- endorse the emerging sexual and physical identity
COGNITIVE Intellectual	- dualism and/or extreme relativism - unquestioning acceptance of and desire to conform to society's standards - formal operations - recognition of need for system but unable to see system as open to change	- from relativism to committed relativism and dialectic thought - to postconventional formalism and postconventional - ability to seek principles underlying rules and laws can - ability to work to change laws which violate principles	- be open to change - show distinction between conventional rules and moral principles - give constant critical examination of existing systems in light of principles
	Self-concept: search for identity: Foreclosed: according to society's demands Diffused: constant experimentation In moratorium: delaying choice - identity still derived largely from group - ambivalent though self-aware	- to achieved identity through commitment to self-chosen values and self-ideal, emerging from story and dream - become aware of distinction between one's roles, career, and one's self; I am not my roles; I have those roles	- be mentors who clearly distinguish in themselves, their roles and their selves - present career opportunities consistent with chosen values - present variety of options and opportunities
	View of others - moving from extreme dependence to counter-dependence - able to others seeing self - still needing and using others more than mutual giving	- to intimacy and mutuality of relationship - to participation in the larger society - to fidelity, love and commitment to others' service	- be models of life-long intimacy and participation in society - present "causes" and institutions worthy of commitments - show sensitivity to, and awareness of, the less privileged
	View of transcendent - synthetic-conventional or unquestioning emotional adherence - negative separation from any institutional membership	- commitment to vision, dream and story of an institution based on reflection - I choose this vision - individuative-reflective	- show that the faith vision is lived out consistently in behavior - present community of support and vision
SELF	- I can be faithful to or - I will be faithful to my commitments	- to making and keeping commitments of career, relationships and values - as called by the transcendent reality of God - to know and respect groups with different customs, values and vision - to an awareness that, although they must fit into society, they can be apart from it and help shape it	- only support the search - respect the commitment - reveal one's own commitment - give experiences of other cultures - give example of transcending, though working within the environment

	WHERE THEY ARE	WHERE THEY CAN GO	WHAT ADULTS CAN DO
YOUNG ADULT (Ages 25-40)	**VITAL:** ·mature genitality ·fulness of bodily energy and development	·love of life ·to be for life in self and in subsequent generations	·encourage their vitality
ENVIRONMENT: work world, school world, political world, social world, financial world, starting family; all conflicting	**COGNITIVE:** **Intellectual** ·greater acceptance of ambiguity or compartmentalized relativism ·challenged by their principles which can conflict with societal values & career goals	·morality of care and responsibility ·greater consistency between principles and actions ·greater clarity of hierarchy of values	·models who live up to principles even at some cost of material success ·colleagues with similar courage and consistency
	Self-concept: ·competence and career choice should enforce sense of autonomy ·career and role success could be career dependence and role conformity not autonomy ·extreme concern with external signs of success	·distantiation from career ·broadening of goals to include contribution to larger society ·self-transcendence more than self-actualization ·dream-to create a better society rather than to have more	·give dream ·create society where autonomy is encouraged and goals are more than power, status, or material goods
	View of others ·intimacy and solidarity ·period of greatest relationship to spouse, children, colleagues ·struggle between career demands and family	·expand areas of concern beyond here and now to future generations ·to underprivileged ·generativity	·support when relationships and/or career falter ·models of generativity ·offer opportunities for generativity
	View of transcendent ·for some, after period of indifference, desire to share faith vision and values with children ·return to faith community for the children	·deeper understanding of faith commitment ·for some, growth in prayer and relationship with God ·acceptance of institutional limitations	·offer faith community-all seeking to grow in understanding-courses, reading ·an institution that serves rather than demanding service ·older adults who live their faith commitment
	Self: ·I am defined by whom I love and what and whom I care for. I am my commitments to others and to God.	·generativity: I have the strength to be generative ·to bring forth potentials in others and in the material world. I need to share God's love with others by giving of self	·can never help directly, but only by creating facilitating environment
	<------------------------> EXPANDING ENVIRONMENT	·to criticize accepted values ·integration of worlds around values ·I can shape the world even thought I am shaped by it to some extent	·a nation, city, society open to reexamine values ·environment based on respect for each person

	WHERE THEY ARE	WHERE THEY CAN GO	WHAT OTHERS CAN DO
MIDDLE AGE (40-60 years)	**VITAL:** -mature generativity -beginning of declining strengths	-integrity in spite of declining strengths -openness to death, illness	-encourage the sensible care of health
ENVIRONMENT work world home, other countries OR narrowing world to work & home	**COGNITIVE** **Intellectual:** -moral decision based on care and respect for rights -Increasing powers of synthesis and dialectical operations -dialectic of social and psychological dimensions can occur	-can continue to grow in ability to accept contradictions -to generate multiple solutions -to tolerate continual change -to care, be responsible	-ask questions to generate multiple solutions -help openness to change by keeping change gradual -help distinguish between changing social conventions and stable moral principles
	View of others -either impersonal, isolated, avoiding intimacy, or in -superficial relationships -or developing deeper friendships, shared thoughts, feelings -either constricted view of society, or openness to views and feelings of more and more groups	-generativity: hoping to share with others one's dream; or -self-preoccupation; -sense of continuity with future generations -or role-domination and job routinization	-differing generations seek and support each other -show that "No man is an island"
	View of Transcendent -either synthetic conventional or unquestioning conformity to the institution, or -Informed commitment to it	-to conjunctive faith or awareness of limits of any institution's expression of faith vision -Lives and acts between an untransformed world & a transforming vision	-community of like persons seeking to live out a vision and pass on vision and commitment to children
	SELF: I am: -what survives of me -all I have been & will generate	-to be through having been -I am concerned with life in face of death -Integrity	-call forth their generativity and care for future generations; help them separate their roles from their committed selves
	──────> EXPANDING ENVIRONMENT	-to become a world citizen -global village -I am a part of a world that is interdependent, economically	media that emphasizes -likeness, common humanity -rituals that downplay nationalism and ethnicity

LATE ADULTHOOD

(Ages 60 and over)

ENVIRONMENT
relocation can cause stress or invigorate; important for autonomy more than for comfort

<-->

CONSTRICTING ENVIRONMENT

WHERE THEY ARE

VITAL
- diminished psychomotor and sensory functioning;
- slower physical reactions compensated by skill and experience

COGNITIVE

Intellectual
- going beyond pure logic to pragmatic logic
- concern with concrete pragmatics and social system stability

Self-concept
- maintaining consistency
- self image more important than facing impending death

Awareness of others
- little research
- some institutionalized persons have low empathy and high distrust in order to maintain sense of self

Awareness of an ultimate
- little research
- elderly found on all faith levels
- commitment to meaning chosen by themselves possible and evident in some

SELF
- wisdom, integrity and mature faith characterize the healthy self
- to be through having been

WHAT OTHERS CAN DO

- accept and support their reactions as different, not necessarily inferior

- recognize that concern for pragmatics and stability may result in loss of some details and pure logic

- enable them to care for and contact others who will affirm self-image

- create institutions which foster sense of autonomy, and trust of others

- give opportunities for continued learning so they can continue to reformulate their commitment to meaning

- help them become aware that the spirit can grow stronger and deeper as the body grows more frail

INDEX

A

Abhishiktananda 234
Abraham 13
Absolute 23-27, 32, 34, 38, 41-44, 53, 75, 95-96, 107, 124, 128-129, 134, 136, 139, 141, 146-147, 157-159, 166, 174-176, 188, 198-201, 204-213, 215-219, 224-230, 254, 272-281, 294, 297-298, 307-320, 342-45, 355, 365, 372-375, 393-401, 404, 406, 410
Abulaylah 26
Abyss 19, 125, 201, 369, 391-394, 403, 406
Accommodation 358, 419, 426
Adler 29, 47, 182, 233, 328, 377
Adorno 412
Aesthetic 66, 111-113, 130-131, 212, 225, 281-282, 332-333, 340, 360, 363, 366
Africa iv, 3, 78, 88-89, 93, 104, 128
Agrawala 138, 160
Albert 1
Alexander 26, 47, 165, 193, 284
Alexandria 186, 242
Alienation 39, 296
Allen 49, 323, 413
Alszeghy 193, 284
Ananda 226
Anaximander 47, 171, 192
Anglo-Saxon 262, 356
Animal 15, 17, 68-69, 82-83, 86, 90, 101, 103, 116, 118, 335, 346
Anscombe 48, 322
Anselm 42, 49, 290- 291, 298, 322-323

Anthropology 64, 78-86, 91, 95-96, 103, 115, 284, 327
Anxiety 400
Aquinas 1, 7, 12, 27-28, 31, 46, 69, 95, 101, 167, 185, 187, 198, 200, 228, 232, 235, 255, 262-265, 273-276, 280, 284, 290, 319, 337
Archimedean 344
Aristotle 12, 18, 24, 27, 29, 32, 34, 46-47, 68-69, 71, 80, 96, 98, 101, 125, 141, 167-168, 171, 174-175, 177-194, 206, 331, 337, 347-355, 364, 370, 378-379, 395, 411
Arjuna 148-158
Asia 1, 3, 6, 49, 97, 102, 186, 323
Aspell 46, 47, 131, 192, 193, 234, 284
Atheism 320
Augustine . 12, 32, 71, 93, 145, 186, 195, 212, 220, 238, 245, 255, 290, 393, 406
Autocracy 208
Averroes 1, 26-28, 31, 165-167, 185-186, 235, 243, 255-256, 260-261
Avicenna 1, 7, 27, 166, 235, 247
Awareness *passim*
Axiology 336, 341

B

Bacon 266, 345
Balasubramanian 104, 160
Barth 383
Beauty 11, 45, 68, 113-114, 148, 168, 199, 207, 225-227, 244, 282, 320, 333, 339, 340, 376
Behavior 55-57, 62-66, 77, 83, 119,

159, 207, 343, 417, 420, 425-429
Bergson 26, 165, 280
Black 122, 129
Bodhisattva 321
Boethius 46, 216-218, 383
Bolivar 359
Bonaventure 4, 278, 290
Bose 228, 233
Bradley 309, 310, 313
Brahman 80, 99, 103, 115, 137, 148, 157-161, 192, 231, 392
Brhadaranyaka-Upanisad 413
Browne 82, 84
Bruhl 15, 46, 65, 73, 86-93, 104, 115
Buber 307-308, 321, 348, 406
Buddhism 169, 321
Business 30, 182, 206, 222

C

Caputo 378
Carmel 4
Carnap 309, 317, 324, 328, 344, 377-378
Catholic iv, 4, 11, 12, 205, 207, 232-233, 283, 356, 383, 413
Cenkner 49, 323
Chaos 17-21, 122-127, 142-143, 227
Children 18, 20, 36, 43, 62-65, 92, 100, 121-123, 126-127, 207, 222, 292, 313, 321, 347, 374, 418, 422, 427-428
Christ 112, 128, 176, 182, 184, 191, 200, 214, 221, 226, 233, 265, 271, 347, 383, 408- 410
Christianity iii, 1, 3, 6-7, 12, 27-34, 40, 95, 115, 138, 165, 180, 193-

199, 201, 204-205, 214-215, 221, 224-227, 230-238, 255, 268, 273-279, 281, 284, 293, 298, 309, 322, 325, 331-332, 383-387, 408-415
Chu Hsi 360, 364
Churchill 112
Cicero 339
Civil society iii, 293, 327, 334-363, 368, 373-375
Civilization iv, 2-5, 9, 25, 38, 40, 65, 72, 78, 124, 147, 238, 294, 296, 340-341, 371-372, 378
Cognition 29, 54-60, 63-71, 85-86, 90, 103, 111, 118-120, 133-134, 167, 177, 180, 210, 250, 273, 311-314, 318, 344, 346, 360, 365, 371, 386, 395, 398, 403, 405, 412, 417, 420
Cold War 88, 267
Collective 86, 89-90, 427
Commitment 12, 24, 146, 191, 203, 282, 312-313, 343-344, 359, 386, 411
Common good 351-355
Communication 25, 147, 217, 222, 229, 310, 314-315, 321, 341, 343, 350, 352, 426, 427
Communion 98, 232, 308, 313-314, 320-322, 389
Communism 88, 383
Community 15-16, 88-93, 101, 176, 207, 214, 238, 248, 262, 313, 336, 338, 340-344, 346-347, 350-362, 367, 385
Compartmentalization 90
Composite 34, 179, 197-198, 201-202, 209-213, 216, 219, 223, 227-231, 272, 276, 340, 354

Conceptualization 79-80, 395
Confident 24, 146, 222, 225, 246, 282, 342
Confucius 41, 112-113, 207-208, 214, 225, 298, 359, 366
Consciousness *passim*
Crawford 130
Creator 206
Critique 32, 82, 108, 111-113, 130-131, 195-196, 2225, 237, 241, 260, 274, 281, 327, 330, 332, 373, 386
Cronus 18, 20, 122-123, 126-127, 222
Cua 49, 323, 347, 356, 359-360, 364-365
Cusa 85, 217, 279, 393

D

Daniel 102
Dasein 37, 71, 257, 293, 300-307, 332, 367
Dasgupta 104, 160, 170, 193, 231, 234, 316, 325
De Mazenod iv
Death 30, 90, 92, 121-122, 139-140, 150-154, 158-159, 182-184, 203, 206, 225-226, 240, 242, 244, 247, 282, 312-313, 347, 382-385, 400-404
Democracy 73, 226, 328, 342, 351, 357-358, 368, 371-372, 379
Depersonalization 318
Descartes 46, 54, 68-69, 89, 96, 101, 109, 157, 200, 245-253, 258, 266, 283, 290, 344-346, 378, 398
Deussen 193
Dewey 267

Dialect iii, 5, 8, 32, 47, 79, 111, 134-135, 177, 193-195, 233, 239, 310, 328, 333, 377, 381-386, 389-390, 393-404, 408, 411-412, 414
Dialogue 49, 177, 206, 233, 323, 368, 370-373
Dibadj 380
Dirk 412
Divine *passim*
Dynamism 115, 98, 294

E

Earth 11, 17-18, 25, 118-127, 140-142, 147, 150-160, 182, 220, 225, 245, 347
Ecstasy 339, 366, 403-405
Education 65, 75, 124, 240, 246, 252, 315, 323
Ego iv, 13, 27-28, 36, 43, 59-60, 68, 80, 84-87, 89, 103, 109-112, 127, 131, 148, 158-159, 165-167, 170, 180, 184, 220, 237, 258, 290, 299, 381, 393 418-420, 426-432
Elkin 82
Emotion 378
Emotion 56-59, 83, 152, 336, 338, 400, 409, 420- 422
Enlightenment 1, 3, 26, 30, 53, 89, 165, 183, 266-267, 310, 344-345, 356, 368, 373
Epistemology 37, 108, 145, 237, 240, 252-256, 275, 327, 388, 390, 393
Equilibrium 55-57, 62, 64, 115-117, 133-134, 157, 179-180, 315, 373, 419-424, 431, 433

Equipment 91
Erikson 124, 132
Eros 18, 20, 42- 45, 122-128, 144, 191, 346, 375-376
Esteller 137, 140, 141, 160
Ethnic 363, 407
Europe iv, 19, 88-89, 124-125, 138, 142, 148, 186, 238, 331, 356, 379, 383-384, 412
Evil iii, 2, 8-9, 17, 20-21, 69, 90, 121, 126-129, 149-151, 159-169, 204-207, 226, 245, 251-252, 278, 310, 320, 364, 381, 383, 398
Existence 5-8, 12, 14, 20, 28-34, 37-38, 42, 44, 46, 54, 76, 79, 84-87, 92, 95, 97, 99-102, 108, 114, 126, 134, 136, 139-145, 157-159, 167, 180-190, 19-202, 209-219, 226, 229-235, 240, 247-250, 264-282, 290-294, 299-334, 339, 344-348, 358, 375, 383, 385, 390, 396-410, 414-417

F

Fabro 30, 47, 48, 183-184, 194, 200, 232, 276-277, 285
Faith 11, 13, 22-26, 35, 73, 99-100, 146, 165, 172, 189, 192, 194, 198, 245-249, 253, 259, 261-264, 277-279, 282-283, 291, 308, 325, 339, 365-367, 405-410, 415
Fall 398
Family 21, 37, 56, 87, 92, 97, 100, 108, 127, 137, 144, 149-150, 179, 186, 191, 208, 214, 216, 222, 249, 293, 311, 336, 342-343, 354, 404
Farabi 1, 27, 166, 235, 247, 260, 275, 277

Farm 16, 30, 56, 116, 182
Fate 123, 154, 241, 308, 400, 401
Ferguson 336
Ferrand de Piazza 131
Fichte 393
Fidelity 21, 27, 128, 166, 237, 312- 313
Firth 84
Flick 193, 284
Fork 173, 237
Fortes 84
Fowler 62, 70, 73
Freedom 25-33, 37, 40-47, 97, 109, 112-114, 147, 154, 157, 165-166, 179, 182-183, 193, 196, 208, 212-216, 220, 223-226, 235, 264-267, 271, 277-282, 293, 296-299, 305-307, 310, 313-318, 327-334, 338-339, 342-363, 367-368, 372-376, 381- 383, 394, 398-401, 408, 411, 414
Freud 16, 116, 300, 303
Friendship 203, 324, 352, 354
Fuchs 102
Fulfillment 3-4, 13, 35, 206, 224, 232, 236, 245, 257, 272, 282, 289, 303, 329, 335-339, 357, 363, 400, 409

G

Gadamer 37, 104, 293, 356, 359, 378, 380
Gandhi 323, 411
Geertz 340, 378
Geiger 200
Ghandi 77, 322

Ghazālī iii, 6, 26-27, 31, 165-167, 185, 235-264, 268-269, 275-278, 282-286, 289
Gift 35-46, 48, 143, 159, 206, 224-226, 250, 294-299, 323, 344, 374-377
Goebbels 222
Golden Age 65
Goodness 198-199, 206, 210-215, 223-226, 229, 281-282, 308, 317, 321, 339, 340, 358, 363, 367
Gorman iii, 63, 73, 435
Governance 327, 338, 350-356, 362, 371, 373
Graham iv
Greek *passim*
Griaule 91, 104
Griffith 160, 325
Ground 381- 415
Gueye 53
Guilt 399-404
Guthrie 172, 193

H

Habermas 113, 131
Happiness 150, 206, 219, 246, 249, 337, 350-351
Harappa 78
Harmony 39-40, 43-44, 112-115, 156, 160, 204-208, 218, 224-226, 296, 331, 333, 342, 358-359, 373-375, 385
Hatred 226, 282
Havel 120, 283
Heaven 17-20, 207, 231, 304
Hegel 5, 12, 53-54, 79, 213, 223, 309, 349, 379, 398, 401, 415
Heidegger 37, 71, 73, 78-81, 84-86, 96-98, 102-103, 107, 168, 257, 268, 293, 295, 299-307, 315, 317, 323-325, 337, 356, 358, 367-377
Henle 194
Hermeneutics 25, 28, 71, 78, 81, 84-86, 96, 104, 131, 137, 147, 167, 258, 316, 340, 344-348, 365-370, 373, 380
Hesiod 17, 21, 46, 47, 108, 120-123, 125, 129, 132, 137, 142, 169, 230, 347, 378
Heteronomous 62, 329, 430
Hindu iii, 6-7, 12, 20, 40, 49, 83, 90, 95, 115, 126, 133-135, 145, 148-151, 168-169, 192, 211-212, 215, 233, 267, 273, 296, 323, 332
Historicism 388
Hitler 381, 383
Hobbes 128, 329, 346, 393
Holiness 223-224, 240, 251, 332, 388
Homer 21, 47, 230
Horse 67, 101, 129
Human capabilit 64, 67, 117, 120
Human dignity 57, 90, 226, 280, 324, 343, 346, 402
Human mind 14, 26, 76, 95, 108-109, 135, 145, 165, 188, 211, 230, 272, 277, 279, 290-291, 330, 346, 392, 405
Human person 26-27, 32-33, 37, 54-55, 112, 134, 166, 179, 195, 206, 212, 214, 217, 225, 232, 263, 265, 270-272, 275, 277-281, 293-294, 307, 310, 327, 332-333, 355, 357, 362, 365, 387, 405, 408

Human spirit 36, 108, 134, 237, 264, 290, 330, 339-340, 367, 386, 412
Human thought 13-14, 24-25, 75, 133, 138, 142, 146-147, 174, 180, 209, 269, 284, 309
Human Understanding 21, 318, 377
Humanity 90, 107, 174, 176, 204, 221, 230, 265-266, 307, 318-319
Hume 328, 345, 377
Husserl 37, 293, 307, 350

I

Idealism 188, 267, 309-310, 321, 381-382, 384, 387, 391-395, 410
Identification 27, 81, 114-115, 166, 319, 385, 392
Ideology 92, 98, 112-113, 120, 184, 222, 267, 329, 386
Imagination 14-17, 20-23, 65-70, 76, 107-119, 126, 128-129, 134-137, 145, 168-169, 173, 330-333, 345, 424, 430
Incarnate 182, 221, 241, 362, 410
India iv, 12, 76, 100-104, 138, 145, 148, 160-161, 169, 226, 231, 234, 316, 379, 411
Individualis 88
Individualization 262, 387-390, 394, 397-398, 402
Infancy 57, 97, 417, 420, 426
Infinite 12-13, 20, 23-29, 33-34, 48, 64, 118, 126, 134-135, 146-147, 156, 166, 173-175, 180, 196-197, 200, 205-210, 213, 217-218, 221, 225, 231, 262, 268-269, 272, 275-276, 311, 319, 361, 367-368, 371, 387, 392-394, 396-397, 401, 403, 407

Intelligence 56-62, 172, 350, 419-421, 430, 432-433
Intelligibility 19, 96, 109, 125, 144, 172, 209, 217, 220-223, 228, 319
Internal sense 14, 21-23, 67-71, 76, 108, 119, 128, 170, 173
Interpersonal 16, 40, 360, 421-422, 426-427
Iqbal i, iii-iv, 3, 11-14, 17, 20, 24-48, 75, 96-97, 107, 116, 126, 146-147, 161, 165-167, 180, 184-185, 192-198, 232, 236, 268-269, 280, 282, 284, 289-294, 296-299, 322-323, 343, 375, 377
Islam i, iii, 11, 13, 26-28, 31-36, 40, 46, 75, 95, 115, 165-167, 185-186, 192, 195, 198, 227, 232, 235-239, 243-244, 247, 252-256, 259-268, 277-279, 284-285, 290, 296, 332
Islamic 165-167, 185-186, 192

J

Jaeger 46, 47, 132, 192, 193, 229, 234
James 113, 131, 233, 413
Jefferson 218
Jesus 4
John Paul II 46, 49, 194, 264, 277, 284-285, 377, 380
Judaism 95
Judeo-Christian 204
Judgment 110-113, 177, 188, 210-213, 219, 222, 240, 253-254, 260, 277-282, 330, 332, 338-339, 345, 357, 370, 372

Justice 22, 46, 62, 94, 158-159, 171-172, 207, 214, 222, 226, 237, 262, 271, 308, 317, 337, 339, 346, 354-358, 363-365, 377, 383, 425, 428

K

Kaegi 160, 161
Kairos 382
Kant 29, 36-37, 42, 108-113, 130-131, 182, 213, 224, 225, 281, 291-293, 298, 327-332, 363, 381, 386
Keith 78, 102-103, 136, 141, 160-161, 233
Kennedy 205
Kierkegaard 169, 383, 388, 398
King 68, 127, 149-152, 359, 385, 398, 411, 416
Kinship 86-87, 92, 311
Kirk 19, 46, 47, 125, 132
Kohlberg 54, 62-63, 70, 73, 114, 133
Kondoleon 233
Krishna 141, 148-152, 157, 161

L

Lahore i, iv, 3, 46, 101, 232
Language 20, 22, 37, 59, 68, 125-126, 136, 138, 141, 171, 209-211, 276-277, 293, 342-343, 350, 395, 421, 425-429
Leclerc 377
Leibniz 17, 42, 121, 200, 298
Liberation 131
Limitation 17, 32-33, 37, 80, 84, 116, 134, 188-189, 195-196, 204-205, 209-218, 229, 236, 254, 256, 272, 275-276, 281, 293, 310, 318, 328, 359, 413
Lincoln 359
Little 194, 200
Locke 36, 172, 266, 292, 328, 329, 344, 345, 377, 417
Logic *passim*
Logos 30, 65, 169, 171, 173, 183, 189, 215, 221-222, 274, 391-392, 394, 396
Loiacono 131
Lombard 148
Lonergan 85, 103, 192
Love iv, 18, 27, 30-33, 38, 42-46, 56, 72, 78, 87, 93, 114-118, 121-124, 128, 146, 149, 155, 159, 166-168, 182, 191, 195-196, 200, 206-208, 214-215, 220, 223-229, 237, 244, 281-282, 294, 299, 307-308, 312-314, 320, 339, 344-347, 357-358, 374-377, 381, 405, 411, 415-416
Lutheran 381, 383

M

MacDonell 130, 161, 233
MacIntyre 356, 359
Mahadevan 12, 99, 104, 413
Mahal 359
Majumdar 102
Malinowski 82
Marcel 308-312, 321-325, 348
Marriage 15, 82, 87, 203, 244, 312
Marx 12, 16, 48, 89, 116, 267, 323, 383, 386, 388, 391, 398,

401, 404, 411
Materialism 99, 109, 141, 188, 258, 317, 320, 384
Mathematics 22, 39, 69-71, 170, 191, 247, 266, 295, 311, 347, 387
Mathieu 377, 378
McLean i, iv, 46-48, 73, 131, 160, 192-193, 232, 234, 283-285, 323, 377-378
Meaninglessness 258, 264, 383, 386, 388-390, 400-405, 411
Mechanism 22, 170, 343, 346
Mediation 69, 188, 242, 244, 249, 257-258, 266, 415
Mehta 377
Metaphysics iii-iv, 6, 12, 22, 27-37, 42, 48, 70-71, 78, 80, 83, 96-102, 109, 137, 139, 144, 159, 166-167, 170-171, 174, 178, 183-192, 195-198, 200-201, 209-217, 221, 228-232, 236-237, 243, 255, 257, 262, 268, 272-276, 289, 293, 295, 299, 309, 322, 327, 334, 365, 367, 385, 424, 431
Middle Ages 6, 7, 27, 69, 167, 235, 238, 243, 316, 331
Millennium 1-2, 11, 14, 167, 186, 264-265, 271-272, 411
Milton 1
Mohammed 265, 271, 298
Mohanjodaro 78
Molina 131
Monism 98, 145, 391
Montgomery 411
Moral iii, 49, 54, 62-64, 73, 113, 124, 131, 159, 214, 330-331, 335-340, 346, 356, 359, 363-365, 373, 378-379, 386, 388, 399-400, 410, 422-425, 430, 435
Moslem 239
Mourelatos 47, 284
Movone 379
Mukherji 102
Muses 17, 121, 122
Myth iii, 6, 8, 14, 17-24, 28, 32, 62, 65-66, 70-71, 76-81, 91, 93, 97-98, 107, 115-121, 124-137, 141, 144-146, 158-159, 167-171, 173-174, 177, 180, 191, 195, 216, 222, 228, 268, 269, 345, 395, 398, 432

N

National Socialism 308, 382
Naturalism 247, 384-388
Nazi 308, 381, 382, 383
Nedoncelle 48, 203, 232, 323
Nietzsche 53, 383, 388, 391, 398
Nothingness 22-23, 172-174, 199, 201, 209, 216, 219, 400

O

Objectification 60, 93
Objectivity 369, 393, 410
Ogden 48, 322
Ogotemmêli 91, 104
Ojha 138
Olympus 17, 121, 122
Ontology 34, 144, 176-177, 197, 220, 271, 279, 301, 311-314, 321, 335, 387-390, 393-395, 399-400, 406, 410, 412, 415
Organization 57-58, 65, 70, 121, 267, 305, 373, 423
Origin *passim*

Owens 47, 178, 193, 194, 233

P

Panikkar 233
Panini 137
Pantocrator 181, 270
Paradigm 215, 220, 229, 323, 347, 359, 379
Pardon 46, 377
Parmenides 22-23, 32, 34, 40, 43, 47, 49, 171-176, 179, 181, 185-198, 201, 209, 212-221, 230, 233, 254, 272, 280, 284, 296, 299, 309, 317, 323, 334, 365
Participation 15, 31-34, 38, 47-49, 72, 81, 90-95, 98-100, 127, 139, 160, 167, 169, 175-181, 184-202, 205, 208-210, 216-221, 224-232, 255, 271-276, 279, 285, 294, 308, 311-322, 348, 349, 352-355, 385-390, 396-397, 402-403, 410-413
Pascal 169
Peace 25, 46, 131, 147, 152-160, 225, 265, 282, 308, 334, 342, 346, 377
Pegoraro 131
Pelican 365, 380
Perfection 13, 30, 43, 143-144, 156, 174, 176, 182, 189, 200-208, 216, 219, 223-224, 227-229, 252, 284, 317-320, 328, 332-335, 338, 353, 358-359, 362-368, 374, 389, 396, 409
Personality 35, 49, 55-57, 236, 289, 323, 359, 382, 417, 423-424, 431
Pessimism 320
Phenomenon 53, 75, 79, 87-88, 133, 145
Physiology 55-57, 159, 417
Piaget iii, 54-64, 66, 70-73, 85, 103, 108, 114-115, 133, 417
Piazza 131
Plato 12, 15, 28, 30-34, 43, 49, 76, 79, 96-98, 104, 175-189, 191-199, 212, 220, 230, 235, 247, 255, 260, 263, 271-274, 279, 299, 309, 311, 316, 323, 330-333, 337, 346-349, 352, 355, 361, 365, 379, 393, 395
Plenitude 47, 81, 84, 86, 93-100, 107, 131, 143, 160, 168-169, 185, 189, 202, 209-211, 216, 223, 227-229, 311, 314, 317-322
Plotinus 29, 42, 181, 193, 212, 223, 270, 284, 298
Pluralism 98, 145, 217, 315, 368, 372, 391
Poem 17-18, 22, 121-123, 148, 171, 175, 217, 272, 280, 300-301, 305-306, 366
Polish 382-383
Polytheism 98
Poseidon 119
Positivist 36, 37, 267, 292, 293
Pragmatic 37, 82, 113, 128, 131, 237, 258, 267, 293, 310, 343, 359, 367, 384, 391, 409
Praxis 39, 296
Prejudice 226, 314, 370, 372
Prophet 24-25, 29, 31, 34, 36, 77, 146-147, 184, 198, 236, 238, 243-246, 249-254, 257, 265, 277, 290, 306, 347
Protestant 381
Psychoanalysis 59-60, 421

Psychology 53-55, 67, 73, 82-85,
110, 114, 133
Pusalker 102
Pythagoras 171

R

Radhakrishnan 141, 227, 233, 413
Rahner 37, 293
Raja 78, 100, 102, 105, 131, 160-161
Rajagopalachari 367
Ramanuja 273, 317
Raven 19, 46, 47, 125, 132
Rawls 329, 356
Readdy 131
Reasoning 12, 31-32, 41, 54, 65, 71, 80, 96, 99, 133, 136, 170, 171, 177, 188, 192, 195, 199-200, 212, 229, 236, 240, 246, 248-249, 253-255, 260, 269, 273, 275, 281, 291-292, 297, 349, 422
Reconciliation 13, 26, 35, 46, 360, 376-377, 385, 408
Redemption 183, 191, 384
Relativism 63, 78, 157, 345, 357, 363, 365, 366, 384, 409
Representation 86, 89-90, 110
Responsibility 27-28, 30, 45, 166-167, 182, 330, 338, 351, 354, 376
Resurrection 226, 248, 381, 385
Resurrection 184, 255, 260, 262, 277, 279, 281, 381, 383, 385, 390, 412
Revelation 402, 408, 415
Revelation 24, 27, 99, 146, 191, 192, 214, 228, 244, 260, 265, 269, 274, 277, 279, 283, 307, 308, 337, 402, 403, 405, 406,

408, 409, 410
Rg Veda 107, 108, 117, 130-145, 148, 168, 220, 227
Rhea 18, 122, 123, 127
Richardson 49, 306, 323, 324
Ricoeur 71, 85-86, 104, 311
Riedel 350, 379
Rishis 136, 138
Ritschl 381, 383, 388
Rogue.34 330
Roosevelt 112
Ross 194
Rosthal 325
Royce 26, 267
Russell 36, 292

S

Sacred 2-6, 14-16, 31, 68, 72, 76-77, 82-83, 91, 95, 98-101, 116, 118, 120, 134-135, 151, 169, 184, 222, 252, 261, 270, 277, 381
Sadra 6-7, 235, 264-268, 270-285
Sage 57, 91, 98, 103, 117, 134, 136, 139, 144-147, 151-157, 169, 183, 251
Sankhya 154, 157
Sanskrit 137-138, 161
Sartre 53
Schelling 382, 393, 395, 398, 414
Schleiermacher 383
Schmitz 48, 49, 323, 380
Scotts 336
Scotus 27, 167
Scripture 80, 99, 231, 155, 228
Sensibility 113, 172, 177, 214, 236, 331, 378
Sensorimotor 59-60, 420, 426-427,

Shankara 12, 143, 169-170, 233, 273, 280, 284, 317, 325
Shils 359, 379
Simon 225, 233
Sister 200, 321
Skeptics 188, 248, 275, 315, 405
Smith 130, 336, 412
Social Gospel Movement 384
Socialism 39, 295, 308, 382, 386, 389, 394
Socrates 46, 79, 98, 132-133, 167, 193, 219, 229, 247, 339, 341,
Solidarity 82, 352-356, 360, 373, 374, 383
Solipsism 384
Solzhenitsyn 386
Soul 97, 150-156, 177-178, 184
Soviet 383
Spinoza 200, 223, 229
Spirit 28, 36-37, 40, 44-46, 53, 68, 83, 85, 97-98, 103, 108, 134, 135, 136, 150-154, 158, 167, 168, 180, 182, 213-215, 221, 224-225, 231, 237-250, 253-264, 277-282, 290-296, 300-301, 305-306, 316, 322, 330, 339-340, 356, 366-367, 375-376, 386, 400-401, 408, 410, 412
Spirituality 28, 167, 256
Stanley 232, 283, 337, 377
Stoics 18, 124
Strauss 71, 82-85, 92, 103, 104
Structuralism 83-85, 92, 103
Subjectivity iii, 36-37, 72, 169, 232, 249, 257, 289-293, 299-300, 307-308, 327, 331, 359, 377, 393, 401, 410
Subsidiarity 352-357, 360, 373-374

Substance 91, 110, 141, 178-179, 205, 211, 247, 250, 273-274, 279-281, 370, 392, 418
Summa 12, 54, 57-58, 60, 62, 199, 225, 227, 231-235, 243, 261-263, 271, 325, 337
Supernatural 14, 75, 103, 403
Sutra 12-13, 46, 75, 80, 90, 103-104, 131, 148, 192, 194, 233, 284
Syllogism 187, 254, 275

T

Tagore 49, 77, 83, 102, 107, 323
Tatar 380
Technolog 318
Technolog 27, 33, 166, 179, 196, 222, 231, 263, 290, 315, 318-321, 353
Teleological 112
Tempels 65, 73
Teresa 4
Theogony 17, 19, 20, 46, 108, 118-127, 132, 137, 142-148, 171, 347, 378
Theologian 12, 99, 239
Theonomous 407
Theresa 263, 359
Thomas Aquinas 200, 232
Tillich 12, 65, 117, 131, 232, 273, 283-284, 355, 381- 413
Totem iii, 5, 8, 14-16, 21-24, 32, 66, 70-71, 75-76, 79, 81-103, 107-108, 115-118, 120, 128-129, 133, 138, 141-146, 151, 159, 167-168, 174-177, 195, 199, 216, 269
Transcendent 3-4, 6-7, 16-17, 20-

22, 27, 29, 41, 45, 200-208,
211-212, 215-218, 221-222,
225-226, 229-231, 241, 250-
251, 262, 269, 277, 279, 297,
309, 313, 317, 321, 358, 361,
366, 371, 376, 383-385, 393,
398, 405, 410
Tribe 15-16, 21, 82, 84, 86-88, 90-
94, 101, 103, 116, 128, 151
Trinitarian 72, 182, 191, 192, 226
Trinity 46, 101, 182, 191, 215,
224, 226
Troeltsch 381, 383
Truth *passim*
Tylor 378

U

Ultimate Concern iii, 8, 73, 284,
381, 386, 392, 396, 405, 406-
408
Unity *passim*
Universalization 179
Upanishads 77, 78, 80, 98, 102,
137, 148, 160, 168, 170, 193,
231, 392, 413
Utilitarian 15, 83, 94, 101, 237,
315, 355

V

Vedanta Sutras 192
Vico 266, 268, 360, 379
Violence 26, 46, 156, 222, 241,
329, 334, 346, 359, 377, 383
Virtue 44, 56, 72, 136, 193, 213-
215, 220, 327, 332, 337, 339,
341, 347, 349, 356, 364, 374,
375, 379-380, 400, 419

W

Whitehead 26, 36, 79, 165, 176, 280,
292
Wicker 48, 322
Williams 119, 378
Wisdom 33, 41, 72, 78, 99, 117, 138,
140, 144-145, 148, 152, 154-160,
168, 187, 196, 220, 221, 227-228,
240-241, 260, 298, 315-316, 340-
344, 347, 349, 357, 360
Wittgenstein 36, 292, 356
Women 27, 150, 166, 264, 307, 315
Wright 233
Wurzer 131

X

Xenophanes 21, 47, 128-130, 158,
169, 228

Z

Zen 133
Zephyr 119
Zeus 18, 121, 123, 347

COUNCIL FOR RESEARCH IN VALUES AND PHILOSOPHY MEMBERS

S. *Avineri*, Jerusalem
R. *Balasubramaniam*, Madras
M. *Bednár*, Prague
P. *Bodunrin*, Ibadan
K. *Bunchua*, Bangkok
V. *Cauchy*, Montreal
C. *Pan*, Singapore
M. *Chatterjee*, Delhi
Chen Junquan, Beijing
M. *Dy*, Manila
I.T. *Frolov*, Moscow
H.G. *Gadamer*, Heidelb
A. *Gallo*, Guatemala.
K. *Gyekye*, Legon
T. *Imamichi*, Tokyo
A. *Irala Burgos*, Asunçion
J. *Kellerman*, Budapest
M. *Kente*, Dar es Salaam
J. *Kromkowski*, Washington
J. *Ladrière*, Louvain

P. *Laleye*, Dakar
A. *Lopez Quintas*, Madrid
H. *Nasr*, Teheran/Wash.
C. *Ngwey*, Kinshasa
J. *Nyasani*, Nairobi
Paulus Gregorios, Cochin
O. *Pegoraro*, Rio de Jan.
T. *Pichler*, Bratislava
C. *Ramirez*, San José
P. *Ricoeur*, Paris
M. *Sastrapatedja*, Jakarta
J. *Scannone*, Buenos Aires
V. *Shen*, Taipei
W. *Strozewski*, Krakow
Tang Yijie, Beijing
J. *Teran-Dutari*, Quito
G. *Tlaba*, Maseru
Wang Miaoyang, Shanghai
M. *Zakzouk*, Cairo

BOARD OF DIRECTORS
Kenneth L. *Schmitz*, University of Toronto
Richard *Knowles*, Duquesne University
Richard T. *De George*, University of Kansas

SECRETARY-TREASURER
George F. McLean

ASSISTANT SECRETARIES FOR:
Research Design and Synthesis: Richard A. Graham
Moral Education: Henry Johnson
Research and Programming: Nancy Graham
Publication: Hu Yeping

THE COUNCIL FOR RESEARCH IN VALUES AND PHILOSOPHY

PURPOSE

Today there is urgent need to attend to the nature and dignity of the person, to the quality of human life, to the purpose and goal of the physical transformation of our environment, and to the relation of all this to the development of social and political life. This, in turn, requires philosophic clarification of the base upon which freedom is exercised, that is, of the values which provide stability and guidance to one's decisions.

Such studies must be able to reach deeply into the cultures of one's nation -- and of other parts of the world by which they can be strengthened and enriched -- in order to uncover the roots of the dignity of persons and of the societies built upon their relations one with another. They must be able to identify the conceptual forms in terms of which modern industrial and technological developments are structured and how these impact human self-understanding. Above all, they must be able to bring these elements together in the creative understanding essential for setting our goals and determining our modes of interaction. In the present complex circumstances this is a condition for growing together with trust and justice, honest dedication and mutual concern.

The Council for Studies in Values and Philosophy (RVP) is a group of scholars who share the above concerns and are interested in the application thereto of existing capabilities in the field of philosophy and other disciplines. Its work is to identify areas in which study is needed, the intellectual resources which can be brought to bear thereupon, and the financial resources required. In bringing these together its goal is scientific discovery and publication which contributes to the promotion of human kind in our times.

In sum, our times present both the need and the opportunity for deeper and ever more progressive understanding of the person and of the foundations of social life. The development of such understanding is the goal of the RVP.

PROJECTS

A set of related research efforts is currently in process; some were developed initially by the RVP and others now are being carried forward by it, either solely or conjointly.

1. *Cultural Heritage and Contemporary Change: Philosophical Foundations for Social Life.* Sets of focused and mutually coordinated continuing seminars in university centers, each preparing a volume as part of an integrated philosophic search for self-understanding differentiated by continent. This work focuses upon evolving a more adequate understanding of the person in society and looks to the cultural heritage of each for the resources to respond to the challenges of its own specific contemporary transformation.

2. *Seminars on Culture and Contemporary Issues.* This series of 10 week cross-cultural and inter-disciplinary seminars is being co-ordinated by the RVP in Washington.

3. *Joint-Colloquia* with Institutes of Philosophy of the National Academies of Science, university philosophy departments, and societies, which have been underway since 1976 in Eastern Europe and, since 1987 in China, concern the person in contemporary society.

4. *Foundations of Moral Education and Character Development.* A study in values and education which unites philosophers, psychologists, social scientists and scholars in education in the elaboration of ways of enriching the moral content of education and character development.

The personnel for these projects consists of established scholars willing to contribute their time and research as part of their professional commitment to life in our society. For resources to implement this work the Council, as a non-profit organization incorporated in the District of Colombia, looks to various private foundations, public programs and enterprises.

PUBLICATIONS ON CULTURAL HERITAGE AND CONTEMPORARY CHANGE

Series I.	*Culture and Values*
Series II.	*Africa*
Series IIa.	*Islam*
Series III.	*Asia*
Series IV.	*W. Europe and North America*
Series IVa.	*Central and Eastern Europe*
Series V.	*Latin America*
Series VI.	*Foundations of Moral Education*

THE COUNCIL FOR RESEARCH IN VALUES AND PHILOSOPHY

VOLUMES ON

CULTURAL HERITAGE AND CONTEMPORARY CHANGE

VALUES AND CONTEMPORARY LIFE

Series I. Culture and Values

Vol. I.1 *Research on Culture and Values: Intersection of Universities, Churches and Nations,*
George F. McLean,
ISBN 0-8191-7352-5 (cloth); ISBN 0-8191-7353-3 (paper).

Vol. I.2 *The Knowledge of Values: A Methodological Introduction to the Study of Values,*
A. Lopez Quintas,
ISBN 0-8191-7418-1 (cloth); ISBN 0-8191-7419-x (paper).

Vol. I.3 *Reading Philosophy for the XXIst Century,*
George F. McLean,
ISBN 0-8191-7414-9 (cloth); ISBN 0-8191-7415-7 9paper).

Vol. I.4 *Relations Between Cultures,*
John Kromkowski,
ISBN 1-56518-009-7 (cloth); ISBN 1-56518-008-9 (paper).

Vol. I.5 *Urbanization and Values,*
John Kromkowski,
ISBN 1-56518-011-9 (cloth); ISBN 1-56518-010-0 (paper).

Vol. I.6 *The Place of the Person in Social Life,*
Paul Peachey and John Kromkowski,
ISBN 1-56518-013-5 (cloth); ISBN 1-56518-012-7 (paper).

Vol. I.7 *Abrahamic Faiths, Ethnicity and Ethnic Conflicts,*
Paul Peachey, George F. McLean and John Kromkowski
ISBN 1-56518-104-2 (paper).

Vol. I.8 *Ancient Western Philosophy: The Hellenic Emergence,*
George F. McLean and Patrick J. Aspell
ISBN 1-56518-100-X (paper).

Vol. I.10 *The Ethical Implications of Unity and the Divine in Nicholas of Cusa*
David L. De Leonardis
ISBN 1-56518-112-3 (paper).

Vol. I.11 *Ethics at the Crossroads: Vol. 1. Normative Ethics and Objective Reason,*
George F. McLean,
ISBN 1-56518-022-4 (paper).

Vol. I.12 *Ethics at the Crossroads: Vol. 2. Personalist Ethics and Human Subjectivity,*
George F. McLean,
ISBN 1-56518-024-0 (paper).

Vol. I.13 *The Emancipative Theory of J. Jürgen Habermas and Metaphysics,*
Robert Badillo,
ISBN 1-56518-043-7 (cloth); ISBN 1-56518-042-9 (paper).

Vol. I.14 *The Deficient Cause of Moral Evil According to Thomas Aquinas,*
Edward Cook,
ISBN 1-56518-070-4 paper (paper).

Vol. I.16 *Civil Society and Social Reconstruction,*
George F. McLean,
ISBN 1-56518-086-0 (paper).

Vol.I.17 Ways to God, Personal and Social at the Turn of Millennia
The Iqbal Lecture, Lahore
George F. McLean
ISBN 1-56518-123-9 (paper).

Vol.I.18 *The Role of the Sublime in Kant's Moral Metaphysics*
John R. Goodreau
ISBN 1-56518-124-7 (pbk.)

CULTURAL HERITAGES AND THE FOUNDATIONS OF SOCIAL LIFE

Series II. Africa

Vol. II.1 *Person and Community: Ghanaian Philosophical Studies: I,*
Kwasi Wiredu and Kwame Gyeke,

ISBN 1-56518-005-4 (cloth); ISBN 1-56518-004-6 (paper).
Vol. II.2 *The Foundations of Social Life: Ugandan Philosophical Studies: I,*
A.T. Dalfovo,
ISBN 1-56518-007-0 (cloth); ISBN 1-56518-006-2 (paper).
Vol. II.3 *Identity and Change in Nigeria: Nigerian Philosophical Studies, I,*
Theophilus Okere,
ISBN 1-56518-068-2 (paper).
Vol. II.4 *Social Reconstruction in Africa: Ugandan Philosophical studies, II*
E. Wamala, A.R. Byaruhanga, A.T. Dalfovo, J.K. Kigongo, S.A. Mwanahewa and G. Tusabe
ISBN 1-56518-118-2 (paper).

Series IIA. Islam

Vol. IIA.1 *Islam and the Political Order,*
Muhammad Saïd al-Ashmawy,
ISBN 1-56518-046-1 (cloth); ISBN 1-56518-047-x (paper).
Vol. IIA.2 *Al-Ghazālī, Deliverance from Error and Mystical Union with the Almighty (al-Munqidh min al-Dalāl)*
Arabic text established and English translation
with introduction by: Muhammad Abulaylah;
Introduction and Notes: George F. McLean
ISBN 1-56518-081-X (Arabic-English Edition)
ISBN 1-56518-082-8 (English Edition.)
Vol. IIA.3 *Philosophy in Pakistan*
Naeem Ahmad
ISBN 1-56518-108-5 (paper).
Vol. IIA.4 *The Authenticity of the Text in Hermeneutics*
Seyed Musa Dibadj
ISBN 1-56518-117-4 (paper).
Vol. IIA.5 *Interpretation and the Problem of the Intention of the Author: H.-G. Gadamer vs E.D. Hirsch*
Burhanettin Tatar
ISBN 1-56518-121 (paper).
Vol.I.6 *Ways to God, Personal and Social at the Turn of Millennia The Iqbal Lecture, Lahore*

George F. McLean
ISBN 1-56518-123-9 (paper).

Series III. Asia

Vol. III.1   *Man and Nature: Chinese Philosophical Studies, I,*
Tang Yi-jie, Li Zhen,
ISBN 0-8191-7412-2 (cloth); ISBN 0-8191-7413-0 (paper).

Vol. III.2   *Chinese Foundations for Moral Education and Character Development, Chinese Philosophical Studies, II.*
Tran van Doan,
ISBN 1-56518-033-x (cloth); ISBN 1-56518-032-1 (paper).

Vol. III.3   *Confucianism, Buddhism, Taoism, Christianity and Chinese Culture, Chinese Philosophical Studies, III,*
Tang Yijie,
ISBN 1-56518-035-6 (cloth); ISBN 1-56518-034-8 (paper).

Vol. III.4   *Morality, Metaphysics and Chinese Culture (Metaphysics, Culture and Morality, Vol. I)*
Vincent Shen and Tran van Doan,
ISBN 1-56518-026-7 (cloth); ISBN 1-56518-027-5 (paper).

Vol. III.5   *Tradition, Harmony and Transcendence,*
George F. McLean,
ISBN 1-56518-030-5 (cloth); ISBN 1-56518-031-3 (paper).

Vol. III.6   *Psychology, Phenomenology and Chinese Philosophy: Chinese Philosophical Studies, VI,*
Vincent Shen, Richard Knowles and Tran Van Doan,
ISBN 1-56518-044-5 (cloth); 1-56518-045-3 (paper).

Vol. III.7   *Values in Philipine Culture and Education: Philippine Philosophical Studies, I,*
Manuel B. Dy, Jr.,
ISBN 1-56518-040-2 (cloth); 1-56518-041-2 (paper).

Vol. III.7A   *The Human Person and Society: Chinese Philosophical Studies, VIIA,*
Zhu Dasheng, Jin Xiping and George F. McLean
ISBN 1-56518-087-9 (library edition); 1-56518-088-7 (paper).

Vol. III.8   *The Filipino Mind: Philippine Philosophical Studies II,*
Leonardo N. Mercado
ISBN 1-56518-063-1 (cloth); ISBN 1-56518-064-X (paper).

Vol. III.9   *Philosophy of Science and Education:*

Chinese Philosophical Studies IX,
Vincent Shen and Tran Van Doan
ISBN 1-56518-075-5 (cloth); 1-56518-076-3 (paper).

Vol. III.10 *Chinese Cultural Traditions and Modernization: Chinese Philosophical Studies, X,*
Wang Miaoyang, Yu Xuanmeng and George F. McLean
ISBN 1-56518-067-4 (library edition); 1-56518-068-2 (paper).

Vol. III.11 *The Humanization of Technology and Chinese Culture: Chinese Philosophical Studies XI,*
Tomonobu Imamichi, Wang Miaoyang and Liu Fangtong
ISBN 1-56518-116-6 (paper).

Vol. III.12 *Beyond Modernization: Chinese Roots of Global Awareness: Chinese Philosophical Studies, XII,*
Wang Miaoyang, Yu Xuanmeng and George F. McLean
ISBN 1-56518-089-5 (library edition); 1-56518-090-9 (paper).

Vol. III.13 *Philosophy and Modernization in China: Chinese Philosophical Studies XIII,*
Liu Fangtong, Huang Songjie and George F. McLean
ISBN 1-56518-066-6 (paper).

Vol. III.14 *Economic Ethics and Chinese Culture: Chinese Philosophical Studies, XIV,*
Yu Xuanmeng, Lu Xiaohe, Liu Fangtong,
Zhang Rulun and Georges Enderle
ISBN 1-56518-091-7 (library edition); 1-56518-092-5 (paper).

Vol. III.15 *Civil Society in A Chinese Context: Chinese Philosophical Studies XV,*
Wang Miaoyang, Yu Xuanmeng and Manuel B. Dy
ISBN 1-56518-084-4 (paper).

Vol. IIIB.1 *Authentic Human Destiny: The Paths of Shankara and Heidegger*
Vensus A. George
ISBN 1-56518-119-0 (paper).

Series IV. Western Europe and North America

Vol. IV.1 *Italy in Transition: The Long Road from the First to the Second Republic: The 1997 Edmund D. Pellegrino Lecture on Contemporary Italian Politics*

Paolo Janni
ISBN 1-56518-120-4 (paper).

Series IVA. Central and Eastern Europe

Vol. IVA.1 *The Philosophy of Person: Solidarity and Cultural Creativity: Polish Philosophical Studies, I*,
A. Tischner, J.M. Zycinski,
ISBN 1-56518-048-8 (cloth); ISBN 1-56518-049-6 (paper).

Vol. IVA.2 *Public and Private Social Inventions in Modern Societies: Polish Philosophical Studies, II*,
L. Dyczewski, P. Peachey, J. Kromkowski,
ISBN 1-56518-050-x (cloth). paper ISBN 1-56518-051-8 (paper).

Vol. IVA.3 *Traditions and Present Problems of Czech Political Culture: Czechoslovak Philosophical Studies, I*,
M. Bedná, M. Vejraka
ISBN 1-56518-056-9 (cloth); ISBN 1-56518-057-7 (paper).

Vol. IVA.4 *Czech Philosophy in the XXth Century:*
Czech Philosophical Studies, II,
Lubomír Nový and Jirí Gabriel,
ISBN 1-56518-028-3 (cloth); ISBN 1-56518-029-1 (paper).

Vol. IVA.5 *Language, Values and the Slovak Nation: Slovak Philosophical Studies, I,*
Tibor Pichler and Jana Gašparíková,
ISBN 1-56518-036-4 (cloth); ISBN 1-56518-037-2 (paper).

Vol. IVA.6 *Morality and Public Life in a Time of Change: Bulgarian Philosophical Studies, I,*
V. Prodanov, M. Stoyanova,
ISBN 1-56518-054-2 (cloth); ISBN 1-56518-055-0 (paper).

Vol. IVA.7 *Knowledge and Morality:*
Georgian PhilosophicalStudies, 1,
N.V. Chavchavadze, G. Nodia, P. Peachey,
ISBN 1-56518-052-6 (cloth); ISBN 1-56518-053-4 (paper).

Vol. IVA.8 *Cultural Heritage and Social Change: Lithuanian Philosophical Studies, I,*
Bronius Kuzmickas and Aleksandr Dobrynin,
ISBN 1-56518-038-0 (cloth); ISBN 1-56518-039-9 (paper).

Vol. IVA.9 *National, Cultural and Ethnic Identities: Harmony beyond Conflict: Czech Philosophical Studies, IV*

Jaroslav Hroch, David Hollan, George F. McLean
ISBN 1-56518-113-1 (paper).

Vol. IVA.10 *Models of Identities in Postcommunist Societies: Yugoslav Philosophical Studies, I*
Zagorka Golubovic and George F. McLean
ISBN 1-56518-121-1 (paper).

Vol. IVA.11 *Interests and Values: The Spirit of Venture in a Time of Change: Slovak Philosophical Studies, II*

Tibor Pichler and Jana Gasparikova
ISBN 1-56518-125-5 (paper).

Series V. Latin America

Vol. V.1 *The Social Context and Values: Perspectives of the Americas,*
O. Pegoraro,
ISBN 0-8191-7354-1 (cloth); ISBN 0-8191-7355-x (paper).

Vol. V.2 *Culture, Human Rights and Peace in Central America,*
Raul Molina, Timothy Ready,
ISBN 0-8191-7356-8 (cloth); ISBN 0-8191-7357-6 (paper).

Vol V.3 *El Cristianismo Aymara: Inculturacion o culturizacion?,*
Luis Jolicoeur
ISBN 1-56518-104-2 (paper).

Vol. V.4 *Love as the Foundation of Moral Education and Character Development*
Luis Ugalde, Nicolas Barros, George F. McLean
ISBN 1-56518-080-1 (paper).

Vol. V.5 *Human Rights, Solidarity and Subsidiarity: Essays towards a Social Ontology*
Carlos E. A. Maldonado
ISBN 1-56518-110-7 (paper).

FOUNDATIONS OF MORAL EDUCATION AND CHARACTER DEVELOPMENT

Series VI. Foundations of Moral Education

Vol. VI.1 *Philosophical Foundations for Moral Education and*

Character Development: Act and Agent,
G. McLean, F. Ellrod,
ISBN 1-56518-001-1 (cloth); ISBN 1-56518-000-3 (paper).

Vol. VI.2 *Psychological Foundations for Moral Education and Character Development: An Integrated Theory of Moral Development*,
R. Knowles,
ISBN 1-56518-003-8 (cloth); ISBN 1-56518-002-x (paper).

Vol. VI.3 *Character Development in Schools and Beyond*,
Kevin Ryan, Thomas Lickona,
ISBN 1-56518-058-5 (cloth); ISBN 1-56518-059-3 (paper).

Vol. VI.4 *The Social Context and Values: Perspectives of the Americas*,
O. Pegoraro,
ISBN 0-8191-7354-1 (cloth); ISBN 0-8191-7355-x (paper).

Vol. VI.5 *Chinese Foundations for Moral Education and Character Development*,
Tran van Doan,
ISBN 1-56518-033 (cloth), ISBN 1-56518-032-1 (paper).

The International Society for Metaphysics

Vol.1 *Person and Nature*
George F. McLean and Hugo Meynell, eds.
ISBN 0-8191-7025-9 (cloth); ISBN 0-8191-7026-7 (paper).

Vol.2 *Person and Society*
George F. McLean and Hugo Meynell, eds.
ISBN 0-8191-6924-2 (cloth); ISBN 0-8191-6925-0 (paper).

Vol.3 *Person and God*
George F. McLean and Hugo Meynell, eds.
ISBN 0-8191-6937-4 (cloth); ISBN 0-8191-6938-2 (paper).

Vol.4 *The Nature of Metaphysical Knowledge*
George F. McLean and Hugo Meynell, eds.
ISBN 0-8191-6926-9 (cloth); ISBN 0-8191-6927-7 (paper).

The series is published and distributed by: The Council for Research in Values and Philosophy, Cardinal Station, P.O. Box 261, Washington, D.C. 20064, Tel. 202/319-5636; Tel. message/Fax. 202/319-6089 and 800/659-9962; e-mail: cua-rvp@cua.edul; website: http://www.acad.cua.edu/phil/rvp.

Prices: -- Europe and North America: cloth $45.00; paper $17.50; plus shipping: surface, $3.00 first volume; $1.00 each additional; air, $7.20. -- Latin American and Afro-Asian editions: $4.00 per volume; plus shipping: sea, $1.75; air, Latin America $5.70; Afro-Asia: $9.00.